*Her Words*

# Her Words

*Diverse Voices in Contemporary
Appalachian Women's Poetry*

*Edited by*
*Felicia Mitchell*

The University of Tennessee Press / Knoxville

Copyright © 2002 by The University of Tennessee Press / Knoxville.
All Rights Reserved. Manufactured in the United States of America.
First Edition.

Quotations are credited in the permissions section in the back of this book.

This book is printed on acid-free paper.

**Library of Congress Cataloging-in-Publication Data**

Her words: diverse voices in contemporary Appalachian women's poetry /
edited by Felicia Mitchell.— 1st ed.
    p. cm.
Includes bibliographical references and index.
ISBN 1-57233-195-X (cl.: alk. paper)
ISBN 1-57233-196-8 (pbk.: alk. paper)
  1. American poetry—Appalachian Region, Southern.
  2. American poetry—Appalachian Region, Southern—History and criticism.
  3. American poetry—Women authors—History and criticism.
  4. American poetry—20th century—History and criticism.
  5. Women and literature—Appalachian Region, Southern.
  6. Women—Appalachian Region, Southern—Poetry.
  7. Appalachian Region, Southern—In literature.
  8. Poets, American—20th century—Interviews.
  9. Appalachian Region, Southern—Poetry.
10. Women poets, American—Interviews.
11. Mountain life in literature.
12. Mountain life—Poetry.
  I. Mitchell, Felicia, 1956–

PS554 .H47 2002
811'.540809287'0975—dc21                          2002002860

To Brigitte N. McCray

_____

*and in memory of Bennie Lee Sinclair*

# Contents

# Acknowledgments

I first have to thank all the writers and poets who participated in the development of *Her Words*. They *are* the book.

Thanks also go to poet E. Ethelbert Miller for encouraging me to speak about Appalachian poets redefining place for an Associated Writing Programs conference in 1997. That paper was the catalyst for this book. Joyce Harrison of the University of Tennessee Press listened to my early ideas about focusing on women's poetry and encouraged me through this project. A poem by George Ella Lyon published in *Catalpa* (Wind Publications, 1993) inspired the title.

A number of individuals and organizations have inspired my interest in Appalachia over the years: John Lang, director of the Emory & Henry College Literary Festival and editor of the *Iron Mountain Review*; the Emory & Henry College Literary Festival, annually celebrating writers with roots in Appalachia; Rita Sims Quillen—poet, teacher, and scholar; Ann F. and Larry Richman, publishers of *The Sow's Ear Poetry Review* and Sow's Ear Press; Steve Fisher, social activist and director of the Appalachian Center for Public Policy and Community Service at Emory & Henry College; Nancy Garretson, a fiber artist working out of Washington County, Virginia, whose work celebrates place; my colleague Charles Goolsby, an artist whose work has made me look at my region in a new way; the Appalachian Center for Poets and Writers, located in Abingdon, Virginia; Virginia Highlands Community College, whose Arts Array in Abingdon, Virginia, has introduced me to a number of writers over the years—most recently, thanks to Ben Jennings, Patricia A. Johnson; Joyce Dyer, who edited *Bloodroot: Reflections on Place by Appalachian Writers* (Univ. Press of Kentucky, 1998); the Appalachian College Association for all it has done to help me connect with colleagues across the region; the Hindman Settlement School in Kentucky, where I have visited the Writers Workshop and hope to return; my students, too numerous to mention, though I will name poets Justin Black, Brigitte N. McCray, and Will Mullins; and writer Barbara Kingsolver, whose vision of Appalachia has guided me to take a closer look at this world around me.

I want to recognize the staff of Kelly Library at Emory & Henry College, a library that has supported my projects and research in many ways over the years, and the college's Academic Council, for professional development funds that supported the book proposal process during the summer of 1999. Additional thanks go to all the helpful people at the University of Tennessee Press.

Finally, heartfelt personal thanks go to my husband, Barry A. Love, and my son, Guy B. Mitchell Love; my friends Sophia Caparisos, Susan C. Cate, and Ann F. Richman; my mother, Audrey E. Mitchell; and poet Albert Huffstickler.

# Introduction

## Felicia Mitchell

The Merriam-Webster definition of *Appalachian* is "a white native or resident of the Appalachian mountain area" (1888).[1] This "American" dictionary, used by people nationwide, does little to broaden outsiders' perceptions of the diversity within Appalachia, and its implicit assumption about ethnicity reflects some trouble within. Appalachians are often seen as a monochromatic subculture within white America. Robert Snyder, in "Image and Identity in Appalachia," remarks on such a "curious inner division of the WASP identity."[2] Rodger Cunningham, in "Writing on the Cusp: Double Alterity and Minority Discourse in Appalachia," operates under the assumption that ethnic Appalachians are white, going so far as to comment about "Appalachians along with blacks."[3] Of course, it is true that when people outside Appalachia think of Appalachia—and "hillbillies"—they think of the descendants of Scots-Irish settlers, a picture that films such as "The Guid Scots Tongue," a part of the BBC series *The Story of English* widely broadcast in the United States, reinforce with their stereotypical depictions of Appalachia.[4] Unfortunately, shows such as *The Beverly Hillbillies* have been even more influential.

In his essay "Hicks, Hillbillies, Hell-Raisers, and Heroes: Traditional Mythic Types of Southern Appalachia," published in *Appalachian Literature: Critical Essays* a number of years ago, Robert J. Higgs suggested that not only such derogatory stereotypes but also a wholesale loss of identity had been threatening the writing of southern Appalachia. He wrote, "What is needed at this time for Appalachia, the South, and the World are new myths for a new age or old myths made viable in an age of revolution."[5] In the twenty-plus years since he penned these words, Appalachia has seen the appearance of a number of notable writers whose voices and vision are viable. Among these writers is a diverse group of women whose voices have expanded the possibilities for poetry both within and beyond the Appalachian region. Representatives of these women include Maggie Anderson, Marilou Awiakta, Kathryn Stripling Byer, Jo Carson, Lisa Coffman, Lou V. Crabtree, doris davenport, Nikki Giovanni, Patricia A. Johnson, Leatha Kendrick, George Ella Lyon, Linda

Parsons Marion, Irene McKinney, Lynn Powell, Rita Sims Quillen, Rita Size-more Riddle, Bettie Sellers, Betsy Sholl, Bennie Lee Sinclair, and Barbara Smith. Their poetry is as diverse as their ethnic backgrounds.

Jo Carson—whose writing defies easy categorization as her poems are simultaneously stories, monologues, plays—has gone far to reinvent old myths and to turn stereotypes of Appalachia on their head. Jennifer Mooney, writing about how Carson creates dialogical communities with her "people pieces," analyzes Carson's work to show how she "intentionally sets out to elevate common people, their stories and their language to the level of art, without making the product inaccessible or denying the authenticity (or authority) of its sources." What better way to counter popular misconceptions of Appalachia than to have "common people" talking for themselves to the broader audience Carson has found within her performances and publications? Carson's poem "Faith in Words," which precedes Mooney's essay, reminds us just how malleable words are as they reflect a world that is not static. Appalachia is a region full of paradoxes, especially to people with stereotypical perceptions.

George Ella Lyon, according to Roberta T. Herrin's essay, uses "the power of poetry to mitigate the cultural paradoxes of the region." John Lang has called Lyon's poetry "notable for its varied voices, its strong narrative elements, its moving portraits of family relationships, its investigation of the interconnections between nature and art, and its focus on the role that memory plays in defining our identities."[6] As Herrin contrasts Lyon's poems published in Catalpa with poetry that has been adapted for children's books, Herrin shows how Lyon translates memories and personal experience into poetry and then into "picture books," which provide a format that "suits her poetic style." With her audience including both adults and children, Lyon is able to reach a wide audience outside the region with her poems rich in Appalachian tales and language. Her roots, as she established in her first chapbook, Mountain, are "here."

Lisa Coffman's roots are also "here," in her case in East Tennessee. According to Patricia M. Gantt, "Coffman's Likely offers reflections from a profound new poetic talent with firm grounding in her native Appalachia, as well as in the larger world of her actual or intellectual wanderings." Appalachian influences show up in her choice of subject matter and in her language. Family history is found in poems such as "Maps," a poem about the Smith Mountain Dam Project in Roanoke Valley, just as an awareness of regional issues is found in others. Gantt shows just how frank Coffman is in her poetry, as in "The Small Town," where dead fish are rotting from chemical dumps or in

"Pulled Down," which describes destruction of native timber. Because of Coffman's roots, it is easier to read her depictions of mill workers and shabby coal mining towns as realistic and believable. Along with this appraisal of ugly elements in Appalachian life, the beauty of the landscape is found in a number of poems as well, as in "The Small Town," with its image of "the powerful flanks of the mountains."[7]

In addition to recognizing the landscape and roots, contemporary Appalachian poets may rely on colloquial and idiomatic usage at times to honor roots and frame stories. Rita Sims Quillen notes how models like Fred Chappell first helped her to honor her dialect and roots. As she discusses her early efforts at writing fiction, and her more recent success writing a screenplay, we find poetry at the heart of a creative process that was ignited when she discovered that writers like Chappell existed to give her a kind of permission to use her own voice and her own Appalachian experience for the material of her poems. Don Johnson's interview with Quillen leads us into a discussion of stylistic techniques and what for her is at the center of poetry: story. She notes that poetry "was ideal for my very visual way of thinking and seeing drama in the mundane. . . ." Seeing drama in the mundane is what poets of all ages have tried to do. The frank description of hard times in "Counting the Sums," with its image of "the mouth-drying grief / of a busted radiator" enriches a legacy of family history.[8]

This strong tie to family, often found in Appalachian poetry, is integrated with new conceptions of family in the poetry of Linda Parsons Marion. In an essay about Jim Wayne Miller's poetry, Don Johnson discusses "the Appalachians' obligation to re-claim their heritage through the recreation of the oneiric cabin."[9] Linda Parsons Marion, in quite a different way, uses her poetry to define for herself "what home is." Jeff Daniel Marion observes, in his interview with Marion, that he thinks "the central metaphor in [her] writing, that writing itself, is an attempt to provide the anchor that daily life did not provide. . . ." Going back to a childhood during which she moved around "a good bit," attending "nine schools in twelve years," Marion shows how writing poetry is a way of providing stability through life's changes such as her childhood and a later divorce, when she began writing about herself as mother and caretaker but moved on to express anger as she questioned her own need to leave a home she "had painted and papered and raised my children in." "House Holder" values property in a way men who take property for granted cannot do: "To live within these bounds / is world enough for now."[10]

Contemporary women poets have also expanded the physical boundaries of Appalachia. Geographically, Appalachia may be found from Alabama to

Maine. However, the central environs of Appalachia more often have come to be associated with the term in literary contexts. This region includes sections of Ohio, Kentucky, West Virginia, Virginia, Tennessee, North Carolina, South Carolina, and Georgia. But Appalachia is more than a geographical region: it is a terrain without boundaries inhabited by poets such as Kathryn Stripling Byer who live there now; poets such as Betsy Sholl who once passed through; poets like Rita Sizemore Riddle and Rita Sims Quillen, whose family roots go deep; and poets—including Lisa Coffman, Marilou Awiakta, and Nikki Giovanni—whose lives straddle multiple worlds. The Appalachia of the imagination is as diverse as the poets represented within this volume.

The native landscape, the rich oral tradition, and strong traditions influencing native poets inevitably influence writers who settle into Appalachia and call it home. Kathryn Stripling Byer is one poet who moved to western North Carolina a number of years ago, and since then her poems have become saturated with the imagery, language, and folk tales of her adopted Appalachia. Ann F. Richman writes about linguistic elements such as the modified ballad stanzas in poems in *Black Shawl* and the musical effects "in line length and phrasing, with frequent use of enjambment, and in sound devices such as alliteration and assonance" in other poems. The influence of ballads on subject matter is found in poems cited from *Wildwood Flower* as well. Richman also shows how "the women in Byer's poems usually reject the possibility of consolations some find in the church and, instead, seek meaning in earthly gifts—love, the natural world, making beautiful and useful things, singing— as they struggle often alone to survive on their subsistence gardens."

Bettie Sellers is another writer who moved into the region to teach. In "Brasstown Valley," she proclaims, "How fair the mountains / when willows green-out on the valley floor."[11] Sellers has found herself at home in the mountains of North Georgia, becoming a fine example of a folk artist who takes her material from the people and landscape of her community. Fred Chappell has defined "folk artist" as someone who helps his or her reader to become situated easily and comfortably within the narrative of the poem. In a sense, the folk artist presents the narrative as something "for the reader to look through, not at."[12] While she has taken on traditional Appalachian subject matter for her poetry, focusing on nature and community and religion, Sellers is unusual, Robin O. Warren believes, because of the way she avoids "all the hoary stereotypes of the worst Appalachian writing." Unlike writer Lillian Smith who lived in the neighboring Rabun County but felt "little more than contempt for the people of Rabun County," Sellers—like Byer—has used her poetry to celebrate the spirit of Appalachia.

Barbara Smith is yet another poet who moved to Appalachia and never left. As an "outsider" who became an insider, she also expands the Appalachian definition of identity. A longtime teacher who moved to West Virginia years ago, Smith notes, "I have felt most at home in West Virginia, rural and with hills and rivers and trees and mountain people." Writers, she notes in her interview with me, have to find a perspective that is "rooted somewhere." It is inevitable that writers living within Appalachia will be influenced by its natural surroundings, people, places—things. But one need not adopt the stereotypical voice of Appalachia to gain an identity. Rather, the poetic moments that present themselves will grow out of an intense, spiritual interaction with one's surroundings, as in "Folksong in a Cemetery." Smith's reliance on "sympathetic connections and then words" grows out of such a sentiment.

Ties for poet Betsy Sholl, who spent six years living in what she considered a relatively isolated area, are less tangible but strong enough for her to be called "Appalachian" in certain critical contexts. Although Sholl says she is not certain what influence her time had on her writing itself, she acknowledges a huge debt to Appalachia for her "writer's life." She notes in her interview with Richard Jackson, "For sure, there are poems I'd never have written without that landscape and those years." Being immersed in another culture, learning to love another sort of landscape, experiencing the life of an outsider—these influences were strong but no more so than living in such relative isolation. "I had to confront a lot of my own shadows," she acknowledges. Sholl remarked in "Big Stone Gap," her essay in *Bloodroot: Reflections on Place by Appalachian Women Writers*, of the people she met: "They will always be bigger than I can define, they will haunt me and call me back, remind me of all I don't know and all I do, my instructors in how to love both the visible and invisible world."[13]

A number of the poets represented in this volume are "natives" whose roots are deep. Such writers offer three-dimensional appraisals of Appalachia, forsaking the stereotypical for the realistic as they highlight positive and negative elements of their region. Parks Lanier says in *The Poetics of Appalachian Space* that "Appalachian writers claim to be the same type of 'regionalists'" as James Joyce, Mark Twain, and William Faulkner—writers whose regionalism gave rich identities to their work but whose work transcended time and place.[14] As Cecille Haddix, herself a native of Appalachia, has said, "Appalachia is as much a region of the heart as of geography. Appalachia is a way of looking at life, a community of faith and spirit and legend unique in America."[15]

One element of the Appalachian South is its seeming reliance on fundamentalist religions, though in reality the inhabitants of Appalachia include a broad spectrum of Christian and other believers. John Lang shows how Lynn Powell addresses the role of "religion in the mountain south" and yet resists "the dualistic impulse in traditional Christianity that tends to denigrate this world in its eagerness to embrace the next." Her poems in *Old & New Testaments*—which build on images of "mother and child, of hearts and hands, of loving family relationships, and mortality—acknowledge a faith built in "the cathedral of air" of "Epithalamium."[16] Powell's deep religious questioning does not denigrate her roots but ties her to a broader tradition, including the company of Emily Dickinson, Robert Morgan, and Kathryn Stripling Byer.

Although language is key to regional identity, it is also a way of helping writers to transcend time and place. Maggie Anderson comments on how "language for those of us from this region is a very complicated business" in the profile prepared by Ellesa Clay High. As Anderson talks about her experience teaching, she says she has read "poems by young men from the coal fields of West Virginia which gnarl the idiosyncratic grammar of this region into shapes that sound like self-parodies, shapes that show how deeply they have internalized the shame of poverty and isolation and exploitation." Anderson's own poems document and imagine her own life, weaving her "home" language with the language of school. In "Long Story," she says, "History is one long story of what happened to us, / And its rhythms are local dialect and anecdote."[17]

Migration is another characteristic associated with the Appalachian region. Irene McKinney, a poet who has lived both within and outside the region, believes that her own "push-pull motion in relation to this region . . . is the primary subject matter." In his interview with Irene McKinney, Jeff Mann acknowledges the importance of her homeplace as he also notes how "much Appalachian writing seems tinged with the struggle between Going vs. Staying." Poems such as "The Jewelry Box," from *Six O'Clock Mine Report*, are about a type of homesickness. This poem uses the image of a dusty television screen, a symbol of city life, to contrast with images in memory from the farm: a cat, a Persian rug. McKinney notes that when she did move back to her home, a friend asked what she was going to "do down there in isolation, in the country." Her response: "I'm going to think about community." One of the big influences of isolation, however, and "one of the great cultural forces in Appalachian life is to teach you to live with your own company."

Poets like Bennie Lee Sinclair have used that isolation to great advantage. William B. Thesing and Gilbert Allen's essay on Sinclair presents a study of a poet who shaped her life to revere her native soil. Sinclair's love for her native land compelled her to combine her poetic vision with attention to the environment, which is perhaps why in her life she received "more attention from the general public than from the literary community." Sinclair of South Carolina, who passed away while we were preparing this book, spent her life in Appalachia. The engagement with place in her poetry touches on the "destructive, ahistorical violence of technology" and "emphasizes the need for responsible stewardship." In "The Arrowhead Scholar," Sinclair wrote, "Out of the grounded ark / God led each lesser pair / . . . and delivered them / into our care."[18] This sense of responsibility that leads to polemical elements in poems such as "The Arrowhead Scholar" distinguishes Sinclair's poetry from the purely pastoral.

How they denote "Appalachian" is just one of many ways in which the writers are diverse. One might ask, however, how much diversity can exist if this book includes only women. Women writers in general in this past century have had to work against literary and social constraints such as those articulated in Sandra M. Gilbert and Susan Gubar's No Man's Land: The Place of the Woman Writer in the Twentieth Century.[19] George Ella Lyon amplified this challenge in "Appalachian Women Poets: Breaking the Double Silence," an essay published in American Voice in 1987, in which she noted the challenges women poets in Appalachia faced. Lyon said, "To speak as an Appalachian woman means to push two hands away from your mouth, to break a double silence. For, if you are female, you are outside the mainstream of literature as it is published and taught. Your experience is seen as trivial, narrow, other. Likewise, if you are Appalachian, you are perceived outside the parade of American culture."[20] Stereotypes of Appalachia have hurt both men and women, but women writers risk double jeopardy because that which may be essentially female may blur the boundary between stereotype and universal. Like Lyon, Joyce Dyer also affirms this in Bloodroot: Reflections on Place by Appalachian Women Writers. Dyer comments, "Few groups of women writers have suffered as many literary injustices as those from the southern hills. They have had to bear injustices caused by their gender as well as by their place."[21]

David Huddle has called Rita Sizemore Riddle "an Appalachian feminist with a polemic."[22] To expect more for women than women's traditional lot is to be a feminist, Riddle believes. When Riddle writes "I found out / There was more to marriage / than making beds and biscuits," the sense of drama Parks Lanier finds in her work is at its understated best. In her interview with Lanier, Riddle acknowledges hard times and notes how she uses traditional Appalachian scenarios for backdrops in her poems such as "Hole in the Sky." "I hunger for a hunk of hot cornbread / like Mama used to make, with country butter," that poem begins. Riddle's lesson is that the poet can take the commonplace and sentimental and imbue it with a spiritual depth that makes the poem more than a catalog of old-time words and feelings: the secret is to provide an understated yet outspoken commentary in a simple language that honors roots. Something as simple as a can of potted meat can evoke memories of home—and hard times. In both "Potted Ham and Crackers" and "Hole in the Sky" Riddle provides a turn in the last lines of each poem to take her reader from the mundane to a moral. Her poems resonate with a rich awareness of struggles women in Appalachia have to make.

Best known outside the region for a collection of stories, Lou V. Crabtree takes her same themes and concerns into her poetry. According to Dan Leidig, "Within the vast range from romantic exuberance to tragic flaw to adventures in the realms of space, the poet's deft hand, guided by the wisdom of experience, explores with wit, candor, and pathos the ageless arenas of childhood, love, belief, nature, tragedy, and death."[23] Judy K. Miller's profile of Crabtree shows just how she does that, with its focus on a long-lived poet who is just as likely to contemplate the many euphemisms for masturbation as the nature of outer space—two subjects not traditionally associated with Appalachian women. "He Cut My Garden Down" is a stark contrast to sentimental folk poetry. With its ballad-like story interwoven within a lyric poem with the repetition of the line "He did not have to cut my garden down," this poem captures the poverty and brutality of an earlier life with no sentimentality attached.[24] It is a "feminist" poem as much as it is an Appalachian tale.

Leatha Kendrick, who calls herself a northern southerner, often uses traditional "female" experiences and imagery as she imbues her poetry with philosophical depth, taking the reader into a novel way of perceiving the ordinary. "Zen Laundry" fuses the idea of washing machines as Buddhas with "female / openings accepting what is placed in them" and reflects, "Love has put me here. . . ."[25] Michael McFee's interview with Kendrick leads the reader to pay close attention to Kendrick's craft and writing process as they discuss *Heart Cake*, the most recently published of the books discussed in this volume. Like many of the other poets, Kendrick also acknowledges a debt to her grandmother, the archetypal yet homespun figure often found in Appalachian literature.

This book also highlights women because it is among women writers of Appalachia that we find another kind of diversity that has often been ignored or underplayed in traditional studies of Appalachia. Patricia D. Beaver noted in "Women in Appalachia and the South: Gender, Race, Region, and Agency," an essay in a 1999 issue of the *National Women's Studies Association Journal*, that "mythologized conventions of a static and homogeneous (white) society have dominated the literature on the southern Appalachian region."[26] I would add "of" to that: on and of the Appalachian region. Scholars of Appalachian studies while addressing problems distinctive to the white population have often ignored the greater diversity, including people with Cherokee and African roots—roots often intertwined with those of the Scots-Irish.

Marilou Awiakta's Cherokee and Scots-Irish roots have helped to create the Appalachian heritage that informs her poems. Awiakta's poetry interrelates many of the themes discussed up to this point, as it acknowledges the value of perceiving earth as Mother and is grounded, literally, in a specific geographic region. Her poetry also confronts the stereotype that Appalachia is a backward place out of touch with technology, as *Abiding Appalachia: Where Mountain and Atom Meet* grew out of Awiakta's childhood in the shadow of Oak Ridge National Laboratory, where plutonium for the Manhattan Project was extracted. Grace Toney Edwards's essay shows how Awiakta's poetry defies categorization. Reading Awiakta's poems, one finds a sense of stewardship that helps to reconcile the ancient and modern forces at odds within her native lands. "An Indian Walks in Me" proclaims, "Long before I learned the / universal turn of atoms I heard / the Spirit's song that binds us. . . ."[27]

The poetry of doris davenport is informed by her African American and Cherokee roots, along with her own exploration of lesbian-feminist issues. James A. Miller calls davenport a "Visionary/Mystic/Seeker" in his essay and shows how davenport's poetry evolved to include stronger and more explicit connections with her northwest Georgia roots. Some of davenport's poems resonate with the voices of people who populated her native landscape, just as others help to locate her "radical/lesbian/feminist consciousness squarely within her experiences as a southern black woman."

Lyon, in an introduction to *Old Wounds, New Words: Poems from the Appalachian Poetry Project*, acknowledged that "paradox is as indigenous to Appalachia as the coal: wealth and poverty (personal, cultural, ecological), beauty and ugliness, the stereotype with its wink of truth."[28] And, she said, poetry can acknowledge and heal paradox. Patricia A. Johnson, a native of Elk Creek, Virginia, writes poetry that evokes strong family ties and rich native landscapes but also chronicles the racial injustices of southern Appalachia. In her conversation with Christina Springer, she focuses on her Appalachian roots and racial identity. Johnson's poetry invigorates Appalachian literature with its direct treatment of racial issues while its strong oral roots connect with both African American and Appalachian models. Citing poems about ethnic identity, church burning, and killing, Springer helps readers to see the horrific experiences about which Johnson writes without leading them to dismiss such acts as essentially or negatively Appalachian. In "In a Place Where," a poem about the burning of G. P. Johnson in rural Grayson County, Virginia, Johnson leads the reader from a striking description of rural beauty to the image of a man "burned alive and decapitated . . . in a place where / I call home."[29]

Another poet who embodies paradoxes is Nikki Giovanni, who now lives in Blacksburg, Virginia. Her Appalachian roots are deep and strong. Using the metaphor of the quilt to analyze Giovanni's poetry, Virginia C. Fowler notes how Giovanni's "quilt is a metaphor for the struggles, the creations, and the beauty of black women." Giovanni grew up in Cincinnati, "Gateway to the South," and Knoxville, her family straddling rural and urban worlds as it worked for a better life outside the South, yet a life that brought with it a certain loss. In "Knoxville, Tennessee," Giovanni writes of "what was lost by African Americans in their migration to the North and the necessity to retain connection to it." Giovanni's poetry, including her more recent "Train Ride," has maintained strong connections with an element of the Appalachian South that should be acknowledged.

Another reason to write about women is to fill a gap in the critical literature. There are excellent critical studies that highlight the work of the sons of Appalachia. Articles abound on the work of the well-known writers Fred Chappell, Robert Morgan, and Charles Wright. Rita Quillen's critical study of Appalachian poetry, published in 1989, highlights the work of four male writers: Fred Chappell, Jeff Daniel Marion, Jim Wayne Miller, and Robert Morgan. *Looking for Native Ground: Contemporary Appalachian Poetry* used the work of these four poets because they best illustrated Quillen's thesis: "By synthesizing their personal past, present, and imagined future, Chappell, Marion, Miller, and Morgan transcend the region and bring a wider understanding of the mountain culture in a state of flux."[30] Any book, like Quillen's or like this one, by necessity must establish parameters. Poets represented in this volume join these four well-known writers to carry Quillen's thesis further, as well as to expand it with attention to Lyon's point about authenticity of voice in women's poetry.

Lyon has commented that "the accommodating thing to do, the thing women usually do early on for survival, is to muffle their authentic voices, write at a distance from themselves; write, if at all possible, like men."[31] In their quest to develop their authentic Appalachian voices in diverse ways, the writers highlighted in this book write like themselves. In that sense, they join a larger community of writers in the latter part of the twentieth century. Alicia Suskin Ostriker suggested in *Stealing the Language* that "an increasing proportion of . . . work is explicitly female in the sense that the writers have chosen to explore experiences central to their sex and to find forms and styles appropriate to their exploration."[32] Just as she believes that women writers in general "are challenging and transforming the history of poetry," women in Appalachia should be noticed for their own contribution in honoring roots, transcending boundaries, and writing well-crafted, dynamic contemporary poetry.[33]

In *The Hillbilly Vampire*, scholar Amy Tipton Gray satirizes academic exploitation of Appalachia with poems that offer biting caricatures of people who write about the mountains as if Appalachians are as exotic as vampires.[34] Within *Her Words*, the critical voices are as diverse as those of the poets honored. In some cases, poets enter into dialogues with other poets and writers so their natural voices as well as their poems can be heard. In other cases, critics have examined the poetry to acknowledge literary contributions and to make broader connections. Throughout, however, the central goal has been to provide diverse perspectives on diverse voices in contemporary Appalachian women's poetry. There are no vampires lurking in the background but instead honest, open-minded critics whose balanced analyses help to shed light not only on Appalachian women's poetry but also on a segment of contemporary poetry that is far richer than some people yet know—but will, if this book does its job.

## Notes

1. *Merriam-Webster's Collegiate Dictionary.* S.v. "Appalachian."
2. Robert Snyder, "Image and Identity in Appalachia," *Appalachian Journal* 9 (1982): 124–33.
3. Rodger Cunningham, "Writing on the Cusp: Double Alterity and Minority Discourse in Appalachia," in *The Future of Southern Letters*, ed. Jefferson Humphreys and John Lowe (New York and Oxford: Oxford Univ. Press, 1996), 44.
4. "The Guid Scots Tongue," part 3 of *The Story of English*, BBC TV co-production with MacNeil-Lehrer Productions in association with WNET (Chicago: Public Media Video, 1986).
5. Robert J. Higgs, "Hicks, Hillbillies, Hell-Raisers, and Heroes: Traditional Mythic Types of Southern Appalachian," in *Appalachian Literature: Critical Essays*, ed. Ruel E. Foster (Charleston, W.Va.: Morris Harvey College, 1976), 11.
6. John Lang, "The Editor's Page," *Iron Mountain Review* 10 (1994): 2.
7. Lisa Coffman, "The Small Town," in *Likely* (Kent, Ohio: Kent State Univ. Press, 1996), 10.
8. Rita Sims Quillen, "Counting the Sums," in *Counting the Sums* (Abingdon, Va.: Sow's Ear Press, 1995), 21.
9. Don Johnson, "The Appalachian Homeplace as Oneiric House," in *The Poetics of Appalachian Space*, ed. Parks Lanier Jr. (Knoxville: Univ. of Tennessee Press, 1991), 41.
10. Linda Parsons, "House Holder," in *Home Fires* (Abingdon, Va.: Sow's Ear Press, 1997), 39.

11. Bettie Sellers, "Brasstown Valley," in *Westward from Bald Mountain* [1974], 49.

12. Fred Chappell, "Two Modes: A Plea for Tolerance," *Appalachian Journal* 4 (1978): 338.

13. Betsy Sholl, "Big Stone Gap," in *Bloodroot: Reflections on Place by Appalachian Women Writers*, ed. Joyce Dyer (Lexington, Ky.: Univ. Press of Kentucky, 1998), 260.

14. Parks Lanier Jr., introduction to *The Poetics of Appalachian Space*, ed. Lanier (Knoxville: Univ. of Tennessee Press, 1991), 1.

15. Cecille Haddix, foreword to *Who Speaks for Appalachia?* ed. Haddix (New York: Washington Square Press Pocket Books, 1975), ix.

16. Lynn Powell, "Faith" and "Epithalamium," in *Old & New Testaments* (Madison: Univ. of Wisconsin Press, 1995), 66.

17. Maggie Anderson, "Long Story," in *A Space Filled with Moving* (Pittsburgh: Univ. of Pittsburgh Press, 1992), 21.

18. Bennie Lee Sinclair, "The Arrowhead Scholar," in *The Arrowhead Scholar* (Cleveland, S.C.: Wildernesse Books, 1978), 26.

19. Sandra M. Gilbert and Susan Gubar, *No Man's Land: The Place of the Woman Writer in the Twentieth Century* (New Haven and London: Yale Univ. Press, 1988).

20. George Ella Lyon, "Appalachian Women Poets: Breaking the Double Silence," *American Voice* 8 (Fall 1987): 63.

21. Joyce Dyer, introduction to *Bloodroot*, ed. Dyer, 2.

22. David Huddle's comment is found on the cover of Riddle's *Aluminum Balloons* (Blacksburg, Va.: Pocahontas Press, 1996).

23. Dan Leidig, foreword to *The River Hills and Beyond* (Abingdon, Va.: Sow's Ear Press, 1998), i.

24. Lou V. Crabtree, "He Cut My Garden Down," in *The River Hills and Beyond* (Abingdon, Va.: Sow's Ear Press, 1998), 18.

25. Leatha Kendrick, "Zen Laundry," in *Heart Cake* (Abingdon, Va.: Sow's Ear Press, 2000), 56.

26. Patricia D. Beaver, "Women in Appalachia and the South: Gender, Race, Region, and Agency," *NWSA Journal* 11, no. 3 (1999), par. 20. Online. Infotrac.

27. Marilou Awiakta, "An Indian Walks in Me," in *Abiding Appalachia: Where Mountain and Atom Meet* (Memphis: St. Luke's Press, 1978; reprint, Bell Buckle, Tenn.: Iris Press, 1995), 14.

28. Lyon, "Old Wounds, New Words: Sources and Directions," in *Old Wounds, New Words: Poems from the Appalachian Poetry Project* (Ashland, Ky.: Jesse Stuart Foundation, 1994), 14.

29. Patricia A. Johnson, "In a Place Where," in *Stain My Days Blue* (Philadelphia: Ausdoh Press, 1999), 17.

30. Rita Quillen, *Looking for Native Ground: Contemporary Appalachian Poetry* (Boone, N.C.: Appalachian Consortium Press, 1989), 7.

31. Lyon, "Appalachian Women Poets," 62.

32. Alicia Suskin Ostriker, *Stealing the Language* (Boston: Beacon Press, 1986), 7.

33. Ibid.

34. Amy Tipton Gray, *The Hillbilly Vampire* (1989; Blacksburg, Va.: Rowan Mountain Press, 1992).

# Maggie Anderson

## *Marginal*

This is where I live,
at the edge of this ploughed field
where sunlight catches meadow grasses
and turns them silver-yellow
like the tines of the birches
at the rim of the forest, where
lumps of earth are scabbed over
with rust colored pine needles
and one noisy crow has been
traversing them all morning.
Deep in these woods
his feathers have fallen so often
in some places they have started
to pile up like black snow.

I prefer it here, at the line
where the forest intersects
the field, where deer and groundhog
move back and forth to feed
and hide. And on these juts and outcroppings
I can look both ways, moving
as that crow does, all gracelessness
and sway across the heaved-up fields,
then tricky flight between
the overhanging branches he somehow
manages to scrape against.
This life is not easy,
but wings mix up with leaves here,
like the moment when surf turns into
undertow or breaker, and I can
poise myself and hold
for a long time, profoundly
neither one place nor another.

## Self-Portrait

I was far outside the frame, beyond
the pale, lost in the margins, smudged
like a fingerprint and frankly, nervous
about holding my own. I knew what was coming:
you, toward me, your arms open,
preparing to wrap them around my neck
with the clear determination some people
bring to learning anthropology. I was not
about to be moved, to be swept off my feet
by your exotic bracelets. I'll admit
I sometimes incline toward
the minute particulars of a scene
but never have I been undone by a woman
on account of her accessories. Until now,
when I come into the picture, captivated
by black coral beads, the gold wire of an earring,
the rustle of red scarf against a neckline,
as this pull, this great tug at my heart,
forklifts me into the foreground
at the center of the photograph
of empty beach, empty that is except for
you, and pine and manzanita,
the silver rings and necklaces of white surf.

# Maggie Anderson
## Two Languages

### Ellesa Clay High

> I prefer it here, at the line
> where the forest intersects
> the field. . . .
>
> Maggie Anderson
> "Marginal," 1992[1]

When I met Maggie Anderson in 1986, *Cold Comfort* had just been published and I was impressed with it. In the first of what would be several conversations about her poetry, I commented that she seemed to be a writer of the "in between" of dusk, autumn, grayness. After a moment of reflection, she laughed quietly and agreed. That description still seems apt today, as evidenced by *Windfall: New and Selected Poems* (Univ. of Pittsburgh Press, 2000), which provides a timely overview of her work.

As she acknowledged in the interview remarks transcribed below, her earliest remembrances were of living between two worlds, of being born in New York City to parents still connected through language and kin to the central Appalachian hills of Pennsylvania and West Virginia. In "Two Rivers," an essay which appeared in *Liberating Memory* in 1994, Maggie recalled that "they had worked out some ways of carrying the mountain culture with them": "My father sang West Virginia songs and union songs, and he taught them to me. My mother made small vegetable gardens on the fire escapes of every apartment building we lived in. Every summer we went back to West Virginia to visit the family. It was important to my parents that I know the world they had come from, but they clearly had other ambitions for my life."[2]

These plans were sidetracked, though, when her mother became ill with leukemia and, after a two-year struggle with the disease, died when Maggie was almost nine. A lingering memory of Maggie's childhood was when her mother "took me to the Bronx Botanical Gardens and to parks in New Jersey where she taught me how to tell a maple from an oak by the shape of the leaves . . . she wanted me to know the names of trees and flowers and plants."[3]

At the age of thirteen, she moved to West Virginia with her father, who did "what all good mountain people do when there is trouble: he came back home." Part of their extended family still lived in the northern part of the state, and through "the convincing social pressures of adolescence and the shared parenting of my father's brothers and sisters, I became a West Virginian." These were a people she would love "fiercely, with all the complicated angers and sorrows of kin."[4]

Later, she would earn both her B.A. (1970) and her M.A. (1973) in English from West Virginia University, fulfilling a generational aspiration:

> Both of my parents had been chosen from their families of
> origin to get "the education," and everyone else worked so that
> they might achieve. The strongest lesson they passed on to me
> was that the individual from the working class achieves for the
> group, on behalf of, and because of, the sacrifices of a com-
> munity of others. . . . From the world my parents were born
> to and the one my father took me back to, I learned determi-
> nation, humor, the harsh lessons of class in our country, and a
> sense of community.[5]

While a student at W.V.U., she worked in creative writing with such professors as Judith Stitzel and Winston Fuller, who still remain friends and colleagues today. Then she co-founded and edited with Winston and Irene McKinney a magazine of poetry and poetics entitled Trellis, which was based in Morgantown, and she worked for ten years as an artist in the schools throughout West Virginia, as well as holding many poetry residencies throughout the state, including at the West Virginia Penitentiary in Moundsville.

Her own poetry also began to appear in print. In 1979, a limited edition chapbook, The Great Horned Owl, was published by Icarus Press and named as one of the best small press books of that year by the American Library Association. The next year, her first full-length book, Years That Answer, appeared from Harper & Row, followed by Cold Comfort (1986), A Space Filled with Moving (1992), and Windfall (2000), all from the University of Pittsburgh Press. In addition, she co-edited A Gathering of Poets (1992) and spent an extended period editing Hill Daughter: New and Selected Poems (1991), one of the last books published by then West Virginia poet laureate Louise McNeill—with whom she developed a literary friendship eloquently described in her essay, "The Mountains Dark and Close around Me," included in Bloodroot: Reflections on Place by Appalachian Women Writers, edited by Joyce Dyer.[6] In recent years, Anderson has lived in Ohio, where she is a professor at Kent State University, directs the Wick Poetry Program there, and edits the Wick Poetry Series published by Kent State University Press.

The narrative included below has been selected from approximately sixty pages of unpublished material gathered in an interview I conducted with Maggie in my home on October 27, 1986, and from a lecture she gave to my Appalachian literature class a few days later on October 30 at West Virginia University, where she was holding a weeklong residency in poetry. It provides a window to a time when Maggie was centrally involved with our region and when *Cold Comfort*, her most Appalachian of books, was freshly published. Her concerns as a writer expressed here—for unearthing the "true facts" of place in a voice that accurately reflects those facts—can be seen working later in one of her finest poems, "Long Story":

> History is one long story of what happened to us,
> and its rhythms are local dialect and anecdote.
> In West Virginia a good story takes awhile,
> and if it has people in it, you have to swear
> that it is true. . . .

> (*Space*, 21)

Such material requires matching poetic structures, as Maggie observed in an article in *Poetry East*:

> I want to feel the freedom to work in, and to invent, forms which help articulate the truth of my feelings. I want forms which accommodate the speech rhythms of my region . . . I want forms like walks, where I can choose to go down one street and then change my mind and go down another, choose to walk with dogs or children or to go unaccompanied, where I can make things up along the way. Most of the rhythms of my feelings seem to me more circular than linear, more like a square dance than a box step, more like a garden than a train.[7]

In addition to the above concerns, she also discusses the responsibilities she has felt as a writer from a region whose local dialect still is equated "with ignorance" and from a culture associated with "the shame of poverty and isolation and exploitation." She remains acutely aware of the challenge all artists face as constructors of realities and the special obstacles they confront when handling material the "outside world" may consider quaint or foreign. Anderson's shifting relationship to Appalachia—at times "in it but not of it," or later "of it but not in it," both observer and observed, focal point and border, the subject and verb of remembrance—has underscored such pieces as the "Walker Evans" series of poems in *Cold Comfort*, "Marginal" in *A Space Filled with Moving*, and "Self-Portrait" in *Windfall*, a poem which begins:

> I was far outside the frame, beyond
> the pale, lost in the margins, smudged
> like a fingerprint. . . .

Yet a few lines later, she reveals that a "great tug at my heart, / forklifts me into the foreground / at the center of a photograph. . . ."[8]

Despite the fact that little of our region surfaces in the nineteen new poems collected in *Windfall* (excepting, perhaps, the landscape and cadences in "These Greens"), I believe that Anderson's roots remain strong here, and I hope that her writing will return to these mountains in the future. As she expressed in the opening and closing stanzas of "Abandoned Farm, Central Pennsylvania," from *A Space Filled with Moving*,

> In the middle of my life,
> orphaned, childless,
> I am perched on a promontory
> of genealogy, where branches
> fade from the yellowed pages
> and the farm goes back to the wild
> where it came from.
>
> (31)

She concludes,

> I'm as at home as any of us
> likes to think we are,
> in our saving up for later,
> in the solitary repetitions of our labors.
>
> (35)

The "road to Ohio" never has been closed to two-way traffic. In the fall of 2000, Maggie returned to West Virginia University to give a reading as part of the Eberly College of Arts and Sciences Second Annual Distinguished Visitors Program. Just as she had done so generously fourteen years before, she kindly guest-taught one of my classes, this time in creative writing, where she demonstrated that she still has "something of particular value to offer the first- or second-generation working-class men and women who are my students."[9] Some of my students responded on paper to her reading and class visit, and to her poetry:

> Maggie's poems are like thoughtfully composed pictures. Considering this, I understand why, being a photographer myself, I like her poetry as much as I do. She seems to share in the idea of the significance of a single moment which, when recorded, can symbolize a much larger period. If a picture is worth a thousand words, so too are Maggie's poems. They generally are narrative and very informal, which is inviting to a reader who may be intimidated by the notion of poetry. Once inside, the reader meets with powerful imagery and a certain playfulness that peeks out of even the more serious pieces.
>
> Abby Aikens

> I appreciate "Spitting in the Leaves" and its honest description of West Virginia boys—tight jeans and muddy cowboy boots. At one time this was much more the norm and in some places it still is: men doing something for the sake of upholding tradition, because it is the right thing to do but they don't know why. "Long Story" also is excellent. I was walking through Cassville in my mind. If it is beautiful to me—one who has seen such sights a million times—imagine the one who never thought of such things. I especially like the description of the "vinyl chairs and curled linoleum" that can be seen by the glow of the television. After reading this one I thought, "My, she is talented."
>
> Lauren Vineyard

> To be able to converse with a distinguished and accessible artist such as Maggie was an extremely beneficial experience. I tended to ask her more technical questions about specific poems and rhetorical devices because it seemed like a real chance to get some honest feedback from a master of her craft. Her telling of the creative process behind "Long Story" was enormously helpful in grounding me about how long it can take to create—just imagine, ten years for one poem! I admire her for working hard to establish her own true voice and not veiling it behind subterfuge or something she is not. I am not a soft critic either.

If I didn't like Maggie's poetry or thought she was a phony, I would say so. But thankfully, she is a very real artist who makes it seem practical to be a poet.

Mat Hogg

As she spoke, I listened carefully as she answered all of the questions I had planned to ask, before I even asked them. I noticed the warm, familiar Appalachian in her, and it seemed like I had known her for quite some time. I then felt proud and relieved to know that, yes, a West Virginia girl from a small town can be successful and be heard—that it's okay to show others who are ignorant of my heritage what it was really like growing up here. She gave me a sense of home, inspiration, and hope.

Leslie Barrett

After class, Maggie and I ate lunch in the student union, and following refills of iced tea and distilled conversation covering years, we turned to a draft of this article which I had sent to her for review. Her suggested revisions filled the page margins with sideways text. I was even more pleased when she handed me the written response I had requested from her to add as an update to the interview. I read:

> To look at one's own spoken words in print after a period of fourteen years is bracing. It's as if I am at two removes from myself: one, the distance of time and the other, the distance that print always creates around what was originally talk. "Remarks are not literature," as Gertrude Stein remarked, and I am very aware, as I read this compilation of transcribed speech, that there is nothing particularly literary about what I have said.

> Still, I am willing to give my permission to publish them now because I still find some things here of value and possible interest to others. And I am surprised to discover that I still feel much the same way. Of course, a number of things I would now say differently, and a couple of particulars no longer pertain (e.g. many of the closed steel mills in Pennsylvania in the 1980s have now been razed and replaced by computer software companies, another turn on economic disempowerment).

> But self-representation and false representation of certain groups through art has, if anything, become a topic of *more*

interest to artists and cultural critics than it was in the 1980s. And my own experience of speaking two languages and feeling challenged as a teacher and an artist by the dominant negative view of West Virginians has only been exacerbated by my last ten years of living in Ohio. Here, stereotyping, discrimination against, and hatred of those who live in the "hillbilly ghettos" of Akron, Youngstown, Columbus, Cincinnati and Cleveland, are commonplace.

So, while probably many things have changed for the better since 1986, my own awareness of the "outsiders'" perception has grown more painfully acute since I now live outside the region, but not far enough from it for the embarrassment, or perceived shame of proximity and personal heritage—many of my neighbors here are from West Virginia or Kentucky—to have transformed.[10]

I put down the pages and looked across the table at Maggie. We both smiled, comfortable, yet also shared a brief, hard glance meant to anchor us in this moment. Well over fourteen years of involvement with our region in writing trailed behind us, and inevitably fourteen future years swirled up close to our chairs. Would we sit together once more then, and if we did, what would our voices sound like? And what Appalachia would they reflect? My mind shifted to what Maggie had written in "Two Rivers": "I am always wary about what I assert that I understand. I know the lives of the working poor and the unemployed in West Virginia because they are the lives my people lived. But I have known something of the lives of privilege also, because, for a brief time in my early childhood, I was a marginal insider in those worlds. I have felt largely protected from the harsh labor of my family and the economic tenuousness they lived with. Yet, I never felt 'marginal' to them."[11]

As we took our leave from one another, I felt grateful to Maggie, that as a poet she had, as she wrote in "The Artist," "past her hunger . . . brought out these things / of beauty and of memory, and began to play."[12] These mountains would always be her home. And I hoped that by the next time we met, she would have come home for good.

# Comments

## Maggie Anderson

My work as an artist, as a poet, has to do with language. And language for those of us from this region is a very complicated business. Our familial language, our own native Appalachian dialect—which is getting diluted now that we're all more likely to talk the way everybody talks on television—is one that the rest of the world tends to equate with ignorance. So for a writer, that means that at some point in our lives we're going to have to deal with this question of two languages.

When I grew up, my parents lived in New York City, though my mother originally was from western Pennsylvania and my father was from Preston County, West Virginia. They had met and married, and gone to live and work in New York City, where I was born. I was thirteen years old when we moved back to West Virginia, so I had grown up in New York speaking two languages. One was the language I used at school. The other was the language I used at home with my parents and during summers when we came back to West Virginia to visit family.

The characteristics of those languages were that the school language was grammatically correct. It was considered a plus in school in New York to be witty, to be quick with language. And it seemed to me that this language was more rational, that when you talked with people you were supposed to develop your conversation logically—a thing I have never been comfortable with.

My home language often was grammatically *incorrect*, as in "We come up, just now, from Stansbury Hall." And it also was metaphorical, and to me more imaginative. And it worked—when it worked—a kind of cleverness. It was a cleverness of situation, of anecdote. It didn't seem to matter, with my aunts and uncles in the summers, how long it took to tell a story. The point wasn't really even the end of the story, but the detours you took on the way.

And I worked these two languages pretty successfully—though with some pain, obviously, until I was thirteen and moved to West Virginia. There, more of my classmates and teachers spoke the way I did at home, so I had a brief merging of these languages at that point. Then I started college at West Virginia University, and I learned the old lesson again. As an English major if I wanted to do well in classes, I had, once again, to be logical in my term papers, for example—witty, linguistically clever, and certainly grammatically correct.

So this schism of two languages, I think, has been one of the major issues I've dealt with as an Appalachian writer. It is particularly crucial for poets, because in poetry what you are really writing about—whatever else you are writing about—is language. And I want a poetry that incorporates the rhythms and some of the idiosyncrasies of that dialect of the Appalachian region—which has always sounded to me like the truth. That may sound simplistic, but when somebody tells me something in our West Virginia dialect, I know I can believe it.

I also don't want to deny what I learned in college, what I've learned by reading, and what I love about the intricacies of language: long words, beautiful words, and the rhythms of the most exalted speech. Now that's a pretty tall order. How am I going to weave together those two languages so that I don't ever deny where I came from, but also never deny what I've come through?

There is a kind of poetry that bothers me as it is sometimes written by the people of this region. This is the poetry which pretends they never heard anybody say, "We come up just now from Stansbury Hall"—that pretends they never heard that dialect or rhythm. And they write in a language that, to me, seems alien to them. One of the things we have to ask of our poems, and more particularly about our lives, is "Is what we are saying true? To our experiences, and to our feelings? And does it fit into a language that for us makes sense?"

And so as poets we're always asking, "Is this true? Is it true to the feelings of our lives?" And I don't mean facts, now. I mean "true facts." True facts are the ones that mesh with our feelings. All the time we have to check our truths—for compromise, and if we're from this region especially—for timidity. Are we afraid to say what we really think? Dissembling? And conformity—are we trying to talk the way somebody told us to talk?

Recently, I wrote this in a special "Poetics" issue of *Poetry East*:

> In recent years I have seen in university writing classes and workshops too many poems by young women in which the truth of their feelings is buried under artful music and some skillful imagery within a metered line, in which the things they know are being handled with the clunkiest of asbestos gloves. I have seen poems beginning with four dependent clauses and

no subject to avoid using the pronoun "I," to avoid confronting rage. I have also seen poems by young Black poets written in iambic pentameter lines and in a diction no *white* person has used since the nineteenth century. And I have seen poems by young men from the coalfields of West Virginia which gnarl the idiosyncratic grammar of that region into shapes that sound like self-parodies, shapes that show how deeply they have internalized the shame of poverty and isolation and exploitation.[13]

What concerns me in the poetry that's written in a kind of exalted voice—what we think of as the "poetic" voice—is that it has no connection to the truth of our lives. And when we write that way what we're saying is "all those people from the outside are right. We're dumb and ignorant. So we better write like they write." And that's just not true.

Another kind of poetry that disturbs me is poetry written by well-educated young people from this region totally in the language rhythms, the "pure" dialect my grandparents spoke. Now I think that's all right if you're assuming a voice, but I guess I wonder, "What did you learn yourself on the way?" I think it's avoiding the problem if you simply go back into that old language in a kind of nostalgic reaching for the way things were. We have a real struggle, now, to bring together those things—education, which we must never deny because for many of us it was an opportunity our parents and grandparents never had. On the other hand, it is wrong to forget that other language entirely.

Growing up in this region we also get a wonderful connection to the landscape that is, for the poet, a tremendous asset. I remember being in a workshop with a lot of older people, and the young man leading the workshop was from New York. A woman read a poem where she named six different flowers, about seven kinds of trees, and three different kinds of birds. Now there were some things about the poem that maybe weren't as wonderful as one would have liked, but this young poet from New York just shook his head and said, "I'd kill for that knowledge of the natural world." I thought that was a really good response.

So many of us have that connection, and a strong connection to the past—not only through our own families, but through the *smallness*, the very smallness of the community. And the isolation of communities has given us in this region, I think, a very valuable connection to the past. Our obligation then, as writers and as people, is to make sure that it really *is* our past—not somebody else's interpretation—and that it's accessible to us.

Appalachian families tend to be very close-knit families, and that has its good and bad aspects. A good aspect is that family can provide a support system for most of us that is like an endless well of affirmation of ourselves. The negative side is that family always brings obligation. If your family is like mine, that can mean problems, including a tendency—because of our isolation—not to believe that things can be done.

I have an aunt who lives in Parsons, West Virginia, and when I told her I was going off to Penn State to teach for a semester, her response to my declaration was simply, "Well. . . ." For some reason that day, I was aggravated. You know that West Virginia "well . . ." that sort of slides in the air? And I said, "What do you mean, 'well . . .'? I'm going off to teach at this big university!"

She said, "Where is it again?"

And I told her it was in the middle of Pennsylvania.

"Lot of snow up there," she said.

"Yeah," I said, "but I don't have to drive. Once I get there, I'll be all right."

"Uh-huh. When are you coming back?"

"In the spring."

"Well . . ." she said.

What I finally figured out is that she didn't believe I could go up there, do all that, and come back. Some part of her—and it didn't have to do with her being elderly because she felt that way when she was forty—thought "you can't do it, you can't get there or, if you do, you won't come back." As a writer—this is on a more personal level now—that's an important attitude to work against. On the other hand, I wouldn't trade my own experience of family for anything. There's a playwright from McDowell County, Jean Battlo, who says she likes to think that what's so special about her family's love is that they support her *even though* they don't understand the things she's doing as a writer.[14]

Louise McNeill has a poem called "Hill Daughter," and it's addressed to her male ancestors, so it is about family, among other things.[15] She is telling them, in a somewhat ironic voice, that she has done at last what is required to save the farm—she has brought a son into the world. I love much of Louise McNeill's work, and I think what I love most is how she goes back to the most ancient of poetic rhythms in which she weaves her own distinctive Appalachian voice. And in "Hill Daughter" the voice is that of a crazed goddess in a way—exalted but angry, and the rhythms are some of the most sophisticated you can hear in any poem.

Another poem with a very different voice is "pickens" by Jayne Anne Phillips.[16] She grew up in central West Virginia, in Buckhannon. And Pickens is way up in the mountains in Randolph County—you have to climb a number of dirt roads to get there. The poem ends up not being too much about Pickens, actually, but about a woman in a bar—a midwife. And what amazes me about this poem, again, is the West Virginia language, and yet you know every minute that this is not an uneducated person writing it. She is not in any way denying the fact that she's had a lot more education than this Elva, who is the heroine in the poem. So she's using both languages.

Language and landscape—I'm thinking right now of another poem by Louise McNeill called "Deserted Lumber Yard" about how the timber industry stripped all the trees off the hills and then closed down and left, abandoning whole towns.[17] So it's about an abandoned logging camp—very depressing— and what interested me about the poem is that it's very much like one of mine in Cold Comfort called "Gray," which is about driving through the Monongahela Valley and seeing the closed steel mills (10). One of the things we have to do as writers in this region is document what happens to us. What has often happened is that economic interests come in and make a big BOOM for us: everybody's got jobs and trailers and lots of places to go. Then when it's all done and they pack up and leave, we have abandoned towns and a raped landscape.

I was doing a residency in Pennsylvania, driving through the Monongahela Valley up to Johnstown. There's a little place up above Johnstown called Westmont, where you can look down an incline, like the one they have in Pittsburgh. And you're looking down on all these closed steel mills with "For Sale" signs on them. That's the set-up of "Gray," and the grayness that settles over us in January and stays until May. The hardness of the landscape here compounds in our lives and in the writing of our region.

My aunt from Parsons was in that terrible fall flood in 1985. Of course there were lots of civic groups cleaning up downtown areas in Parsons, but in terms of getting mud out of houses, it really was pretty much up to the people themselves. My aunt was eighty-six years old—clearly not a mud shoveler. So I did what a lot of other people did—I took a group of friends there to shovel mud. But I'd never seen anything like that and I hadn't the foggiest idea what to do. There were three men and three women with me, and we had brought shovels and water and stuff to keep warm. When we went into the house, there were mud and debris and logs up to the second floor. Windows were broken and doors crashed, and the mud . . . the mud! I will never forget it.

We stood there awhile and just looked. But I think the fact that we were all from this region allowed us to do what we did. I said, "What are we going to do?" Then this one guy with me, who actually was from Boone County, said, "We're going to get those shovels and shovel mud." And that's what we did. And I think that's one of the things I'm talking about in "Gray." That city's been rebuilt three times after a flood. What we have learned here is something like the "poise of affliction." We get our shovels . . . and shovel mud.

Writing often comes out of such hardness. You know, my mother was very sick from the time I was six until she died right before I turned nine. And when that happened, my whole life changed, and a lot of it had to do with language. I started writing after my mother died—they weren't actually poems, but more like stories. Then I got scarlet fever, and when I recovered, I was totally unable to read or write. Sometimes this happens when there is a severe trauma with a child, or an accident or a death. I had been reading way above grade level and writing, and then for about six months I simply couldn't do either one. I can still remember the feeling of it—I could see all those little marks on the page, but they made no sense. They just didn't register in my brain. Then it all came back as suddenly as it had left.

That sounds very dramatic, and it was. But after that I not only read all the time, but I wrote. I didn't necessarily show these little poems to anybody—actually I didn't. I wish I had some of them today—I have a feeling they were interesting, what I was writing when I was eight, nine, ten. They're all gone. Somehow they got lost in the move to West Virginia, so I don't even know what they were about.

I guess that's one function of poetry—at least for me: to remember what happened. A New York poet, Dick Gallup, has a line in a poem somewhere that just says something like, "remember what happened."[18] And I think that a lot of the poets I admire most are poets who are rememberers. When I recently taught an Elderhostel class on the art of the journal, somebody brought up the point that in the novel 1984, the first subversive act that Winston Smith does is write in a journal.[19] If poets and other writers aren't writing down what happened—chronicling our daily lives—then we're in trouble. It's so important for us to keep writing out of our region, documenting and imagining our own lives, for our own reasons, and in our own language, once we find out what that really is.[20]

Morgantown, West Virginia, October 1986

## Notes

1. Maggie Anderson, "Marginal," in *A Space Filled with Moving* (Pittsburgh: Univ. of Pittsburgh Press, 1992), 11. Subsequent references to this book are presented parenthetically in the text.
2. Anderson, "Two Rivers," in *Liberating Memory: Our Work and Our Working-Class Consciousness*, ed. Janet Zandy (New Brunswick, N.J.: Rutgers Univ. Press), 144.

3. Ibid., 146–47.

4. Ibid., 145.

5. Ibid., 148,149.

6. Anderson, "The Mountains Dark and Close around Me," in *Bloodroot: Reflections on Place by Appalachian Women Writers*, ed. Joyce Dyer (Lexington, Ky.: Univ. Press of Kentucky, 1998), 32–39.

7. Anderson, "Saving the Dishes," *Poetry East* 20 and 21 (1986): 88–95.

8. Anderson, "Self-Portrait," in *Windfall: New and Selected Poems* (Pittsburgh: Univ. of Pittsburgh Press, 2000), 97.

9. Anderson, "Two Rivers," 149.

10. Anderson, correspondence with the author, 29 July 2000.

11. Anderson, "Two Rivers," 149.

12. Anderson, *Cold Comfort* (Pittsburgh: Univ. of Pittsburgh Press, 1986), 28. Subsequent references to this book are presented parenthetically in the text.

13. Anderson, "Saving the Dishes," 92.

14. "Frog Songs," one of Jean Battlo's one-act plays, is available on the internet at Lewis W. Heniford's *Small-Cast One-Act Guide Online* at <www.heniford.net/1234/1m1f_fs.htm>.

15. McNeill, Louise, "Hill Daughter," in *Hill Daughter: New and Selected Poems*, ed. Maggie Anderson (Pittsburgh: Univ. of Pittsburgh Press, 1988), 15.

16. Jayne Anne Phillips, "pickens," in *Sweethearts* (Berkeley, Calif.: Truck Press, 1976), unpaginated.

17. McNeill, 86.

18. To read some of Dick Gallup's poetry, see *Shiny Pencils at the Edge of Things* (Minneapolis: Coffee House Press, 2001).

19. George Orwell, *1984* (London: Martin Secker & Warburg Ltd., 1949).

20. I gratefully acknowledge here the assistance of Beth Cahape, who, as a graduate student at West Virginia University in the late 1980s, spent many hours transcribing tapes of the interview with Maggie Anderson and her class lecture, on which much of this article is based.

# Marilou Awiakta

## An Indian Walks in Me

An Indian walks in me.
She steps so firmly in my mind
that when I stand against the pine
I know we share the inner light
of the star that shines on me.
She taught me this, my Cherokee,
when I was a spindly child.
And rustling in dry forest leaves
I heard her say, "These speak."
She said the same of sighing wind,
of hawk descending on the hare
and Mother's care to draw
the cover snug around me,
of copperhead coiled on the stone
and blackberries warming in the sun—
"These speak."     I listened . . .
Long before I learned the
universal turn of atoms, I heard
the spirit's song that binds us
all as one. And no more
could I follow any rule
that split my soul.
My Cherokee left me no sign
except in hair and cheek
and this firm step of mind
that seeks the whole
in strength and peace.

## Star Vision

As I sat against the pine one night
beneath a star-filled sky,
my Cherokee stepped in my mind
and suddenly in every tree,
in every hill and stone,
in my hand lying prone upon
the grass, I could see
each atom's tiny star—
minute millions so far-flung
so bright they swept me up
with earth and sky
in one vast expanse of light.

The moment passed. The pine
was dark, the hill, the stone,
and my hand was bone and flesh
once more, lying on the grass.

# Marilou Awiakta
*Poet for the People*

## Grace Toney Edwards

When Mary Lou Bonham was scarcely three years old, she composed her first poem in 1939, inspired by a beautiful butterfly in flight that fell dead, suddenly, at her feet. Her mother, always a teacher and nurturer, wrote down her daughter's words to be cherished and savored both then and in years to come:

> Oh, Little Butterfly,
> how I wish you weren't dead,
> so that you could fly
> with other butterflies instead.[1]

Just three years later at the ripe age of six, Mary Lou "published" her first short story, entitled "Mr. and Mrs. Honeybee Find a Home." Written in wartime, when housing for families was at a premium, the topic reveals the powerful influence of social issues even then on the thoughtful little girl. The carefully lettered title page of the manuscript, still extant, contains colorful illustrations of bees and flowers by the author, who also highlighted her name in bright red and blue double underlining. Already the budding young writer perceived the importance of identity and was clearly in pursuit of establishing her own.

Today we know this blooming author as Marilou Awiakta, whose identity continues to be of utmost import in her life and writing. Known as a Cherokee/Appalachian poet, she pulls together the three significant strands of her life: her Cherokee ancestry, her Celtic heritage, and her upbringing on the atomic frontier of Oak Ridge, Tennessee. In a metamorphosis of names, she has moved from the child, Mary Lou Bonham; to the adult wife, Marilou Bonham Thompson; and finally to the author, Marilou Awiakta. After her first publication, she began to use her Indian name, which means "eye of the deer," given to her by her grandfather. She shares the name with the vibrant, hardy flowering plant we know as black-eyed Susan, or "awiakta" to the Cherokee. Awiakta has written, in some form or other, virtually her whole life. In fact, as a youngster she avowed to her mother that she wanted to be a writer. In response, her mother queried: "What will you do for the people?" Awiakta's answer has been the production of three published books and hundreds of published poems, essays, and articles. In demand as a speaker, reader, and workshop leader, she makes frequent appearances on college and university campuses across the nation; in Native American gatherings of various sorts; and in literary, artistic, historical, religious, and civic groups.

Her eclectic interests and versatility of literary forms defy conventional categorization. Indeed, her blending of genres marks her as pioneer of a currently popular form: the prose poem. She wrote prose poems in her very first book, *Abiding Appalachia: Where Mountain and Atom Meet*, published in 1978 by St. Luke's Press and never out of print since then, with the eighth printing by Iris Press of Tennessee. That collection, which she considers to be the eye of her work, contains other poetic forms as well. Her second book, entitled *Rising Fawn and the Fire Mystery* (St. Luke's Press, 1983), is a child's story of historical fiction widely read by audiences of all ages and even used as a text in college classrooms and social therapy groups. Her renowned 1993 publication *Selu: Seeking the Corn Mother's Wisdom* combines poetry, prose poems, myth and legend, fiction, personal essay, and philosophical treatise to create a truly multi-genre book. Yet her perception of herself is as poet. As she put it in conversation with me, "Everything I write is poetry. Life is metaphorical. The form comes from the thought." And even though a piece may appear as prose, in Awiakta's mind it is a poetic expression. Dr. Ernest Lee, in a Knoxville, Tennessee, conference presentation on Awiakta's work in March 2000, commented on his observation of the "power of poetry in her home and in her person" when he visited her along with two college students for the purpose of an interview. To Awiakta, a member of the audience, he said directly, "I think of you as a poem." He continued, quoting her, "The way I feel about poetry is that all of life is poetry. Part of my work as a poet is to listen for the poems in other people and, if they don't want to sing them themselves, to sing for them."[2] And sing she does—for Native people, for Appalachians, for women, for the beleaguered, for Mother Earth, and more.

Awiakta is at her best when she can sing in unison with other people— or perhaps the round format, or call-and-response, is a more appropriate musical analogy. She thrives on interactivity and encourages audience participation in her readings and presentations. In fact, she even asked the publisher of *Selu* to consider leaving blank pages in the book so that readers could respond with their own written thoughts and creative forms. In the interest of costs, Fulcrum Press demurred; nonetheless, Awiakta always invites readers to write in the margins and on the flyleaves of her books.

This proclivity of the author to foster communal engagement in an art form generally considered to be a solo, even lonely, activity leads again to a discussion of categorization. I have asserted already that Awiakta thinks of herself as a poet and writes in the recognized genres of poetry, fiction, essay, and article. But what of the content? Can that be categorized? I submit that Awiakta is a historical/philosophical autobiographer. That is, she writes from and about her own experiences but broadens those to represent her ethnic groups, her gender, her community. In her efforts both to gather material for her art and to share the fruits of it, she leans toward communal engagement; hence the audience participation, the warmth and genuine interest in others, the gifts of word and seed that are trademarks of this poet. As an example of the latter, I offer her practice of circulating personally among her audience, when the size allows it, to put a grain of corn in each person's hand along with her own personal greeting.

In keeping with the designation of autobiographical history/philosophy, I see four major recurring thrusts in Awiakta's writing:

(1) Childhood experiences and Oak Ridge history
(2) Woman's role, conditions, and rights
(3) Nature and science
(4) Native American thought and philosophy

Some of these divisions overlap; some writings easily fit more than one category. Indeed, the last of the four, gleaned from her personal ethnic heritage, infuses all of her writing and will not be treated in this essay as a separate category. Rather, the influence of Native thought and philosophy is discussed as a part of the whole in her various themes, symbols, and images.

## Childhood Experiences, Oak Ridge History, and More: Abiding Appalachia

Born in Knoxville, Tennessee, in 1936 to parents with Cherokee ancestry on both sides, Awiakta spent her earliest years in Nashville and then in Knoxville. During the beginning of the United States' involvement in World War II, a great flurry of secret activity erupted in the misty mountains just west of Knoxville. Soon Marilou's father went to work there, and in time when housing became available, the family moved to live "behind the fence" in Oak Ridge, Tennessee. Marilou was nine and old enough to absorb all the newness, the excitement, the pioneer spirit, the secretiveness, the sense of something hugely important in that place. As she grew, and as time and events brought an end to the war, she thrived in that hub of scientific experimentation and advancement. Her interests leaned toward the artistic and literary, but she recognized the great import of the scientific and appreciated the community culture that acknowledged the essential co-existence of science and art.

At the University of Tennessee Marilou majored in English and French and took with her from the university both a degree and a husband, Paul Thompson, a pre-med student who would eventually take her to live in Laon, France, to fulfill a long-nurtured dream. During the three years in France as a young wife and mother, translator and liaison officer, Marilou immersed herself in the culture and language she had studied. Oddly enough, the strange new sounds and sights began to take her in mind back home, to Oak Ridge, to the Great Smokies, to the mountain people she had grown up among. During a long seventeen-year hiatus from writing poetry, the people and the experiences of her childhood and adolescence gestated until, one day in 1972 to answer a challenge, she wrote "Prayer of Appalachia." The challenge included entering the poem in the Mid-South Poetry Contest. She won first place, the Jesse Hill Ford Award. (Ford himself was a judge). She has written steadily ever since. That poem became part of *Abiding Appalachia: Where Mountain and Atom Meet*, a collection commissioned by St. Luke's Press in Memphis, where Marilou, Paul, and their three children were living by then.

The birthing that occurred with that publication shows clearly both the nature and nurture that constitute the person Marilou Bonham Thompson, née Awiakta. Braiding together the three strands of her personal heritage—Cherokee, Appalachian, and scientific—Awiakta has managed to write history and espouse philosophy that represents the oldest and the newest cultures of a large and diverse group of people. Starting with the natural habitat and moving on to encompass the secrets of the early 1940s, she writes in the opening prose poem:

> My mountains are very old. When the Rockies birthed
> bare and sharp against the sky, the Smokies were already
> mellowed down, mantled with forests, steeped in mist,
> like ancients deep in thought. And to their foothills
> in my childhood days men brought the atom—to split it
> and release a force older than the earth, older, perhaps,
> than time itself. Where mountain and atom meet is
> to some a place in Tennessee—Oak Ridge, a city that
> came suddenly and fenced itself and drew around it
> ridges of oak and pine to guard the reactor that in
> secret split the atom.

She continues with the mystery, the mystical if you will, of the Cherokee influence so prevalent in that place and in the blood of the poet herself:

> But to me, where mountain and
> atom meet is a spirit beyond time and place, a spirit
> that abides in the mountain, in the atom, in the hearts
> of my people—Cherokee and pioneers and other folk
> who through the years have come to call the mountains
> home. I have seen traces of this spirit but the spirit
> itself I have not seen. Like the sacred deer of the
> Cherokee it is from everlasting . . . invisible . . . abiding
> in the quick of mystery. And so I call it by the ancient
> name—Awi Usdi, Little Deer.[3]

The collection has no table of contents to announce its intent but is loosely organized into four parts with topics moving from the Cherokee experience to the Appalachian experience to the atomic experience, and finally to a blending of the three. The poem Awiakta calls her credo, "An Indian Walks in Me," comes appropriately near the beginning and proclaims her heritage and her philosophy: a quest for balance and harmony, for unity and wholeness. She closes the credo poem with these lines:

> Long before I learned the
> universal turn of atoms, I heard
> the spirit's song that binds us
> all as one. And no more
> could I follow any rule
> that split my soul.
> My Cherokee left me no sign
> except in hair and cheek
> and this firm step of mind
> that seeks the whole
> in strength and peace.
>
> (15)

Autobiography, yes, but representative of a greater whole than the poet herself. Following her own identification with the Cherokee, she introduces Little Deer in "The Coming of Little Deer": "From the heart of the mountain he comes, with his head held high in the wind. / Like the spirit of light he comes—the small white chief of the Deer" (18). Revered for his sense of justice, protection, and direction in time of need, Little Deer, or Awi Usdi, plays significantly in the mythology of the Native people. Indeed, Awiakta herself has chosen the emblem of Little Deer leaping inside the orbit of the atom as her personal insignia. She wears, always, this tangible evidence of her blended cultures in a pendant of silver on a background of black. Little Deer with his wisdom and guidance is never far from the heart of the poet.

From Little Deer to the Trail of Tears, from the sad story of Tsali to the mountain settlers who follow the Cherokee, the collection moves toward the Oak Ridge story. In the third segment of the book, Awiakta describes the foretelling of "a city on Black Oak Ridge." The prophet, in a poem by that title, is John Hendrix, a farmer who, around 1900, had a vision of Bear Creek Valley being filled with "great buildings and factories" that "will help / win the greatest war that ever will be" (45). John's neighbors were skeptical, but some forty years later his prophecy came to pass, much as he had described. In "Genesis" Awiakta says, "A frontier was a-borning" on Black Oak Ridge:

> Thousands of people streamed in.
> Bulldozers scraped and moved the earth.
> Factories rose in valleys like Bear Creek
> and houses in droves sprang up among the trees
> and strung out in the lees of ridges.
> A great city soon lay concealed among the hills.
> Why it had come no one knew.
> But its energy was a strong and constant hum. . . .
>
> (47)

To the hum of that frontier, Awiakta's family was drawn to live behind the fence, a symbol not of oppression to the young minds of children but of protection and freedom—freedom to run and play in field and wood, protected "as if our own kin patrolled the fence" ("The Fence," 52). She describes the much-coveted house of their own, a cemesto cabin designated as a "B" for size, indicating two bedrooms to accommodate two adults and two children. The A, B, and D cemestos were single-family pre-fabricated houses, brought in and erected, some say, at the alarming rate of one hundred every thirty minutes. The need to house 70,000 inhabitants in a hurry produced remarkable results. There were other types of dwellings as well, including multiple-family houses, flat-tops, hutments, and barracks. Most of these continue to be occupied today in Oak Ridge, though vinyl may cover cemesto and garages may crowd into basements. Well built to stringent government standards, even in the haste of necessity, they have retained their value and their historical import.

Awiakta's poetry in *Abiding Appalachia* and her prose pieces in *Selu* attest to the significance of the houses and the wooded lanes they sat on in establishing the sense of security and community in that strange, yet familiar, place. One of her favorite stories is about the homecoming to the new house. On a cold December day, just after Christmas, the family made the trip from Knoxville and climbed the ridge to South Tampa Lane. When her father pointed out their house, they saw a wisp of smoke coming from the chimney. The movers had started a fire in the fireplace to greet and warm them on their arrival, and they had set up the beds to provide a place of rest. The men themselves were gone—mountain men, Awiakta is quick to add—for they appreciated the family's need for privacy in this special moment of arrival in a new home.

Another prevalent memory from Awiakta's childhood days is the boardwalk. In the hastily built city with as yet unpaved streets, mud abounded. Boardwalks were laid to provide footpaths and, for an imaginative child, a great resource of sensory images. In her poem "Boardwalk," Awiakta revels in her love of sound, touch, and smell imagery, evident both in the child experiencing and the adult recalling. This piece she dubs "my most Appalachian poem," the one she always asks audience members to participate in. From the echo of steps, both her own and others, to the slipperiness of wet wood, to the smell and touch of drying wood, she contrasts the gifts of this living organic substance with the unyielding nature of concrete. Her poem concludes,

> Boardwalk . . . boardwalk . . .
> Step, step . . . talk, talk . . .
>
> Concrete
> won't talk to me
> won't give to me
> won't play with me
> won't fight with me
> won't do
> for me.

(55)

The playful nature of this poem runs through others spoken from a child's perspective; yet the same reflection on serious issues noted in the six-year-old's "Mr. and Mrs. Honeybee Find a Home" surfaces again and again here. "Test Cow," as an example, indicates the child's knowledge of the dangers of radiation and at the same time her compassion for the radioactive cow "locked / behind a fence. . . . It hurts my heart / that I can't even stroke her head / but as mother said, / radiation's just not friendly" (57). "Cemeteries" lends the welcoming presence of "folks" who don't mind if children "settle on a stone / Like on a lap" and tarry to "talk and play" (59). "Disaster Drill" recalls not only the dangers of living on the atomic frontier in wartime, but other removals from other times—Anne Frank, the Cherokee, Tsal— ". . . [N]ot for real . . . no bomb is falling . . . / no seal broken at the lab . . . a drill. / But we leave school, climb the hill / lie in the ditch—we are removed" (65). And "Mother's Advice While Bandaging My Stubbed Toe" counsels, "If you go barefoot in the world / you have to take bad stubs in stride— / or hide in shoes. 'Be plucky, like an Indian,' / that's what my papa said to me / . . . Be wary, but run on . . . / Go barefoot and feel the joy / and when pain comes, bind up your toe / and go your way again. / 'Be plucky, like an Indian'" (63). To reiterate my argument about a topical category for Awiakta's work, I assert that these poems are clearly autobiographical, but they are also clearly more: they convey history of an important place and time from an insider's point of view; they speak philosophy from considered reflection and perhaps even racial memory.

The last segment of *Abiding Appalachia* comes from the adult poet's perspective. She weaves together the strands of her life experience from childhood into adulthood, including now her children as visitors in the cemesto cabin that has become a white-sided cottage. She revisits the cemetery folks and makes a pilgrimage to prophet John Hendrix's grave. She acknowledges change and loss, but recognizes progress and growth as well. Nostalgia notwithstanding, the emphasis of this section is plainly on the power of the atom and the skill of those scientists who dared to experiment and discover. In a visit to the reactor that actually split the atom, Awiakta describes "The Graphite Queen," also known as the Loyal Lady, in words of royalty and mystery: "Reactor Regina," "a boarded structure, tall and temple-like," "commanding presence," "an altar, majestic, immense," "she met her end— standing, with life itself fading slowly . . . slowly . . . Standing as becomes a queen whose power was of the light itself" (84–85). Despite the fading of the Loyal Lady, she is not gone, we learn, but reigns nearby, a new queen in a new form: "She is a deep pool / clear and still / and from the slender cylinder / of her heart / a blue glow rises, / a glow they call / Cerenkov's fire . . ." (87).

Awiakta closes her collection with a poem she names "Where Mountain and Atom Meet." Representative of both the forces of nature and of scientific experimentation, the poem depicts the mountain and the atom as powerful entities exuding from the "great I Am / that gathers to its own / spirits that have gone before" (89). Finally, serving as an epilogue for the whole book, Awi Usdi, the Ancient White, appropriately is the last character on the stage:

> I see him coming . . .
> leaping from the heart of the mountain
> leaping from the eye of the atom . . .
> the white deer follows an ancient path
> leaving no print on the ground
> . . . . .
> Deep calls to deep
> And the mountains call their children home
>
> (91)

While I have labeled this section "Childhood Experiences, Oak Ridge History, and More," clearly other designated themes abound: Cherokee myth, legend, and philosophy as evidenced in the lines just quoted; a reverence for the advances of science as depicted in the poems about the splitting of the atom. Even though I have not pointed specifically to poems about women, Awiakta's awareness of and admiration for her own gender are plain. It is, however, to the next collection that we turn for precise attention to this theme.

## Woman's Role, Conditions, and Rights: Selu—Seeking the Corn Mother's Wisdom

Choosing as her title character the powerful image of Selu, the Cherokee Corn Mother who has analogues in other Native cultures as well, Awiakta explores the giving nature of this female prototype. The Cherokee myth of Selu's birth shows her stepping down, a full-grown woman, from a stalk of corn, bringing with her an ear of the sweet vegetable and singing a lovely song. She befriends Kanati, the lonely, bored solitary male, who heretofore has sought solace in excessive hunting for game. She prepares him a meal, using his meat and the sweet corn she has brought with her, and thus is born a marriage of balance and harmony, mutual respect between male and female, a take-and-give-back philosophy between nature and humankind. This is the lesson Selu teaches throughout Awiakta's book. In the author's own words, "Woman and man represent cardinal balances in nature. Among these balances are: the balance of forces—continuance in the midst of change; the balance of food—vegetables and meat; the balance of relationships—taking and giving back with respect."[4]

The myth of Selu continues with her demise in human form but her regeneration in a stalk of corn growing from her grave—hence the Cherokee word *Selu* meaning both *Corn-Mother* and *corn*. Her death comes as a consequence of her grandsons' breaking the law of respect in regard to her; however, she offers them instructions on how to redeem themselves by preserving and planting the corn that will grow from her grave. Upon following her instructions, they produce abundant corn. And even today Selu continues to feed the people the whole world round with her plentitude (10–14).

While the Selu story is a straightforward Native American myth of origin, the origin of corn, the teachings of Selu offer a philosophy of life that anyone would do well to emulate: strength, balance, harmony, respect. As for the condition of women in the early Cherokee society, that too begs enviable emulation. In the poem entitled "Song of the Grandmothers," Awiakta makes this proclamation:

> I am Cherokee.
> My people believe in the Spirit that unites all things.
>
> I am woman. I am life force. My word has great value.
> The man reveres me as he reveres Mother Earth and his own spirit.
>
> (93)

Throughout the book *Selu*, Awiakta stresses the participation and leadership of the Cherokee women in the Great Council, in the sacred dances, in the home, in the marriage, in the field, even in battle. It is the coming of the white man and his concept of woman's place that bring change. In one of her most poignant poems depicting the circumscribed role of women, "If the Hand That Rocks the Cradle Rules the World," she asks,

> If the hand that rocks
> the cradle rules the world,
> why does the mother pace
> row on row of white crosses,
> seeking the one that
> stakes her son motionless
> in his lidded box?

In ongoing queries about unpunished rapists and starving babies, she concludes with this powerful image:

If the world wants the hand
that rocks the cradle to rule,
why does it slam its Council door
on the mother's wrist,
        watching as she strains
        her other hand toward
        a cradle that rocks slower
            slower
                slower. . . .
                    (85)

In "Anorexia Bulimia Speaks from the Grave," Awiakta assumes one of her most activist positions as she recounts "busting out" consequences of bound feet, bound breasts, bound waists. But to contemporary young women she says, "They've got your soul in a bind. . . ." They want you to starve yourself to fit some unnatural societal image; they don't want you "to take on weight" because "you might start throwin' it around." Her resounding crusade cry is

        Feed your body.
        Feed your soul.
        Feed your dream.
        BUST OUT!!!
            (193–94)

Awiakta's humor energizes her poetry, even with subject matter as serious as this. In my mind's ear I hear her reciting "Anorexia Bulimia" with great vigor and enjoyment, just as she does the tiny vignette called "On Being a Female Phoenix": "Not only do I rise / from my own ashes, / I have to carry them out!" (135). Alongside the sparkling humor that wends its way through *Selu*, a reader also discovers sensitive poetry addressing love and sacrifice between the sexes. "Motheroot," in both of Awiakta's collections, was written in 1978 for her husband Paul. It speaks of sacrifice and support within a marriage but can certainly apply to numerous other relationships as well. Brief and simple, its message is profound:

        Creation often
        needs two hearts
        one to root
        and one to flower

One to sustain
in time of drouth
and hold fast
against winds of pain
the fragile bloom
that in the glory
of its hour
affirms a heart
unsung, unseen.

(184)

Another love poem that clearly has personal overtones appears in both texts. In *Selu* the poem is titled "Selu and Kanati: Marriage" and carries a note identifying the mountainous twin peaks known as the Chimney Tops in the Great Smoky Mountains. Awiakta writes in the note, "One peak is softly rounded, one is sharp. Their beauty is their balance." The poetic description is of a spectacular natural landmark; the title suggests human counterparts:

Two peaks
alone . . . apart . . .
yet join at the heart
where trees rise green
from rain-soaked loam
and laurel's tangled skeins
bear fragile blooms
and wind, a honing, ceaseless
sigh, blends with mirth
of streams defying heights
to wend their way unquenched.
Two peaks
they stand against the sky
spanned by a jagged arm of rock
locked in an embrace
elements cannot destroy
or time erase.

(117)

The poem gains in autobiographical significance when one knows that the Chimney Tops was the spot at which Paul Thompson proposed to Marilou Bonham and presented her with an engagement ring that would lead to marriage some months later. As Awiakta the poet writes of the balance in the two separate peaks joined at the heart, surely Marilou the woman must be considering the two individuals joined in a union of mutual support and sustenance: "Creation often / needs two hearts / one to root / and one to flower ..." (184).

## Nature and Science: Selu and Abiding Appalachia

Just as Awiakta enjoys celebrating the female gender, so does she enjoy celebrating nature. Indeed, she sometimes combines the two as in "Smoky Mountain Woman," a poem attributing feminine characteristics of strength and persistence to the mountain. She could be speaking of either entity, woman or mountain, when she pens her final line: "Time cannot thwart my stubborn thrust toward Heaven" (*Abiding*, 27). In an even more poignant female/nature comparison, she writes in a poem entitled "Women Die Like Trees":

> Women die like trees, limb by limb
> as strain of bearing shade and fruit
> drains sap from branch and stem
> and weight of ice with wrench of wind
> split the heart, loosen grip of roots
> until the tree falls with a sigh—
> unheard except by those nearby—
> to lie ... mossing ... mouldering ...
> to a certain softness under foot,
> the matrix of new life and leaves.
> No flag is furled, no cadence beats,
> no bugle sounds for deaths like these,
> as limb by limb, women die like trees.
>
> (*Abiding*, 35)

In a conversation with me about this poem, Awiakta noted that it took four years to write, to come to maturity. For her, the sentiment describing women's gifts of life and nurture and the toll these exact could only be expressed in poetry, never adequately in prose. She uses exact and near rhyme in a way that pleases the ear as well as the mind and the heart. The imagery she evokes compliments the strength and function of both woman and tree, despite the death knell both must hearken to.

In a more active mode, Awiakta the environmentalist warns of dire results from an incautious and disrespectful use of natural resources in "When Earth Becomes an 'It,'" instead of Mother (*Selu*, 6). "Dying Back" chillingly describes the "standing people" on the mountain turning "brown in the head" from "acid greed / that takes the form of rain / and fog and cloud." At the same time the "walking people" in the valley are "blank-eyed" and "dying back / as all species do / that kill their own seed" (*Selu*, 5). The poet's humor flashes in "Mother Nature Sends a Pink Slip," but her message is grim. In memo format, the address reads,

> To:   Homo Sapiens
> Re:   Termination

The memo poem gives the reasons for this drastic action as non-compliance with management goals and objectives. Three warnings over the past decade have not brought about change; hence, the final lines of the memo:

> Your failure to take appropriate action
> has locked these warnings into
> the Phase-Out Mode, which will result
> in termination.      No appeal.
>
> (*Selu*, 88)

Bleak as this message is, Awiakta's hope springs eternal. Just as she recognized while but a child the power of the atom to destroy as well as to help and heal, she acknowledges again and again in *Selu* the curative powers of restoring balance and harmony in our relationship to the earth and to one another. One entire section of her book is entitled "When the People Call Earth 'Mother'"; it is filled with anecdote, legend, myth, historical account, interview, personal narrative, and more, exemplifying repeatedly obedience to the law of respect, restoration of balance and harmony, unity in diversity. Awiakta calls on the good nature and common sense of her Native people; she points to the thoughtfulness and generosity of wise statesmen; she applauds the respect, caution, and daring of cutting-edge scientists. Finally, in the conclusion of her multi-genre book, she entitles her penultimate section "Selu Sings for Survival." It is here where she celebrates the remarkable work of Dr. Barbara McClintock, corn geneticist, who discovered the process of "jumping genes" among chromosomes, who preached the philosophy of considering the wholeness of the organism rather than only isolated parts, who won eventually a Nobel Prize for her groundbreaking work. According to Awiakta, McClintock knew first-hand Ginitsi Selu, the corn and the Corn-Mother. She knew the wisdom, the philosophy, and the grain itself. McClintock helped the modern world to accept and understand the gift:

> Awi Usdi, Little Deer
> Ginitsi Selu

Corn, Mother of Us All
in perfect balance
in perfect union.

The Creator offers us a gift. . . .
(*Selu*, 326)

And so the story comes full circle—from a sacred origin myth of the Cherokee to a singularly important scientific discovery, brought to fruition in each case by a female protagonist. The "telling" comes from Awiakta, a Cherokee/Appalachian female poet who, in the words of scientist Rupert Cutler, may provide for the ethnic/gender equality movement, and consequently the environment, an impact similar to that rendered by Rachel Carson's *Silent Spring*.[5]

## Personal Connections

I cannot conclude this essay without a personal note. I first came to know Marilou Awiakta's work and then the person in 1984. Since that time our professional association has steadily continued, and our friendship has flourished and grown. One of the most exciting professional linkages relates to the development of the Selu Conservancy at Radford University. By invitation, Awiakta offered in 1989 the name Selu to the 375-acre parcel of land given to the Radford University Foundation and designated as a culture and nature conservancy. The name honors the gifting legacy of the property through the years. Awiakta conducted the first workshop for writers on the site, has participated in various launchings and dedications at the Conservancy, and today serves as an honorary member of the Selu Steering Committee. She has taken part in numerous readings, classes, and writing workshops at Radford University, including the year-long celebration of corn and culture in 1996–97. It has been my good fortune to have a close alliance with each of these events, to become better acquainted with Awiakta and her remarkable warmth as person and author.

On an even more personal note, it was also my fate to stand by with friends and supporters in April of 1998, several hundred miles removed from Awiakta, while we awaited news of the outcome of her surgery for breast cancer. The surgery and subsequent treatments, including the healing powers of nuclear medicine which grew out of research in her own Oak Ridge frontier town, have brought her back to health and happiness—renewed, strengthened, balanced.

On January 1, 1999, Awiakta called on a day that was one of the darkest for me. My mother had died in the still hours of the night, just after the birthing of the new year. Marilou said, "Grace, I want to give you a gift in honor of your mother. It is a poem called 'Cora's Patchwork,' and I will say it for you":

It takes more than saying
to make love so.
It takes being and doing
as stitch by stitch
Love makes a pattern
that endures.

No more fitting tribute could have been offered to Cora Green Toney, who sewed her whole life to clothe a houseful of daughters and one lone son, who put together many a patchwork quilt to guard against the cold, who stitched love into every garment and covering over the course of her almost ninety years. Awiakta had never met my mother, but somehow she knew intuitively the person and the poem that fit. The poem became part of a written memorial tribute and of the funeral service itself. Of course, it had been published years before under the title of "Patchwork" in *Abiding Appalachia* (31), but only in this personalized context did I come to know its full significance.

I include this personal narrative as a final example of the kind of gifts Marilou Awiakta offers to her readers, listeners, family, and friends. She is an author who does not separate herself from her subject matter, nor from her audience. She is part and parcel of that which she writes about and for. To reiterate a point made much earlier in this essay, she writes autobiography, but not just about herself. It is the history, the philosophy, the autobiography of an ethnic group, a community, a habitat. It is what she does in answer to her mother's question posed so long ago: "What will you do for the people?" Awiakta's answer today might well be: "I tell their story."

## Notes

1. The poem is mentioned in "Sound" in *Bloodroot: Reflections on Place by Appalachian Women Writers*, ed. Joyce Dyer (Lexington: Univ. Press of Kentucky, 1998), 47–48. Biographical details are from an interview by the author (Memphis, Tenn., Sept. 16, 1999). Subsequent references to biographical information are from this interview if not otherwise noted. An earlier version of this essay entitled "The Hum of Black Oak Ridge in the Poetry of Marilou Awiakta" was presented at the Appalachian Studies Association's Annual Conference, Univ. of Tennessee, Knoxville, Tenn., Mar. 24, 2000.

2. Ernest Lee, "Sources of Light in Awiakta's *Selu*" (paper presented at Appalachian Studies Association's Annual Conference, 2000).

3. Marilou Bonham Thompson, *Abiding Appalachia: Where Mountain and Atom Meet* (Memphis, Tenn.: St. Luke's Press, 1978), 13. Subsequent references to poems in this book are presented parenthetically. The most recent printing of this book, the eighth edition, is by Iris Press of Bell Buckle, Tenn. (1995), under Marilou Awiakta.

4. Marilou Awiakta, *Selu: Seeking the Corn Mother's Wisdom* (Golden, Colo.: Fulcrum Publishing, 1993), 25. Subsequent references to this book are presented parenthetically.

5. Rupert Cutler, review of *Selu: Seeking the Corn-Mother's Wisdom*, by Marilou Awiakta, *Now & Then* 12, no. 1 (Spring 1995): 37.

# Kathryn Stripling Byer

## *Wildwood Flower*

I hoe thawed ground
with a vengeance. Winter has left
my house empty of dried beans
and meat. I am hungry

and now that a few buds appear
on the sycamore, I watch the road
winding down this dark mountain
not even the mule can climb
without a struggle. Long daylight

and nobody comes while my husband
traps rabbits, chops firewood, or
walks away into the thicket. Abandoned
to hoot owls and copperheads,

I begin to fear sickness. I wait
for pneumonia and lockjaw. Each month
I brew squaw tea for pain.
In the stream where I scrub my own blood
from rags, I see all things flow
down from me into the valley.

Once I climbed the ridge
to the place where the sky
comes. Beyond me the mountains continued
like God. Is there no place to hide
from His silence? A woman must work

else she thinks too much. I hoe
this earth until I think of nothing
but the beans I will string,
the sweet corn I will grind into meal.

We must eat. I will learn
to be grateful for whatever comes to me.

## Black Shawl

around me,
unraveling its garland
of snakeroot
and cobweb, her
black thoughts made
manifest night
after night as she
labored, her silver
hook gleaming by
candlelight. Memory
chained unto
memory: hawk
sailing, smoke curling
out of the burned
fields, her name
written fancy in black
ink, the words
in her letter, the two
words, *Remember*
*me.* Nights I can't
sleep I hear
wind shove the dead
leaves along like my own
thoughts, those rag
taggle gypsies she sang
about, all of them black
shawled and stealing
away to their dirty
work, digging as
always past earthworm
and ground water,
tremor of mine
shaft where rocks bear
the imprint of ancient
anemone. They bring
her back piece by

piece to me, even the sound
of her breath in my
oldest dream. "What
will you make
of this?" they whisper,
filling my arms
with a snatch of her
hair, muddy ribbons, this
tangle of black roots
that drags my hands down.

# Singing Our Hearts Away
## The Poetry of Kathryn Stripling Byer

Ann F. Richman

When I first heard Kathryn Stripling Byer read the Alma poems, some twenty years ago, the strong impression she made was created both by her vision of an isolated mountain woman whose inner and outer lives she evoked so feelingly and by the songlike language that is the trademark of this poet. In her three published books of poems—*The Girl in the Midst of the Harvest* (1986), an Associated Writing Programs award series selection; *Wildwood Flower* (1992), winner of the Lamont Prize; and *Black Shawl* (1998)—she displays both the imaginative power of a novelist in creating different personae and the linguistic sensitivity of a poet in singing the stories in varied voices.[1]

Although she was born in South Georgia, Byer is at home in Appalachia, where she has lived since moving to the mountains of North Carolina in 1968 and where she is now poet-in-residence at Western Carolina University in Cullowhee. There she found inspiration in the life of a grandmother who had moved from and was never able to return to the Blue Ridge that she loved, who is clearly the muse of the first book. In fact, in her essay "Deep Water," Byer reflects, "Sometimes I think that all of the poems I have written since I came to the mountains have been an attempt to find a song that would sail her away, out of the sad story in which she had become trapped, back to the mountains where she belonged and longed to be." The comment highlights her major themes of singing, entrapment, and the overarching isolation, the deep water of Emma Bell Miles's metaphor, "Solitude is deep water," cited by Byer and from which she draws the essay's title. In Byer's view, "No one who has lived for long in these mountains can doubt the power of that solitude. It can cause a woman to sink into its depths and never rise again. It can drive her crazy trying to break its hold on her, all the while drawing her closer and closer to the edge of some jump-off, the distance rising up before her like a vision of freedom."[2]

Byer's poems are unapologetically regional; but after all, as William Stafford once said to William Mooney of *The Tennessee Poetry Journal*, "All events and experiences are local, somewhere. And all human enhancement of events and experiences—all the arts—are regional in the sense that they derive from immediate relation to felt life. It is this immediacy that distinguishes art."[3] That Byer is more than a local colorist and transcends the merely regional is affirmed in a review of Black Shawl, her most recently published book. Penelope Scambly Schott writes, "Byer is not a limited 'regional' poet, retailing folksy atmosphere. Yes, her poems are set in Appalachia, even in the Cullowhee Valley where she lives, but she combines her local scenery and Cherokee lore with poetic strands that go back as far as the early Middle Ages. As she ties the past to the present, she gives us what is eternal in the souls of women."[4]

In Byer's first book we find a double vision. The opening section of The Girl in the Midst of the Harvest presents a young girl living in the second half of the twentieth century and looking forward while at the same time remembering her childhood in Georgia. The girl in the corn is, as Jennifer Johnson puts it in a review, "the harvest of what was planted long ago by her ancestors" and her voice "sings of how much it is looking toward the future. . . ."[5] That cheerful, hopeful voice is heard in "Cornwalking," singing "What is the world but our song?" (5). It is also in "Daughter," proclaiming,

> When I look up the future's a field for me.
> I am the girl in the midst of the harvest.
>
> I am the harvest.
>
> (7)

The girl who sees herself as the harvest in the opening poem, "Wide Open, These Gates," sings winningly, "Going down the road feeling good, I snap / my fingers" and ends "The gnats sing, and I'm going / to sing. One of these days I'll be gone" (3).

Not all the poems in Girl are joyful. Byer, lacking the source materials, the letters and diaries, that are often the only "histories" of women, fictionalized her grandmother and great-grandmother and placed them in the American West. The grandmother goes there to search for her mother (her history) and by implication to search for meaning in her life. The final section, "I Inherit the Light of My Grandmother's House," seems to offer, as a tentative answer to the question of how to live, the celebration of daily existence, but even there in some poems a desire to escape lends a sober undertone.

In both joyful and sober poems, some of the strength of Byer's lyrics comes from her use of open forms with unrhymed lines of varying lengths.

She finds her musical effects not in rhyme or in meter but rather in line length and phrasing, with frequent use of enjambment, and in sound devices such as alliteration and assonance. The only rhymes are slant rhymes such as *pits/fished, shoes/glue* in "Peaches" (61) or *creek/feet* and *cloth/thoughts* in "Kitchen Sink," also worthy of mention because it ends the book with the important theme of the grandmother:

> The reward of a long life is faith
>
> in what's left. Dishes stacked on a strong table.
> Jars of dried beans. Scraps of cloth.
> And the ten thousand things of her own thoughts,
> incessant as creek water. She has been able
>
> to lay up her treasures on earth,
> as if heaven were here, worth believing.
>
> (73)

The first quoted line above is the last line of the second stanza and seems at first to make a complete statement, but in an effective use of enjambment the line runs on into the next stanza with the phrase "in what's left," which alters the meaning. That rather long assertion with its alliteration (*long, life, left*) is followed by three short phrases naming some of the material things that are left and then a fourth much longer phrase descriptive of her inner life: "thoughts / incessant as creek water." Then again the last line of the stanza runs on into the following stanza. The last sentence of the poem is four lines long in a return to the rhythm of the opening stanzas. The effect is to create an expectation of a traditional sort of poem embodying homely "kitchen" truths but then to shake the ground under the reader's feet. This poem offers a philosophy beyond "kitchen" wisdom, a philosophy that might be called, with no intention to minimize, "kitchen existentialism."

In the second book, *Wildwood Flower*, much of which "exists because of Appalachian ballads,"[6] that influence is more on subject matter than on form. The poet uses a greater variety of forms than in the first book—varying stanza patterns and even including one villanelle, "Lost Soul" (16). Her meters are still irregular, as are line lengths, and she continues to create her music with rhythms and the sounds of words. One example of her use of sound to reinforce meaning occurs in "Thaw," following the passage describing the discovery of a mule frozen in the pasture:

                                               I thought
                       how I too might have simply stood

                       still and become ice, I was that
                       tired of lifting cold water.
                       Today the road's shedding
                       its ice like a snakeskin,

                       like my own calloused skin
                       I will scour this very night,
                       though the almanac says spring
                       is six weeks away.
                                               (12)

The repetition of "s" sounds combined with harsh consonants like the hard
"c" in cold, calloused, scour, and almanac and the "k" sounds in like, snakeskin, skin,
and weeks creates a dissonance in the passage that reinforces the meaning of
the poem—the discouraging effect of a long, cold winter filled with hard
work. The poem's context and its meaning are inseparable, meeting a stan-
dard set by Dave Smith: "The poetry is the music which evokes, creates,
releases, controls, and clarifies feeling in the dramatic context."[7] This music
with its enjambed lines breaking normal speech rhythms, its sibilance, and
its hard consonants is a highly crafted discordance.

     Wildwood Flower opens with "At Kanati Fork," an invocation to the pres-
ence Byer felt while hiking the trail:

                       At Kanati Fork
                       she was a face fading back into hemlock.
                       . . . . . . . . . . . . . . . .
                       She was the wind in my ears,
                       singing "Sail away, ladies,"
                       and setting the maple leaves spinning,

                       a lone woman haunting the trail
                       till it ended in chimney-stone. . . .
                                               (n.p.)

She gave to that identity the name Alma, which Byer explains as both the
name of a real woman, Mrs. Alma Pressley, and "the metaphor of soul that
could encompass a woman's spiritual journey as well as her literal one."[8] By

creating a life for Alma, a woman living at the beginning of the twentieth century high on a mountain where the soil is thin, the wind cold, Byer embodies in carefully wrought lyrics some of the womanly experiences that she feels need to be remembered, including desire for the love and companionship of men, the suffering as well as the joy of motherhood, loneliness and disappointed love, and extremities of cold, hunger, pain, and loss.

In "Trillium" Alma says, "Though we spoke of love, / I know now it means little / but loneliness" (22). And in "Midnight" she remembers,

> I lay waiting for you
> to come back from the spring
> house and say, "Hear
> that whippoorwill singing
> its heart away?" I should
> have wrapped you in words
> like a soft blanket.

(9)

The poems grouped under the heading "Christmas" are poems of motherhood. In "Mary" Alma imagines the life of the pregnant Virgin and dreams of her in the cold stable. In "Whippoorwills," with her baby kicking in the womb, Alma sits on a bucket in her own cold barn and remembers her grandmother singing: "She promised me / wonders if I'd but believe them, the elderbush / blooming in snow, and at daybreak / a barn full of whippoorwills singing" (26). Those wonders are things of this world, not miracles of the supernatural. In the last poem of the group, "Snow," she identifies the snow she dreams of as "the light in the darkness the preacher says / faith is . . ." (27). She can think of faith only in terms of the things of this world.

Of extremity Alma knows a great deal. In "Lost Soul" she thinks, "Against solitude I have no aid" (16). The poem "Extremity" begins, "Pity my cold feet in bed" and ends with "Nothing can come / to me now. I have no blessings to count. // I count my cold fingers and toes" (13–14). That Alma sees things differently at times is clear in the contrast between "Extremity" and the poem "Wildwood Flower," which ends with an image of Alma in her garden, hungry after a winter which has "left / my house empty" and thinking that she must work because "We must eat. I will learn / to be grateful for whatever comes to me" (3).

The women in Byer's poems usually reject the possibility of consolations some find in the church and, instead, seek meaning in earthly gifts—love, the natural world, making beautiful and useful things, singing—as they struggle often alone to survive on their subsistence gardens. John Lang, in a paper entitled "Means of Grace," informs us that in a letter to him in 1996 Byer said she had grown up with a Presbyterian view of God as "distant, judgmental, cold." Lang concludes that Alma rebels against that God and "seeks to affirm the spiritual significance of the senses, of the body, and of nature itself."[9] Lang—looking closely at four poems from *Wildwood Flower*, "Cobwebs," "Easter," "Amazing Grace," and "Afterwards, Far from the Church"—finds they reveal a "distrust of a religion that deprecates both the world of the senses and women themselves." As an example, he quotes the full text of "Easter," which includes the perception that dogwood blooms are "like white flesh this man [the preacher] claims / is devil's work . . ." (44). Lang concludes that [i]t is by way of nature and the body that Alma feels most directly connected with the Creator's spirit at work in the world . . ." and that the poems are an effort to transcend the traditional link of women to physical phenomena.[10]

One way women in Byer's poems seek transcendence is by making art out of necessity—quilting, crocheting, weaving, and especially singing. For example, Alma's grandmother sings an old ballad of shipwreck in "Weep Willow" to pass on something important to a grandchild: "At night she watched the road / and sang . . . / near ninety verses full of grief" (37). In "Bittersweet," Alma, the nursing mother, rocks her baby to sleep "singing, "'Little bird, / little bird under my wing'" even though her voice cracks and she believes "My sweet songs / have all blown away, / one by one, down the mountain" (29).

At times it seems that, as Rilke proclaimed in the third of his *Sonnets to Orpheus*, song is being.[11] Rilke's belief lends weight to Johnson's comment that to Byer "life is to be lived and to be told to others; it is the singing of the world to the world."[12] The interest in music and the attention paid to sounds of words are not surprising in a poet who says that growing up she wanted to be a singer. She studied singing for two years, sang at church, and occasionally elsewhere. Noting that she wanted to become a singer, she believes that "much of poetry is song: praise and celebration in the face of loss and death."[13] Her poems, however, are not simply songs but frequently are songs about singing. The voices of women singing their way out of solitude form a web of interconnections symbolized by the lacy handwork of a crocheted shawl, the "Black Shawl" that appears in *Wildwood Flower* and then becomes the title for the next book. In "Deep Water" Byer describes the shawl that haunted her as a "black shawl that gathers up all of these voices into its complicated, endlessly evolving pattern."[14]

The web metaphor has its counterpart in the real world in the connections between Kathryn Byer and other women—poets, novelists, photographers, and quilters. In "Deep Water," she writes that the work of Emma Bell

Miles and Lee Smith gave her clues to the identity of the felt presence who became Alma. Lee Smith then used Byer's "Weep Willow" at the beginning of her novel *Fair and Tender Ladies* as a kind of verbal frontispiece opposite a second title page, which quotes the line, "Oh Ivy, sing ivory, rosebud and thorn . . ." from "Ivy, Sing Ivory," a Byer poem in *Wildwood Flower* (50). The connections multiply. Smith's main character is named Ivy, and she like Alma is making sense of her life by telling her story, though through the medium of letter-writing rather than singing.

This kind of interaction is something women may have dreamed of and idealized more than actually experiencing, but it is encouraging and instructive to observe it in practice with real women like Kathryn Byer and Lee Smith living full lives of commitment to family, to teaching, and to writing. The interaction contributes to a creative process that may aptly be described by the shawl metaphor. Byer seems to connect material in a way similar to the way a needlewoman uses her crochet hook to create chains and patterns that then loop back to connect to previous creations while the entire piece moves toward wholeness and completion.

The material she works with in *Black Shawl* is strongly influenced by ballads. Part two, "Blood Mountain," opens with a prologue invoking the legend of the Creek and Cherokee wars which left the mountains "stained / with their warriors' blood," and suggesting in contrast a woman's perspective:

> but if you ask
> the old woman threading
> her loom on the outskirts
> of town how this
> place got its name,
> she says one story's
> good as another
> so long as there's
> blood in it.

(n.p.)

A woman's tale of blood is not of warriors but of menstrual blood, blood of childbirth, children's injuries, gutted wild game, or butchered pigs as in "Let's Say":

> Old blood and first
> blood and bad blood and cold blood and blue
> blood and blood in her mouth
> from a bit tongue

(29)

That is, "bite your tongue" rather than say what you really think. The black thoughts in these poems suggest the shawl crocheted by Alma's grandmother in the poem "Black Shawl" in *Wildwood Flower*. Her silver crochet hook produces "memory / chained unto / memory," as "her / black thoughts made / manifest night / after night . . ." (41). The shawl, to Alma, becomes the grandmother's name

> written fancy in black
> ink, the words
> in her letter, the two
> words, *Remember*
> *me.*
>
> (41)

Surely those words are the cry of all those who have been left out of history.

In her informative essay "Having Become Their Own Voices," Julie Kate Howard examines the influence of the ballad on *Black Shawl*, which she describes as a "weave of blood lines, song lines, and Indo-European language lines."[15] One of the poems Howard illuminates by reminding us of the life of Queen Anne is "Wild," which presents the queen "trapped" in her tower with her ladies-in-waiting, not by the king but by the eighteen failed pregnancies that produced no living child. Reading the poem again after reading Howard, I saw the queen as literally a lady-in-waiting herself. The poem's jarring metaphor contrasting her immobility with the movement of the wild carrot also known as Queen Anne's Lace which is "strewn along crossties and fenceposts / or stitching its stubborn way through / to the edge of each backcountry road" (42) is a disturbing image of biological destiny reducing a human being to a condition with less freedom than a plant which bears the same name.

Many of Byer's poems could fit into the pattern of entrapment and escape or the longing for escape. James Byer, in his essay "Woman's Place," notes that certain poets, including Byer, write of women who see the house as a haven but also as a cage.[16] Kathryn Byer confirms that "in my work the domestic round is both inviting and claustrophobic, and that I seek my reconcilements in the poetry itself, with its long historical and mythic perspectives."[17] Many of the poems in *Black Shawl* refer to traps which women have found hard to escape. In "Bone" the trap is kinship—being surrounded by relatives: "What good to run away into some dark night // where every lamp signified kinsmen?" (23). The trap in "Storm" is marriage to a man who becomes brutal when drunk (24). In "Phacelia" it is delusion about love, a love that leaves "every sweet / nothing melting away" as the poem compares the snowy white flower phacelia to the bride's veil of "*Sheer / Illusion*" (25).

Some poems in *Black Shawl* are in a modified ballad stanza but without the regular meter (common meter) of traditional ballads. In other poems Byer experiments with stanzas of varying lengths as, for example, in "Timberline," with its nine-line stanzas of irregular line lengths (37), or in "Snow Breath," which has nine stanzas, six with the same first line—"Snow on the mountains"—then three with a variation of the first line, ending with these lines:

> . . . after so long,
> a woman's soul searching
>
> through snow on the mountains
> will sink, out of breath, in the silence
> of nothing more, nothing less.

> (12)

In Byer's work grandmothers are a key to the past, their stories a kind of history that is central to Byer's poetics. One statement of that view is found in "Mountain Time," a prologue to *Black Shawl*, in which Byer responds to a "famous poet" at the Library of Congress who said poetry would no longer be read by the year 2000. Byer rejects the thesis that American poets will become extinct. She sees the poet as storyteller passing on words of earlier storytellers who might be saying the world "keeps calling us back to beginnings" (x).

It is that call that I believe affected me so much in my first hearing of the Alma poems. The poems are such rich evocations of feeling and so completely convincing in their authenticity that they made me think in a new way about my own beginnings, at least as far back as my great-grandmother. I tried to imagine her life that, while it seems quite remarkable to me, was no doubt not that unusual at the time. She at the age of six moved from North Carolina to Arkansas in a wagon train with her father and her six older sisters, their mother having died giving birth to the youngest girl, Margaret. The lives Byer imagines of mountain women seem similar in many ways to the lives of many of those pioneer women who endured hardships unimaginable to us. My great-grandmother's story is known to me only through a few notes she wrote in the margins of her Bible and through a page or two written down by her daughter, my mother's mother, of what her mother had told her. The stories of the women in my family are closely related to the lost voices that Kathryn Byer is trying to recover. Her work serves an important purpose in filling in some of the details of the largely unknown territory on the map of human experience—that territory of women's hopes and feelings, their thoughts and searches for meaning.

In an interview for *Mossy Creek Journal*, Byer commented on the way she has seen her work: "When I first discovered that I wanted to 'be a poet,' I saw that as a way of escaping from the sort of feminine role I'd been unable to master in girlhood and young womanhood. You know, the Southern Belle, the cheerleader, the prom queen. I also saw it as a way out of the claustrophobic world of marriage and family, the traditional roles of my mother, grandmother, and great grandmothers, *ad infinitum*. Now I see poetry as a *way into* a more realistic expression of the feminine. . . . I've felt my share of conflicts and frustrations."[18] Her way of expressing conflict and frustration has been to create characters who experience them, to employ dramatic devices to a greater extent than do most lyric poets, and to strive for what she considers a realistic view of women's lives and history despite obvious differences between her own life and the lives she depicts.

In her new collection, *Catching Light*, Byer has been able to write first-person lyrics from the point of view of a much older woman, demonstrating once again her ability to bring alive a persona and to make real for us the poignancy of daily life for a woman no longer waiting for someone to come home, or for something exciting to happen, but waiting now for the end.[19] With this collection, Byer completes a kind of life cycle of the human female from girlhood through young womanhood, maturity, and old age. The cycle is hardly chronological as it moves through time from mid to early to late twentieth century, but it records aspects of women's lives ranging from youthful high spirits to a more subdued spirit shadowed by experience of the world.

To her credit, Byers asserts the importance of women's experience and seems to share the view of Lee Smith, who when asked about being called a southern, or Appalachian, or feminist writer responded, "I will probably write mostly about women because I know better about how they think. . . . And I don't think it's any lesser. I mean, I think that things that women have often written about, which are deep kinds of rituals or families or relationships, I think that those things are as important as slogging through some battle. I really do—as important as some traditionally male thing."[20] Byer has said that she sees her poetry and, in fact, "all poetry, as a struggle against amnesia." She describes the poems in *Girl* as "attempts to save from the rubble of the past the memories that will enable one to find a self that is one's own." She believes that we are all "in danger of becoming amnesiacs" and losing our connections "with the past, with family, with the land itself. . . ."[21] She has taken it upon herself to reinvent some of the history of ordinary women by combining memories, fictionalized biographies, and ghost stories. In her work memory is history, and she is the historian of unremembered, solitary women. She is a poet who calls us back to beginnings and who insists in her beautifully crafted poems on the significance and validity of women's feelings and thoughts.

## Notes

1. Kathryn Stripling Byer, *The Girl in the Midst of the Harvest* (Lubbock, Tex.: Texas Tech Press, 1986); *Wildwood Flower* (Baton Rouge: Louisiana State Univ. Press, 1992); *Black Shawl* (Baton Rouge: Louisiana State Univ. Press, 1998). Subsequent references to Byer's poems are in the text.
2. Kathryn Stripling Byer, "Deep Water," in *Bloodroot*, ed. Dyer, 63. The previous quotations in this paragraph are also from this page.
3. William Stafford, "The Tradition of Total Experience," in *First Person Singular*, comp. Joyce Carol Oates (Princeton, N.J.: Ontario Review Press, 1983), 223. Stafford's remarks were first published in *The Tennessee Poetry Journal*.
4. Penelope Scambly Schott, review of *Black Shawl*, by Kathryn Stripling Byer, *Sow's Ear Poetry Review* 8, no. 3 (Sept. 1998): 24.
5. Johnson, review of *The Girl in the Midst of the Harvest*, by Kathryn Stripling Byer, *Mossy Creek Journal* 11 (Spring 1987): 22.
6. Kathryn Stripling Byer, Interview, *Mossy Creek Journal* 11 (Spring 1987): 29.
7. Dave Smith, "Assays," in *First Person Singular*, comp. Oates, 178.
8. Byer, "Deep Water," 69.
9. John Lang, "Means of Grace," paper presented at meeting of South Atlantic Modern Language Association, Savannah, Ga., Nov. 1996, 8.
10. Ibid.
11. Rainer Maria Rilke, "Sonnet to Orpheus 3," in *Sonnets to Orpheus*, trans. C. F. MacIntyre (Berkeley: Univ. of California Press, 1960), 7.
12. Johnson, 23.
13. Byer, interview, 29.
14. "Deep Water," 63.
15. Julie Kate Howard, "'Having Become Their Own Voices': The Third Stream in Kathryn Stripling Byer's *Black Shawl*," *Asheville Poetry Review* 6, no. 1 (Spring and Summer 1999): 38.
16. James Byer, "A Woman's Place," in *The Poetics of Appalachian Space*, ed. Parks Lanier Jr. (Knoxville: Univ. of Tennessee Press, 1991), 161–82.
17. Byer, interview, 31.
18. Ibid.
19. *Catching Light* (Baton Rouge: Louisiana State Univ. Press, 2002).
20. Lee Smith, "Every Kind of Ritual: A Conversation," interviewed by Dorothy Hill, *Iron Mountain Review* 3, no. 1 (Winter 1986): 27.
21. Byer, interview, 29.

# Jo Carson

## Faith in Words

Remember: words are all pretenders,
two together may not mean the same tomorrow,
and three or more coincident are likely
just another chancy fruit of the deception
language was first spoken to disguise.

Remember: if it is true, the very words
that say it may also bear false witness.
Faith in words is not faith at face value.
Faith in words comes by reflection.
Words have the same light as the moon.

## People Piece #11

You know the other day we went over at George's get some eggs?
    No, we went over George's get some beans.
    George ain't got no eggs.
No, we got beans up at Lucille's.
    We took tomatoes to Lucille.
We took tomatoes to Wally.
    Where'd we get the beans?
Lucille's.
    I swear I took tomatoes.
Well, we didn't.
    Now, Wally's got a garden.
    Why we carryin' tomatoes up to him?
His ain't come in yet.
    Lester's has; Lester should'a give him some.
Lester's so tight you couldn't pry tomatoes out of him.
    He give George's boy a little puppy.
It was a stray and it turned around and bit him.
    Who?
Lester.
    Well, at least it wasn't George's little boy.
What'd we get at George's?
    I guess we didn't go to George's.
Oh. Maybe that's why we ain't go no eggs.

# "Room Is Made for Whoever"
## Jo Carson and the Creation of Dialogical Community

Jennifer Mooney

> What I create are not plays in the traditional sense. They are
> more like patchwork quilts of stories which community people,
> not professional actors, play back for the community in public
> performance. Room is made for whoever wants to participate.
>
> Jo Carson, 1996[1]

> Moving from silence into speech is for the oppressed, the col-
> onized, the exploited, and those who stand and struggle side
> by side a gesture of defiance that heals, that makes new life and
> new growth possible. It is that act of speech, of 'talking back,'
> that is no mere gesture of empty words, that is the expression
> of movement from object to subject—the liberated voice.
>
> bell hooks, 1989[2]

> Dialogical texts are marked by a "plurality of independent and
> unmerged voices and consciousnesses, a genuine polyphony
> of fully valid voices . . . a plurality of consciousnesses, with
> equal rights and each with its own world.
>
> Mikhail Bakhtin, 1984[3]

I n the various incarnations of his "Preface to *Lyrical Ballads*," William Wordsworth refutes contemporary neoclassical theory by arguing that true poetry is virtually identical to ordinary speech, differing only by the addi- tion of passion and meter. Based upon such theorizing, he states his intentions to eschew in the collection "poetic diction" and instead "chuse incidents and situations from common life, and to relate or describe them, throughout, as far as was possible, in a selection of language really used by men."[4] Wordsworth's endeavor is noble, but is destined by the prevailing poetical and ideological dic- tates to be only partially successful, a certainty that the poet seems to recognize. With its tone so resoundingly that of an *apologia*, the preface does not endorse fully this language of the common man, but will instead provide a selected or edited "vernacular" more palatable to its discerning readers: it will present not only a "*selection* of language" but one that will be "*purified* indeed from what appear to be its real defects."[5] And, in truth, while such poems as "Simon Lee, the Old Huntsman," "The Last of the Flock," and "The Thorn" do indeed take as their subjects the common man (or woman), their diction and aesthetics remain resolutely poetic, aimed toward a distinctly less-than-common audience. Thus does the potentially subversive implication of Wordsworth's theory remain unfulfilled.

However, by privileging the common person living a common life and arguing for—if not in practice fully accomplishing—the fundamental connection between poetic and real language, Wordsworth's theories laid the foundation for subsequent conceptions of poetry as a democratizing force capable of bridging social divides and speaking to, belonging to, everyone. Yet it has taken two hundred years of practice among the Walt Whitmans, the Langston Hugheses, and the Nikki Giovannis to fully integrate the two halves of that groundbreaking theory, to praise in works deemed "art" the common person speaking in his or her own voice. Among the contemporary writers to actualize the sort of communal, redemptive, as well as defiant, vision only hinted at by Wordsworth's theories is East Tennessee native, self-professed play "quilter," and storyteller Jo Carson. In her plays, essays, short stories, and "found poetry," Carson provides ample space for and celebrates the voices of the common person, creating from her collection of oral histories, remembered events, and overheard conversations a living community of words that makes room for anyone who wishes to speak and bridges the traditional disjunction between written and oral narratives.

As a storyteller, Jo Carson carefully distinguishes her artistic vision, with its emphasis on "real" stories, from that practiced by the professional purveyors of tall tales and Jack tales. The distinction is an important one, for while the real stories are "harder" or more painful, both to write and to hear, they are more valuable. Carson believes deeply that the energizing and redemptive powers of real storytelling, the recording of our everyday, individual lives with their related mythological underpinnings, enable a communal spirit to flourish. Real stories define us as individuals and bond us as communities because "in the telling of these stories are the moments when we come to understand our relationship to those mythic underpinnings."[6] Stories are "how we gain strength from one another, how we come to know one another, how we come to be a community, how we come to be people who have engagement in our own lives and in other people's lives."[7] Thus Carson acknowledges the direct correlations among speech, identity, community, and power, an entwining made possible by engagement.

Such engagement is natural, for, as Walter J. Ong suggests, "the spoken word forms human beings into close-knit groups. When a speaker is addressing an audience, the members of the audience become a unity, with themselves and with the speaker."[8] Because of the story's basis in and its enacting of reality, the experience bonds speaker and audience together in a single continuum. It permits diversity of perspective but also simultaneously and subversively defies social constructions and constrictions, enabling the silenced to speak and the invisible to become visible—in short, creating the sort of empowered community that can come only through the release of the spoken word. "[Y]ou do not know how hard it can be to tell real stories, out loud in front of real people in places where the tradition of silence in such matters is so very, very strong," Carson suggests.[9] To permit her work to speak most effectively, Carson depends on several related practices: the incorporation of multiple voices, the use of direct address, and a comfortable privileging of everyday speech, techniques which both universalize and democratize the stories. Each practice is defiant, subversive in its own way.

In Carson's literary world, there is not a single authoritative voice, but many voices, each with its own inflection, resonance, and beauty. Each has its own story to tell, and it is obvious that in Carson's opinion this is the way it should be. From the philosophical musings she expresses in her interviews to the themes she explores in her poems, short stories, and plays, it becomes easy to discern such principles at the core of Carson's literary theory. No matter what form the written story takes, at the heart of Carson's work beats the human voice. "Everything I write is to be spoken aloud," she recounts in one interview. "If something doesn't fit in my mouth it won't fit in somebody else's head."[10] Rarely can one find in Carson's stories merely a single dominant persona, for even in the found poetry, the speaker addresses a listener whose presence is palpable and thus shapes reception of the material. Most often several voices speak with equal force and emphasis, as found in many of her short stories and countless poems; or—in a way that stretches the dialogical dimensions of "voice"—sometimes two or more will resound as facets of a single character, as in the plays *Daytrips* and "The Brown Dress."

Moreover, Carson's speakers have been known to address an audience directly, thus defying theatrical conventions. In Colquitt, Georgia, where with the Swamp Gravy Project, Carson has helped bring a community's collected oral histories to the stage, the actors "are themselves, in costumes that suggest an older time, telling stories that come from other people . . . and they have, in their choice of attitude and presentation, a comment on the story. [I]t is one of the tricks in the box. And it is moving, right up close to a religious experience—a community experience with real roots in it—when stories have this kind of reality for the players and the audience. The experience is removed from behind a fourth wall."[11] Although this technique immediately bridges the remaining gap created by the theatrical experience, it is neither the most revolutionary nor the most dialogically engaging element of Carson's storytelling.

More important are the voices which occasionally speak from outside the story, as they often have in the Colquitt project. At the end of every evening's production, participants enact a closing ceremony wherein they acknowledge by naming, thanking, and remembering the people whose stories they have told. "There have been nights," Carson says, "when members of the audience have added their own remembers to the list. It was a surprise the first time. Now, I hope for it. I want the experience to be so strong that people are moved to participate."[12] These external voices are not only permitted, but welcomed because they help realize the truly communal, democratizing, and interactive nature of oral history—indeed, they are creating an alternate oral history.

Such an unmerged cacophony of voices would seem challenging to the cohesiveness of any work, but Carson thrives on and in fact expresses preference for nonlinear stories informed by the intersection of multiple narratives and voices. She even conceptualizes her Swamp Gravy plays in terms of chaos theory: "It helps to think about this stuff in terms of Chaos Theory and the fractal images produced by chaos. The oral history material is the chaos and I choose a trunk story . . . from the unpredictable order of it and make the branches of a tree with other stories; or I choose a current—like work—and come out of it in the patterns of turbulence with other stories like spinoffs."[13] Chaos, unpredictable order, turbulence—all of these terms dovetail with what literary theorist Mikhail Bakhtin calls multivoicedness, polyphony, dialogism. The polyphonic nature of Carson's work is not unusual, for as Bakhtin notes, all "[l]iterary language . . . is represented precisely as a living mix of varied and opposing voices, developing and renewing itself."[14] Carson's work thus privileges no speaker, no authority, no single voice. And in the very best, most "people-oriented" examples of her work, the language is forcefully non-literary in style: when the voices speak, they do so in everyday or common speech, replete with colloquialisms and individual idiosyncrasies.

It would be untrue to say that Carson always adopts a common style of diction for her voices, but very true to suggest that her most vibrant examples do. While her plays are unsurprisingly almost exclusively grounded in common speech, some of her short stories and poems bear the touches of elevated stylistics, or what Wordsworth calls "poetic diction"—in common terms, a literary self-consciousness. For example, she writes in the short story "His Father's Work": "When they arrived home, Evan sat in his father's chair, *suffering the common agony of uncompleted things.*"[15] And in the poem "Jump," Carson describes an underwater swim in near-perfect iambic pentameter: "When I fell the mud / packed hard in to the bed / of the river that still / runs inside Boone Lake, / I jumped, a pink frog / who leaned UP, and rose."[16] Such style is, depending upon the context, deliberately literary or poetic, but in either case remains far removed from common language and speech.

Yet, even in the most self-consciously literary or poetic examples of Carson's work, there is quite often a small flash of true-to-life speech, such as informal contractions in the midst of formal language, or a reminder of common, everyday life inserted through the guise of an incorporated genre. Several of the short stories provide such examples. In "His Father's Work," an incorporated genre arrives in the form of the prayer slips distributed by Evan at the welfare office, with slogans written on them like "SINNERS BEWARE OF GOD" and "HIS FROWN WILL DOOM YOUR SOUL TO HELL HIS SMILE IS YOUR TICKET TO HEAVEN" (8–9). Here the encoded message runs counter to the prevailing social aims of the welfare agency by subtly suggesting "Your physical bodies do not take precedence over your eternal souls." Similarly, in "The Last of the 'Waltz across Texas,'" the words of an Ernest Tubb song reverberate in our ears as the wife dances with her alcoholic husband, delivering a musical message to him that this waltz is the final one. The prominence given to such informal, interpolated genres continues Carson's challenging of traditional literary assumptions: they say "We, too, are legitimate forms of speech. We have a bearing on the story. Listen to our messages."

Other stories from the *Waltz across Texas* collection, like "Maybe" and especially "Stories from the Night the Family Received Friends at a Kentucky Farmer's Wedding," offer more completely authentic renditions of common speech. Thus they more fully celebrate the "real" stories of which Carson speaks so reverently in her essays and interviews. In the first story—which focuses on one of Carson's favorite themes, that of relationships—several voices speak contrapuntally, each with its own flavor and rhythm, to tell the tangled story of a love triangle: Dessa, who would not marry Harry; Harry, who "up and marries" Brenda after a two-week fling; and Brenda, the new wife. The speech is colloquial, filled with grammatical glitches, contractions, and interjected expressions. It is also marked by the sort of hushed tone that replicates a story told confidentially. Dessa's speech exemplifies these qualities:

I am not telling this for sympathy. I don't like sympathy and I don't want any of it. Harry'll say I made my own bed and I now have the honor of lying down in it. Well, maybe I did. If I did, what I'm doing now is tucking in the corners like they ought to be tucked in. No call for sympathy here. A body feels sorry for somebody, they feel like they're better than that somebody, that's the truth. Now, I might feel different if Harry had died, but Harry didn't die. Harry got mad at me, went to Nashville, stayed two weeks and come home married to somebody else. What I get is "Oh, poor Dessa, I feel so sorry for you . . ." Well, don't. Feel sorry for Brenda if you want to feel sorry for somebody. She married Harry. (53)

Here, the speech is so authentic that its closing seems naturally punctuated by the flick of ashes from a cigarette and a confidential nod. The story begins in Dessa's voice and ends in Harry's but throughout, the story belongs to them all, verifying an awareness that stories are by their very nature communal and that most of the good ones are, in fact, as nonlinear as real life itself.

"Stories from the Night the Family Received Friends at a Kentucky Farmer's Funeral" perhaps even more successfully translates into written text the primary features of oral speech. Disregard for correct grammar, nonlinear sentences, the presence of contractions and interjections, and the consistent use of dashes to indicate natural pauses are among the markers of true speech that characterize the eight individual stories within the larger one. For example, listen as the first speaker recounts how the farmer they are gathered to mourn once dealt with a recalcitrant mule who wouldn't cross a creek: "It wasn't much of a ford, wasn't much of a creek for that matter, didn't get a bridge for years, but your daddy's old mule, Henry, didn't like to get his feet wet" (25). Later he continues with another sentence that again beautifully replicates the spoken word: "Now I had a car—well, Parker had a car too but he still used them mules for farm work—and I had a place up Hard Creek before they flooded it for the lake, and Parker left John—John was the other mule—left John and Henry standing, come up and asked would I bring my car down and pull Henry through that creek" (25). As authentic as the reality of gathering at a family's house to mourn the passing of one of its members, the voice of the first speaker joins with those of the story's other tellers to resurrect the dead farmer. Through their words and memories, they bring him to life once more before he is finally laid to rest. Carson's story ultimately performs a double memorial service: in celebrating the farmer's life, it also honors the regional custom of the funeral visitation.

Thus in many of her short stories Carson does manage to blur the boundaries between the written and oral narrative, to allow the free play of usually marginalized voices, and to create from this chaos a community in which all speakers (and listeners) can share. It is in the pieces conceived of as more strictly performance-based, however, that one can see and hear most fully realized Carson's conception of voice as a powerful, galvanizing, and subversive force for change. This conception is most evident in the plays based on oral histories, like those in the Swamp Gravy project, which are driven by social and psychological dilemmas and agendas, but it can also be found in the collection of found poetry or "people pieces" titled *Stories I Ain't Told Nobody Yet*.

Perhaps because of their close ties to the oral storytelling tradition, which is by its nature communal in spirit, the Swamp Gravy and *Stories I Ain't Told Nobody Yet* collections more forcefully articulate the speakers'/narrators' moral bond with the audience: speaker and listener are in this story together and rely on each other to make from it a meaning that will permit them to prevail. Paul Hernadi suggests, "While works outlast the situation in which they were produced, authors and readers live in the WORLD serving for both as a source of motivation and a field of action. Along the axis of communication every text can thus be seen as responding to 'worldly' challenges . . . and in turn challenging the reader to respond . . . in his day and age, under his particular circumstances."[17] The Swamp Gravy plays almost universally address the "hard" issues that Carson finds most promising and nourishing, both for herself as a playwright and for the community as a whole: racial otherness, various forms of abuse (sexual, spousal, child), gender bias, general social hypocrisy and malaise. To acknowledge these issues through the stories that are in fact the community's oral history is difficult but in most cases cathartic. Though they recount one play which failed to be remounted for a second season because of the controversial depiction of its main character, a prominent woman of the town, Swamp Gravy director Richard Geer and fellow writer Debra Jones note the rarity of this occurrence: "While . . . it's no exaggeration that Jo's community performance writing can hurt, it has done a whole lot of healing."[18] That Carson focuses in the Swamp Gravy Project on women's stories—those hard, real stories—suggests her recognition that the plays can engender this healing process. "It is in the telling of women's stories through community performance that Jo Carson reveals her feminist/womanist allegiance," write Geer and

Jones. "[Storytelling] has become the unlikely vehicle for community change and subversive feminism. Through community performance, women are given a voice."[19] Still, despite their obvious feminist leanings, Carson emphatically denies writing purely "female stories" or "male stories," preferring to call them merely "hard stories."[20] Perhaps it is more appropriate to argue that Carson will speak for whichever oppressed voice calls to her imagination the loudest—and that most often those voices belong to women, who traditionally have the most need and the least outlets for expression.

In "The Brown Dress," for example, the first truly "controversial" play staged by Swamp Gravy, Carson brings to life the oral history of an abused woman interviewed by a policeman for the murder of her husband.[21] Because Carson did not want the theater's patrons to ascribe the play's story of spousal abuse to a particular ethnic or racial community, she and director Richard Geer literally split what is a single female lead into two personalities. Although this calls for having two women onstage—one black; the other, white—they portray dimensions of the same character, at times completing each other's sentences and often speaking simultaneously:

> BOTH: He beat us, all of us.
>
> WOMAN ONE: His sisters saw that, too, but they didn't worry about that.
>
> WOMAN TWO: They were here,
>
> BOTH: both of them,
>
> WOMAN ONE: the nights all three of my children were born, and they'd look at those babies when they came out of my body and try to decide whether or not they looked like him.
>
> WOMAN TWO: They were his,
>
> BOTH: all of them. (Pause) He beat me the night the third one was born because they didn't think she looked like him. And he beat her. Not that night, but as she grew. She's nine years old, and she has scars all over her back where her clothes cover them and you can't see them.
>
> WOMAN ONE: He was careful about that. I've got scars
>
> WOMAN TWO: on my back, too.
>
> BOTH: We all do.
>
> (44–45)

The effects are multiple and startling. Clearly, the decision to have two women share the role of a single female lead effectively coalesces two voices into one, which ultimately universalizes what began as a single woman's story into the story of all abused women. Beyond that interpretation, though, lies an additional one that speaks directly to issues of speech, identity, and power. As the abused woman tries to convince the policeman to change the dispassionate method, steeped in legal language, with which his training demands he record her deposition, her resolute iteration of her story—far more than the shooting of her tormentor—indicates her gradual reassumption of control and power over her own destiny. Although she fails to prevail against the policeman's official language, she has by her very vocal challenging of it reassumed stature as an individual.

In a similar vein, "Thou Shalt Not Covet," a piece from the play *The Gospel Truth*, also makes room within a single story for multiple voices.[22] Although it foregrounds what Carson calls "an encounter/conversation between a woman and her younger self," which occurs at the funeral of the man who sexually molested her when she was a child, the speaking roles are not limited to these two but can in fact be assumed by as many as twelve women ("Out Loud," 45). Carson herself indicates that the play works best not with two speakers, but with at least four to six ("Out Loud," 46). Obviously, the play relies on the adage that there is "safety in numbers" regarding the theme, but there is more to it than that. In an even more forceful way than in "The Brown Dress," the multiple voices of "Thou Shalt Not Covet" create by their shared experiences, unified adult front, and common speech a community of power capable of overcoming the imprisoning past. In a haunting roll call at the end of the play, the various speakers name those children abused by the man who has died:

> —I want to look Sara and Alice and Jane and Morgan in the
> eyes and know he isn't there,
> —Forty years before you begin to wonder what happened to
> —Sara
> —and Alice
> —and Jane
> —and Morgan

> (46–47)

The litany is heartbreaking, but it is also freeing: by naming the victims, the speakers return to them their stolen identities. Carson alludes to this potential for liberation when writing about the woman from whose history "Thou

Shalt Not Covet" is drawn, a woman who, despite being haunted for years by memories of her abuser, not only told the tale but also courageously performed in the play. Carson says she has informed the woman that "[t]elling the story has taken the power out of him. I tell her it is hers now, that power, or it could be. . . . She does not seem comfortable with the idea of having power at all, but she has changed for telling that story. You can see it in how easily she meets your eyes now with her own, and she is taking back some power from somewhere whether she wants it, or intends it, or not" ("Out Loud," 47). The very act of speech itself brings power, identity, and self-awareness, as Carson's work with the Swamp Gravy Project so clearly illustrates. This equation between speech and liberation does not end with the staging of Carson's plays, however, for it reappears in an even more forceful form in the collection *Stories I Ain't Told Nobody Yet*.

While even Carson's most "oral" short stories clearly conform to generic expectations, and her plays are, through their staging, easily recognizable as plays, the pieces in *Stories I Ain't Told Nobody Yet* defy easy categorization. Are they, too, short stories? Poems? Plays in miniature? They do not conform to the standards of the short story, and, besides that, Carson writes another form of poetry one would call traditionally literary in tone and style. Carson herself has used a variety of terms to describe these pieces, but like the speech acts they are meant to replicate, her definitions remain appropriately fluid. In the introduction to the collection, she refers to the pieces as "monologues and dialogues," terms that are precise but rather distancing.[23] In one interview, she admits thinking of the collection "as a sort of play, because it is performance material. It's supposed to be read aloud."[24] In another place, they become what she calls simply "found poems."[25] Perhaps the best moniker, however, is that of "people pieces" because it appropriately ties the works to Carson's larger, ongoing People Pieces Project, as well as emphasizes the origin of the works themselves, their oral natures, and their intended audience. Like Wordsworth, Carson intentionally sets out to elevate common people, their stories and their language to the level of art, without making the product inaccessible or denying the authenticity (or authority) of its sources.

In her own preface to *Stories I Ain't Told Nobody Yet*, Carson articulates a literary theory that in its embrace of the common person and its appreciation of everyday occurrences is remarkably similar to that of Wordsworth. However, while the majority of Wordsworth's poems are no doubt inspired by such common persons, scenes, or occasions, the text that appears on the printed page derives primarily—almost exclusively—from the poet's imagination. Carson, on the other hand, goes directly to the source, either accidentally hearing the kernel of what will become one of the pieces or deliberately eavesdropping on likely subjects to hear a story from beginning to end. Notes are surreptitiously taken, and later the stories are reconstructed. "The pieces all come from people," she writes. "I never sat at my desk and made them up. I heard the heart of them somewhere. A grocery store line. A beauty shop. The emergency room. A neighbor across her clothesline to another neighbor" (xi). In many cases, what Carson reconstructs is a monologue, although the reader is immediately thrust into the role of the listening audience, a confidante with whom the speaker shares a secret or relieves a burden. On other occasions, she creates dialogues, wonderfully vivid conversations that either tell a complete, coherent story or unfold in a natural, nonlinear way about what initially appears to be nothing important.

As with true speech, however, meaning lies encoded in all of the pieces. Such meaning derives most obviously from their subject matter, but also from, in essence, their forms. Regardless of whether they arrive as monologues or dialogues, they are overheard conversations or gossip, which immediately casts upon them the nature of shared confidences. The stories then invite us to listen in on and participate in the sharing of privileged information. As Carson uses the interceding mask of the play to permit her speakers to introduce difficult subjects and effect change, so does she use gossip or the overheard conversation to provide alternative perspectives and form community. As opposed to what we would call "idle talk," serious talk—terminology that importantly parallels what Carson calls "real stories"—provides, according to Patricia Meyer Spacks, a "resource for the subordinated . . . a crucial means of self-expression, a crucial form of solidarity."[26] Gossip is thus capable of building or strengthening a community, but its value is more subversive when it is interpreted as a challenge to formal, acceptable speech. Gossip is by its very nature dialogical, as it "embodies an alternative discourse to that of public life, and a discourse potentially challenging to public assumptions; it provides language for an alternative culture. Gossip's way of telling can project a different understanding of reality from that of society at large, even though gossip may claim to articulate the voice of the community. A rhetoric of inquiry, gossip questions the established."[27] For Carson, as we will see, gossip thus brings an avenue for both community-building and community pride.

Beyond emphasis on the common person and everyday occurrences, Carson's preface shares another feature with that of Wordsworth's: as in his, in hers Carson states an intention to "remain true to the speaker's thoughts and rhythms of speech and anything else that can be kept somehow in chosen words" (xi). Unlike that of the earlier poet, however, Carson's endeavor proves more consistently successful. Although some of the people pieces seem more consciously poetic, as in the prologue's poem about Willis Comfort, with its resonances of E. A. Robinson, ("Willis Comfort did not outlive / as many enemies as he hoped to"), there is enough embedded in them of "real speech" —"'em" for "them," interjections like "see"—to connect them more closely with the vernacular (3). And while Carson occasionally uses devices that are consciously literary, such as the rapid-fire exchange known as stichomythia, in context such techniques almost determinedly replicate the nature of everyday speech.

Carson's collection is divided into five subject sections: *Neighbors and Kin, Observations, Relationships, Work,* and *We Say of Ourselves.* None of the poems have titles; instead, they are identified by numbers. Of the five major sections, the one titled *Observations* contains the largest number of purely didactic pieces, like #16:

> Mountain people
> Can't read,
> Can't write,
> Don't wear shoes,
> Don't have teeth,
> Don't use soap,
> And don't talk plain.
> . . . . . . . . .
> Well, let me tell you:
> I am from here,
> I'm not like that
> And I am damned tired of being told I am.
>
> (29–30)

Although its message is important and is most certainly—speaking with the awareness of a native—grounded in reality, this poem, like several others in this section, tends to deliver its message with a somewhat heavy hand and remains rather self-conscious. Given the premise of the collection, artistically the most successful poems deliver their messages—about general human and love relationships, the search for identity, the value of family and neighbors, and the changing nature of Appalachia, among others—subtly and in the vernacular.

Piece #10, a monologue, effectively balances two related themes while never losing sight of its origins in common speech. First, it plays with the generalization that all of Appalachia is one big neighborhood, its inhabitants on a first-name basis with each other and constantly visiting. Simultaneously, it reiterates—through their glaring absence from the story—the value of such community and friendships. Loneliness lies at the core of the wistful piece. We listen as the speaker tells about being invited to the home of someone who had just purchased new carpeting. Importantly, the invitation is extended not by "Sue" or "Betty" or even "a neighbor," but instead by the distancing "A lady who lives there close to me" (19). The speaker notes how this lady "wanted me to come and / drink a cup of coffee and admire" (19). The speaker herself can understand this impulse, for she, too, has done something of which she is proud—hanging wallpaper—and "come near to inviting a perfect stranger in to see it . . ." (19). Thus in the first two stanzas we are given an impression of two relatively lonely souls who live near to each other but do not interact on a regular basis, an antithesis of the traditional conception of Appalachia's close-knittedness. When the speaker arrives, she is not greeted warmly but with the admonition to "be careful / how you wipe your feet" and then finally asked to remove her shoes (19). The new carpet—"white. Bleach white."—comes to symbolize the isolation and loneliness of the Lady (19). The piece goes on to reinforce this reading, as the speaker muses how no children will dirty the carpet, no dogs will roll on it, no fresh-cut garden flowers will be carried across it. Its cleanliness, destined to be permanent, is what the Lady admires, but her final words poignantly articulate for the reader a life that is altogether lonely and devoid of human pleasure. She speaks of the carpet as would a mother whose child needs special nurturing: "I'll have to be so careful, / it being white and all" (20). The story closes, and friendship is never gained, nor is a small community built. In retelling the story to us, the speaker—like the ancient mariner in Coleridge's poem—attempts to come to terms personally with its lessons. She also suggests to us that community—particularly one made possible by the joining of women who are alone ("redundant," to use the Victorian phrase) and otherwise have no strong roles in or ties to the dominant society— should be pursued and encouraged for the empowerment it can bring.

On the contrary, piece #11 beautifully reconstructs a community filled, as are all real communities, with a myriad of friends and true neighbors, even counting Lester, who gave George's little boy a puppy that "turned around and bit him" (21). Although the piece seems to go nowhere—like a rambling conversation overheard on the front porch—it strongly reinforces the value of community and celebrates the beauty of human interaction with two speakers who grumble and contradict but clearly love and value each other. This selection is reprinted as it appears in the text in order to remain faithful to Carson's intention to replicate the conversational ebb and flow:

> You know the other day we went over at George's get some eggs?
>> No, we went over George's get some beans.
> George ain't got eggs.
>
> No, we got beans up at Lucille's.
>> We took tomatoes to Lucille.
> We took tomatoes to Wally.
>> Where'd we get the beans?
> Lucille's.
>> I swear we took tomatoes.
> Well, we didn't.

(21)

While Shakespeare uses stichomythia to reveal something like the growing desire between Romeo and Juliet, Carson uses it to describe the easy, relaxed mode of language interaction adopted by people who clearly have lived in their relationship for quite some time. And the listing of who has what produce (or gift, in the case of Lester's puppy) to pass along to which neighbor more than effectively portrays within these people a spirit of true community: they stick together and share their bounty. Whether they are counted among society's movers and shakers or, more probably, are its castoffs, they are strong characters, powerful in their self-awareness and in their sense of community.

These two pieces alone do not begin to adequately represent the gamut of themes and styles Carson incorporates into *Stories I Ain't Told Nobody Yet*. They do, however, indicate that Carson remains faithful to the promises expressed in her preface: to retell real stories spoken by real people and to do so in their own voices.

Since the topic of this essay is voice, what ultimately do her essays and interviews, her short stories, plays, performance pieces, and poetry say about Jo Carson? Perhaps they say no matter what she calls herself—poet, playwright-for-hire, practiced (and practicing) eavesdropper—she is intent that the message, whatever it is, be understood. Whether she wishes to conceptualize her intentions as evidence of political or social activism, or one nearly religious in tone, this attention to transmission of the message can be seen in practically all of her work, in one way or another. It is visible in her attitude about being an Appalachian. It is visible in the way her Swamp Gravy stories deliver the blunt facts of spousal and sexual abuse. It is visible in her care to encompass rather than demarcate ethnic and racial differences. And it is visible in the democratic conception of her work and in her definition of an intended audience. "'One-and-one-half percent of the population goes to the theatre, and that ends up being for the most part the wealthy and well-educated people," she says. "That's not who I write the 'people pieces' for. One of the audiences I like best is the Wednesday night dinner at the Baptist Church."[28]

In Carson's conception and in their execution, her works transcend cultural, geographic, and social boundaries. For example, her play *Daytrips,* which recounts the trials of a woman caring for her mother, stricken with Alzheimer's, and an increasingly elderly grandmother, constantly alludes to towns and highways in East Tennessee. It connects to a regional audience by what Sandra K. D. Stahl calls a "common frame of reference."[29] However, this same play has been staged—and translates effectively—in New York, California, Connecticut, Michigan, Pennsylvania, and Missouri, as well as points south. In Atlanta, despite the fact that its cast was all black, its script remained unchanged, a fact Carson relishes because it underscores the true universality of the work's themes. "It translated culturally," Carson notes. "Love, duty, and madness are human traits, after all."[30] But her works, in whatever form they are found, do more than merely translate well: through their emphasis on multiple voices and privileging of common, everyday speech, they also challenge cultural, geographic, and social boundaries; speak courageously for the oppressed; and extol the virtues of joining together in a powerful community of speakers committed to each other and to change. In the end, what better thing to say?

## Notes

1. Jo Carson, "Out Loud: Telling Real Stories in Front of People Breaks the Tradition of Silence," *Southern Exposure* 24 (Winter 1996): 42.
2. bell hooks, *Talking Back: Thinking Feminist, Thinking Black* (Boston: South End, 1989), 9.
3. Mikhail Bakhtin, *Problems of Dostoevsky's Poetics,* ed. Caryl Emerson (Minneapolis: Univ. of Minnesota Press, 1984), 6
4. William Wordsworth, "Preface to *Lyrical Ballads, with Pastoral and Other Poems*" (1802), in *William Wordsworth: The Oxford Authors,* ed. Stephen Gill (New York: Oxford Univ. Press, 1984), 596–97.
5. Ibid., 597.
6. Jo Carson, "Some Thoughts on Direct Address and Oral Histories in Performance," *Drama Review* 40 (Summer 1996): 115.
7. Jo Carson, "The Wealth of Story: A Conversation," interviewed by Pat Arnow, *Iron Mountain Review* 14 (Summer 1998): 32.
8. Walter J. Ong, *Orality and Literacy: The Technologizing of the Word* (New York: Methuen, 1990), 74.
9. Carson, "Out Loud," 43.

10. Jo Carson, interviewed by Jo Harris, *Appalachian Journal* 20 (Fall 1992): 64.

11. Carson, "Some Thoughts on Direct Address," 117.

12. Ibid.

13. Ibid., 116.

14. Mikhail Bakhtin, "From the Prehistory of Novelistic Discourse," in *The Dialogic Imagination*, ed. Michael Holquist (Austin: Univ. of Texas Press, 1981), 49.

15. Jo Carson, "His Father's Work," in *The Last of The "Waltz across Texas" and Other Stories* (Frankfort, Ky.: Gnomon, 1993), 24. Emphasis added. Subsequent references to the stories in this collection provided parenthetically.

16. Jo Carson, "Jump," *Iron Mountain Review* 14 (Summer 1998): 7. This poem was first published in *Preposterous: Poems of Youth*, ed. Paul B. Janeczko (New York: Orchard Books, 1991).

17. Paul Hernadi, "So What? How So? And the Form That Matters," *Critical Inquiry* 3, no. 2 (Winter 1976): 370–71.

18. Richard Owen Geer and Debra Jones, "Gathering Mayhaws: Jo Carson and Writing for Community Performance," *Iron Mountain Review* 14 (Summer 1998): 28.

19. Ibid.

20. Carson, interview by Harris, 65.

21. Jo Carson, "The Brown Dress," reprinted in "Out Loud," 44–45. Subsequent references to this play provided parenthetically.

22. Jo Carson, "Thou Shalt Not Covet," reprinted in "Out Loud," 42. Subsequent references to this play provided parenthetically.

23. Jo Carson, preface to *Stories I Ain't Told Nobody Yet: Selections from the People Pieces* (New York: Theatre Communications Group, 1991), xi–xii, xi. Subsequent references to this collection provided parenthetically.

24. Carson, interview by Harris, 58.

25. Sean Mitchell, "Eavesdropper Jo Carson Spins a Personal Story," *American Theatre* 7, no. 1 (Jan. 1990): 56–57.

26. Patricia Meyer Spacks, *Gossip* (New York: Knopf, 1985), 5.

27. Spacks, 46.

28. Mitchell, 57.

29. Sandra K. D. Stahl, "Style in Oral and Written Narratives," *Southern Folklore Quarterly* 43 (1970): 107–20.

30. Carson, interview by Harris, 59.

# Lisa Coffman

## Rapture

What is the gear that turns this world?
Bright now, the wall of the east sky like honey
    church chimes off red tenement bricks
      off humped roads where the vans slam down their
        loading ramps
      subway clap in the beams and the window frames shaking.

What's left of the night's in the shadow of things
precise and solid: the cornice tops
    The shadow of that branch so hard I could lift it.

The white-smocked fish-market man bends from the waist
        receiving and flinging boxes from the truck ramp
butt above his head, weight swung
    from bent leg to straight leg now bent
head down, grunting and hugging the boxes—
      the silver, hacked bodies of fish in the window.

Another man sits on an upturned box outside the grocer's
    legs planted on each side of his box like a storyteller.
The motion of his hands breaks and strips beans
      never seeming to put a bean down and reach for the
        next one:
    always the green scrap of bean in his hand.
And the rhythm of stripping is the rhythm of mending
           or weaving a cane-bottom seat.

If the mountains will let me back,
if they will let me back and give me a small house:
    yellow light in winter when the mountains are gray
      the brittle spiked pine scent splayed over me
        in winter.

Now the red-headed boy on our street comes out of his house.
    He has grown up:
I first saw him going to Catholic school with his small head of
    hair slicked back

Once he pushed two boys on our stoop and said *I can kill both*
          *you guys.*
Yesterday he tucked his shirt in and crossed the street
                              where the girls idle in the blue evening.
He looked worried:
     wet dreams and erections have humbled him.

I have thought I might be a hater of Jews
          and I have never met a black man without being afraid.
          I have never met a woman without being afraid.

My brother squealed in the yard. I made up games.
We pulled the dog by a stick; if we fell, he pulled us.
When my brother went in his pants, our mother
               took the shit and smeared it on each of his cheeks.
          I remember the pitch his cry went into.
The dog is old now and staggers and has cataracts like white stars.

Whatever it is, it must be very basic,
we must turn of a piece, or the turning is no good.
We must turn of a piece
                         but there is nothing so good
as the row of furrows cut in the earth,
as the gold block of cheese on the dark shelf.

# On a Mill Worker in Rockwood

### for Thomas Hayes

He'd come home and put his face in his hands,
whiskey and chair by the kitchen door,
while your Mamaw fixed supper he never ate
and small at the table, you watched his bent back.

Whiskey and chair by the kitchen door,
he'd lurch to the stove and pile in more wood
and small at the table, you watched his bent back,
heat bright in the room like hell preached in church.

He'd lurch to the stove and pile in more wood,
face closed as the fist he hit you with,
heat bright in the room like hell preached in church
while your Mamaw whispered you were excused.

Face closed as the fist he hit you with,
"Damn HEAT" he'd cry and kick open the door
while your Mamaw whispered you were excused,
the night shiny black when his shift was up.

"Damn HEAT" he'd cry and kick open the door,
sit coughing and swearing as you went to bed,
the night shiny black when his shift was up:
he'd come home and put his face in his hands.

# A Level Gaze Trained at Life
## The Poetry of Lisa Coffman

Patricia M. Gantt

> Let not what I have be taken from me,
> But let me step new from *was* into *is*.
>
> Lisa Coffman
> "Leaving New York City," 1996

When I first picked up *Likely*, Lisa Coffman's initial collection of poems, I was moved at once by the painting on the cover—Bo Bartlett's image of a young girl with her arm outstretched toward a world lying beyond the edge of the book, her hand outside its frame. That girl's level gaze seems to penetrate the viewer. Turning to the back of the book, I encountered that same honest gaze in the photograph of the poet. Now, having read the thirty-eight poems in the volume, with their reflections on Coffman's internal and external experiences, I see a systemic connection among the painting, the photograph, and the poems: Coffman's writing results from a level gaze trained at life. Her insights—including those based on her Appalachian homeland, other places her experiences have taken her, or regions explored in the landscape of her imagination—constitute a powerful new poetic voice.

Coffman grew up in East Tennessee, a locale that often figures in her work. She studied at the University of Tennessee, and in 1985 earned her undergraduate degree there in English and computer science. The following year she studied at the University of Bonn, Germany, on a Rotary International Fellowship. Returning to the United States, she completed a master's in creative writing at New York University in 1988. Presently she is a member of the English faculty at Pennsylvania State University–Altoona. Coffman's creative imagination takes her to all these actual worlds, as well as to the rich internal one she explores so well. Before writing *Likely*, Coffman "spent six months living in a cabin on the Cumberland Plateau in rural Tennessee absorbing family history, regional color, and the ephemera of the regional dialect."[1]

The poet maintains her ties to the East Tennessee mountains where she grew up, dividing her time between her Bellwood, Pennsylvania, residence and her Rugby, Tennessee, home.

Coffman's poetry has been published in *The Southern Review, The Beloit Poetry Journal, Painted Bride Quarterly, The Village Voice,* and a large number of additional journals. Her poems have been included in a several of anthologies, including *Learning by Heart* (Univ. of Iowa Press, 1999) and *American Poetry: The Next Generation* (Carnegie Mellon Press, 2000). She is certainly no stranger to honors for her work, having won poetry fellowships from the National Endowment for the Arts and the Pennsylvania Council on the Arts, and serving in 1990 as poet-in-residence at Bucknell University.[2] In 1993 panelists including Lucille Clifton selected Coffman as a fellow of the Pew Charitable Trust, an award based on "artistic accomplishment and promise" and aimed at providing financial support "at moments . . . when a concentration on artistic growth and exploration is most likely to have the greatest impact on long-term personal and professional development" in an artist's career.[3] Her most prestigious award thus far, however, is having *Likely* win the 1995 Stan and Tom Wick Poetry Prize, awarded by Kent State University Press for an outstanding first collection of poems. In awarding Coffman's writing the Wick Prize, judge Alicia Ostriker heralded her as "a major poet in the making":

> Imagine a voice that combines heart-of-America brooding like James Wright's with a shaded elegance like Elizabeth Bishop's. Imagine Whitman's spirit somewhere in the vicinity. Imagine a love of small towns ringed by mountains, a shrewd ear for lonely folks' dialogue and a music that seems to pour out of your own life as you read these poems. *Likely* is a book brimming with surprises and beauty; some of the poems— "Rapture," "The Products of Hog," "[The] Graveyard"—left me breathless.[4]

*Likely*'s thirty-eight poems are divided among four untitled parts, each containing from eight to twelve selections. Each part contains both poems previously published—at least three in each section—and those appearing for the first time in this volume. Topics range from seemingly everyday occurrences (e.g. "Learning the Butterfly" or "Cheerleaders") to considerations of the punishment life can bring to people and to the land (e.g. "On a Mill Worker in Rockwood" or "Pulled Down"), or to private meditations (e.g. "Weather" or "Courage, or One of Gene Horner's Fiddles").[5] Allusions, too, are varied and rich—including the Bible; the mountains and mill towns of her childhood; locales as widespread as Nova Scotia, Newark, and Germany; St. Francis of Assisi; and blackberries or buck dancing. The deceptively simple poems in Likely are in fact carefully crafted—unrhymed lyrics and narratives written in a conversational tone that at times confides in the reader and at other times seems to be an individual speaking out loud about deeply felt ideas.

"Likely," the title poem, introduces the first section. It begins, "Magnolia bloom can sex the air / until one thinks for long blanknesses / only magnolia, magnolia" (3). Immediately the reader sees a key marker of Coffman's poetry—the creative use of language both to carry her ideas and to alert us to the originality of her voice, as when she uses sex as a verb and refers to long periods of nothingness as "blanknesses." Coffman frequently extends language in this way, creating new suffixes for words, using nouns as verbs, or inserting common words in unusual places—such as in "Girl/Spit" when she speaks of "the hook-thinness" of a smile or "the flutter of that cheek"; in "In Envy of Migration," when she depicts children who constantly come and go as "orbiting" their mothers' laps; or in "For Sheila's Julia," when she intensifies the image of darkness by calling it "a heaped-on dark" (4, 34, 61).

As "Likely" continues, Coffman depicts two girls heading for branches higher up in the tree, where one of them concentrates on a single magnolia bloom. Something of a tomboy ("raised / to be her daddy's boy"), the girl cuts the bloom, which "floats all night in a glass, / the kitchen lit in other places by the moon" (3). The speaker flows between past and present, using the transition between the present and the time remembered as a frame for the poem. Variation in time also functions like interchapters in a novel, allowing the speaker both to remember and to comment externally on the memory. In the image of the cut bloom, Coffman suggests the hidden life that awaits the young climber: "skin at the lifted clothes, or the shining / averted face of a woman undressing" (3). Coffman's ability to compress life's potential into a single image is reminiscent of Philip Larkin in "High Windows," when he takes an ordinary incident of seeing a young couple together and explodes it into the infinite.[6] The suggestion of inherent potential is a frequent focus for Coffman, figuring in her poems from the earliest ones up to her most recent work.

The speaker in "For Najeema, 6, Who Admitted to Hitting Renee," for instance, invites the little girl to look at her hands, and explores with her all the things those small hands could one day accomplish. She equates the touches that will proceed from Najeema's hands with the latent artistic potential of a block of wood waiting to be carved, with the energy of a dancer, and with the grace of a "floating bird" (56). Najeema's hands, now used crudely to articulate her frustration over some childish disagreement, may one day touch "the faces of the blind . . . the heads of children" (56). Promising the child that new, powerfully productive touches lie "hiding in your hands," the speaker ends with a valediction to Najeema to "Go lay them on" (56). As in this poem, one periodically gets a sense that Coffman is spinning out a positive tension, that something powerful stirring below the surface is about to burst forth. Indeed, the final words of *Likely*, from "For Sheila's Julia," are "born-broken-born," indicative of the constant process of renewal and of implicit hopes for what lies unseen (61).

In "Cheerleaders" Coffman allows us a glimpse into the lives of several people—the beautiful young girl whose sneaker "strikes the wooden boards hard / until the stands start ringing back"; the young male photographer who emotes that "there are no women like that, anywhere"; and the photographer's girlfriend and sisters, who respond to his enthusiasm with ironic stares (6–7). Even while the girl who is the central figure in the poem concentrates on conforming with the "scrubbed citric innocence" of the cheerleader's norm, she appears to be more than the vapid, semi-sensual stereotype she is perceived to be (6). After all, cheerleaders, though "exemplary for beauty" are often "discarded at the end of high schools / excluded from cabinet meetings and businesses" (7). One senses that for this girl, being a cheerleader is just a phase of her life, not its apex. We are told that she is an "oddity of a girl / to whom her own opinions pose a danger," an original thinker more like the photographer's sisters and girlfriend than one may realize (6).

An interesting aspect of Coffman's treatment of the cheerleaders is her language: At several points in the poem she employs an elegance not normally invested in depictions of cheerleaders. Her portrait is both precise in its detail ("hair fanned across the inwardly groaning boy's fourth-period desk / . . . the hairless lotioned calves end in sock folds, / the chest is topped demurely with a carpet letter") and mock-epic in its dimension (6). She introduces her subjects as emerging, "Out of the American provinces / regarded by many as exile," giving them an elevated setting that invites the reader's ironic amusement (6). Coffman knows rural southern towns and the social primacy cheerleaders enjoy there. Yet she contrasts the cheerleaders' precision, "ironed flat" hairdos with the unkempt beauty of Venus rising from the foam and speaks of "troubadours" who broadcast stories of the girls' exploits, clichéd allusions to female beauty and romanticism (6). Both the allusions and the cheerleaders themselves differ markedly from the more realistic women mentioned in the last stanza of the poem, seen reading in the midst of a "magazine- / littered living room" (7). Clearly the speaker has mixed emotions about these lovely girls, perhaps preferring the women the cheerleaders will eventually become, while simultaneously celebrating the moment.

Evidence of Coffman's most mature work is found in "Weather," a brief lyric whose eight lines reflect a speaker dealing with the results of choices made. The weather of the title is the weather of the self, of thought and physical change, of internal and external decisions:

> When I sit teaching among my red-lipped girls sugaring to ripeness
> among the flushed necks prideful as mine has been
> and feel in myself only the new wish
> to lie down in the earliest dark and turn my face
>
> or when I go among pleasured women filling with first child, oh
> when I want to go over what is gone and done
> then I come to my high room that faces the river
> and the wide light the river moves ceaselessly under.
>
> (8)

Here the poet is at her contemplative best. Calling on the language of Coffman's Appalachian beginnings, her speaker sees the "red-lipped girls" as "prideful," aware of the power of their youth and potential (8). Aligning these young girls with other products of the good earth, Coffman depicts them as "sugaring to ripeness," an image that indicates the naturalness of their coming to maturity (8). The speaker, being older and less full of the potential of life—its sugar—simply wishes to exclude herself, to "lie down in the earliest dark and turn my face" (8). Later, she encounters women at another of life's passages; they are ripening in a different way, "filling with first child" (8). They cause her to think once again about the direction she has chosen for her life, exemplified in the children she has not had. Yet, despite being filled with longing when she looks at both pairs of women, the speaker turns back to the life she has embraced and savors its bitter-sweet satisfactions, encapsulated in a light-filled room overlooking the flowing river.

Coffman has a particular gift for capturing the sort of image that flashes and is gone. It is as if she has internalized the secrets of visual acuity espoused in *Pilgrim at Tinker Creek*, Annie Dillard's 1974 hymn to the power of actually seeing what one is looking at:

[T]here is another kind of seeing that involves a letting go.
When I see this way I sway transfixed and emptied. The differ-
ence between two ways of seeing is the difference between
walking with and without a camera. When I walk with a cam-
era I walk from shot to shot, reading the light on a calibrated
meter. When I walk without a camera, my own shutter opens,
and the moment's light prints on my own silver gut. When I
see this second way I am above all an unscrupulous observer.[7]

Coffman combines this capacity for penetrating observations with an ability to
capture a subject in intense, memorable images relying on sight, sound, and
even taste.

The poet has said that she admires "the heaped-up line of Whitman, the
syllabics of Moore so terse in form and lush in detail, the end rhymes of Yeats
set into places like jewels . . . I like poems packed with things from this
world, and described with a focus so tight you see the corners and edges and
colors . . . you see the air, even."[8] These guides are ones she follows in creat-
ing her own poetic lines. When, for example, she depicts the growing dark-
ness of evening in "Maps," she does so through a strong visual: "Did you sing
of the good Christians going to heaven? / Of the sweet one leaned forward
on the porch until all but your white shirt was gone in the dark?" (21). Her
strength with the finely crafted image extends to places, people, ideas—even
creatures, as when she uses "fly and cricket, the thirsty snake" as exemplars
of nature's repetitive harmony in "Glenmary, 1990" (20). In "The Road to
Canso," she describes the darkness of fir trees in Nova Scotia by juxtaposing
them against the blackness of "a widow's skirt in Canceau," rather than the
more usual comparison to some other aspect of nature (26). The actions of
lovers eager to disrobe are captured in "Cold Sunday" by "the dark-colored
pants with the shhh of being shucked off" (33). In "Romeo Collision" Coffman
casts the bitter taste of unresolved arguments as "Tak[ing] the char taste of
fight to bed" (39). She can also undercut her own romanticism, offering the
kind of realistic picture she paints in "The Simple Day," when she describes
the coming of morning: "I rise up with my breasts, bubble and seed, /
smaller than nationally advertised breasts. / [. . .] This is the hour some light
their first smoke / off the stove eye, / pajamas drooping below the butt"
(51). Coffman has acknowledged her delight in word play and imagery: "I
love rhyme, alliteration, assonance, and phrases that are (in sound) excessive
and a delight to say."[9] The Pew Fellowship for the Arts, also noting Coffman's
being "attuned to the nuances of speech and language," says, "In the playful

bendings and curlings of sound, Ms. Coffman's poems speak themselves out loud in the reader's mind."[10]

"Rapture," a poem that Ostriker specifies as leaving her "breathless," contains rich images heaped upon one another.[11] Opening with a global question that frames the poem and is answered only in the last six lines, Coffman asks, "What is the gear that turns this world?" As she details the morning light "like honey" on the walls of the city, the church bells chiming, the "white-smocked fish-market man [who] bends from the waist / receiving and flinging boxes from the truck ramp," the storyteller breaking beans as he sits straddling a box, young boys from her childhood, and her own fears, Coffman takes her reader to the very place of the action and contemplation (11). Coffman concludes that whatever the force is that turns the world, it must be "very basic,"—as basic as our own daily experiences, longings, and fears (12). "We must turn of a piece," she says, in harmony both with ourselves and with others, even those who make us afraid. We must acknowledge the power of the simplicity found in elemental things, which she exemplifies in the closing lines of the poem with "rows of furrows cut in the earth, / . . . the gold block of cheese on the dark shelf" (12). Not all critics find her exploration of the poem's central question satisfactory. Unlike Ostriker, Publisher's Weekly argues that "Rapture" shows Coffman's talent unrealized because she does not adequately deal with the tension she has created: "The poems often end in soft generalizations or safe natural imagery. 'Rapture,' which owns the provocative line, 'I have thought I might be a hater of Jews,' concludes: 'we must turn of a piece / but there is nothing so good / as the row of furrows cut in the earth.'"[12] Yet "Rapture" is not the only poem in which Coffman argues for a return to the elemental harmonies. "Dog Days" and "Learning the Butterfly," too, find the speaker struggling for a balance in her life.

Often compared to Walt Whitman, whose work she admires, Coffman is most Whitmanesque when she is writing about the body and its workings. Particularly notable for this quality are "Leaving New York City," "About the Pelvis," and "Brother Ass," three of a number of poems containing such examinations. In these poems, Coffman truly sings the body electric.

Aching with the physical struggle of packing and moving her belongings from an apartment up several flights of stairs, the narrator in "Leaving New York City" pauses to think about the wonder of the human body and mind: "If I admire my knees, the knobs on the inner side / the fact that they bend, the act of their bending, if I admire the toes that grip / the floor in argument against the falling body, / or I admire the turning head and the fixed spine, energy flashlighting forever out the top, I will have enough"

(53). Again using an unexpected word—"flashlighting"—to characterize the constant workings of the brain, its non-stop production of movement and ideas, Coffman creates an image particular to her style.

"About the Pelvis" is an extended series of definitions and amplifications of this basic bodily structure, given in eight two-line stanzas. Coffman variously refers to the pelvis as a "furnace," "a self-fueler," a "chair that walks," and a connector for "brother legs" (55). One senses that the poet is both musing and having a good time as she explores the functions of the pelvis. The speaker advises us to "Trust the pelvis—it will get everything else there: pull you onto a ledge, push you into a run" (55). Becoming increasingly lyrical, Coffman goes so far as to create names for adjacent body parts, which she terms "the constellations of the pelvis": "Drawn Bow, Flame-of-One-Branch, / Round Star, and Down-Hanging Mountains" (55). As she frequently chooses to do, the poet undercuts her own growing lyricism by bringing the reader resoundingly back to reality in the last pair of lines: "Forget the pelvis, and you're a stove good for parts: / motion gone, heat gone, and the soup pots empty" (55). "Rogue Gene" finds the narrator humorously contemplating dominant and recessive characteristics that show up through the generations in a family. He wonders whether the "genetic mix" includes more than height, a legendary temper, or "mama's fanny on papa's skinny body," but perhaps even concubines, pirates, or prisoners (23). The speaker whimsically deduces, "There's no way of knowing my family: / height, gait, speech—or the presence of the rogue gene" (23). Like all of us, he is inheritor of the physical characteristics and excesses of past generations; both produce strongly ambivalent feelings.

"Brother Ass," supposedly St. Francis of Assisi's affectionate name for the body,[13] presents Socrates debating over which has supremacy, the soul or the five senses. After enumerating the failings of the body, the speaker asks, "Or is it the body that is first of all wise?" (57). In a final stanza strongly reminiscent of Whitman's *Leaves of Grass*, Coffman explains the merit of the body, which does not fret over complexities, but simply reacts naturally:

> The body does not fear: that is the chattering soul's.
> The body knows hurt: it pulls its hand from the flame.
> It covers its backside with a blanket in the cold wind.
> It would not charge the bayoneted enemy line.
> It neither rules nor follows, nor cares to teach:
> it is merely the bear and the paw at the crack of honey.

(58)

Perhaps the body, in its straightforward approach to life, is wiser than either the mind or the soul.

Likely is dedicated to Appalachian women Coffman knows well, her mother and aunts, "the five Wright sisters" (v). Often she turns to family history for the subject of her poems, using her experiences or those recalled by relatives to center her writing squarely in the place of her Appalachian roots. "Maps" is such a poem. Dedicated to her grandmother's cousin, Curtis O. Roberson, the narrative speaks of a task Roberson was assigned by the Appalachian Power Company—"to find and move all graves in a four-county area near Roanoke, Virginia, that would subsequently be flooded by the Smith Mountain Dam Project" (21). This dam allowed the development of a power source for the populous Roanoke Valley, at the risk of those who lived in its path. Roberson and his partner relocated almost fourteen hundred graves in less than three years. This story of the absorption of actual lives, homes, and family places is one that touches intimately on the history of a region too often at the mercy of corporate power. Coffman uses the metaphor of maps as her central idea. The speaker compares the several maps we may be familiar with, those of paper, of lines written on faces, and of the paths of stars above "the root-starred earth" (21). Recalling the days when people were settled throughout the valley that would soon be flooded over, the speaker evokes these mountaineers, who perhaps sing a "little song" in the evening, "free from the burden of work" (21). Gone and forgotten now, these people nevertheless have left unconscious reminders of having passed this way: "loose buttons, / teacups alongside a thigh, wedding bands" (22). A "good Company man" moves each uncovered body into a "two-by-two-by-one-foot box" (22). Thus the people of the valley—so individual in their actual lives—are regularized in death by an uncaring force, the Appalachian Power Company, more concerned with a dubious progress than with the families who surely must pay its cost.

Publisher's Weekly noted Coffman's skill in depicting the Appalachian region: "In long-lined narrative poems steeped in detail, Coffman links the past century's miners', mill workers', and farmers' wives with their present-day descendants, depicting circumscribed lives filled with daily grace and loneliness."[14] However, the same critic argues that Coffman often does not push her images hard enough, but backs off from what could be a startling insight: "In 'Glenmary, 1990,' Coffman writes: 'Summer: one child's in the cellar for lying, / four shout with the high voices of running / where the yard grows dark.' This journey into the soul of working-class, small-town and rural America avoids risky territory, touching on a passive frustration without ever fully exploring it. . . . Coffman is at her best when she refuses to pull her punches."[15]

Despite this criticism, readers will find frank exploration of Appalachia's problems in numerous Coffman poems. In "The Small Town" she at first presents an idyllic picture of a young boy in summer. His rustic swimming hole, however, is the place where the Emory joins the Clinch "into one brown river / . . . cut by boat propellers / and upstream chemical dumpings" that have killed the fish, their rotting bodies revealed as the river pushes away from its banks (9). The river, far from a sparkling current, "drags a fermented smell with it" as it passes the people living in supposed normalcy along its banks (10).

Each section of Likely contains references to the hard work and poverty of the region's people, often contrasted with the majestic beauties of its natural setting. "The Boy with the Blueberries" focuses on a young boy who cannot find a sense of home in the city, but returns "into the blue mountains / that secure the horizon" to try to make a living (17). There he soon "becomes cheap labor timbering / where woods lock darker onto what was town," ironically being forced to destroy the very thing—the mountains—whose call has brought him home (17). Coffman touches, too, on the problem of out-migration, saying, "the clever ones plead to leave, then leave" (17). In "Pulled Down," Coffman portrays the lives of those living in shabby company towns in a "land down under the mountain," working long hours in the paper mills or in the mines whose exploitation destroys their home (18). Inevitably a mine shaft collapses, leaving the workers "sealed in" and the survivors so filthy from coal dust they must bathe twice before feeling fit to carry the tragic news to the victims' families (18). Coffman ends on no positive note here, but with the Hiwassi Land Company's further destruction of native timber: they "sprayed the oaks so they died standing" to make way for a pine forest and a new paper mill (18). This poem constitutes one of Coffman's strongest statements about the devastation of the land.

Notable also for its poignant insights is "On a Mill Worker in Rockwood," which depicts the home life of a man who works a shift in the local mill. He is perpetually exhausted and embittered by his life. The poem is told from the viewpoint of an external narrator, who speaks to a person seen only as a quiet child, fading into the background and trying to stay out of the way of the mill worker, presumably the father. The remaining character is the child's "Mamaw," or grandmother, who cooks and unobtrusively tries to protect the young child. From the moment the man gets home, "the night shiny black when his shift was up," his despair is evident (25). His arrival brings with it a heavy tension that pervades the entire poem. This home is no refuge, but a bleak place of darkness, violence, and stunted hopes.

Several lines repeat, forming a chain of thought from an early stanza to a later one. "He'd come home and put his face in his hands," "whiskey and chair by the kitchen door," "he'd lurch to the stove and pile in more wood," "face closed as the fist he hit you with," "heat bright in the room like hell preached in church," "while your Mamaw whispered you were excused," "Damn HEAT," "he'd cry and kick open the door," and "the night shiny black when his shift was up" appear again in subsequent stanzas (25). Having eight of the poem's only twenty lines given twice makes their effect inescapable. Along with the repeated use of "lurch" and "cry" to describe the mill worker's actions, these refrains indicate the habitual nature of his behavior and the dull, repetitive monotony of his life (25). Nor is this worker unique: In the mills, we may assume, his name is legion.

Coffman's love of the Appalachian mountains forms a thread that runs throughout her work. Although she does not devote a single poem to their consideration, she frequently refers to the way they look and the effect they have on her spirit and her aspirations. Her pictures of the mountains vary: In "The Small Town" Coffman makes "the powerful flanks of the mountains" her final image (10). "The Graveyard" carries another view of the power of the hills, "each one bigger than the one before: / bigger than all the heavings to drums, than the noises of deep drum throats / to the stories of giants" (46). Whether bold, dark, or powerful, the mountains can also offer solace. In "Rapture," the speaker longs to return to the mountains and says, "If the mountains will let me back, / if they will let me back and give me a small house: / yellow light in winter when the mountains are gray / the brittle spiked pine scent splayed over me in winter" (11). Evidently such a reunion will compensate for what is missing in the speaker's life far away from the hills. Of this, the reader is certain.

One final aspect of Coffman's poetry cannot go without mention, her ability to take a tiny moment and use it microcosmically to explore life's essential matters. Coffman does so skillfully in a pair of poems placed next to one another in the final section of the collection, "In Trout Season" and "Courage, or One of Gene Horner's Fiddles." "In Trout Season" uses a common occurrence for its poetic occasion, an imagined trip to the riverbank to join a crowd of people gathered to fish. The speaker takes his "breath and clay self," the essence of his body, along the path leading to the water, remembering the many other times his feet have traveled there (60). He recalls the joy he felt when he was a "scuff-heeled loiterer" heading this same way (60). The second stanza seems a marked departure from the first, a sudden expression from the interior voice of the speaker, commenting on the fearsome nature of the beauty found in "the curl of the duck's tail / or the first buds spread in a sheerness / like the veil the new bride lies in, / the one thing she wears" (60). This stanza serves as a bridge between the first stanza and the final one, in which the speaker will emerge from memory to focus on the fishermen who stand in a line along the riverbank. They, rather than the fish, are spoken of as being "in season" (60). Several of them, "inked by the tattoo needle," resemble the spotted trout; their tattoos suggest a kinship between man and fish (60). As the speaker continues to observe the human line along the river, he expands his thinking. In the shining river, the trout swimming in it, and the people waiting to catch the trout, he sees an affinity. They look to him like "prayers might look in ascension / on a wire for carrying prayers / or as the spirit shines when it extends in ecstasy past the body / but walks on with the body. Or sits, fishing" (60). For the speaker in this poem, the real connotes the spiritual and the ties between the body and the eternal.

There are only three characters pictured in "Courage, or One of Gene Horner's Fiddles," Catherine Osborn, an invalid; Gene Horner, the fiddle maker; and the speaker, cast as a writer. Just after putting a self-indulgent line onto paper ("My face burned and I wanted to cry"), the speaker happens to look up and see Catherine making her way "slowly by the canal, with the jerking motions of a small boat / when the people in it move or change places on their knees" (59). Recalling that Catherine has been "on oxygen all winter," the speaker implies her admiration for the woman's powers of endurance, her ability to push herself onward when many would acquiesce to illness (59). Next, once again feeling sorry for herself on a dull, rainy day, she goes to the fiddle maker's shop with the intention of buying a "dark maple fiddle" (59). There she is treated to a demonstration song, played by Gene Horner himself. In the hands of its maker, the fiddle produces such sweet music, "such a pure sound," that it seems to "rise from the frets of my wrists, my curled hands" (59). The woman's endurance and the strains of the fiddle combine to bring the speaker out of herself and consider the nature of true courage. It is not a bold, flashy thing, she decides, and says, "We are wrong about courage. It is closer to music. / It rises from us simply as we move in this life, or submit" (59). The fourteen lines of this poem are all Coffman needs to enable her speaker to arrive at a fresh definition of courage, one that embraces both the effort and the song.

In The Philosophy of Travel, George Santayana speaks of having been guided by "the rooted heart and the ranging intellect."[16] These twin guides have served many Appalachian writers like Lisa Coffman who, although distinctly rooted in their homeland, have ranged afar in their travels and in their writing. Coffman's *Likely* offers reflections from a profound new poetic talent with firm grounding in her native Appalachia, as well as in the larger world of her actual or intellectual wanderings. The poems contained in this first volume indicate that Coffman's talented voice is one we will hear from again. We await the fulfillment of that promise with eagerness and wonder.

## Notes

1. Pew Fellowship for the Arts web page: <www.pewarts.org/abpfmaintcxt.html>.
2. Pennsylvania State Univ.–Altoona English Dept. faculty web page: <www.personal.psu.edu/faculty/k/a/kaw16/Facultybiographies.htm>.
3. "Lisa Coffman," Pew Fellowship for the Arts web page: <www.pewarts.org/93/Coffman/main.html>.
4. Alicia Ostriker's critique appears on the back jacket of *Likely*.
5. Lisa Coffman, *Likely* (Kent, Ohio: Kent State Univ. Press, 1996).
6. Philip Larkin, *High Windows* (London: Faber and Faber, 1974), 17.
7. Annie Dillard, *Pilgrim at Tinker Creek* (New York: Harper & Row, 1974), 31.
8. Lisa Coffman, "Judges Notes: Poetry," from the *Philadelphia Citipaper.net* web page: <www.citypaper.net/articles/122895/article009.shtml>.
9. Pew Fellowship for the Arts web page.
10. Ibid.
11. Ostriker.
12. Review of *Likely*, by Lisa Coffman, *Publisher's Weekly*, Nov. 25, 1996, 72.
13. Coffman, *Likely*, 62.
14. Review of *Likely*, 72.
15. Ibid.
16. George Santayana, "The Philosophy of Travel," in *"The Birth of Reason" and Other Essays*, ed. Daniel Cory (New York: Columbia Univ. Press, 1968), 171.

# Lou V. Crabtree

## Husband

I never saw my husband
    naked
For all his years we were
    under eyes, taboos, codes
    Just that one time
I saw his yellow back
    as I helped him
    with his bath
when the liver cancer
    had him.
Not even in dreams
    does he ever come
Gloriously in naked good health.

## He Cut My Garden Down

       making it so
this winter was hard
so hard I sent the girl
borrowing a bit of lard
to make the water gravy

       making it so
the boy hung to me
       past his years
my blue drop of milk
       barely passing
the blue of his lips
until his skin glistened
and his leg shanks lengthened
and I wrapped him and held him
through the day as we
took on the snow's whiteness.
I walked the girl
       seven years is young
to be put with strangers
her dangers clamped on me
I walked her on the high ridge
until I saw a house in the far valley
       "Go there,
Go to that house. Try to stay the winter."
I watched her go in the snow
until she was a dot through the gate.

*He did not have*
       *to cut my garden down*
It was not the women in town
       or the liquor
or my crocheted doily he snatched
       off the mantle
       and burned in the stove

It was not the cold stove
        he stood around
        and kicked the cold stove
        cold from no wood
until the dog slunk away
        from older kicks.

They said—
        The black mare reared and
        dragged him
        as he raced up Main Street in town
        Some men brought him in
        and prepared him
        and asked did I want to look
        I did not want to see who it was
        cut my garden down.

They said—
        I must look and helped me in
        and pulled back the sheet
        so I could see where the black mare kicked
        with his black hair crushed
        and wet in the bruises
        in a pale face where all
        the rage seemed gone.

Old granny honed me
        "Don't let his rage into you"
I said
    *He did not have to cut*
    *my garden down.*

In nightmares someone comes at me
        Awake I am glad
        *someone* is dead
They did not have to cut my garden down.

# What Kind of Egg Are You?
## A Profile of Lou V. Crabtree

Judy K. Miller

L ou V. Crabtree, born in 1913, has lived most of her life in Washington Country, Virginia. Her career has included school teaching, farming, directing a band, and lecturing. Her first book, a collection of short stories entitled *Sweet Hollow*, was published in 1983 by Louisiana State University Press after writer Lee Smith "discovered" Crabtree during a visit to Virginia. The book is now in its fourth printing. Crabtree has won many awards for her writing, including a PEN/Faulkner award and poetry awards from *Shenandoah* and the Poetry Society of Virginia. In 1988, she was declared a "Laureate in Literature" of Virginia. In 1998, the Sow's Ear Press published a collection of Crabtree's poems entitled *The River Hills and Beyond*, which was named the Virginia Center for the Book's Poetry Book of the Year in 1999.[1]

But there is more to Lou than awards and accolades. Her lessons to generations of writers, including me, remain a major contribution to letters in our region.

"Seeing yourself in a mud puddle."

"The smell of home."

"The squishy mud that the frog knows."

"The long teeth of winter's icicles."

"Hearing a rocket blast off . . . try to hear a butterfly walking."

These are Lou Crabtree's words to students of writing. She teaches them how to see, how to hear, how to move to move in and out, in and around, words.

Some years ago, not long after the publication of *Sweet Hollow*, Lou Crabtree visited my classroom to talk with some of my students. The students were college freshmen and Lou was in her seventies. Innocently enough, Lou began. "Seeing yourself in a mud puddle. The smell of home. The senses are important," she said. "Now, how many senses are there?"

This was good. Already, we had talked about how good writing is sensual and had worked through appropriate writing exercises. Lou talked a short time about sight, sound, smell, taste, touch: "See the birds circling in the sky.

They are the spirits of all unborn babies." Her images were sharp, character-istically original; then, much to my dismay, Lou had my adult students stand, form a human train and march around the room, playacting, as she called it. Well, okay, I could go along with it. After all, I reminded my stuffy academic self, Lou did teach high school drama for years, and quite successfully, I might add.

I watched my students chug around the room, Lou the chief engineer, as she asked them to add whooping sounds and to hop from foot to foot. "Oh, lord," I thought, "student evaluations!" What visions I had of my students being forever intellectually scarred! In a surge of Darwinian intellectual self-preservation, I muttered to the class. "You know, she was a drama teacher."

I still do not know if anyone was listening to me. I hope not because they were in fact having the time of their lives playacting—learning things that I had yet to learn. These days, years later, because Lou says her "ole knees get stiff" and keep her close to home, I take the class to her house, instead of having her come to the classroom. When I took students from an Appalachian Literature course for a visit, she took us on an imaginary bear hunt.

"Are you ready?' she asked. " Here we go." We marched in place in her bedroom, which also serves as a sitting room in cooler months. We marched through a Jell-O factory, through a candy store, and through a dark forest. I watched the different students' reactions. Some were over thirty, some under twenty. All had fallen under Lou's charm. We each found our own bear. Finally, I was beginning to learn what Lou had tried to teach both my students and me years ago in that first classroom visit time: Motion. Playacting. Laughing. Be not afraid.

Lou insists not enough poets and writers pay attention to motion. "They might have pretty words," she says, "but there's no movement. " To illustrate what she means by motion, she reads examples from scraps of paper where she has "scratched out" a line here and there as it has occurred to her, maybe in the middle of the night, maybe as the result of a conversation with a friend: "Keeping peas on your knife when you're eating," "your flower pot turning over," "your wash blowing on the line."

While these examples show everyday physical motion, much of Lou's sense of motion is far more complex. For example, consider how the following lines from the unpublished "Tears" use movement to evoke emotion:

> I learned tears
> from raindrops
> falling from roofs

From a boiling kettle
Popping sizzling falling
Dancing on a hot stove

In her writing, Lou often pushes the laws of science to their fantastical and whimsical limits even as she pushes words to theirs. "We learn that energy can be harnessed," she says. "I hope that in the future my dog's tail can be harnessed and that my heart's beat can plug into and run my car." And she writes:

What keeps me from knowing
that from the particles
of my hurting knee
a tree is sprouting

What kind of a mind would dare imagine such possibilities? Surely a fearless one. A while back a group of poets was sitting around one evening when Lou Crabtree's name entered the conversation. "She is one of the most fearless writers I know," one of the poets said. While others in the group asked for further clarification, I knew immediately what he meant. Fearless, indeed.

When it comes to her writing, Lou forbids no idea, no word. When Lou writes, anything and everything goes. Recently, Lou was sitting, as she often does, on her front porch. In fact, almost without notice, Lou Crabtree's front porch has become one of Virginia's finest institutions of higher learning where poets, writers, Viet Nam boat people, climbers of Mt. Everest, Buddhists, and others have gathered for years; and I have been one of the fortunate ones to have a chance to study there. On this particular day, the sweet scent of wisteria warmed in the sunshine. Somewhat selfishly, I stopped by for a pick-me-up visit. Casually, I asked, "So, Lou, what are you working on these days?"

She answered without hesitation, "Masturbation. I've been keeping a list of all the different ways they have of saying it." And she read off a few: "Circle jerk, wash your butterfly quickly, whackin' your wiener." There was that same mischievous twinkle that I'd sometimes seen at poetry readings right before she enticed the audience with a promise of some censored stuff, "if there's time," and of course the audience always insisted that time there surely would be.

"Censored material, such as sex, is part of life," Lou says, but her writing career did not begin with this censored material. Instead, she admits to beginning at the same place where most writers begin—with love. "My first attempt at writing was an Hawaiian love story," she says. "I knew zero points about love." The first poem she remembers writing was about her mother. "I thought it was pretty good," she says. "When I showed it to my boyfriend, he said, 'You didn't write that!' He wasn't my boyfriend any more!"

"Once I wrote about love as in the teen age years. When I was thirteen I thought Black Holes were filled with chocolate," Lou says chuckling, "then I progressed to the twenties when children are born. In your work life, you support them, then in the fifties maybe there is a divorce or a death. In the sixties if there is money, women take a cruise or go back to school, and then in the eighties you have a great time with the senior citizens, going places, eating with them. Now in my porch years of spiritual life and great peace, I learned along the way that love is not as one thinks as a teenager, but is transferred to friends, animals, the land, students and work, books, and that the future is an achievement."

Much of her poetry reflects her changing insights about this most illusive of emotions and include the light-hearted verse in "Love No. 3":

> A life-long romance
>> is always in my mind
> In the softness
>> in the mouse's ear
> in the bubby bush
>> beside my kitchen door
> in the kisses and murmurs
>> and whispers among leaves
>
> (14)

And then there is the charged expression of relations in "Nit of a Louse":

> I am the coyote
>> bringing game
> to my mate
>> caught in a trap
>> in her need to eat.
>
> (45)

While love may continue to be one of the themes that manifests itself in her work, Lou says that "Now in my porch years, I am pursuing two things at this late time in my life: spiritualism and space." In order to learn all that she could about the universe, Lou enrolled in a graduate level astronomy course and every Saturday morning drove to class in her little vintage VW Beetle. She was in her eighties at the time.

In her space poems Lou blends the lyrical with the scientific. The following stanza from the unpublished "Space" is powered by its own motion:

> In life or death
> Light or darkness
> we dance
> To wavelengths of the Sun.

Space remains a primary interest these days, finding its way into poems about mortality such as one from "Lost in Space":

> I look back to see bleached bones
> My bequest to the stars . . .
> Only this eternity of no beginning
> With no end to loneliness
> Is real.
>                      (50)

I remember well my first introduction to Lou's Space poems. It was that same summer when she was enrolled in the astronomy course. Sitting on her front porch on a sunny afternoon, I casually asked Lou to read me one of the poems she was working on, and she obliged by reading "Space Poem # 6." I was stunned. This particular poem combined science, spirituality, and sexuality in a way that only Lou Crabtree can do. Although the exact words of the poem are lost in the chaos of the papers in her house at this writing, its impact remains with me.

This exploration of space has helped Lou expand her understanding of spirituality. "I have a new way of thinking about God," she says. "A man scientist told me that he thought of God as mixed up with all of the laws of science and astronomy and physics. In my spiritual life, I have put away all of the artists' pictures that show God as a man. I thought of God as a man all of my life, and even as a woman from old religious statues like Juno and Venus."

From her scientific study of astronomy and poetic exploration of space, Lou has arrived at her own interpretation of paradise expressed in a poem entitled "Paradise" where she puts a unpredictable twist on the phrase "growing old":

> Growing young and younger
> Scientists and scripture agree
> Upon breaking the speed
>        Of sound
> One grows younger
>        And time stops

Currently, she is working on a collection of writings about Abingdon as a paradise and about angel women she has known. She plans to put a seal on this work until the year 2075. At first, I thought she was teasing, but she explained, "I don't want my friends to think that I'm writing about them," she said. "When my book of stories first came out," she says, referring to *Sweet Hollow*, "one of my friends told me she knew who every single one of my characters was. I told her I was glad she did because I sure didn't. I don't want that sort of thing happening again."

How can one reconcile Lou's hope in Paradise with the loneliness that permeates the loss in some of her poems? A touching and more personal one is the poem "Gone," written upon the death of her daughter, Sara Taylor, who died November 12, 1996:

> Gone
> In God's Law of Change
>    Leaving
>      Shadows beckoning
> Footsteps behind
> A button uncovered
>      Under a drainpipe
> Lonely forever
> For one
> Gone Gone

As a whole, Lou's poetry does not dwell on loneliness, but it is a theme she does not avoid. She says, "Loneliness we pursue all of our lives. We are born lonely and we die lonely." Loneliness is one of those big life questions that poetry allows us to explore. She says, "A poem should begin with a question about life and end with a bigger question. The bigger the question, then maybe the poem is immortal."

The image and themes of cycles and circles have long had a prominent place in Lou's work. Her short story "The Jake Pond," which could just as easily be classified as a prose poem, includes the following sentence in its introduction: "And spring vaulted into summer; summer slipped into fall, making cycles like the circles left on the face of the pond, where insects lifted or the boy tossed a pebble out" (69). The movement in these circles is the movement of nature itself, the cycles of life. Even in its ending, the story circles back: "The scents of the locusts blooms and mating blacksnakes wafted in gentle circles to meet circles of peppermint over the breast of unfathomable waters, of the ever and forever Jake Pond" (75).

Though not as eloquent in language as "The Jake Pond," Lou's poem "God's Law of Circles" examines the same types of images:

> George laughing at cow flops
> And horse turds . . .
>
> To old John lost in a circle
> Finding his way home

That image of the circle, whether, directly or indirectly, consciously or sub-consciously, evokes a sense of change.

She says that the best sentence she ever wrote came from another one of her short stories from the *Sweet Hollow* collection, "Little Jesus." The sentence, which was cut from the book before publication, read, "Come back Little Jesus and I will give you my golden catalpa and my red flame maple and all the judas trees high on the persimmon ridges above the red gashed sand gullies." The persimmon ridge and red flame maple evoke imagery similar to earlier examples.

A favorite poem about change is "The Man in the Moon," and often when I visit Lou I ask her to read it to me. This poem features the Apache Kid, torn from a magazine, lounging faithfully on a shelf near her bed:

> Times they be a-changin
> I'm sayin
> Cut me a new un
> Out'n that catalog
> Cut'n a new picture
> Of a new boyfriend for me
> Apache Kid
> Ugly Ole Indian
> Your picture I'm likin
>
> Now it's me a changing
> In these changin times
> Old Indian man Apache Kid
> He be steady
> Keep me steady Apache Kid like you is
>
> Moon Man
> Don't be messin
> Wid me
> It's me to now no
> I be one a changing.

This poem reflects her characteristic wit and attitude about change, but it also offers a sampling of another one of Lou's favorite topics, Native Americans. Not only has she written many stories and poems about them, but in the 1980s Lou was adopted into the Cherokee tribe. Because of her sensitivity about their cultural heritage, she was given the name of Grandmother Wolf Woman.

"Where will poetry fit in?" Lou asks, changing the subject. Then in a characteristic, yet unexpected zinger, she says, "Some people say that poetry is between hallux or the big toe and the next one. Smart people never refer to the big toe as the hallux. Ha! Who is going to read that!" A profound statement about poetry.

"If you have the right words, you can get by with a lot of hard luck," Lou Crabtree says. "If you have the right words, you can have peace with your children, you can get by with ill feelings, bad tempers, with wars. We could get along with Russia, with China. No word is bad," she says, "if it is used by the right person in the right place." Surely this is just the sort of thing that writers everywhere are obligated to say; but to illustrate her point, Lou tells a little story about some teenage boys who drive by her house. It is a story I have heard before, but I must say it is not one I have fully appreciated.

"They are showing off and having a good time," she says, "and they holler at me, 'Hiddy, bitch.' I wave at them." She plugs her thumbs in her ears and wriggles her fingers. "I throw them a kiss. I smile at them. We enjoy each other."

But . . . but . . . but . . . I cannot help but object to the rudeness, to this obvious lack of respect by these young boys. Yet when I tell Lou how angry I feel toward the boys, she is genuinely surprised at my reaction. "They don't mean anything by it. They're just out having a good time. Some years ago if someone called you a bitch, it was a fighting word, but these days, it doesn't mean the same as it once did."

And I realized that for a short while I had slipped back to my stuffy academic self, that I was taking myself too seriously, that I had forgotten motion. Language moves the moment. I had missed the point.

Of course the boys probably thought that Lou was just some crazy old woman, never once realizing her genius. I could not help but remember that classroom of students from years ago, hopping from foot to foot, whooping while I tried to apologize for Lou's dramatic introduction to the senses and the movement of learning. "Without movement, there is no learning," Lou says. "You are dead."

I remember one of Lou's whimsical little poems, "The Egg," that whacks me to attention:

> What kind of an egg are you?
> Hard-boiled     Cracked
> Deviled     Scrambled
> Sunnyside up
> Spoiled     Soft boiled

What kind of egg am I, indeed? What kind of egg are you?

## Note

1. Lou V. Crabtree, *The River Hills and Beyond*, introd. by Lee Smith (Abingdon, Va.: Sow's Ear Press, 1998). References to Crabtree's poems from this book are found within the text. Other poems cited are unpublished at this time.

# doris davenport

## *And that's another thing*

People in Gainesville
not all that different
from Cleveland, Bean Creek, Cornelia,
Clarkesville, or Toccoa. They cared about
what they cared about. Mainly
each other, and each other's business.
Put a lot of stock, and time,
into looking good, living as good as they could,
and doing the best they could
with what they had.
And they, like the rest of us,
liked where they lived.
Must have. They still there,
ain't they? Unless they dead—
and some of them so nosey, they
still hanging around.

> *Who? Who you know*
> *still hanging around,*
> *and been dead? You*
> *start talking that*
> *foolishness, and I'm leaving.*
> *I'm outta here, soon's*
> *you get started,*
> *with that.*

## Ceremony

Soquee is a Cherokee word for the hill,
cross the railroad track, in Appalachian foothills,
where madness runs like possums. Like honeysuckle
kudzu
taking over everyone
insane and acceptable all the time
all the time, Soquee sits playing tricks
on minds

hainted.

■

Sak Wi-Yi. Sounds Inflected

in rhythmical air
in a sacred place

■

Don't mess with the sacred
It will get you every time.

# Coming Home to Affrilachia
## The Poems of doris davenport

James A. Miller

> they call me a
> two-headed woman,
> but sometimes i got three.
>
> —doris davenport, 1980

Educator/writer/performance poet; African American/southern/Appalachian; Lesbian-feminist/revolutionary/iconoclast—doris davenport has always resisted easy classification throughout a public career that now spans more than two decades. The price for her unwillingness to claim convenient, tailor-made identities has often been critical neglect. During the late 1960s, davenport explains, her work was rejected by African American "little" magazines, because she ". . . didn't fit the party line." And she encountered problems with lesbian-feminist publishers, too: "I ran into the biases of editors and publishers, in our alternative reality, as well. For some wimmin editors, my poems weren't overtly lesbian or feminist enough. For others, my poetry didn't advocate 'victimology' (my word, not theirs) enough. Ironically, for some I was either not black enough or too black. . . . I did not fit any of the publishing pigeonholes; I did not fit any of their ideologies comfortably enough. . . ."[1]

davenport has also observed, "There is not yet a place (or even the concept, for most people) for little African-American girls who are born mystics/ philosophers/intellectuals. I had no choice but to try to live in what has been called the 'real' world, one that has ever been, mostly, unreal to me— except in northeast Georgia."[2] Visionary/mystic/seeker, davenport has crisscrossed America since she graduated from Paine College, armed with a B.A. in English, in 1969. San Francisco; Buffalo, New York; Institute, West Virginia; Orangeburg, South Carolina; New Haven and Hartford, Connecticut; Los

Angeles; Iowa City; Norman, Oklahoma; Bowling Green, Ohio; Charlotte, North Carolina; Sautee, Georgia—all of these landscapes have figured in her odyssey; all of them appear in her poetry; but, in retrospect, one constant in her work has been her "Affrilachian experiences"—after the poet Frank X Walker who coined the term "Affrilachian" to convey the particular experiences of African Americans from the Appalachians.[3] "Some aspect of the people or the place appears in everything, prose and poetry, as anecdotes, allusions, single poems, and entire manuscripts . . ." davenport has written. "Northeast Georgia determined my worldview, behavior, and value system."[4] In the final analysis, davenport's poems always point in the direction she calls home—a state of mind as well as the physical setting of her beloved northeast Georgia mountains.

davenport announced her presence with it's like this, self-published in 1980. Best read/heard as a response to the open-ended greeting "what's happening?," "what it is?" or, most recently, "whassup?," it's like this introduces a voice that is alternately laconic and wry, lyrical and reflective—but always deeply personal, consistent with the feminist maxim: the personal is the political. "Sojourner, you shouldn't have done that . . ." establishes the mood and tone of the entire collection:

> you told them what was what, i guess.
> you really made your point,
> you stood 'em on their heads but
>
> i got one question. why did you bare
> your chest? you set an awesome precedent.
> now, everytime they see us coming,
>
> they get ready for a show,
> they get ready for a comedy.
> or a tragedy, to some. but entertainment,
> to most. . . .

For davenport the black woman's body is the stage upon which American society projects its deepest fantasies, but this sense of being under constant public scrutiny and siege should not be confused with a claim for victim status—a posture she never assumes; like Zora Neale Hurston, davenport is too busy sharpening her knives. And she has plenty to aim daggers at. Writing out of an unabashedly black woman-centered universe davenport casts a sardonic eye on all sides of the racial/gender divide in "Vision I: Genesis for Wimmin of Color":

white boys run america.
black boys run period.
white girls run the wimmin's movement
& everyone runs over and from
black wimmin.

Against the mediocrity she sees surrounding her davenport pits her own "two-headedness," with its associations of traditional African American beliefs in hoodoo and conjure; and, ultimately, her own personal mythology, drawing upon references from the panoply of Yoruba orishas—Isnya Oye, Damballah, Erzulie-Oshun—and, in later poems, the legendary voodoo priestess Marie Laveau. Within this tradition, davenport casts herself as a goddess, too—as in "the abolitionist, 9979":

i want to free your minds
from centuries of slime
semantic disenfranchisement
and semen.
from seeing yourselves as others do
free you from the prisons of the
penis people.
i want to loosen the chains
of pettiness, pretense, & distorted
perceptions.

davenport's second collection, *eat thunder & drink rain*—its title adopted from Nina Simone's "Obeah Woman"—continues in a similar vein. Many of the poems are mood(y) pieces, often cast in the form of dialogue or letters to friends—as in "Mercy Mercy Me/Things Aint What They Used To Be—for Jeanie" and "For Edjohnetta."[5] Others are blues lyrics. davenport continues her critical assault on the world around her, however, taking aim at heterosexual norms in poems like "Lord if you take him away/I don't wanna live" (11) and "straight people" (25) and criticizing some of the practices of the lesbian community as well. At the center of *eat thunder & drink rain* stands "DOG-MATIC DYKES," a manifesto of sorts that challenges lesbians who adopt patriarchal attitudes towards other gay women:

i am tired of being oppressed
by dykes in male clothing
of being bought with presents of
ivory, bean pies, tea cups, & gold

who say it's natural
and skirts are uncomfortable and shirts
are so comfortable,
who agress me like men

(41)

"A cynical response to the concept of 'the common reality of wimmin' (dedicated to some dykes I knew in L.A.)" speaks for itself in its relentless critique of uncritical and unreflective assertions about the shared experiences of women across the boundaries of race and class (47). These are ideas davenport develops forcefully and eloquently in her essay that appears in Cherrie Moraga and Gloria Anzaldua's *This Bridge Called My Back*, "The Pathology of Racism: A Conversation with Third World Wimmin." Here davenport speaks directly and graphically about the experiences she has encountered with some white feminists:

> A few years ago in New Haven, I tried to relate to feminism through a local womon's center. . . . I was politely informed that I should "organize" with Black wimmin. In other words, get out. . . . In short, white only. Then, the socialist study group I was interested in suddenly closed just at the time I wanted to join. And once, in a wimmin's group when a discussion of men came up, it was revealed that half the white wimmin there feared black men, which included me (from the way they glared at me). In other words, *nigger, go home.*[6]

Characteristically, davenport is less interested in recording grievances than she is in exploring the deep sources of the problem; and this means airing the areas of deep aesthetic, cultural, and social/political aversion that often lead to antagonisms between black and white women. While acknowledging that these attitudes exist and that she, too, has participated in them, davenport nevertheless argues that the burden of her critique must fall upon the shoulders of white feminists who ". . . cling to their myth of being privileged, powerful, and less oppressed (or equally oppressed, whichever it is fashionable or convenient to be at the time) than black wimmin."[7] As much as she would like to believe that centuries of racial/psychological conditioning can be overcome through deep conversation *and* humor, davenport concludes it would be naive to invest much hope in these efforts—except in those ". . . rare and individual cases where the person or group is deliberately and obviously evolved mentally and spiritually . . . we really do have a lot more to concentrate on beside the pathology of white wimmin."

This essay clearly resonates with some of the themes of *eat thunder & drink rain* and sheds additional light on a poem like "ON (MY) BEING A SEPARATIST":

> i have wandered
> for years
> outside anyone's
> comprehension. . .
> outside the "normal"
> circles of respect / kindness / love. &
> like a wolf is
> drawn to camp / fires
>
> (75)

In her early collections, references to davenport's hometown of Cornelia, Georgia, are brief and understated. "121 Soque Street" (an address whose full significance becomes clear in *Soque Street Poems*) appears in *it's like this*, and *eat thunder & drink rain* includes the haiku-like "Georgia in my mind":

> green plum bushes
> the railroad track
> bare
> brown feet,
> red dirt.
>
> (63)

But davenport has not yet begun to mine her Southern Appalachian experiences the way she will in subsequent poems.

In the last poem of *eat thunder & drink rain*, "'Certain Sounds in Time,'" she reflects about growing up in a small town:

> Folks in small towns
> love to bear grudges
> the older, the triter,
> the better.     they live,
>
> it seems, to bear grudges.
> to pull tight lips back
> in disapproval of everyone
> except oneself
>
> . . . . .

---

Certain sounds linger on in the
minds of those who
heard them. . . .

. . . . .

i lived in a smalltown lis-
tening to hear / what they
listened to.

i left a small town
carrying a sound:
clear dots of
infinity swirling in space
a sound / clear & blue.
translucent blue.

(84–85)

The "clear dots of / infinity" in this poem lead directly to the ". . . little pieces
of infinity / floating around / like clear dots" in "draft of another short
story," one of the opening poems in a special issue of a "little" magazine, DAY
TONIGHT/NIGHT TODAY, dedicated to davenport's poetry.[8] These poems, many of
which will reappear in her third collection, VOODOO CHILE: *slight return*, mark an
important transition in davenport's work—a much more concerted and self-
conscious effort to imaginatively reclaim the South as her spiritual home.[9]

    With its invocation of the raucous, gut-bucket sound of the soul musi-
cian Jr. Walker as its epigram, VOODOO CHILE travels "way back home" through
most of the poems in part one of the volume. davenport's poem "Sisterhood"
locates her radical/lesbian/feminist consciousness squarely within her expe-
riences as a southern black woman:

"understand this.
my basis for loving wimmin
is my love for
five younger sisters, my
momma and myself. . . ."

"apart from five sisters /
    i also practice southern
    hospitality. i *am*
from Georgia. . . ."

(6–7)

From this vantage point, davenport conjures up childhood memories in poems like "Gainesville, Georgia" and "Gainesville, too"; or is transported to Georgia by experiences in other landscapes, as in "Poem for a Varnette Honeywood Painting (The Beating Poem)." Most noticeably, in this sequence of poems davenport adopts a range of voices and angles of vision as she begins to map the geography of Northeast Georgia. In "way back home," she alludes to:

> . . . a jook joint on
> nobody's map except the
> map of memory and that
> one the private possession of
> a few & even one of them, now
> & then, will say,
> yeah—where *was* that? . . .
>
> (26)

This "map of memory" leads her back to her maternal grandparents' house, where "spiders live at / 103 Soque now / silently they move / between what was & / what is"; along the route from Cornelia to Clarksville, Georgia, "8 miles of honey suckles & / wild roses dripping fog / & dew, of clouds / on hill people's houses & / minds . . ."; back to some of the eccentric people who inhabit Cornelia, most notably Miz Anna, who ". . . done seen / all kindsa things."

davenport, too, moves between "what was & / what is," mining memories, but dancing with them as well. She writes in "where did our funk go?":

> i dance alone.
> i know, *these* days,
> i dance      alone.
> but me & these memories & ghosts
> gone party
>      on.
>
> (38)

This sequence of poems in VOODOO CHILE: *slight return*, though not published beforehand, sets the stage for davenport's most recently published—and best— collection of poems, Soque Street Poems. Here, for the first time, davenport devotes herself wholeheartedly to reclaiming the Southern Appalachian foothills as her ". . . sacred place of mental, physical, spiritual, and psychic renewal."[10]

Although some of the poems in Soque Street Poems had their genesis in davenport's experiences in Los Angeles in the early 1980s, the volume really began to take shape when she returned to Cornelia in 1992. davenport has said,

These poems are based in fact but most of them have some—ahem—poetic embroidering. Their intention is to celebrate us. To recreate, preserve, and remind us that we had (and have) viable, culturally rich communities; that that sense of kin and connectedness is a living legacy, especially for young folk growing up as I did—economically poor, sometimes frustrated and lost, but with abundant, exuberant creative energy. These poems are love poems, praise songs of the unique African-American communities of Southern Appalachia.[11]

In VOODOO CHILE: *slight return* davenport invokes the spirit of Zora Neale Hurston in "—Janie to Jody as he lay dying . . ." (from Hurston's *Their Eyes Were Watching God*) where she rewrites Janie's final words to her second husband:

> You wanted my pace confined
> To blocked and finite squares
> On a chessboard that fit
> In your pocket          ah
> You wanted, exactly,
> To run off with me—
> When I wanted
> To run
>
> (9)

The spirit of Zora Neale Hurston (and Toni Morrison, too) hovers over *Soque Street Poems* as well, this time in the presence of the artist as cultural insider/outsider. In these poems the i/eye of davenport's earlier work gives way to the voices and personalities that inhabit Soque Street. This shift is reflected in both the style and content of the poems—most notably davenport's adoption of long, prose-like lines and stanzas—in sharp contrast to the short sentences and sometimes staccato phrasing of her earlier work.

Three important symbols/motifs form part of the visual iconography of *Soque Street Poems*. Two of them are drawn from the Cherokee—the medicine wheel and the dream catcher—as an acknowledgment of their abiding presence and their spiritual legacy in their ancestral homeland. They also function as symbols of davenport's own Native American forebears. The third is the African American love knot: "These three symbols represent my Northeast Georgia: an ancient spirituality and mysticism, a dreamlike isolation and eccentricity, a passionate love that binds us to each other and to these hills."[12] Within this iconography, davenport spins her own particular form of "magical realism."

Part One/The Book of Fannie Mae introduces a family genealogy, of sorts, through the ruminating voice of "Miz Fannie Mae Gibson Shueburgh," who has countless stories to tell about the Gibsons (davenport's maternal family), including the marriage of her niece, Ethel Mae, to Claude Davenport; and the circumstances of the birth of their first child, Doris, who was born with a veil (5–6), or caul, a sign of spiritual significance.

Miz Fannie Mae's rambling story is followed by that of Lutecia Brown, a "two-headed woman" (7) who arrived in Gainesville, Georgia, and set up her practice under the sign of a red-hand. Any questions about Lutecia Brown's presence in the saga of the Gibsons are quickly answered when she reveals that she has had a sexual liaison with the audacious and irrepressible Claude Davenport:

> . . . Well, we was friends at first. I'd listen to him tell his
> dreams. He wanted him a good woman, he said, not like his
> Ma. He wanted him a house full of boys and then, he changed his tune.
> And mine.
> Shouldn't have listened, but I did.
> You know, even a two headed woman can get weak in the head
> (and the knees) sometimes. Well, things happened like they happened.
> He sang that tune all the way into my bed, then changed it, again.
> Said he just wondered what a conjure woman's . . .
> stuff was like. He said that, to my face! And laughed.
> I saw red so bright,
> I thought my brain had exploded.
> I saw red, *heard* red, and tasted red, choking me. Claude now,
> getting dressed, telling me this woman he found from Cornelia. How
> she gone have all them boys for him.

> (7–8)

Lutecia Brown takes her revenge by "fixing" Claude so that "girls is all he got from that woman" and haunting his dreams until the end of his days (8). In this way—through bits and pieces, snatches of anecdotes, and extended reminiscences—the community of Cornelia, and particularly the extended Gibson family, slowly reveals itself.

In part one, the voice of Miz Fannie Mae often intervenes, commenting upon the affairs of her neighbors like a Greek chorus, as she does, for example, in "Fannie Mae, #1,001":

Well, if Susie had asked me,
before she shot her husband,
I could've told her. It wouldn't
do a bit of good. Not in
the head, where she shot him.
You can't hurt no man by shooting him in
the head! You got to get 'em somewhere else,
where they can feel it.

(13)

But part one is populated with other vivid and affectionately drawn characters, too: Goatman Joe Harris, Mr. Arthur Wright and Miz Maggie Wright, Maggie Wright's daughter, Amy, Claude's mother—the extended network of kin whose bloodlines converge in the poet.

Part Two/Crossroads (with its suggestion of the Yoruba deity Eshu-Legba, the embodiment of the crossroads) briefly recounts the whirlwind romance of davenport's parents, Claude and Ethel Mae, then segues into the heart of the collection—Soque Street itself and the African American community of "the Hill" in Cornelia. This section is filled with memorable characters: Cleo Smith and Miz Zelma (Shankle) Crow; davenport's grandmother and grandfather, Elvira Juanita Smalls and John Alexander Gibson; Mr. PoppaDock Williams; and others. And it revels in reminiscences of Cornelia Regional (Colored) High School (which covered grades one through twelve), Sally's Lunchroom, Fred's Tavern, and the Grand Theater; and the sounds and tastes of very precise memories—like eating a pig foot in Fred's Tavern, just the way Bessie Smith commanded it:

jukebox music
a pig foot, and a bottle of beer.
To be precise,
a champale and a
pickled pig foot,
wrapped in wax paper, & held
just so, so a little
juice could leak out
& run down y'r hand
& arm, so then, you
had to lick it off.

(52)

*Soque Street Poems* is filled with moments such as these, a poetic memoir rich in language and the texture of the experiences it lovingly recalls and celebrates. In this respect, *Soque Street Poems* represents not only a literal homecoming to the setting and people who are central to davenport's work, but it also signals the consolidation of her considerable poetic gifts around a project that will sustain her for some time into the future: The poems in *Soque Street Poems* have been culled and edited from a much longer manuscript, and davenport has completed another collection of poetry about being home in Cornelia, Kudzu.[12] Readers can expect more in this vein in the future.

## Notes

1. doris davenport, correspondence with the author, Aug. 13, 2000.
2. doris davenport, "All This, and Honeysuckles Too," in *Bloodroot: Reflections on Place by Appalachian Women Writers*, ed. Joyce Dyer (Lexington, Ky., Univ. Press of Kentucky, 1998), 90.
3. See Frank X Walker, *Affrilachia* (Lexington, Ky.: Old Cove Press, 2000).
4. davenport, "All This, and Honeysuckles Too," 88.
5. doris davenport, *eat thunder & drink rain* (Los Angeles: privately printed, 1982). Subsequent references to poems in this book are given parenthetically.
6. doris davenport, "The Pathology of Racism: A Conversation with Third World Wimmin," in *This Bridge Called My Back: Writings by Radical Women of Color*, ed. Cherrie Moraga and Gloria Anzaldua (Watertown, Mass.: Persephone Press, 1981), 85.
7. davenport, "All This, and Honeysuckles Too," 87–88.
8. Ibid., 89–90.
9. DAY TONIGHT/NIGHT TODAY 21 (1984). This magazine is based in Hull, Massachusetts.
10. davenport, "All This, and Honeysuckles Too," 89.
11. doris davenport, introd. to *Soque Street Poems* (Sautee-Nacoochie, Ga.: Sautee-Nacoochie Community Association, 1995), iv. Subsequent references to poems from this book are presented parenthetically.
12. Ibid.

# Nikki Giovanni

## *Knoxville, Tennessee*

I always like summer
best
you can eat fresh corn
from daddy's garden
and okra
and greens
and cabbage
and lots of
barbecue
and buttermilk
and homemade ice-cream
at the church picnic
and listen to
gospel music
outside
at the church
homecoming
and go to the mountains with
your grandmother
and go barefooted
and be warm
all the time
not only when you go to bed
and sleep

# Train Rides

(for William Adkins and Darrell Lamont Bailey)

so on the first day of fall only not really because it's still early
October you sort of get the feeling that if you wear that linen
blouse with that white suit one more time someone from the
fashion police will come and put some sort of straitjacket on
you or even worse CNN *Hard Copy Politically Incorrect* will come
film you and there you will be shamed before the world caught
in the wrong material after the right season has passed and
though you have long ago concluded that jail might make
sense for folk who drink and drive and jail certainly makes
sense for folk who beat their wives and children and there
could be a good case that jail would be significant to folk who
write bad checks or don't pay their bills you know for a fact not
just in your heart that there is no excuse for prison unless you
just want to acknowledge that building anything at all is good
for the economy but if that is the case why spend the money
on building prisons when a region a state a community won't
spend the money on building houses schools recreation centers
retirement complexes hospitals and for that matter shelters for
hurt neglected and abused animals so it's not just the building
but actually what is being built though you can't always tell
that from watching roads go up since roads always take so long
to build by the time they are built they are obsolete and we
could have had a wonderful rail system if we hadn't been more
interested in Ferguson winning instead of Plessy and the entire
system collapsed under the weight of racism you are glad you
do not go to jail but rather are shamed or more accurately fear
being shamed into proper dress but on the first day of fall
when you know it's time to break down the deck and put the
flowerpots away since you could not actually afford to pur-
chase all-weather flowerpots and when you gave it a second
thought you said to yourself I don't think I should throw this
good soil away and you now in order to save money are on
your way to Lowe's where you will purchase a big thing with
a top that fits and stupid you you never even remembered that
you can't possibly carry the soil down so in order to save the
soil that you can't afford to replace you now have to hire two
young men to carry the aforementioned soil-loaded thing with

the tight top down the stairs to place it under the porch only your dog has been scratching and barking and moaning and you fear no really you know that little mother mouse is back and last year it was quite a dilemma for you since mother mouse started coming to the inside deck and you and the dog kept seeing these little nuts and of course those mouse droppings and you were actually going to kill her but your nose was running so you went to the tissue box and the tissue was all chewed up so you lifted the box and there clearly was something in it and to be very honest you were scared because no matter what we say human beings don't do well with other life-forms but something made you peer down into the box and there were two bright eyes looking back and you really expected her to run only she didn't and then you realized it was because of the babies which you more sensed than saw and even though you have to admit to yourself you are afraid you take the box and place it in a hollow log in the meadow because even though you don't want to kill her and even though you are a mother and understand why she did not run because you wouldn't have left your baby you know you cannot live with mother mouse though of course now that you have paid to put the soil under the porch you understand you have put a sign out: MICE WELCOME

and this poem recognizes that

so when you find yourself on the first day of fall which is not actually the first day but simply early October and because it has been such a dry hot summer the leaves aren't really turning so it looks enough like late spring to make you think back to when you and your sister used to catch the train from Cincinnati to Knoxville to go spend the summer with your grandparents and you thought you were pretty well grown because Mommy didn't have to travel with you and the two of you were given money which is not exactly true because your sister was given money and you were told to ask her if you wanted something and we couldn't wait to get to Jellico because the man came on the train with ham sandwiches which were made with butter instead of mayonnaise and ice cold little Cokes in a bottle and we had enough for that though we always shared the potato chips and we didn't have a care that the world was not a warm and welcoming place but we didn't realize that all up and down the line there was a congregation of Black men looking out for us that no one said or did anything to disturb our sense of well-being and what a loss that more Black men are in prison than on trains which don't exist protecting two little girls from the horrors of this world allowing them to grow up thinking people are kind so even though we lived in a segregated world and even though everybody knows that was wrong that band of brothers put their arms around us and got us from our mother to our grandmother seamlessly

and this poem recognizes that

and I do have a lawn jockey next to the river birch just a bit to the back of the birdbaths besides the bleached cow's head the ceramic elephant the rabbit and the talking dogs and you can easily see that I collect foolish things but they make me happy and I was ecstatic to see *Emerge* put Clarence Thomas the poster boy for lawn jockeys on the cover because I agree with the folk who say give Scalia two votes and save a salary since Thomas must surely be causing Thurgood Marshall many a turn-over in his grave while he talks about the disservice done to him by affirmative action though old Clarence didn't sell hurt until the nazi right was buying and I really don't understand how some people can take advantage of every affirmative initiative from college to law school to EEOC to the Supreme Court and say these programs do not work and even old foolish Shelby Steele was saying his children didn't need a scholarship as if the existence of the scholarship should be eliminated since he didn't and what kind of sense is that when you take a pitiful little dumbbunny like Armstrong Williams who says things like my parents taught me to work hard and behave myself as if other parents give lessons: *Now, Kwame, I want you to practice laziness today. You were far too busy yesterday* or worse: *Now, Kieshah, I expect loose morals from you. All last week you was studying and cleaning the house and helping out at the church and visiting the sick in the hospital and we just can't have none of that* and that is why those little lawn jockeys for the far right are so despicable because they lack not only good sense but common compassion and like the old jokes about Black people being just like a bunch of crabs the Black right is pulling people down because they think if they don't knock Black people down they will not be able to stay where they are and they are of course right because the only usefulness they have is to stand in opposition to progress

and this poem recognizes that

so your back hurts anyway but you have to close things down as winter will be here and no matter what else is wrong with winter the little lawn jockeys get covered the mice find a home and little girls travel back and forth with the love of Black men protecting them from the cold and even when the Black men can't protect them they wish they could which has to be respected since it's the best they can do and somehow you want to pop popcorn and make pig feet and fried chicken and blueberry muffins and some sort of baked apple and you will sit near your fire and tell tales of growing up in segregated America and the tales will be so loving even the white people will feel short-changed by being privileged and we call it the blues with rhythm and they want it to be rock and roll and all the thump thump thump coming from cars is not Black boys listening to rap but all boys wishing they could be that beautiful boy who was a seed planted in stone who grew to witness the truth and who always kept it real and lots of times there is nothing we can do through our pain and through our tears but continue to love

and this poem recognizes that

# And This Poem Recognizes That
*Embracing Contrarieties in the Poetry
of Nikki Giovanni*

## Virginia C. Fowler

## *ONE*

The most appropriate metaphor to describe Nikki Giovanni's work is
perhaps the quilt; she herself invokes this metaphor frequently to
describe "*Michelle-Angelo's* contribution to beauty" (*Selected*, 246).[1] Although the
quilt as a metaphor for women's writing has become "commonplace" today,[2]
it has most frequently been applied to women's fiction, where its connec-
tions to various aspects of postmodernism are evident. Elaine Showalter has
argued that "the patchwork quilt came to replace the melting-pot as the cen-
tral metaphor of American cultural identity."[3] Even more recently, artists and
scholars like Deborah Gray White, Faith Ringgold, and Patrice Kelly have
demonstrated the centrality of quilt making by African American women
during slavery, and the connections between this activity and African weav-
ing and textiles; as Angela Dodson has pointed out, "When we dig deep in
our history we find people whose livelihoods have been linked to textiles,
making and shaping them into long ribbons of colorful cloths we now know
as kente, or the neutral tones of mudcloth. The thin strips produced on treadle
looms necessitated piecing together smaller fragments."[4] A quilting aes-
thetic informs the work of many African American women writers, includ-
ing Nikki Giovanni. In many unique ways the quilt is an apt metaphor for
Nikki Giovanni's conception of art; further, the quilt best symbolizes those
values and meanings that she associates with black female identity.

When Giovanni makes explicit reference to quilts in her poetry, the
attribute she most frequently highlights is their structural composition; in a
gesture, perhaps, toward her own southern/Appalachian roots, she nearly
always invokes quilts of a log cabin pattern. Even in an early poem like "My
House," Giovanni identifies women as the makers of quilts and love as the
spirit that urges them on:

i spent all winter in
carpet stores gathering
patches so i could make
a quilt
does this really sound
like a silly poem
i mean i want to keep you
warm

(*Selected*, 149)

Central here and elsewhere is the fact that the quilt is a whole made of
patches or fragments. Equally important is the quilt's ability to provide spir-
itual and emotional as well as physical warmth, a quality she also wants her
poetry to possess. "A Very Simple Wish," for example, opens with her expres-
sion of this desire: "i want to write an image / like a log-cabin quilt pattern /
and stretch it across all the lonely / people who just don't fit in / we might
make a world / if i do that" (*Selected*, 172).

In a somewhat later poem, "Hands: For Mother's Day," Giovanni's cele-
bration of women is actually a celebration of those qualities she associates
with black women. The poem initially suggests that gender can bridge the gulf
often created by race: "The wives and mothers are not so radically different"
(*Selected*, 245). But eventually the speaker acknowledges that "I yield for
women whose hands are Black and rough" (*Selected*, 245). At the heart of the
poem is one of Giovanni's few extended uses of the quilt metaphor; in the
following passage we see that for her the quilt is a metaphor for the strug-
gles, the creations, and the beauty of black women:

> Some people think a quilt is a blanket stretched across a Lincoln
> bed . . . or from frames on a wall . . . a quaint museum piece to
> be purchased on Bloomingdale's 30-day same-as-cash plan . . .
> Quilts are our mosaics . . . *Michelle-Angelo's* contribution to beauty
> . . . We weave a quilt with dry, rough hands . . . Quilts are the
> way our lives are lived . . . We survive on patches . . . scraps . . .
> the leftovers from a materially richer culture . . . the throwaways
> from those with emotional options . . . We do the far more
> difficult job of taking that which nobody wants and not only
> loving it . . . not only seeing its worth . . . but making it lovable
> . . . and intrinsically worthwhile . . .
>
> (*Selected*, 246)

What Giovanni finds remarkable about black women is their ability "to make a way out of no way," that is, to create something of beauty and comfort out of the "scraps" thrown away by those who are "materially richer." These are the kinds of qualities Giovanni repeatedly attributes to and admires in black women; significantly, she most frequently envisions these black women as southern and old—as, we will see, her grandmother.

Finally, the quilts made by these women bring spiritual warmth because they incorporate the past, family history; one of Giovanni's recent poems, "Stardate Number 18628.190," written in celebration of "the Black woman . . . in all our trouble and glory," elaborates on the historical function of quilts:

> This is a summer quilt . . . log cabin pattern . . . see the corner piece . . . that was grandmother's wedding dress . . . that was grandpappa's favorite Sunday tie . . . that white strip there . . . is the baby who died . . . Mommy had pneumonia so that red flannel shows the healing . . . This does not hang from museum walls . . . nor will it sell for thousands . . . This is here to keep me warm
>
> (*Selected*, 19)

The quilt incorporates the vicissitudes of a family's history; it brings together joy as well as grief, fear as well as hope. It is art designed to comfort and protect, not to be showcased or made unavailable to average people by its exorbitant price (Alice Walker's short story "Everyday Use" develops this same theme).[5] The "This" of the opening line refers to the poem Giovanni is writing, and we can see once again that she views the quilt as an appropriate metaphor for her own art. The particular language here is notably personal, "grandpappa" and "Mommy" being the nomenclature Giovanni actually uses for her grandfather and her mother, and it can hardly be surprising that Giovanni's own quilt collection was recently featured in a photograph of her and her mother as a part of Roland Freeman's *A Communion of the Spirits: African-American Quilters, Preservers, and Their Stories*.[6] As I hope to make clear in the following pages, the quilt is a gendered, racialized, and even region-specific trope for Nikki Giovanni. Until very recently, the love and strength of black (southern) women it represents in Giovanni's poetry are adequate bulwarks against a world (usually white and male) that is often treacherous. Some of the poems she has written since her encounter with lung cancer, however, seem to question the effectiveness of these bulwarks. Simultaneously, as we will see, some of her most recent poems have begun to celebrate black men.

## TWO

Certain aspects of Giovanni's biography are not unique to her but common to several generations of African Americans. Born in Knoxville, Tennessee, she moved with her family to Cincinnati, Ohio ("Gateway to the South"), in 1943, when she was only two months old. She and her family were a part of what we now call the Great Migration of blacks from the rural South to the urban North. Like many others, Giovanni's parents migrated north to pursue better job opportunities and to escape the racial conditions of the South. In Knoxville, Giovanni's father could find only low-paying, menial jobs, despite the fact that he had a college education. In Knoxville, his children's lives would be constricted by segregation's many rules and regulations. In Cincinnati, where he had moved with his mother when he was himself only a child (a part of an earlier wave of black migration from the South), Gus Giovanni was offered a job at a home for black boys as well as opportunities for future, better-paying professional employment.

Like many other children whose parents migrated to the North but left family in the South, Giovanni and her sister and cousins all returned to Knoxville for summer vacations; moreover, Giovanni lived with her grandparents in Knoxville from the time she was fourteen until she was seventeen, when she left Austin High School and went to Fisk University as an early entrant. Her grandparents' home at 400 Mulvaney Street becomes in Giovanni's work the enduring symbol of safety, happiness, warmth, and security. Even after its literal destruction, it remains, at least imaginatively, her refuge from a hostile world. Importantly, most of the values inscribed throughout Giovanni's poetry are associated with her maternal grandparents. More powerfully than their home at 400 Mulvaney, which was ultimately destroyed in the wake of "urban renewal," her grandparents live on in her poetry as ancestral figures offering wisdom, comfort, and love.

As this brief summary of some of the biographical details of Giovanni's life suggests, both because of her parents' roots in the South and because of her ties to her grandparents, Giovanni may have grown up in the North (although Cincinnati is in reality and not just in name the "Gateway to the South"), but many of the values instilled in her as a child were southern and Appalachian. Like many other African American writers of her generation, however (for example, Toni Morrison), Giovanni tends to identify these values sometimes as "Southern," but more often simply as "Black." When she wants to celebrate black women, for example, her images are most often of southern black women. Although white Americans rarely acknowledge it, many elements of southern culture have some of their deepest roots in Africa. The abiding presence and importance of the past, the significance, even sacredness, of place, the centrality of food and food rituals, the importance of oral tradition—these were central to West African cultures. Similarly, quilts and quilting, which I have suggested are central tropes in Giovanni's poetry, also have African roots. While African American and feminist historians have made significant corrections to the traditional white, male version of southern history, few would venture to assert—as Nikki Giovanni repeatedly does in her lectures—that southern culture, at least in terms of these values, is black.

The process by which black American culture becomes white was definitively described by Langston Hughes in a poem entitled "Note on Commercial Theatre": "You've taken my blues and gone—."[7] White failure to recognize or even to see the ultimate source of some of America's most treasured cultural artifacts stems directly from an overwhelming need to deny both the theft and the original owner; as Hughes's poem indicates, white people have taken black creations and incorporated them into art which is for and about white people and their stories. Black contributions to American culture have been systematically appropriated and then denied. Thus, southern cooking, which incorporates many African features and which also reflects the work conditions of the slaves, is generally viewed (in cookbooks and cooking magazines) as white, while southern black cooking is known as "soul food."[8] The point made in Hughes's poem has frequently been reiterated by Giovanni. In an early essay, for example, she writes about this kind of cultural theft in regard to music: "The blues didn't start with Dixieland or work songs or Gospel or anything but us. . . . Dvořák's 'Fifth,' commonly called 'The New World Symphony,' is nothing but our music" (Gemini, 117). Similarly, in her recent poem "When Gamble and Huff Ruled," she states, "I dislike other people for taking our music our muse and our rap to sell their cars and bread and toothpaste and deodorant and sneakers but never seeming to have enough to give back to the people who created it" (Love, 51). Not only is it the case that "Black people don't get paid for anything that we do," Giovanni argues in a very recent poem, but "we watched the white folks record our music . . . take our dance to the Great White Way . . . and then turn around and ask why we couldn't come up to their standards" (Blues, 39). Among the more frustrating and infuriating aspects of American racism is not simply the denial of the horrors of slavery and, in modern times, of racism, but also the erasure of its products; the reality consistently erased is that America, and especially the South, was built from the sweat, the toil, the skills, and the intelligence of black people.

In an essay first published in Gerald Early's *Lure and Loathing: Essays on Race, Identity, and the Ambivalence of Assimilation*, Giovanni argues that, for her, when the categories of race and national identity are brought together, "the noun is Black" while "american is the adjective."[9] Not only is race central to Giovanni's identity, but it seems always to have been a source of pride. Undoubtedly because of her parents and maternal grandparents, Giovanni recognized from the time she was quite young that privilege and value or merit have no necessary relation to each other. In lectures, she frequently speaks of the many ways her father found to counteract the forces of racism by helping his children actually feel superior to apparently privileged white people. For example, he would take them on Sunday drives to some of the wealthy white neighborhoods of Cincinnati, where the large houses made them feel sorry for the inhabitants because, clearly, heating such large spaces would be impossible. In *Gemini*, Giovanni writes of the fact that her mother asked her "to read three books, one of which was *Black Boy*. I took it to school in the seventh grade and the nun called it trash. Which was beautiful. Because I could intellectually isolate all white nuns as being dumb and unworthy of my attention" (141). Clearly, the self-hatred described so definitively by Toni Morrison in *The Bluest Eye* never factored into Giovanni's sense of self. Some of her best-known poems, in fact, inscribe and celebrate black self-love; "Nikki Rosa," for example, asserts that "Black love is Black wealth," while "Ego-Tripping" presents the black woman as being "so hip even my errors are correct" (*Selected*, 42, 93).

As the latter poem exuberantly illustrates, a large measure of Giovanni's pride in her racial identity is due to her perception and experience of it as a female. Gender, however, is a good deal more complicated category than race, at least for students of Giovanni's work, if not for Giovanni herself. Karen Jackson Ford, for example, has recently written of the pivotal role played by the trope of masculinity in the Black Arts movement, which created special problems for women writers. These women writers (including Giovanni), states Ford, "were faced with the impossible task of being revolutionary poets, who were aggressive, irreverent, and menacing, while being supportive black women, who were submissive, reverent to black men, and feminine. The two personae could not comfortably inhabit the same poem, and their contradictions would trouble African-American women's poetry for the next decade."[10] Although Ford goes on to praise "Giovanni's independence of thought and courage of conviction in rejecting the sexism of the Black Arts movement," she concludes by castigating Giovanni for her failure to "dismantle the structures of masculinity and femininity that undergird"

the problems afflicting the Black Power movement: "Like many of her con-
temporaries, Giovanni rejected the excessive masculinity of the black libera-
tion movement but sought refuge in an excessive femininity that left the
oppressive categories of gender securely in place."[11]

By reading selectively in Giovanni's early work, by ignoring much of
Giovanni's biography, and, most important, by considering gender in isola-
tion from race, Ford offers a reductive analysis that proves less than useful.[12]
Even a cursory glance at Giovanni's poetry—early or recent—reveals her
refusal to "read" categories like "femininity" and "masculinity" in (white)
traditional ways.[13] As Barbara Ellen Smith reminds us, "the social ideology of
white supremacy tended to construct two races but four genders."[14] The
"contradictions" disturbing to Ford do not necessarily disturb the author of
Gemini; indeed, to be black in America has always entailed living with con-
tradictions. In her own personal life, Giovanni has consistently challenged
traditional gender expectations, both those based on white norms and those
based on black ones. Virtually all of the important people in her life have
been women. From her grandmother, who is probably the single most
important influence in her life, Giovanni learned that women are the leaders
for social change, the activists; in part, this was the result of her grand-
mother's particular personality, but it was also, more importantly, the result
of racial history in the South. As Smith points out, during segregation, when
violence against blacks was frequent and widespread, "Southern black
women of all classes emerged as important voices for social reform" because
"outspokenness on the part of black men could result in death."[15]

Until relatively recently, Giovanni's celebrations of blackness have tended
to be highly inflected by gender, so that "black" seems to become almost
synonymous with "female" (though "female" is not synonymous with
"black"). In her last two volumes of poetry, however, she has begun to
reassess and celebrate black men in such poems as "And Yeah . . . This Is a
Love Poem" (for the Million Man March) and "Train Rides." In these more
recent poems, Giovanni develops a greater awareness not only of the burdens
imposed on black men by their socially denied access to (white) gender def-
initions but also of their efforts to be men notwithstanding; as she states
toward the end of "Train Rides," for example, "even when the Black men
can't protect them [little girls] they wish they could which has to be respected
since it's the best they can do" (Blues, 63). Giovanni has been, as she fre-
quently states on stage, a "chauvinist" when it comes to being a black woman,
but she has started to regard black men with greater awareness and empathy
than she perhaps did when she was younger.

## THREE

Race and gender are, then, both closely intertwined and highly central components of Nikki Giovanni's sense of identity. To use her own figure, they are both nouns, not adjectives. As we have seen, "black" and "southern" are in some important ways identical to her, but ultimately "southern" and "Appalachian" would have to be regarded as adjectives, not nouns; they are, however, extremely important adjectives for they imbue both "black" and "woman" with historicity. Giovanni recently commented that the "most Southern" thing about her is her love of storytelling, while the most "Appalachian" thing is her sense of independence and individuality.[16] Trying to differentiate for me between her sense of these two regions and what characterizes them respectively, she emphasized that she sees the southern mentality as a herd mentality. She herself has always believed that she could think what she wanted to think, take actions based on that thinking, and stand up for her opinions; she has never thought that she needed other people to think for her. This concept of freedom and independence is, she stated, uniquely Appalachian. Giovanni concluded with the observation that, beyond her love of storytelling and her concept of freedom, she sees herself as an urban writer who has lately been "accessing" her rural roots; this latter statement seemed to refer to the fact that some of her recent poetry has focused on the destruction of rural settings by unethical real estate developers.

Although Giovanni certainly is an urban writer in many important ways, her distinction between urban and rural suggests an opposition which may be somewhat misleading. Giovanni, like many black Americans, was for much of her life a transplanted southerner. But the urban culture created by black migrants from the South contains remnants of the South. In her study of black migration narratives, Farah Jasmine Griffin demonstrates the ways in which, in migration narratives, the migrant incorporates something from southern culture into the northern cityscape for nurturance and strength. Expanding Toni Morrison's concept of the ancestor, Griffin argues that "the ancestor is present in ritual, religion, music, food, and performance. His or her legacy is evident in discursive formations like the oral tradition."[17]

In Giovanni's poetry, both early and recent, the ancestor (always female) is an important presence often represented in food and always associated, like the quilt, with comfort, warmth, and safety. Consider, for example, the early and justly famous poem, "Knoxville, Tennessee." The poem details "corn," "okra," "greens," "cabbage," "barbecue," "buttermilk," and "homemade ice-cream" as important reasons the child speaker of the poem "always" likes "summer / best" (*Selected*, 48). Complementing these foods, which are eaten "at the church picnic," are the various other activities associated with summer: listening to gospel music, going "to the mountains with your grandmother," and being barefooted. These foods, the love with which they are served, and the presence of the grandmother combine to create the warmth which the final lines of the poem celebrate: "and be warm / all the time / not only when you go to bed / and sleep" (*Selected*, 48). The warmth attributed by the speaker to summer, like the warmth associated with quilts, is quite clearly a figurative warmth generated by the presence of her grandmother; when she is with her grandmother, she can be warm—safe, secure, peaceful—"all the time," not just when she is in bed asleep. Significantly, although the poem ostensibly focuses on the reasons summer is the best time of the year, it is not entitled "Summer Poem," but rather, "Knoxville, Tennessee." Even lacking biographical information about Giovanni, the reader of the poem would eventually recognize that if summer is somehow equated with Knoxville, then Knoxville is probably not the child's home. But knowing something of Giovanni's personal history as well as of American history allows us to see the ways in which this poem speaks of what was lost by African Americans in their migration to the North and the necessity somehow to retain connection to it. The ancestor, present here in the food as well as in the actual grandmother, provides the warmth and safety lacking in the everyday world of the North.

After the death of her grandfather, Giovanni realized that her grandmother would find life difficult. Indeed, her grandmother's desire to live was diminished not only by her husband's death but also, and perhaps more greatly, by "urban renewal" and "progress," which destroyed her home at 400 Mulvaney. The new home which the family found for Grandmother Louvenia was, Giovanni writes, "pretty but it had no life" (*Gemini*, 10). The reason it had no life is that it had no memories, no living past, no ancestral whispers. Giovanni describes her own desperate efforts to somehow be her grandfather, and recreate 400 Mulvaney: "And I made ice cream the way Grandpapa used to do almost every Sunday. And I churned butter in the hand churner. And I knew and she knew there was nothing I could do. 'I just want to see you graduate,' she said, and I didn't know she meant it. I graduated [from Fisk] February 4. She died March 8" (*Gemini*, 10–11). Significantly, when Giovanni and her mother, sister, and nephew drove to Knoxville after they received news of Louvenia's death, Giovanni could not get warm: "And I ran the heat the entire trip despite the sun coming directly down on us. I couldn't get warm" (*Gemini*, 11).

The need to preserve her grandmother and all she represented is apparent in another early poem, "Legacies," where, again, food plays a central role. The opening poem of the pivotal volume, *My House*, "Legacies" describes the effort of the grandmother to teach her grandchild "how to make rolls" (*Selected*, 113); that the rolls are one of the grandmother's specialties is reflected in the pride in the grandmother's voice: "'i want chu to learn how to make rolls,' said the old / woman proudly.'" The granddaughter, however, says, "'i don't want to know how to make no rolls' / with her lips poked out." What is important in the poem is the reason the little girl refuses to learn how to make the rolls: "but the little girl didn't want / to learn how because she knew / even if she couldn't say it that / that would mean when the old one died she would be less / dependent on her spirit" (*Selected*, 113).

Other ancestral figures also appear throughout Giovanni's work, and they are consistently associated with the South or Southern Appalachia. In early humorous poems such as "Alabama Poem" and "Conversation," the speaker is a young, northern urbanite who thinks she is somehow superior to the old, southern country people she encounters. She discovers, however, that she really has little sense of her own racial identity; as the old woman in "Conversation" tells her, "you better get back to the city cause you one of them / technical niggers and you'll have problems here" (*Selected*, 118).

"A Theory of Pole Beans (for Ethel and Rice)," which is dedicated to an elderly couple in Southwest Virginia, celebrates the courage and determination of the ancestors through using the trope of pole beans. The "segregation and hatred and fear" experienced by the black couple were unable to destroy them, just as the "small towns and small minded people" failed "to bend [their] taller spirits down" (*Love*, 67). The title metaphor is presented in these lines:

> pole beans are not everyone's favorite
> they make you think of pieces of fat back
> cornbread
> and maybe a piece of fried chicken
> they are the staples of things unquestioned
> they are broken and boiled
>
> (*Love*, 67–68)

The ancestors celebrated in this poem are, like pole beans, plain, simple, and unsophisticated; the conditions in which they have lived have been difficult and yet, just as pole beans are "staples" that nourish, this elderly couple "bought a home reared a family / supported a church and kept a mighty faith / in your God and each other" (*Love*, 68). They possessed, in other words, the qualities that enabled black people not simply to survive racism but to resist and survive it whole, and the seed they planted will continue to be fruitful: "your garden remains in full bloom" (*Love*, 68).

Thus, although Giovanni is without question an urban poet (especially in the rhythms of her poetry), she is also without question an urban poet for whom the (rural) South—meaning the various values that cluster around it in her imagination—has enormous significance. The South of slavery, of segregation, of racism exists in her poetry, where it is the source of the anger that suffuses much of her work. John Oliver Killens, with whom Giovanni studied at Fisk, describes the black southern literary voice as one "distinguished by the quality of its anger, its righteous indignation, its reality, its truthfulness."[18] With clear ties to the oral tradition of the black preacher, the black southern literary voice described by Killens clearly and accurately describes one of Giovanni's literary voices. Certainly her conception of the poet and poetry is consistent with this description, for throughout her career she has stated that the poet speaks the truth as she sees it in an effort to change the way people look at the world and situations in it; the writer writes, in fact, out of anger at the way things are: "I have been considered a writer who writes from rage and it confuses me. What else do writers write from?" (*Sacred*, 31).[19]

The South, then, is not an idealized place in Giovanni's poetic imagination. As we have seen, the "herd mentality" of the South is antithetical to her own "Appalachian" sense of independence and freedom. But the racism of the South is not, for Giovanni, limited to the South; it can be found everywhere in America. The ties to family, love, and safety, however, which are among the values most important in Giovanni's life and work, *are* exclusively associated with the South. And as we have seen these are values associated in her imagination with black people, especially black women. Again, Killens's comments have clear application to Giovanni: "The people of the black South are much closer to their African roots, in its culture, its humanity, the beat and rhythm of its music, its concept of family . . . and its spirituality."[20] In Giovanni's work, what Killens identifies as African qualities in southern culture rarely are brought together with the ugliness of southern racism.

The food imagery that recurs frequently in Giovanni's poetry is her primary trope for the ancestor and the South. In "My House," for example, the speaker says, "I want to fry pork chops / and bake sweet potatoes / and call them yams / cause I run the kitchen / and I can stand the heat" (*Selected*, 149); notice here the insistence on using the African "yam." When food images occur, then, they are generally images of what are traditionally southern

foods: cornbread, ham, biscuits, fried green tomatoes, blackberries, chitter-
lings, barbeque, bread pudding, greens, pinto beans, fried chicken—these
are typical of the specific food references found in Giovanni's poetry. A recent
poem makes explicit the connections between food, women, and the ances-
tral figure, while it also delineates the symbolic values of food. Written in
celebration of the birthday of the famous country cook, the poem is entitled
"The Only True Lovers Are Chefs or Happy Birthday, Edna Lewis," and the
title's meaning is revealed in the third stanza:

> but this is about love and there can be no better loving than
> bread pudding oh sure I know some people who think bread
> pudding is just food but some people also think creamed corn
> comes in a can and they have never known the pure ecstasy of
> slicing down the thicker end of an ear of silver queen that was
> just picked at five or six this very same morning then having
> sliced it down so very neatly you take the back of the knife and
> pull it all back up releasing the wonderful milk to the bowl to
> which you add a pinch of garlic and some fresh ground pep-
> per which you then turn into a gently lit skillet and you shim-
> mer it all like eggs then put a piece of aluminum foil over it
> and let it rest while you put your hands at the small of your
> back and go "Whew" and ain't that love that soaks cold
> chicken wings in buttermilk and gets the heavy iron pot out
> and puts just the right pat of lard in it at a high temperature
> so that when you dust the wings with a little seasoned flour
> the lard sizzles and cracks while the wings turn all golden on
> the outside and juicy on the inside and yes I'd say that's love
> all right cause that other stuff anybody can do and if you do it
> long enough you can do it either well or adequately but cook-
> ing / now that is something you learn from your heart then
> make your hands do what your grandmother's hands did and
> I still don't trust anyone who makes meatloaf with instru-
> ments cause the meat is to be turned with your hands and
> while this may not be a traditional love poem let me just say
> one small thing for castor oil and Vicks VapoRub and "How is
> my little baby feeling today?" after a hard day's work so yes
> this is a love poem of the highest order because the next best
> cook in the world, my grandmother being the best, just had a
> birthday and all the asparagus and wild greens and quail and

tomatoes on the vines and little peas in spring and half run-
ners in early summer and all the wonderful things that come
from the ground said EDNA LEWIS is having a birthday and all of
us who love all of you who love food wish her a happy birth-
day because we who are really smart know that chefs make the
best lovers . . . especially when they serve it with oysters on
the half shell. . . .

(Love, 39–41)

I have quoted extensively from this poem in order to allow the reader to hear
its rhythms and its colloquial, spoken-language patterns. The poem is at once
a celebration of this particular black woman, who happens to be a famous
chef, and a celebration of all the black female ancestors who showed their
love through the food they prepared, food intended to nurture not simply
the body but the spirit. That is why the heart is the instrument of knowledge
of cooking, and that is why imitating the actions of grandmothers is the real
education one needs.

## FOUR

How strong and effective are the values associated with the South and with
black women? Will their quilts always suffice to keep us warm? In her most
recent volume, Blues: For All the Changes, Giovanni seems to find those values
increasingly fragile and inadequate. This collection contains many powerful
poems, but it is perhaps Giovanni's darkest and angriest to date. In poem after
poem, the love, courage, and strength found in the female ancestor of her
earlier work are threatened or destroyed by or found insufficient to protect
the speaker from the horrors of her world. It is difficult to ignore the likely
autobiographical roots of the tone and mood of this collection of poems.
Written during the first few years following Giovanni's encounter with lung
cancer in 1995, Blues illustrates the way such an experience can often lead to
a reassessment of one's world and those who have been a part of it, as well
as of one's past and the stories one has created about it.

The initial poem of the volume, "The Wrong Kitchen," explicitly finds
"Grandmother" inadequate to protect the speaker from the frightening spec-
tacle of domestic violence. Because of its pun on "kitchen," the poem is
perhaps Giovanni's most exclusively "black" poem; that is, unless or until the
reader/ listener knows that "kitchen" is the term used by African Americans
to describe the hair at the nape of the neck, much of the poem's meaning

will be lost. This is a poem Giovanni has read frequently on stage over the last year or so, and she uses her introduction of it to highlight the ways in which white people are oblivious to and ignorant about black culture. Usually to a good deal of knowing laughter from the black members of her audience, and nervous laughter from white ones, Giovanni explains the time, energy, and pain black women experience in order to straighten their hair and make it seem more "white." Because of perspiration, the hair at the back of the neck, the "kitchen," is what "goes back" most quickly; when she was a little girl, Giovanni recounts, every adult woman in the community felt free to offer to "touch up" her kitchen for her. Giovanni's comments make explicit the poem's implicit meaning, that is, that people have worried about "nappy" hair when what they should have worried about is "nappy" lives.

This short yet powerful poem juxtaposes the speaker's grandmother's values to the brutal realities of the speaker's life; those values, the poem suggests, were inadequate to help or protect the speaker:

> Grandmother would sit me
> between her legs
> to scratch my dandruff
> and unravel my plaits
>
> We didn't know then
> dandruff was a sign of nervousness
> hives tough emotional decisions
> things seen that were better
> unseen
>
> We thought love could cure
> anything a doll here a favorite
> caramel cake there
>
> The arguments the slaps the chairs
> banging against the wall
> the pleas to please stop
> would disappear under quilts aired
> in fresh air
> would be forgotten after Sunday School
> teas and presentations for the Book Club
> We didn't know then why I played
> my radio all night
> and why I kept a light burning

We thought back then it was my hair
that was nappy

So we—trying to make it all right—
straightened the wrong kitchen
(Blues, 3–4)

One only has to think back to "Knoxville, Tennessee" and recall the power of
the grandmother to keep the speaker "warm / all the time / not only when
you go to bed / and sleep" to realize how much the perspective on childhood
has shifted. The grandmother in "The Wrong Kitchen" misapprehends the
causes of the behaviors she sees in her granddaughter. Moreover, the grand-
mother's solutions to life's problems are, in retrospect, childish in their irrel-
evance and ineffectiveness. All of the things that in earlier poems Giovanni has
found a defense against the treacheries of the world are inefficacious here:
"love," "a doll," "a caramel cake," "quilts aired in fresh air," church, reading.

Perhaps more devastating than these failures is the inability of the "we"
of the poem to understand correctly the reality that the "I" was experienc-
ing. Because the poem concludes with the statement that "we—trying to
make it all right" were the ones who "straightened the wrong kitchen," I am
inclined to identify the "we" as all the black women with whom the speaker
came in contact when she was a child, including the grandmother. The poem
thus suggests that because these women were blind to the realities of the
child's life, the child has had to construct her own defenses (the radio and
the burning light) against the violence in her home.

The powerlessness of the grandmother in "The Wrong Kitchen" becomes
the speaker's own powerlessness in some of the subsequent poems in Blues.
When Giovanni stated that she thinks of herself as an urban poet who is "cur-
rently accessing her rural roots," she probably had in mind the dominant
presence of the natural world in this volume. Although nature or the natural
world is invoked infrequently in Giovanni's earlier work, when it does appear,
it is generally seen as southern. The lovely poem "Walking Down Park," for
example, which was first published in Re: Creation in 1970, equates urbaniza-
tion with white capitalist hegemony, and inquires, "ever look south / on a clear
day and not see / time's squares but see / tall Birch trees with sycamores /
touching hands / and see gazelles running playfully / after the lions" (Selected,
81). Looking back past the genocide of Native Americans and the enslavement
of Africans to the continent of Africa, the poem insists on the parallels
between the destruction of the natural world and the enslavement / oppres-
sion of African Americans.

Many of the poems in Blues revisit these themes from a rural vantage point; whereas "Walking Down Park" is set in the city, which allows the speaker to envision places where urbanization has not stripped the world of green, these recent poems present particular rural spaces which she is viewing as the last green on earth—and they are in the process of being destroyed. These green spaces are both gendered and racialized; repeatedly, the speaker identifies with nature or creatures in the natural world, especially birds. The speaker, like the birds, is trying to maintain life in a world governed by white men whose greed supersedes all other considerations. "Me and Mrs. Robin," for example, makes explicit the link between the poet's cancer experience and a handicapped baby robin whose mother insists that it should fly, but whose handicap results in its falling to the ground. Watching the drama from her living room window, the speaker of the poem acknowledges that "for the first time in my life I was angry with God" (Blues, 75). The speaker of many of the poems in this volume sees herself, like she sees the robin, as vulnerable and powerless, a condition that generates her anger; as the speaker states in "Road Rage," "what is really happening is that no one is listening to you and no one cares about your concerns and you have no rights that anyone is bound to respect and you are finally made to realize that you are just a small colored woman trying to protect her home and that will not be allowed" (Blues, 46). The systematic destruction of the natural world is also the systematic destruction of black people, black women in particular; not surprisingly, it is also the destruction of art. The final poem in Blues is entitled "The Last Poem," in which Giovanni asserts that "The Last Poem on the last day will be a love poem"; it will be, however, a love poem that will "scream" and ultimately kill "to try to make it right" (Blues, 99, 100). Destruction of the white men who are "developing" the land is, the poem asserts, the only solution to the evil they represent. The speaker has seen a mother bird fly out of her tree to get some worms for her nestlings, and has watched in dismay as excavators take down the hill on which the tree stands, turning the tree with its nest and nestlings under a huge mound of earth. How else does one respond to the ultimate horror of watching the mother bird peck at the dirt which has buried her babies?[21]

## FIVE

Several poems in Blues strike a more optimistic note. Of these, the finest is without question "Train Rides." This poem also provides an appropriate conclusion to some of the ideas about Nikki Giovanni's poetry that I have been exploring in this essay. As we have seen, Giovanni frequently uses the quilt as a metaphor for her own writing, but there are few of her poems which so perfectly resemble the quilt in terms of structure as "Train Rides." The rhythms of the poem, its title, and the title of the whole volume suggest, however, musical metaphors. Although I have not addressed the connections between Giovanni's poetry and music in this essay, certainly those connections have been extremely important. Indeed, her reading of her poetry in juxtaposition to gospel music on the award-winning album, Truth Is on Its Way, helped bring Giovanni national attention and fame.[22] Her later work has taken on qualities often associated with jazz: the apparent formlessness, the fragmentation, the improvisation. Yet the ease with which one could describe a poem like "Train Rides" as either a quilt or a jazz composition allows us to see just how closely related these two art forms can be. In many ways, a quilt—especially, for example, a crazy quilt—is the visual equivalent of a jazz piece by someone like Charles Mingus or Thelonius Monk. As Houston A. Baker Jr., and Charlotte Pierce-Baker point out in their discussion of Alice Walker's "Everyday Use," "the crafted fabric of Walker's story is the very weave of blues and jazz traditions in the Afro-American community, daringly improvisational modes that confront breaks in the continuity of melody (or theme) by riffing. The asymmetrical quilts of southern black women are like the off-centered stomping of the jazz solo or the innovative musical show-manship of the blues interlude."[23] The structure of "Train Rides" similarly invites us both to envision a quilt and to hear a jazz solo.

"Train Rides" is divided into four sections of unequal length, each of which is followed by the one-line refrain, "and this poem recognizes that" (Blues, 60). The first section of the poem begins with the outrageous idea that the speaker fears being "shamed" for wearing a linen blouse as late in the season as "early October." This allusion to the violation of a fashion "rule" allows the poet to segue into an improvisational interlude about jails and prisons, about what our society builds and why, about the guaranteed obsolescence of new roads, and about the fact that "we could have had a wonderful rail system if we hadn't been more interested in Ferguson winning instead of Plessy and the entire system collapsed under the weight of racism" (Blues, 59). Here we receive the first hint of the title's meanings. The allusion to the 1896 Supreme Court decision in Plessy vs. Ferguson is central to the poem's themes. This case, in which the Supreme Court ruled that Tennessee's policy of "separate but equal" facilities for whites and blacks on trains was constitutional, heralded the official beginning of Jim Crow segregation in the United States. Plessy was the law of the land until the 1954 Brown vs. Board of

*Education* decision set the 1896 ruling aside by stating that separate was inherently unequal.

For the benefit of live audiences, when Giovanni reads this poem on stage she generally provides another piece of historical information often unknown to people unfamiliar with the history of the Civil Rights movement. *Brown vs. Board of Education* was pivotal in many ways, but most especially because it provoked a backlash of white violence in the South. The violent episode that proved to be the most historically significant was the murder of fourteen-year-old Emmett Till, whose mother sent him from Chicago to Mississippi to spend his 1955 summer holidays with his great-uncle, Mose Wright. The story of what happened just a few days after young Emmett arrived in Mississippi is not entirely clear. He apparently had in his billfold a photograph of a white girl, and he may have claimed to his cousins that she was his girlfriend. "Up North," he may have bragged, black boys can date white girls. His cousins apparently dared Emmett to speak to a white woman in Mississippi. Whether he whistled at Carolyn Bryant, who was working in the country store she owned with her husband, Roy Bryant, or said something to her like "Bye, baby," is not clear; in her remarks, Giovanni generally emphasizes the fact that Emmett stuttered and had a gimpy leg. What is known is that Roy Bryant and his brother-in-law, J. W. Milam, came during the night to Mose Wright's home, and took young Emmett away. They brutally beat, stripped, and then shot him, weighted his body down with a fan from a cotton gin, and put him in the Tallahatchie River.[24]

What was done to Emmett Till was not significantly different from what had been done to hundreds of black boys and men across the South since the end of the Civil War, although it is only recently that the full truth and complete documentation of lynching in America has begun to be published (see, for example, *Without Sanctuary: Lynching Photography in America*, published in 2000). What was unique about the Emmett Till case was that his mother, against the express orders of the Mississippi sheriff in charge, and therefore at great personal risk, had his body brought back to Chicago, opened the casket, and invited the world to see what had been done to her boy—whose face and body had been so badly battered and mangled that he could be identified only by the ring he wore on his finger. Photographs of Till's body, published by *Jet* magazine, drew the world's attention to the scene of the crime, Money, Mississippi, where Bryant and Milam actually stood trial for the murder, though, of course, the all-white jury found them not guilty.

In recounting this history for her audiences, Giovanni emphasizes the several aspects of the case that she considers most relevant to her poem, which is itself a celebration of the Pullman porters. First, Pullman porters were responsible for helping Mrs. Bradley defy the sheriff's orders by shipping her son's body back to Chicago. Second, one of the results of the publicity the Till case generated was that black people across the South were emboldened by Till's own courage. Till was murdered in August 1955, and that December, just a few short months later, Rosa Parks refused to move to the back of the bus, and the Montgomery Improvement Association was launched as an umbrella association to organize the Montgomery bus boycott. Because he was relatively young and new to town, Reverend Martin Luther King Jr. was named president of the new Association. Giovanni emphasizes the fact that one of the key civil rights workers in Montgomery, who in fact posted bail for Mrs. Parks, was E. D. Nixon, a former chairman of the Alabama NAACP, and a Pullman porter. Nixon was the one who conceived of the boycott and the best strategy for making it successful, but he of necessity had to find others—clergymen—to carry out the boycott since he, as a Pullman porter, had to make train runs.

The presence of the Pullman porters in these beginnings of the Civil Rights movement is the principal historical context for "Train Rides." The key parallel between the Emmett Till case and the central memory articulated in the poem is also, of course, the Pullman porters. Till was not unique in traveling from a northern city to the South for summer vacation; as we have seen, this movement is crucially important both to Nikki Giovanni's early poem, "Knoxville, Tennessee," and to the childhoods of countless African Americans. Giovanni likes to emphasize to her audiences that Emmett Till was safe as long as he stayed on the train, because there were Pullman porters all along the way who looked out for him—just as they did for Giovanni and her sister on their journeys from Cincinnati to Knoxville.

If we return to the first and longest section of the poem, we can see that, following the initial allusion to Plessy vs. Ferguson, the poem goes off on what initially seems an irrelevant tangent about finding a mother mouse and her babies in a tissue box on Giovanni's screened-in back porch. The second, thematically central, section of the poem recounts the speaker's memories of traveling on the train with her sister to Knoxville. The third section addresses the anti-progressive ideology of black conservatives. And the final, and shortest, section brings the earlier elements of the poem together in a celebration of black men. In addition to the history of civil rights in America, there are several other recurring, unifying motifs in the poem. One of the most important is the relationship between parents and children, in particular, the desire and determination of parents—both human and non-human—to protect their children. For black Americans, however, this desire to protect their young is often thwarted by the racism which has systematically attempted to destroy black men. Societal power and societal institutions (such as racism) can and will overpower individual desires and individual goals. The failure to recognize that no one can be free until all are free is presented in the poem as a major impediment to progress. Thus, for example, white America's determination to maintain a visible white privilege through segregation—even after segregation was made illegal—has meant that America has no effective public transportation system: "we could have had a wonderful rail system if we hadn't been more interested in Ferguson winning instead of Plessy and the entire system collapsed under the weight of racism" (Blues, 59). Similarly, those privileged black Americans who argue against affirmative action after they have benefited from it (Clarence Thomas, whom the poem references as a "poster boy for lawn jockeys") are merely the pawns of white people; "the only usefulness" of such black conservatives "is to stand in opposition to progress" (Blues, 62).

The central theme of the poem, however, is the beauty and wonder of black men like the Pullman porters. What makes them worthy of celebration is not simply the physical safety and protection they provided the Emmett Tills and Nikki Giovannis of America; more importantly, they allowed these children "to grow up thinking people are kind so even though we lived in a segregated world and even though everybody knows that was wrong that band of brothers put their arms around us and got us from our mother to our grandmother seamlessly" (Blues, 61). The real threat of segregation to black children is to their apprehension of the world in which they live and the people who inhabit it. We as a society want all of our children to believe that the world is essentially a good, kind, and safe place, for if the world's terrors are experienced by children at too early an age, they erect barriers and defenses to protect themselves from the good as well as the bad. One thinks of Toni Morrison's character, Nel Wright, in Sula, and of the way in which watching her mother be insulted by a white train conductor forever alters Nel's sense of her mother and of herself. The Pullman porters protected many black children from that kind of devastating experience.

The temporal context of the poem reinforces these meanings. The poem begins in early October, with the speaker's putting away the outdoor furniture and flower pots in preparation for winter. Because she is doing these activities, she is inclined to think of it as "the first day of fall" even though "it's still early October." But her memory of childhood is triggered by the fact that this early October day bespeaks a different season altogether:

"because it has been such a dry hot summer the leaves aren't really turning so it looks enough like late spring to make you think back to when you and your sister used to catch the train from Cincinnati to Knoxville" (Blues, 61). The poem celebrates the Pullman porters because they did all they could to preserve the innocence and safety and security of childhood for little girls like the speaker and her sister; their "fall" into a realization of life's horrors was delayed until adulthood.

Thus, as the final section of the poem makes very clear, the Pullman porters not only preserved and protected the speaker's childhood, but by doing so, they ensured her power to retain/create positive memories of that childhood past: "and somehow you want to pop popcorn and make pig feet and fried chicken and blueberry muffins and some sort of baked apple and you will sit near your fire and tell tales of growing up in segregated America and the tales will be so loving even the white people will feel short-changed by being privileged" (Blues, 63). In much the same way that Giovanni has spoken of her father's efforts, the Pullman porters allowed her to grow up celebrating the world she inhabited, which provided her the necessary armor as an adult to confront that world, and all the injustice in it, without succumbing to the racist ideology underpinning it. Notice the echoes in these lines of earlier poems like "Knoxville, Tennessee"; food, warmth, safety, and happiness have been made available to the speaker by those loving and graceful black men, the Pullman porters. But the final section of the poem expands to include not just those specific Pullman porters who encountered the speaker, but all black men: "no matter what else is wrong with winter . . . little girls travel back and forth with the love of Black men protecting them from the cold and even when the Black men can't protect them they wish they could which has to be respected since it's the best they can do" (Blues, 63). The desires of black men to "protect" children from the "cold" of "winter" are as important to acknowledge and celebrate as the actual protection. Although "Sound in Space," the second poem in Blues, addresses the "distance between want and able" (Blues, 5), "Train Rides" also acknowledges that such a gap exists, especially for black people, but argues that it should never prevent one from loving or from recognizing love. Giovanni is certainly not alone in her implicit suggestion that the psychological attack on black Americans— and particularly black men—has been fueled by their lack of power to fulfill desire. Stated more simply, the poem suggests that all black men would be like the Pullman porters who protected the speaker—if they could; but the fact that they continue to want to protect even when they cannot is also deserving of recognition, respect, celebration.

The final lines of this final section of the poem invoke the late Tupac Shakur, to whom Giovanni's *Love Poems* was dedicated, as the ultimate symbol of the indestructibility of the black male spirit confronting the many facets of white racism:

> and we call it the blues with rhythm and they want it to be
> rock and roll and all the thump thump thump coming from
> cars is not Black boys listening to rap but all boys wishing they
> could be that beautiful boy who was a seed planted in stone
> who grew to witness the truth and who always kept it real and
> lots of times there is nothing we can do through our pain and
> through our tears but continue to love
>
> and this poem recognizes that
>
> (Blues, 63)

Unlike many of the poems in *Blues*, "Train Rides" expresses a belief that somehow even seeds planted in stone can and will find a way to bloom. And it is this spirit, which is embodied by black men, that *all* men wish they could possess. Thus, even though white men steal and then rename black music, that action is motivated by their recognition of the beauty of and their desire to themselves be black men. The unifying riff in the poem—"and this poem recognizes that"—emphasizes the speaker's ability to acknowledge *all* of these complicated truths about being black in America. If whites have "taken my blues and gone," it is because my "blues" are so beautiful and wonderful; that fact does not mitigate the crime, but it does allow me to celebrate myself.

## Notes

1. Quotations from Nikki Giovanni's work are cited in the text with abbreviations: *Blues for All the Changes* (New York: William Morrow, 1999); *Gemini: An Extended Autobiographical Statement on My First Twenty-Five Years of Being a Black Poet* (1971; reprint, New York: Penguin, 1985); *Love Poems* (New York: William Morrow, 1997); *Racism 101* (New York: William Morrow, 1994); *Sacred Cows . . . and Other Edibles* (New York: William Morrow, 1988); *Selected Poems of Nikki Giovanni* (New York: William Morrow, 1996).
2. Cheryl B. Torsney and Judy Elsley, introd. to *Quilt Culture: Tracing the Pattern*, ed. Torsney and Elsley (Columbia: Univ. of Missouri Press, 1994).
3. Elaine Showalter, *Sister's Choice: Tradition and Change in American Women's Writing* (New York: Oxford Univ. Press, Clarendon Press, 1991), 169.
4. Angela Dodson, "Patches: Quilts as Black Literary Icons," *Black Issues Book Review* 1, no. 3 (May–June 1999): 42. In Africa, weaving and textiles were the provenance of men.
5. Alice Walker, "Everyday Use," in *Love and Trouble: Stories of Black Women* (New York: Harcourt Brace Jovanovich, 1973).
6. Roland Freeman, *A Communion of the Spirits: African-American Quilters, Preservers, and Their Stories* (Nashville: Rutledge Hill Press, 1996).

7. Langston Hughes, *The Collected Poems of Langston Hughes*, ed. Arnold Rampersad (New York: Random House, Vintage Books, 1994), 215–16.

8. One of the dominant features of much southern cooking is the long, slow process by which food is prepared. Clearly, this feature is related to the slaves' long workdays, "from sunup to sundown."

9. Nikki Giovanni, "Racism, Consciousness, and Afrocentricity," in *Lure and Loathing: Essays on Race, Identity, and the Ambivalence of Assimilation*, ed. Gerald Early (New York: Allen Lane, Penguin Press, 1993), 54.

10. Karen Jackson Ford, *Gender and the Poetics of Excess* (Jackson: Univ. Press of Mississippi, 1997), 192.

11. Ibid., 196, 196, and 199.

12. Barbara Ellen Smith reminds us of the necessity of seeing race and gender in relation to each other. She points out, for example, that "the social, symbolic, and literal emasculation of black men meant that their power as men was exercised primarily in relation to black women and children; it also lent a masculinist character to their counterassertions of power and integrity." See her essay "The Social Relations of Southern Women," in *Neither Separate nor Equal: Women, Race, and Class in the South*, ed. Smith (Philadelphia: Temple Univ. Press, 1999), 15.

13. See, for example, "Poem (For Anna Hedgeman and Alfreda Duster)":

> thinning hair
> estee laudered
> deliberate sentences
> chubby hands
> glasses resting atop ample softness
> dresses too long
> beaded down
> elbow length gloves      funny hats
> ready smiles
>       diamond rings
> hopeful questions
> needing to be needed
> my ladies over fifty
> who birthed and nursed
> my Blackness

> (*Selected*, 145)

This poem presents a series of images that many traditional white feminists of the early 1970s would have deplored because of the apparent restrictions they placed on the women. But the outward appearance of these women—a cultivated middle-class appearance—indicates nothing about their inner strengths. From such women, the poet asserts, came her own sense of and pride in her racial identity.

14. Smith, 22.

15. Ibid.

16. Giovanni made this statement in a private conversation on April 9, 2000, and she later reiterated it in a lecture at Longwood College in Farmville, Virginia, on April 20, 2000.

17. See Morrison's "Rootedness: The Ancestor in Afro-American Fiction," in *Black Women Writers at Work: A Critical Evaluation*, ed. Mari Evans (Garden City, N.Y.: Anchor Press, 1984), 339–45. See also Farah Jasmine Griffin, *"Who set you flowin'?": The African-American Migration Narrative* (New York: Oxford Univ. Press, 1995), 5.

18. John Oliver Killens, introd. to *Black Southern Voices: An Anthology of Fiction, Poetry, Drama, Nonfiction, and Critical Essays*, ed. Killens and Jerry W. Ward Jr. (New York: Meridian, Penguin, 1992), 1.
19. For a full discussion of Giovanni's theory of poetry and the poet, see my volume *Nikki Giovanni* (New York: Twayne, 1992), 125–34.
20. Killens, 3.
21. Space does not allow me to do full justice to Giovanni's poems about the environment in *Blues*; the volume should be of considerable interest to scholars engaged in ecofeminist studies.
22. Giovanni, *Truth Is on Its Way* (Philadelphia: Collectibles Records, 1993). Audio CD.
23. Houston A. Baker Jr. and Charlotte Pierce-Baker, "Patches: Quilts and Community in Alice Walker's 'Everyday Use,'" in *"Everyday Use" / Alice Walker*, ed. Barbara T. Christian (New Brunswick, N.J.: Rutgers Univ. Press, 1994), 163.
24. For a full account of the Till case, see Stephen J. Whitfield's *A Death in the Delta: The Story of Emmett Till* (New York: Free Press, 1988).

# Patricia A. Johnson

## *The Kink Fell Out of My Hair*

They killed G.P. and the kink fell out of my hair
He was my cousin, blood brother, bond of felicity.
They said, "Another nigger dead; white folks don't care."

Here a Negro not knowing his place is rare,
Been trained since slavery to smile, nod, and agree.
They killed G.P. and the kink fell out of my hair

Four white people and broken black G.P. unaware
That party was his garden of Gethsemane.
They said, "Another nigger dead; white folks don't care."

Trussed like a pig, doused in gasoline, set afire.
White cross or clothesline T, it was a gallows tree.
They killed G.P. and the kink fell out of my hair

Reeling in the blaze, only his body for pyre,
A maul extinguished his plea, "Why don't you shoot me?!"
They said, "Another nigger dead; white folks don't care."

Like rain in the desert, dissipates, so did his air
They hewed him, hacked his head off, then watched TV
They killed G.P. and the kink fell out of my hair
They said, "Another nigger dead; white folks don't care."

## My People

Earth passes over my fingers
And I feel my ancestors
Pass through them

My feet sink into the land
I cannot tell where we end
Earth the color of my skin
God made me of yellow clay
From this West lot of Eden
Carrier of the water bowl
I turn my face within

Cousin Letchar with blue gums
Comes from that patch
A few feet South
Soil rich and dark as oil
He sounds with the wind
The rhythms of our soul
Keeper of the drum

Uncle with no name
White, bloodless
Rises up in the North
Like a dead man from the sand
Where creeping vines crawl
Roots bleached in the sun
He holds the mirror

Grandma Bones
Weaving spider panes
Comes from that bank
Sporting red clay in slates
Carrier of fire
Rising in the East
She sings to our spirit

Blood of this land
Water of these creeks
Dust and ground bone

My people.

# Witness, Testify, Recall
## A Conversation with Patricia A. Johnson

Christina Springer

I n 1996, Patricia A. Johnson of the small town of Elk Creek, Virginia, placed first in the individual championship in the National Poetry Slam. Johnson, who has written poetry since the age of four, grew up in this rural Grayson County community, where she helped to integrate Grayson County High School after attending an elementary school for "colored children" in the sixties. After graduation from high school in 1970, she attended and graduated from Ferrum College and later received a second degree in Theatre Arts from Virginia Commonwealth University. Johnson has read and performed all over the world, including at the 2000 Ironweed Festival sponsored by the Appalachian Women's Alliance. For a number of years, she was a member of the Poetry Alive! performance group based in Asheville, North Carolina. In 1999 and 2000, she toured under the sponsorship of the Virginia Commission for the Arts. Winner of the 1999 Sonia Sanchez Award, *Stain My Days Blue* (Ausdoh Press, 1999) followed Johnson's chapbook *Spirit Rising* (S.P.A.R.K.S., 1999) and has brought even more attention to the poet. In 2001, she received a Mid-Atlantic Arts Foundation Artist as Catalyst 2001 award. Johnson makes her living through performance and recordings. The following interview was conducted while she was in residency for the Sun Crumbs Poetry Series and the Pittsburgh Poetry Slam in Pennsylvania in June of 2001.

*It is noon. Sunlight fills the room all the way up to its brown, twelve-foot high ceiling. Barefoot and cozy, Patricia Johnson and I sit together near my desk. Despite having been up for hours, we are still drinking the morning's coffee. We are surrounded by art, books, scraps of collage, unfinished canvases, and bric-a-brac. Patricia Johnson has been a poet-in-residence in Pittsburgh, Pennsylvania, for two-and-a-half weeks, comfortably and quietly sharing my studio.*

*From time to time the words "I got a poem" ring out, breaking the silence. We must celebrate. We count metaphors and alliteration like mothers count toes and fingers on a new baby. These new poems are not perfect, but we work with what we have. Patricia's poems have a tendency of starting out with solid features and sweet temperaments. They only ever need a dash of lipstick, maybe a slight trim. One or two needed a rigorous diet. A few others surprised us by becoming twins. During the arduous editing process, these poems always grow up to be beautiful, strong, or insightful. Like Patricia, some end up being all three.*

*During this time together, we have had many conversations. This is one.*

SPRINGER: Tell me a story about Patricia Johnson, the little girl who grew up in Elk Creek, Virginia.

JOHNSON: The one with the pigtails? [Johnson laughs.] I was always into something.

Mama would plait my hair the night before. Mama would put a dress on me in the morning; send me out to school and expect me to come home like that. I'd come home with my hair down, my dress torn at the waist. I didn't have sense enough to cry as I walked in the house and say how sorry I was. I didn't even notice it. I was so busy. So busy. She did! She expected me to return just as I left.

I knew the switch well. I knew the language of the switch well. It's whiz. It's crack and it's snap. Boy, switches talk!

SPRINGER: What do switches say?

JOHNSON: Stop all that running! Sit down! Cross your legs! Be still! Girls don't sweat! All the things mamas say.

SPRINGER: Your parents and family are distinct characters in your work. What is so special about them, that you are compelled to document them? What makes you need to hold them forever in poems?

JOHNSON: I don't talk about what they're not. I try to truthfully tell what they are and have been. What stands out to me is that they are fateful.

My mother was able to surround us in a quilt of security and wealth and love and warmth. I was in high school before I discovered we were poor. I remember when we were little I went with my mother to a center for Appalachian families where they offered classes in nutrition, sewing, rug weaving. I was excited about it! When we got home, I asked Mom when we would be going back. She told me that it was a center for Appalachian people and that we were not Appalachians . . . that Appalachians were poor white people. Though we lived in Appalachia, I knew we weren't white and I knew we weren't poor. Mama always told us we were rich because we were happy. I equated wealth with joy. [Laughter.]

The poem "Snow Cream" came out of that period in my life: "if you had told me then / I would not have believed, / we were poor."[1]

We didn't know that Mama didn't have the money to buy flour and sugar for a cake. We got eggs from the chickens and butter from the barn down the road. But you had to buy flour and sugar. Mama made that snow cream and we sang happy birthday! We were so excited, like kids are when they go to MickeyD's today. [Laughter.]

Reading Lucille Clifton made it possible for me to accept that story as a poem. You know how you tell people stories about growing up? You're talking a poem the whole time! But, you don't know it's a poem.

It amazes me how my parents can get up everyday and sit in the same chairs; drink from the same cup; eat from the same plate; say the same words to the same person. Everyday! Like it was the first time they ever did it. It amazes me!

SPRINGER: I assume from this, Patricia, that you find this an alien concept.

JOHNSON: [Laughter.] Yes. I don't move furniture around. But I do move Patricia around quite a bit. It's hard for me to stay in the same place. I don't even sleep on the same side of the bed every night. Sometimes, I put my head at the foot of the bed.

SPRINGER: Wait! That's supposed to be bad luck. . . .

JOHNSON: Who's superstitious? If it feels good. If it feels right. That's where I need to be.

SPRINGER: It's surprising to discover that you are such a nomadic soul, given the way in which your poems seems so grounded in specific geographical places.

JOHNSON: Though I travel, from east to west, from coast to coast and abroad, I take Elk Creek with me everywhere I go. It is fixed in my mind's eye. I relate everything back to that place.

SPRINGER: In essence, your poetry always takes you home.

JOHNSON: Exactly! That's it! It does, maybe that's why I'm never homesick.

SPRINGER: When I read "In a Place Where" (16), I am breath-taken by the lush imagery and resounding sense of location. The imagery is so natural I didn't catch the clues regarding the poem's shocking ending until the second reading. The tension you create with language begins with the first line and does not release the reader until the end.

This poem exhibits a definite mastery of craft. Did you purposefully lull the reader so that you could shock them with the ending?

JOHNSON: No. No, I didn't. I was simply walking the reader through my own experience. I wanted them to see what I saw. And for them to know what happened in a place where all of those things exist.[2]

SPRINGER: But lines such as "crepe myrtle *hangs*," "hills and mountains / *carve* out the sky," "sweet peas and joe-pye weed / *choke* the roadside," and "the smell of hog killing hangs in the air" seem so calculated (16–17).

JOHNSON: Those are intentional verbs. They foreshadow the ending. But you don't kill hogs in July. That line is the red flag that lets the reader know something is wrong. After the incident happened, the way I saw things changed. My vision changed.

I would look at a tree and all I saw was a beautiful tree. I didn't notice the spiders devouring the other insects in the tree. I didn't notice the termites devouring the tree. All I saw was the external beauty. I didn't see the internal play with all of its conflict, its protagonist and antagonist.

Yusef Komunyakaa said to me—when he heard me in performance—he said that my work would benefit from finding the terror as well as the beauty. I didn't understand it. I didn't understand what terror was. I know now.

You can read my poems and tell which ones were before G.P.

[We sit quietly for a time. Patricia's eyes well up with memory.]

SPRINGER: Tell me a story about G.P. that doesn't have savior cows.

JOHNSON: What are savior cows?

SPRINGER: "The cows that were" your "redemption," you know, the "Breath on My Fingers" cows (19).

JOHNSON: Oh, [laughter] . . . redeeming cows. That's one of my favorite poems because you can feel the poem and smell it. You can feel the cold. You can smell the hay. The feel of thawing out. You can see the breath of the cows. It's just a nice poem. It feels womb-like when you read it. It feels like you are entering a womb.

Miss Pearl was G.P.'s mother. She told us . . . all the kids . . . that she was going to be bringing a son home. We were all really excited. Not just because there was going to be another baby, but because finally Miss Pearl's stomach was going to go down! [Laughter.]

Miss Pearl left. She came home. When the car came up the hill, we went flying down the road to see the baby! And to see Miss Pearl. They lived next door to us. She got out. G.P. was in her arms. He was so beautiful. But when she stood up her stomach was still the same! After we all kissed the baby and went home, my mother explained that G.P. was adopted. He didn't come out of Miss Pearl's belly. That was so funny!

Miss Pearl didn't have a fat belly like all the other women. She had a big Buddha belly, a pregnant belly. I don't know if that story is really about G.P. But, we would have never gotten it, if it hadn't been for him.

I earned my first dollar babysitting for G.P.

SPRINGER: Now we know the beginning. It's hard to be part of a story when it begins at the end. Holding "In a Place Where" next to "The Kink Fell Out of My Hair" (37), I am struck with the differences between these two poems about your cousin. Share the way in which you conceived these two pieces.

JOHNSON: "In a Place Where" was written from emotion. It was written the day after. I would walk five miles everyday. I wrote the poem down when I returned from my walk. All of the images which registered with me from that walk are in the poem.

"The Kink Fell Out of My Hair" is what happened. It's taken from talking with people in the community and actual statements that the perpetrators made. Actual statements and statements taken from testimonies during the trial.

It's written in the form of a villanelle. I chose the form to place parameters and to force myself into a discipline. [Pause.] There would be no room to get carried away with rhetoric.

SPRINGER: "Stain My Days Blue" (61–62) is sprinkled with abundant and refreshing amounts of form, like G.P.'s villanelle, and the sonnet "Manna" (46). But I couldn't help noticing, you choose tanka, haiku, and blues more frequently. These are forms which originate in the cultures of people of color. Is this a specific and conscious choice?

JOHNSON: I have worked extensively with Lenard D. Moore, who is known as "The Haiku Dude." I have read and loved the work of Sonia Sanchez, who writes tanka and haiku extensively. The use of nature in those forms attracts me. The haiku is just like second nature to me.

The writing of haiku is such a spiritual experience. You are forced to turn inwards. It should be you are forced to turn in-words in the moment. Be in nature! That's good for the soul! Listen:

> my mouth waters
> poison oak lines the steep bank
> full of black berries
>
> (53)

I saw those blackberries and my mouth did water and I couldn't have them unless I was willing to suffer weeks of discomfort. That's just the way life is. You have to choose. Do you want to suffer for it? Do want to suffer the discomfort to have it all?

Writing haiku is a psychologically healthy endeavor. Even if you don't get a good haiku, you've done something for yourself.

SPRINGER: Your deep, spiritual connection to nature is obvious in all of your poems. You open the poem "My People" with the following stanza: "Earth passes over my fingers / and I feel my ancestors / pass through them" (31). Are you saying something so direct as you feel your ancestors in the granules of dirt?

JOHNSON: In granules of the earth, not the dirt. Yes, that simple and that complex. Standing in a plowed field, reaching down and picking it up, to smell, inhale, I feel them. I know that they are there. Just as when you eat a vegetable that's been cooked right after its been harvested. You can taste the earth in it. I think that just as earth is imbibed in the fruit and vegetables, it is in us. God made us from the dust of the ground.

SPRINGER: You include so many types of people in this poem: "Uncle with no name / White, bloodless / Rises up in the North" (31) and "Grandma Bones / Weaving spider panes / Comes from that bank / Sporting red clay in slates" (32).

JOHNSON: Each stanza of the poem reflects a racial heritage that is a part of my ancestry: African, European, Native American and Asian. The poem begins in Genesis. And then I included the different racial heritages in each stanza and after I had written the first draft of the poem I noticed that it paralleled a Native American creation song, with the directions and colors. I went back and revised the poem and tightened it up to reflect that.

Sometimes, you think you are writing one thing and it turns into something else. When that happens, you have to just move out of the way and let the poem arrive.

One thing I did with that poem is change the four directions. The directions go clockwise in the creation song: North, East, South, West. But in "My People," the images do not adhere to that strictly, if the poem were to be viewed like the creation song. Recognizing that I would be performing the poem, I just could not relent or give up Grandma Bones chanting those lines at the end. Just like a Native American chant: "Blood of this land / Water of these creeks / Dust and ground bone / My people" (32). I sing it three times. I do the steps that the Native American women do while their men are out there dancing . . . dancing like birds! The women use very simple movements that call no attention to themselves. It's like they are the bass for the dancing birds.

[Patricia rises. She dances and chants the last stanza.]

SPRINGER: During the time I've known you, I've come to understand that you are a woman filled with light. I see this light shining most radiantly in the poem "Somebody's Child" (8–10). Why would you write such a forgiving poem about such a vile person?

JOHNSON: Because that is what happens in the Black church and has throughout our history. The history of the Black church is not to become mired . . . but to rise up from it. Forgive. Not for the person who has hurt you or destroyed you. But to forgive for yourself. Forgiving does not release the offender from the consequences. Having forgiven you can move forward. Go on. Rebuild.

I tell you, some of the people . . . the old "thin haired deacons" and "grey-haired sisters" in the poem and in the African American community are filled with so much wisdom (8). Often we want to dismiss them, but when things get tough we end up turning to them because we recognize that wisdom. They've learned how to deal with the helplessness that can descend on us like fleas in summer.

It was amazing when I was in the process of writing that poem, I would ask people—Black people in particular—"who do you think is doing this?" I was amazed . . . not amazed . . . jaw-dropped shocked . . . that the response that older people whispered and younger people just said flat out "some Black child don't have respect for nothing." "Don't know where he's from." It was awful! That hadn't even crossed my mind! I just knew they were going to say somebody in a white sheet.

The thought that somebody who has genes from the beginning of time—we were the first—you know—could destroy something with so much significance, the person clearly had to be ignorant of that. Sad.

In the poem, I tried to do a couple of things. I tried to do as James Weldon Johnson did in *God's Trombones* and bring the voice of the Black preacher to life in the poem.[3] Secondly, through images, I teach the importance of our cultural history.

SPRINGER: I've seen you perform that poem. It is as emotional on the page. There is a precision and accessibility to your poems which resonates with voices such as Lucille Clifton, Robert Hayden, Langston Hughes, and James Weldon Johnson. Why is it so important that these poems be performed since they do their job on the page?

JOHNSON: I'm glad you recognized those influences. James Weldon Johnson and Langston Hughes were the first. They were the poets of my youth. Samuel Allen. I call them the Negro Poets. They went about performing their work. They had a little circuit they traveled on, just like the slam poets! They would stop at churches and give performances of their work. You know, they had to be good to take up the preacher's time!

The poet who truly influenced me to write was Nikki Giovanni. In the early seventies she came out with an album, *Like a Ripple on a Pond*.[4] It changed my view of who poetry was written about and for. Because she wrote about the women who sat on the front porch, the people in the church, the men on the street corners. She wrote about the people I knew. She gave them an exalted place in literature. It was profound for me.

Later, I read Lucille Clifton, Margaret Walker, Robert Hayden, and Alice Walker.

Two other writers who have influenced my style are Stanley Kunitz and Mary Oliver. They parallel nature with human experience. I think people miss a level of the work when they read silently. In order to hear the music of the birds that the writer has encoded in its rhythms, you have to say it aloud.

So many people have been brutalized by good teachers who were incompetent at sounding the simple rhythms of poetry. So we have a nation of people who HATE poetry. When they hear the word, they cringe! I was blessed to attend an elementary school and a church where poetry reigned with music. Poetry has the ability to express the unspeakable.

When there was a death, somebody would stand up and recite a poem. The people would cry and wail. Then somebody would get up and sing to soothe the wails. Poetry had a job to do, to open hearts. It opened hearts.

Nobody that I went to school with said, "What does this poem mean?" You knew by reading it aloud! I'll never forget, sitting in literature class and the teacher laboring over Keats. I just raised my hand and said, "The man was simply trying to get his lover back. That's what it is! It's right there in the poem!" It was so frustrating watching people turn it into something it was not. Trying to turn a simple yearning into a doctoral thesis. [Laughter.]

SPRINGER: Performance poetry can be a zip code driven industry. Sometimes, I sense that there is a notion that you must live in one of the entertainment capitals in order to be taken seriously. How has being southern and rural affected your performance opportunities?

JOHNSON: Well, as far as the slam goes, if you have male judges, a southern accent will take you far! [Laughter.]

All jokes aside, what you just said is not just in performance poetry. It is in everything you do. People think you have to be from New York, San Francisco, Los Angeles, or Chicago to succeed. It's a joke.

We need to grow ourselves where we are! Not uproot ourselves and run off where everybody says you have to be. Wherever you go, you take yourself. Why take yourself somewhere that is going to make you miserable?!?

If you're a writer, you can write anywhere. You don't even need a pen and paper. You don't need a computer. You have your faculties. You have your mind and your memory. Hold it in your memory until you can put it on a piece of paper.

I think it's sad that people think that a well-performed poem is not a good poem. I believe you can perform any poem well. Walt Whitman is easy. Carl Sandburg is easy. Now, John Donne takes a little creativity. Most people are not willing to drop their own voice and be consumed by another.

SPRINGER: I've noticed you don't perform "Chairman of the Bar" often (27). I know that "p" sounds are difficult and there are a lot of "p" sounds in that poem. Is that why?

JOHNSON: Well, I do perform "Chairman of the Bar" usually in the month of February when there is a demand for Black history related poems. I have a number of poems reflecting our African American history, "Chairman of the Bar" being one which nicely illustrates the Jim Crow era. The "p" sounds are difficult, especially when you are using a microphone. They tend to pop. Off the mic, they seem to form a lot of spittle in the mouth. So if the audience is too close, I generally choose not to perform the poem.

What I like about the character, Dr. Poindexter, is that he did not allow his circumstances or where he was in the world to dictate who he was. When we are writing about historical eras that are sensitive—slavery, Jim Crow, Civil Rights movement—fight against the urge to politicize. Using a character such as Dr. Poindexter and allowing him to be a real person rather than a one-dimensional stereotype, I was able to avoid a lot of pitfalls.

One of the things I learned from reading Toni Morrison's work is that in writing about an African American circumstance, community, or individual, write about that specifically and not about how the majority population feels about it.

When I was a little girl growing up in Elk Creek, there weren't any White people in our household. When my father got up and made breakfast every morning he didn't think about anyone other than the people in that household.

He didn't think about White people until he got out of his vehicle and walked into his job. When he got back in his car every evening, he left those White people on that job. He didn't bring them to our house, in his talk or in his demeanor. So, why would they be in my poems about him?

"Cornmeal Mush" is about him (6). Cornmeal mush: a lot of people don't know what it is. The first time my brother walked into a store and saw polenta, he nearly fell out. He couldn't believe so many people would pay so much money for cornmeal mush in a tube. I've been writing a series of daddy poems. I think there is not enough in literature about the African American father who stayed. We always hear about the ones who are absent.

SPRINGER: I agree. I have found that female poets aren't necessarily encouraged to publicly love our men in the fullness of who they are. Nor does the market reward us for doing that.

JOHNSON: As writers, it's our responsibility to tell our own stories and exalt the members of our community to their rightful place. And if there is not a market for the work, we have to create it ourselves.

SPRINGER: Absolutely! I've been lucky enough to see a sneak preview of your next manuscript. Would I be correct if I assumed your work has taken on a new dimension which is almost more intimate than the poems in *Stain My Days Blue*?

JOHNSON: Yes! Well, my goodness, yes! What I'm doing now is new for me. I really don't have a pattern to go by. It's always nice to be able to pick up a basic pattern and then alter it to fit you. But, with this work, I really don't have that luxury.

I simply have to try to make each poem, well, the best that it can be . . . but to have its own integrity. I wrote a poem yesterday that didn't have a single poetic device. Surprisingly, it's clearly a poem. I think what I'm trying to do is wed the spiritual and physical.

Yesterday I was mailing a few of the poems to a friend at home. I made copies at the post office. I accidentally left one of the poems in the copier and got in line to mail my package. When I was leaving, I saw a woman at the copier and asked her if I left anything over there. She said, "Did you write this!" I shook my head. "She said, "I like it! It's really funny!" I told her that I was writing a whole series and I wondered how people would respond. She said, "Well, I have no intention of marrying a saved man or not, but I like that poem." So I think it might appeal to more people than I realized.

SPRINGER: Yes, actually, these poems are very funny. There is just a big, heaping bundle of irony packed into each one.

JOHNSON: Isn't that how life is? I'm writing about experiences that people find themselves dealing with when they are turning their lives around to follow a spiritual path. Their old nature is constantly rising up to bite them in the butt! [Laughter.]

I think that you don't have to be a spiritual person to recognize how difficult it is to change. I think anyone who has ever had a dependency or has left a negative lifestyle will appreciate this work.

In looking over the newer poems yesterday, I noticed that nature doesn't play a big part in them. That's odd for me. There's always a flower, a tree, a rock. Usually a specific type of flower or tree in my poems. The lay of the land was always making its imprint or impression on the page. So this is an untrodden path for me.

SPRINGER: Clearly, people dominate these poems.

JOHNSON: Characters! They are filled with characters. They are character-dominated works. Now, those characters are dependent on place, so I guess I'm not that far from Elk Creek, after all. [Laughter.]

SPRINGER: You've been in Pittsburgh, a northern city for the past two-and-a-half weeks. Do you think the city has crept into your work?

JOHNSON: Yes, I do. The rhythm in these poems is different. They are fast paced. They are relationship based. Man to man or man to woman, rather than woman to nature. And since I've been here, I'm communicating with people rather than nature. At home, I'm alone a lot. I don't feel like I'm alone. I'm outside in the garden, in the woods, watching birds, watching the wind do this and that to this and that. It's better than TV!

I haven't spent a lot of time outside here. I think it's because, even though there is a lot of green, the way man has placed himself in nature here seems so unnatural that I just want to ask the Earth to forgive us. It's a little painful to see it. It's ugly, like a gaping wound, a concrete wound.

I love the Pittsburgh accent. I love to hear the men talk here. You know, sounds fall on different centers in our bodies. And the sounds of men in Pittsburgh rain on an . . . interesting center. I don't think I have to be explicit. [Deep rumbling laughter.] The rhythm of the way they speak, their accent is nice. They sound so manly! No doubt about it, testosterone powers their voices.

SPRINGER: And a new direction for your work. What do you hope people take away from your work?

JOHNSON: At some point I may find a place for their voices in my work.

This sounds trite. I just hope people are blessed by my work and are drawn closer to God. It doesn't matter what people think, but that's truly what I feel.

This interview with you has been an interesting experience because I would answer a question and then start talking to you as a friend. So, in a way, this interview has a lot of intimate conversation in it, a level of intimacy that I would not normally share.

SPRINGER: But, Patricia, we have to see ourselves on history's loom. We have to translate our inner experiences for our audiences. It's through this exchange, this real exchange that people are invited to participate in the artist's process. Our willingness to be vulnerable extends well beyond the page. This is where we bring new vision. This is the cauldron of creativity.

JOHNSON: I have no problem being vulnerable on a stage in performance or in a one-on-one relationship and in writing . . . I peel myself. But there is something different about having a mass audience know what you are thinking in a particular moment when they are not here with you. I feel like I need to be careful. Because after this moment is over, those words still stand. My poems have a life all of their own. But what is being shared in this interview is Patricia . . . a Patricia that is not going to exist for long because I am constantly growing, constantly changing.

## Notes

1. Patricia A. Johnson, *Stain My Days Blue* (Philadelphia: Ausdoh Press, 1999). Subsequent references to poems in this book are found within the text.
2. To learn more about the incident noted in the poem, see Diane Struzzi, "A Trial in Grayson County," *Roanoke, Va., Times*, 15 Feb. 1998, A1.
3. James Weldon Johnson, *God's Trombones: Seven Negro Sermons in Verse*, Rei Edition (New York: Penguin Books, 1990).
4. Nikki Giovanni, *Like a Ripple on a Pond: A Golden Classics Edition*, compact disc (Narberth, Pa.: Collectables Records, 1993).

# Leatha Kendrick

## *Zen Laundry*

Mornings, pulled earthward, I approach
these Buddhas, white and squat, female
openings accepting what is placed in them—
the weight of denim, heft of wet towels.
All passes through them, brought by water
and the heat toward an original state.

A friend of mine once claimed she survived
the dying of her child by doing laundry.
And though I've never had to face that kind
of death, there have been days of crying babies,
everlasting viruses, and loss
when life seemed somewhere else, and the wash
was all I could get done. Over and over
I wonder aloud, "What has this labor
added to the world?" Like purple dresses
or a dark blue shirt, the question fades.

Nighties rumpled full of sleep smells,
t-shirts stained and jeans survive,
demanding to be laundered yet again.
Love has put me here, I muse.
The fairy tale's real end. A cinderella inside out,
I sing, "My love! My endless—laundry."
Among the piles of clothes, I am
a blankness opening
to admit the insufficiency of thought.
The Way of Wisdom.
Go now and wash your socks.

# First, Grief

Death is a hole.
We throw things in it. The body
does not fill it (graves sink) nor all the food after,
the talk before. The laughter of reunion,
cousins rediscovered almost fill it—come the closest.
Death's a closet that absorbs us, clothes and all.

Nothing quite covers
its nakedness, no matter how well-turned-out
we are for the funeral. In uneven procession
the lighted cars wind over roads turned
unfamiliar. They seem to lead into a wilderness
though they end at the same white church,
the graveyard along the creek.

A hole there waiting
for the filling brings back every tear
and tear in the fabric. The first one,
my good dog's static body,
wrapped in a stiff tarp, aslant in a pit
dug in the corner of his pen.

Daddy covered it with dirt
and Mother with red roses—
ramblers to run the fence. Now Mother
is set like a bulb in her oak sheath
at the foot of Grandpa's grave.

The grass lays flat in wind,
and spring wheat leans. With her gone
I thought things would dull, but everything's vivid—
too beautiful! Grief,
like a knife, and then the world, unsheathed,
flashes out, each blade and rock in high relief.

Uncovered by her death,
feet caught in dirt, I'm left. Death's well
—that pit—draws me down until
light blinds the eye. Until the sky spills
into the dark that's always there,
stung with stars.

# "The World So Vivid, Nothing Ends"
## A Conversation with Leatha Kendrick

## Michael McFee

L eatha Kendrick was born in Granite City, Illinois, and grew up in Franklin, Kentucky. She has lived in eastern Kentucky since 1975. Her first book, *Heart Cake*, was published by Sow's Ear Press in 2000. Her poems have appeared in Nimrod, The American Voice, Connecticut Review, The Aurora, Licking River Review, Passages North, Cincinnati Poetry Review, and Now & Then as well as in anthologies, such as *Spud Songs* (Helicon Nine Editions, 1999), and *A Gathering at the Forks* (Vision Books, 1993). She has received fellowships in poetry from the Kentucky Arts Council and the Kentucky Foundation for Women and residency grants from the Vermont Studio Center and the Mary Anderson Center for the Arts. Kendrick has taught poetry and fiction at the University of Kentucky, Morehead State University, and the Appalachian Writers Workshop and has been co-editor of *Wind* magazine.

McFEE: Leatha, I feel like we're just continuing a literary conversation begun years ago at Hindman, one that has continued in Prestonsburg and Chapel Hill/Durham and via e-mail, one that I hope will last the rest of our lives!

It was a great pleasure to re-read *Heart Cake*: I saw it in manuscript several years ago and wrote you about it then.[1] You've reworked it to very good effect, I think. In fact, though it may seem a strange place to start our talk: since you do it so regularly and thoroughly and well, could you say something about the importance of revision—both of individual poems and a book-length collection?

KENDRICK: Revision becomes less and less a matter of "fixing" a poem or fiddling with it, and more an exercise in patience and watching, listening for the poem. Often for me, it is as if the poem were imprinted on a film negative and my job is to help it rise into visibility—to allow it to articulate itself. "Re-vision"—the second seeing. As "creative" as the first, I have come to feel—and fully as satisfying.

It is amazing—heartening—to me to read, for instance, Richard Wilbur's drafts of "Love Calls Us to the Things of This World," a gorgeous, nuanced poem.[2] By publishing his drafts, Wilbur allows us to see how ordinary the poem's language was in early versions and how each successive revision allowed greater and greater lift and depth to the poem's imagery. Each small change he made *allowed* the next change, each an intensifying of the language. His drafts clearly show how the work often gropes toward its true impulse, instead of being propelled by it.

Revising the book manuscript has involved that same kind of groping toward clarity, seeing after the fact what you have written and what it is saying to and about you. One of my writing teachers at Vermont College, Mark Cox, used to say that the poem is always out there ahead of us somewhere.

McFee: Again, before turning to the book itself, I want to ask you about a prefatory page—one that doesn't get much comment from readers or reviewers, usually. In your acknowledgments, you itemize your journal publications, naturally, and it's a substantial listing; but then you also add two paragraphs of "thanks," first to various institutions (some local, like the Kentucky Foundation for Women; some farther afield, like the Vermont Studio Center) and then to a baker's dozen of friends (like George Ella Lyon and Charlie Hughes) for their help in making this book a reality. Could you talk about the importance of support, of a sustaining and validating community, to your persisting and succeeding as a writer?

Kendrick: Along with the myth of the poem sprung fully formed in its first draft (as Athena from the head of Zeus), I have shed the persistent myth of the solitary artist—persistent because it is true and untrue at the same time. Of course, the work is done in isolation, and it must be kept almost secret until it has stumbled toward form. So, the artist must be solitary. Then, however, the work should emerge into the world, ideally into the light of some kind eyes, ones that can see what it may become, what it hopes to be. These eyes are those of trusted writing friends, who are willing to commit the time and effort to read and respond to your work. The friends can be crucial to the work. Even Emily Dickinson exchanged poems with her sister-in-law, attempting to reach out for the kind of validation that we go looking for now at writers' conferences and such.[3] It is hard to continue risking the self—as poetry asks us to do—without a core of sustaining listeners. Besides, we all need someone to call us on our laziness or half-baked imagery. It is too easy to stop short of what the poem could be or not to see the real subject lurking in our lines.

It is also hard to sustain the work of writing day to day. Nothing much in our culture supports the kind of "doing nothing" that writing seems to be, so it is very important to find those kindred spirits who may understand why you are the way you are even before you do. For me, people like George Ella and Molly Peacock, my women writers group, and Charlie (with whom I have worked at *Wind* magazine) and you continue to remind me of the value of being who I am. "Validating" is the right word for it: the people I thank at the book's beginning have taught me that it is "valid" to write.

MCFEE: I'd like to talk our way through *Heart Cake*, looking both at particular poems and at more general points about your oeuvre which they raise. The first section is "My Great Awakening" and the first poem, "Translating Daddy" (1), titles which introduce some of your central concerns. "Translating" is such an arresting word to start a book with, but once I started looking, *Heart Cake* is suffused with language-images: in the first poem alone, there's "tongue" and "language" and "words" and "phrases"; later on there are "letters" and "sentences" and other such terms. Is this book, then, a conscious attempt to find your own tongue or language or voice? (I think of the ending of "Beauty's Bitter Smell" [52] late in the collection.) And to what degree is this poetry a struggle against silence or being "wordless," another word that recurs in the book?

KENDRICK: Though I talked a good deal before I became a poet, I did hardly any speaking at all. The greater part of me was mute. The book is all about coming into language—being able to speak. Of course, I only know that now that the book is finished. As I was writing, I felt stuck a lot of the time, as if I were writing the same thing over and over. And on one level I was. We write not out of our understandings but out of what we don't understand. Writing the poems was a sort of blind battering through thistles and finally looking back and seeing the whole field.

When I was a child, I spent a lot of time pretending to be an animal. As the poem "Translating Daddy" shows, language was a blade that could be unsheathed to do harm (make you feel small or silly). Language also shaped reality (as Dad's scalpel altered reality for the cat). And words could say things were one way when what you were experiencing was something else entirely—as in, "it really does not hurt." So part of me longed for the wordless truthfulness of animals, who simply *were*.

At the same time, I wanted to name things—to translate trees: every twig and every color of the sky through the branches. Poetry, music, painting are all attempts to translate the world and render our experience of it. I ached to do this with an intensity so deep I did not recognize it at all and envied my sister, who knew so clearly that she wanted to be a doctor.

McFEE: The subtitle "My Great Awakening" has religious overtones, obviously, though you don't wrestle with religion as explicitly or self-consciously as many Appalachian and southern writers.

KENDRICK: I guess I have never really thought about why my relationship to religion is not typically southern or Appalachian—although I have been aware of wondering where I might fit as a "regional" poet. I am sort of a "northern southerner" and a "western Kentucky Appalachian," born in Illinois, raised in western Kentucky, married into an old eastern Kentucky family.

I have always known that the most significant religious influence on me growing up was my maternal grandmother. I was very close to her, though she lived in Illinois, three hundred miles from where I did. My younger sister and I stayed for several weeks with my maternal grandparents every summer until we were in our teens. A first generation German American, my grandmother was college-educated and full of what I thought were "old sayings" until I gradually discovered that she had been quoting Pope, Emerson, Lincoln and who knows whom else. She was the most serenely spiritual woman I have ever known. Though she was Evangelical and Reformed by baptism and United Church of Christ by membership, she was clearly a Unitarian and transcendentalist, I realize now. Psalms, Proverbs, and Ecclesiastes were her favorite books of the Bible, and she read to us nightly. I still aspire to her spiritual centeredness.

McFEE: What is the nature of the "ecstasy" (another recurrent word) you're working toward, as in a poem like "The Visible Transformations of a Summer Night" (14)?

KENDRICK: "Visible Transformations . . ." explores both sexual and religious ecstasy—an opening to the boundless, a trusting in love which is more perfect than human love. I want the dissolution that ecstasy is, but I also do not trust it. Emily Dickinson, our fearless poetic foremother, wrote in one of her letters, "The soul should always stand ajar, ready to welcome the ecstatic experience."[4] As a poet and as a person longing for the spiritual to be real in my life, I hope for ecstasy even as I fear its undoing of me as I am.

Of course there is a tradition of ecstatic religious experience as old as religion itself, though it has never been a dominant strain in America. Our historically Protestant and Calvinist religious traditions do not admit the mystic's experience, though groups like the Shakers knew the intersection of bodily (if not overtly sexual) ecstasy and religious fervor. I feel as much descended from Hildegard of Bingen or St. Teresa of Avila as from John Calvin—more, in fact.

From the time I was a child I resisted a pinched-down and too-rational religion, though I was raised in a family and in a Presbyterian church where emotionalism was not a substitute for faith. And I do believe that emotion is not faith and that faith is something that must withstand the ebb and flow of feeling, so I still struggle with the place of *feeling* in religion. Ecstasy is not a feeling, however; it is that state so often entered in childhood when we experience the complete union of ourselves with the place, activity, or object of the moment. That boundless, dream-like state. As a child, I felt God at the level of my skin, as I discovered that the great Puritan preacher, Jonathan Edwards, must have done in those fields as a child and later as a young man reading the Bible. It is a state that cannot be re-entered through theology or logic or mind— and that is the point of the poem "A Life Spent in Contemplation of a Single Thought" (8).

"Visible Transformations . . . ," however, not only examines the unconscious juncture of sexual and religious awakening, but—I understand now—the events of the poems touch on the positive and negative sides of intimacy: intimacy as enlargement or engagement with what is outside the self but intimacy's potential for invasiveness as well. My poems examine, or at least I have come to see in them an exploration of, the varieties of love: compassion, commitment, passion, affection. Filial love, sexual love, agape. How do these interact? What is love, anyway?

MᴄFᴇᴇ: Leatha, a primary strength of your poetry is its sensuality. Even a poem like "Touching the Cat," which looks as if it's going to be about petting a cat, suddenly opens up to the larger animal urge to touch and be touched, "to feel our shape and, felt by hands / or mouths, to know / that we are real" whether cat or prostitute or husband and wife "fallen to the mindless deep / of flesh that hungers for / another, closer gathering in / . . . the ecstasy / of being held all at once / all over" (6–7).

Kᴇɴᴅʀɪᴄᴋ: Part of the point of a poem like "Touching the Cat" is that if we do not allow human contact on the simplest levels to be erotic and yet transcend the merely sexual, we will all suffer the consequences. This "urge to touch and be touched" is not merely *animal*. We need to allow touch to be sacred because it is so deeply human. Audre Lorde's definition of the erotic puts it in the fullest context. In *The Uses of the Erotic: The Erotic as Power*, Lorde says, "The erotic functions for me in several ways, and the first is in the power which comes from sharing deeply any pursuit with another person. . . . Another important way in which the erotic connection functions is the open and fearless underlining of my capacity for joy. In the way my body stretches to music and opens into response, hearkening to its deepest rhythms, so every level upon which I sense also opens to the erotically satisfying experience, whether it is dancing, building a bookcase, writing a poem, examining an idea."[5] It is a fact that in our culture we allow ourselves far too little range for the erotic; thus we have pornography which tries to caricature and corral the sexual into one small province with often grotesque (and certainly dehumanizing) results.

McFEE: Could you address a very fruitful tension in your poetry, between the ideal images of how things are supposed to be—especially for a woman, whether a young girl waiting for Prince Charming (as in "Black Stallion Sleeping Beauty" [12]) or a grown wife/mother (as in section three's poems)—and the difficult realities of struggling to preserve a hard-won sense of self against the endless duties and demands that daily life presents?

KENDRICK: For years, I lived in that ideal, "Prince Charming" world in my head and never measured up to what "ought" to be, no matter how much I tried. I finally allowed myself to be inadequate and—more importantly— to be alone. Anne Morrow Lindbergh (in *A Gift from the Sea*), Virginia Woolf (in *A Room of One's Own*), and other women writers taught me that we win back ourselves in solitude and in the freedom to pursue whatever is our true work.[6] Reading women's poetry—which, despite two degrees in English in the 70s, I did not really do until the 1980s—showed me that my "secret" struggle to become my full self was shared by other women who were trying to not abandon any parts of themselves on the road to self-realization. Then, meditation taught me that if you have stepped into yourself far enough, any work can be true and nothing takes anything from you—as in "Zen Laundry" where the "Way of Wisdom" is simply to "wash your socks" (56). This, of course, echoes the Zen mantra to "Chop wood. Carry water."

McFEE: Section two is "Heart Cake," and contains some of my favorite individual Leatha Kendrick poems. The first one, for example, "Photograph on the Steps before the Dance, 1948" is a real tour de force that gorgeously renders a "favorite" picture of one's parents and yet acknowledges much that is painful and troubling: "vivid as a trumpet vine" is a mixed message for those of use who know how that weed can absolutely take over, and "beautiful as an open / wound" is an almost pathological simile (21). Could you talk about how you managed to sustain the tensions, the negative and the positive in this poem, especially in its ending?

KENDRICK: How did that poem come to be written? Years of trial and error and failed poems. Being haunted by that particular photograph. How did I sustain the tension, you ask? I would say the momentum of the poem sustained the tension. This is one poem that came out almost fully formed while I was attempting to write a sort of sonnet with a very focused center: the photograph. In the process of trying to keep the poem to about fourteen lines, a great deal that I had half-thought or almost written before just came out. It plays off and out of the imagery in poems I had already written at the time, like "Bull Thistle" (27) and others. It also reflects the wound of my mother's death—all her unfinished pain I wanted to take on and heal once and for all, plus the pain she had given me sometimes in life.

As objects in the photograph, my parents were clearly characters whom I could observe with compassion and some distance. The poem also profits from my growing realization that my subject really was the shadowed nature of love. The poem's last line took a while to come right, though. The word "fearful" was finally the only way to say how awesome (awe-invoking?) and huge parental love is for the child, while at the same time acknowledging the fears that played themselves out between the lovers (who were also my parents) as they lived a lifetime together.

MCFEE: We haven't talked much about technique in your poems, but you write very artful free verse, with a particular gift for unexpected diction and word-discoveries—the implications of the word "distressed" in "Knotty Pine," for example (24). Talk a bit about what interests you technically as a poet, about what you're trying to do in your words and phrases and lines and enjambments and stanzas and poems, on the verbal level.

KENDRICK: I do believe that a poem is a "machine made out of words" as William Carlos Williams said, and I want to play with that knowledge.[7] My dad is great with wordplay and word tricks. He takes great delight in language, so I grew up loving puns and word jokes and also experiencing the power of words to surprise you or cause unexpected emotions.

What interests me technically as a poet is intensifying the effects of language, whether that is by echoing a sound, creating an unusual and loaded enjambment, or using an unexpected word. The poem is not its "meaning" or "subject," but its language. There is only "the verbal level." Molly Peacock's poems are filled with the kind of verbal inventiveness that I love. Her poems have given me great permission to be playful while pushing the language of my poems.

The sound of poems matters tremendously to me. The first poet whom I read who made me really want to be a poet was Dylan Thomas, whose poems ride on the sharp edge of the language, impenetrable as scent and yet amenable to understanding if you just read carefully enough. "A Refusal to Mourn the Death by Fire of a Child in London" is an incantation, magical sounding, yet making perfect sense.[8] And, of course, I loved Gerard Manley Hopkins as well, whose work is, at times, pure sound.

MCFEE: The first time I encountered "First, Grief" (36) was when you read it aloud at Hindman. It blew me away, as I told you then; it still does, start to finish. Could you talk about how that poem came to be, about finding the images and the right voice to make the oldest poetic subject, death, new?

KENDRICK: That poem was an outpouring (or an inpouring, to be more exact). I wrote a great deal right after my mother died—most of it very rough prose. In the grief of her loss I lost some of my fear of playing with words in a poem, of letting images unfold like a string of paper dolls. I had nothing more to lose, it felt like, so I would write what pleased me and bring in all the echoes of other losses, all the things that reminded me of her: nice clothes, planting bulbs, warnings about wells. I could just SAY: death is a hole. "First, Grief" is one of the first poems in which I was conscious of *speaking* rather than "writing a poem." Writing that poem took me to a whole different level of expression. That voice, so clear, was my own voice I had never heard. Somehow we hold back out of fear of offending someone by speaking too clearly. This was my "barbaric yawp" and for once I was unashamed of it. Maybe I hoped it could reach across all that had divided me from her in life and even across the hole of death. And I didn't care if it made her mad. I wanted her to hear me.

MCFEE: As I read the poems at the end of section two, I find myself wrestling with a question I asked when both of my parents died: Is being a poet helpful when coming to terms with the death of a parent or loved one? Or is it a guilty distraction? Or is it both?

KENDRICK: Both, I think. You tread that line of exploitation where you wonder at being aware of the intensity of loss as a kind of gift. Feeling so close to the rind of the universe, as if the blackness of NOTHING were just through some thin membrane, carries the exhilaration of terror. The making of poems is a deeply satisfying and saving act against that terror.

Of course, I felt guilty for the pleasure writing gave me, and yet, articulating my loss also comforted me and preserved something of the presence of my mother. I had not only the deep joy of the work of writing but also the poems to keep and to give to my father and my siblings.

McFEE: The last lines of section two—in the "Postcard" poem addressed to your late mother—sum up many of the things we've been discussing: "I am / driving the youngest girl to school or to piano, the sky / the hill the flowers by the roadside and the names you gave them / not disappearing! Leaping out, stubborn, bright. The world so vivid, nothing / ends" (41). Could you chat about that passage a bit?—the domesticity, the lasting power of naming things, the hopeful last two words?

KENDRICK: The persistence of being—things simply going on. How do we make both that and death feel real? Most of our lives are lived in the car, in the kitchen, wondering as we drive or as we dice the onions about where we are going, about nothing less than Eternity (with a capital E). In some ways we never get much past questions like, "Is there a dog heaven?" (wanting to be reassured that there is a people heaven, too). For me there is great joy in seeing that the world is still out there, not really moved by my tempests or losses. I trust that.

McFEE: So far we haven't said a word about the Appalachian dimension of your poems, mostly because it isn't obviously apparent. How has living in this place for so long affected your poetry and your poetic calling? Have you tried to distance yourself from the regional influence, or is it a steady subtext under the surface of your poems?

KENDRICK: The Appalachian dimension of my poetry is still being formed, I think. After all, I have only lived there for twenty-five years! I am still a foreigner! Seriously—it takes decades for a true influence to develop and then some distance from it in order to write about it.

On the unconscious level, the landscape does inform some of my work, though it is not as apparent in this group of poems. I wrote one whole group of poems which became a chapbook called *Sharing a Love of Sunlight*—and realized after I had put the book together that I was light-starved in Eastern Kentucky, living up a hollow and against a hill.[9] Still, the mountains are not my first home, so they do not define home for me in that deep way I see in so many other Appalachian writers. My daughters write poetry, and I have been aware that the shape of this Appalachian landscape is in some sense the shape of the cosmos from which their poems arise.

For me, the regional influence has been people—George Ella Lyon has practically birthed me as a writer. She and her words keep me mindful that, as she is fond of referring to St. Catherine of Siena, all the way to heaven is heaven.[10] There are no words of gratitude adequate to say what she has meant and means to me and my writing. George Ella, Jan Cook, Marie Bradby, Lou Martin, and I met at the Appalachian Writers Conference. Jan, Marie, Lou, George Ella, Ann Olson, and Martha Gehringer are my primary family of writers. They have made all the difference. And, of course, the supportive community of the Appalachian Writers Workshop (which I have called a second birthplace) continues to sustain and enlarge me as a writer and a teacher.

Many individual writers there encouraged me—Jim Wayne Miller, George Ella Lyon, Bob Morgan, Jeff Daniel Marion, to name a few. None of these writers does strictly Appalachian poetry or prose (if there is such a thing). These Appalachian writers draw voices, settings, images from the region, but their work reaches far beyond these. Their writings depend on science as well as soup beans, theology more than "the hillbilly," cosmology as clearly as herbology, not to mention astronomy, mothering, agronomy . . . and on and on, for subject matter and metaphor. I hope to fall more completely under their rich "regional" influence.

McFee: *Heart Cake*'s final section is "Waking Up," a nice surprising way to conclude a collection! In the first poem, "A Simple Thing," there's a lot of power in what remains unsaid, both when the speaker was a girl ("Never acted like I needed to know [how to mash potatoes], / me with my books and / better things to do") and now that she's a mother thinking about what she should tell her daughter ("'Call your sisters down to supper'/ is all she'll hear me say.") (45–46). Though the book as a whole may be about finding a voice and resisting wordlessness, could you talk about the value of *not* saying things sometimes, especially as a poet?

Kendrick: It's all about white space, isn't it? Like that dark matter that makes up 90 percent of the universe, but no one can find it. Poems, of course, work by implication. The unsaid often ought to be the real subject of the poem, demonstrated in its images and even its line breaks and cognitive moves. Just to show these two generations of mother/daughter pairs interacting (or not), remaining silent while projecting expectations, became the point of the poem. This one I rewrote over several years, taking things out mostly. In the interim between the time I first wrote this out and when it came into the final form, I was learning that we must leave space for our readers, if we are writers, or for our daughters, if we are mothers. It is, again, the empty cup that can be filled.

McFee: "Beauty's Bitter Smell" is wonderfully vivid. Could you talk about getting all the senses into your poetry, which you do so well?

Kendrick: In writing "Beauty's Bitter Smell" I tried to write first from the body and then the mind. Smell evokes the wholeness of the past. An odor returns us to a piece of time. Once the body was engaged in recalling that odor, the visual and tactile parts of the poem came with intensity. In my way of thinking, in poetry the ideal is really to write from the body first or from some combination of body and mind that does not think but experiences. I don't consciously try to get the senses into my poems, but I am conscious of trying to write from the physical as well as the mental part of myself. (I don't exclude ideas, but I hope to embody them.)

Even though I've planted the bulbs of the paperwhite narcissus every winter, eager for their beauty, I had always resented their sort of "in-your-face" smell. By the end of the poem, I wanted to own that smell, along with the beauty that the narcissus also embodies. I realized that it could be a good thing for us all to claim our stink as part of our beauty.

McFee: "Zen Laundry" has forever changed the way I look at a washer and dryer ("these Buddhas, white and squat, female / openings accepting what is placed in them," [56]). It's a very witty poem. Could you say something about humor's presence in your poetry?

Kendrick: I value humor in other poet's work tremendously, but I cannot set out to write a "funny" poem. Such humor as happens into my work does so as a result of distance: the ability to make myself a character in my poem and then smile at how seriously this woman takes her struggles, how blind she is to what is holding her back or even to the gifts in her life. "Zen Laundry" did not start out as a humorous poem, but as a cry against the "weight of denim, heft of wet towels" which I lifted over and over, wondering, "What has this labor added to the world?"—feeling completely stuck in that house. But as I wrote and rewrote, the poem began to float up on the possibility of a duel between Cinderella and the Buddha.

So these poems (and there are only a few of them so far) depend upon a fundamental sense of PLAY at the heart of writing. Not just wordplay (though that is part of it), but of what if. What if I were really Cinderella? What if the washer were a Buddha statue? After all, I do so often bow down before the dryer!

MCFEE: *Heart Cake* ends on a series of love poems—not a "happily-ever-after" sort of resolution, but a conclusion that embodies what you earlier called "the shadowed nature of love," the tremendous tensions inherent in desire. Why close the book this way?

KENDRICK: It is absolutely essential that I allow all the misgivings and fears that shadow love to be present in the poems. They are there, though often unacknowledged or played out in destructive ways in our lives. Dissolution and containment, driving away toward the city, then returning to "the dog sighing on the carpet": the desire to be broken and the need to be mended are the twin impulses of the last section of the book.

We are back to the debate between *feeling* and *faith* that informs the first section's poems and to a questioning of the nature of love. Long-term love relationships—familial or passionate—cannot depend upon the steadiness of feeling, which ebbs and flows. They are sustained by acts of will. Yet still the feeling will break through, disrupting as often as it reinforces relationship. I have been married for twenty-seven years. I have lived in the same place for twenty-five years. This final section of the book reflects my convictions that the whole world is wherever we are and longing is the constant condition of being alive.

MCFEE: What books or writers outside Appalachia have influenced you the most?

KENDRICK: Two early influences that seem important enough to name, and they are John Donne and Madeleine L'Engle. John Donne's love poems are the model to which I aspire. They seem to me nearly perfect. Madeleine L'Engle's book, *A Wrinkle in Time*, which I read when I was twelve, created a whole series of possibilities in me, making me think for a long time that I wanted to be a scientist (like the mother in the book), when she was really inspiring me to be a writer. Most importantly, like Donne and Hopkins, Madeleine L'Engle's writing set Eternity inside ordinary time, teaching me the Eternal is here and now. At twelve I felt Heaven outside my window. I continue to look for it there as I grow past fifty.

MCFEE: Finally, Leatha, in your amazing *American Voice* essay, "No Place Like Home," you say, "I want to leave a legacy for my daughters—some possible model of how to be a self and a daughter wife mother hostess crusader friend lover writer worker."[11] That's an awfully admirable and ambitious legacy! By way of conclusion tell us what work is left undone in that model list, what you most want or need to do in the coming years.

KENDRICK: Writer. Worker. That is where I am now. Teacher more than "crusader." I most need to give myself to the work of writing. All the rest of my work follows from that. Writing is my mother now, I guess.

Coming off a three-week writing retreat a couple of years ago, I felt so full and contented, I realized I would never really be lonely again because writing is my true companion. Out of the fullness of this work, I am able to be present more clearly to the rest of my life. I want my daughters—and my students—to see that life is long and there is time to be many things. I want to be more at ease with that pronouncement myself. I want to contain the contradictions. So, to that list I say, "Yes!" and "More."

## Notes

1. Leatha Kendrick, *Heart Cake* (Abingdon, Va.: Sow's Ear Press, 2000). Subsequent references to poems are in the text.
2. Richard Wilbur, "Love Calls Us to the Things of This World," in *New and Collected Poems* (San Diego: Harcourt Brace Jovanovich, Harvest, 1988), 233. Portions of the drafts of this poem are published in Robert Wallace and Michelle Boisseau, *Writing Poems*, 4th ed. (New York: HarperCollins College Publishers, 1996), 284–90.
3. Emily Dickinson, *Emily Dickinson, Selected Letters*, ed. Thomas H. Johnson (Cambridge, Mass.: Belknap Press, 1986), 161–63.
4. Dickinson, *Letters of Emily Dickinson*, ed. Thomas H. Johnson (Cambridge, Mass.: Harvard Univ. Press, Belknap Press, 1958), 140.
5. Audre Lorde is quoted in *Cries of the Spirit: A Celebration of Women's Spirituality*, ed. Marilyn Sewell (Boston: Beacon Press, 1991), 210. See also Audre Lorde, *The Uses of the Erotic: The Erotic as Power* (Milford, Conn.: Out and Out Books, 1978).
6. See Anne Morrow Lindbergh, *A Gift from the Sea* (New York: Random House, 1991), and Virginia Woolf, *A Room of One's Own* (New York: Harcourt, Brace, and Company, 1989).
7. Quoted in Robert Diyanni, *Modern American Poets, Their Voices and Visions* (New York: Random House, 1987), 256.
8. Dylan Thomas, "A Refusal to Mourn the Death by Fire of a Child in London," in *Collected Poems* (New York: New Directions Books, 1957), 112.
9. Leatha Kendrick, *Sharing a Love of Sunlight*, self-published chapbook, 1992.
10. For more on the philosophy of St. Catherine of Siena, see *Dialogue of St. Catherine of Siena*, designed by Algar Thorold (Rockford, Ill.: Tan Books and Publishers, 1991).
11. Kendrick, "No Place Like Home," *American Voice* 49 (1999): 96–106.

# George Ella Lyon

## Archaeology

I am digging
with a soft brush     a pen
at the site of my founding city
                    Mothers

                                    Fathers

I am listening
where the dirt flakes
from the dish chip
for a song my great-great
a hundred greats grandmother sang
way up the chromosome chain
                    Shularoon

                                    Shularoon

And the mountain speaks through its clay flute
and feet dance up and down its back
brushing off the light of this page
to sift through dark rooms
dust of a house I never entered
by the window where I make my bread.

## Papaw

They told him, the youngest,
that babies came from coal mines
so when the Wilders up the creek had their last
he went to see.
He didn't take the mine road
but chose the path by the tipple.
Some journeys shouldn't be easy even in the dark.

At daybreak
when he came in the yard
Dillard and Minnie were smiling.
It aint true, he said,
coal dust streaking his face.
I been there and there aint no tracks.

# From Poetry to Picture Books
## The Words of George Ella Lyon

Roberta T. Herrin

A s a poet, novelist, and dramatist, Kentucky writer George Ella Lyon initially wrote for an adult audience but was drawn into the children's book market through happenstance and effort. When she was working with Paul Janeczko on his anthology *Strings: A Gathering of Family Poems*, he inquired, "Where did you get such a strange name?"[1] She wrote him that she was "named for my mother's brother and sister. He liked my letter, and he sent it to Dick Jackson, who was his editor, and Dick liked it and wrote a note to me saying, '. . . I like the way you write. If you write for children, send me something, and if you don't, think about it.'"[2] She answered that she did not write for children, "but hold on," she said. "I'll try."[3]

Lyon quickly put to use what she learned from poet Nancy Willard at a Women Writers Conference at the University of Kentucky: that "poems are the closest genre to picture books."[4] Willard, she says, "opened my eyes to a whole new way of seeing": "She talked about the economy of words, the music of the language, the necessity of considering the rhythm of the page turn, the way you think about the line break, how you can have a wordless spread that's like a stanza break."[5] Exploring this natural affinity between the two genres, Lyon has found that the picture book format well suits her poetic style. Over the last fifteen years, the result has been a major collection of adult poetry, *Catalpa*,[6] and more than a dozen picture books for children.

The title of George Ella Lyon's autobiography for children—*A Wordful Child*—could well be her mantra. Words are her lifeblood, her stock in trade, a fact she understood at an early age. While this may be true for all poets, it is more self-consciously true for Lyon than for most. Her autobiography begins with these lines: "I was a wordful child. My family says I talked before I walked."[7] She then relates a memory from age four when she made a connection between two words that were alike but different: *pickwick* and *pigtail*. "I kept saying them over and over to myself, like you might turn stones in your hand. I knew they were magic."[8] These two sentences encapsulate the paradoxical core of Lyon's uniqueness as a poet: Words are simple objects, like stones or bones—the plain, hard fabric of life—but words are also magic: "Visions / begin with / basics: bones" (*Catalpa*, 54). The magical is wedded to the solid structure beneath.

In her tribute to Virginia Woolf, part three of *Catalpa*, three successive poems make this connection between stones and words: In "Visiting Monks House," Lyon uses this line: "Every stone has a voice" (57). The poem following "Visiting Monks House," "In the Garden," asserts an opposite premise: "Words make stone speak" (59). The poem "1941" ends with "Your words turn to stone" (60). Though taken out of context, these lines nevertheless make the strong connection—an old and mythical one—between the stone and the voice. The interesting point is that in *A Wordful Child*, Lyon makes the connection between stones and words for the child reader. And herein lies a key to her success as a writer for both adults and children. She appropriately pares down the words for the picture book, allowing the illustration to tell its story, but she does not skimp on the depth.

Following "1941" in *Catalpa* is "At the Lodge." This poem addresses the issue of translating experience into poetry:

> I came through the garden
> by the water lily's praise
> saw rooks wheel the deep sky
> Air threads their bones
> ink seeps into my fingers
> How easily the blood turns black
> capillaries loop upon the page
>
> (61)

If bones are Woolf's meat, words are Lyon's meat. In "Evidence," also from part three of *Catalpa*, Lyon speaks of the material culture of Woolf's world: photographs, china, ink, upholstery. The evidence of Woolf's life is "in the tendons of words," she says (56).

The poet's words spring from a deep emotional source wherein blood and ink, poet and page become one; words take on life as visible, living constructs having tendon and bone and blood. In an interview with Rudine Sims Bishop, Lyon explains it in this way: "I feel a strong connection between ink and thought and blood and heartbeat. . . . I just love the shapes of letters."[9] "Border," a poem about the simultaneous birth of a child and the death of a father, makes the connection between heart and word even more explicitly: "I felt my heart / lifted out like a book / opened, pressed flat" (46).

In an interview at the George Ella Lyon Literary Festival (Emory & Henry College, 1994), Jeff Daniel Marion asked Lyon if her "voice" is related to the movement of her hand as she writes and to "the flow of the ink? A sort of tactile quality?" She answered, "It is. And . . . the materials are a comfort. The paper, the color of the ink, the slight resistance that the paper gives. It's part of the journey, moving across the page."[10] In "Thirteen Ways of Looking at a Mean Poem," she says about the poet: "Words to her / are more real / than money."[11] Lyon speaks of words and uses words as though they were part of the material culture of her world. From poetry to picture books, Lyon's words are sensory, tactile objects. They sing, they shine, and their power is generated in paradox, dialectic, healing, and naming.

In her "Sidelights" commentary for her first biographical entry in *Something about the Author*, Lyon explains that she was "born with poor vision and a good ear."[12] Her "good ear," equally attuned to music and stones, can be credited to a number of experiences, all of which have to do with poetry. She says her father sang to her: "He sang everything from 'Barbara Allen' to radio tunes."[13] She also attributes her "good ear" to the stories she heard as a child: "And so those stories and the music, too, came together for me."[14] In high school, Lyon sang and played guitar in a folk group,[15] and she is now married to a musician.[16]

This melding of music and words is clearly key in her art. And the connection between the sound of the word, the singing, and the visual aspect of words on the page is central to the picture book genre: "Almost as soon as I learned to make letters, I became a writing child. I wanted to draw the words I loved, to catch the feeling on paper the way I caught lightning bugs and put them in a jar. The lightning bugs would die if I didn't let them go, but I could keep words forever."[17] The power of words to capture feeling, to freeze the moment (as in stone), is as old as art and has been honored by poets long before Lyon, as in Keats's "Ode on a Grecian Urn."[18] But Lyon expects words also to shine: "Early on I wanted to be a neon sign maker and I still hope to make words that glow."[19]

In "How the Letters Bloom Like a Catalpa Tree," Lyon writes of the poetic process: "How I would like / the words to shine always like sword grass / and be stubborn as thistle and come to you / heady as lilac, as dandelion to the new bee" (23). The poet's work is not unlike the basket maker's. In this poem, Oaksie Caudill must fashion a basket—a statement—out of white oak, a tactile material unwieldy as words:

> Oaksie's trade is this translating
> of straight to curve, of fact to what we need,
> tough as a poem for the burden that outlasts us,
> for a heart leafed with words like a tree.
>
> (24)

Words are synesthetic; they are small objects packed with multiple sensory, emotional, and intellectual forces. They are full of sound and magic and time. Like Oaksie Caudill's white oak basket and Lyon's grandmother's basket, which is the source of the picture book *Basket*, words are seeds encapsulating layers of meaning.

When these seeds fall in fertile ground, the result is a poem or a picture book, such as *Basket*, which tells the story of a white oak basket. Its contents changed as did the grandmother's life; it held eggs, peaches, pot holders, roses, scissors, plums, flashlight, holly. She moved from farm to town and finally lost the basket when she moved to an apartment. "When she died, we found in the closet in the cedar chest wrapped in tissue paper inside a pillowcase her little basket."[20] This reverse encapsulating is effective: in the closet, in the cedar chest, in the tissue paper, in a pillowcase. It took some digging to get to it. Ironically, when it was found, the basket contained only a spool of thread, but the thread then becomes the symbol. The persona inherits the basket—and the spool: "I still keep it in the basket with stories of holly and peaches and flashlights, with memories of feathers and scissors and plums. [page break] I draw out the thread and hear my grandmother sing."

Like a poem or a single word, the basket is infused with life and history. It is an archaeological artifact. It is itself a thread, evoking and stringing together memories and stories and song and experience. Lyon's poem "Archeology" uses this metaphor more directly.

> I am digging
> with a soft brush     a pen
> at the site of my founding city
> Mothers
>
> Fathers
>
> (27)

"Archeology" expresses the role of the poet to uncover layers of meaning, in the same way an archeologist uncovers layers of the past by sifting and sorting through stone and bone, freeing them to speak, to tell their stories (like the basket, lying under layers of closet, cedar chest, tissue paper, and pillow case).Yet, for the persona (and for Lyon), this is not some dead, academic, historical past; it is *her* past: "the site of my founding city" (27). Being a writer who is native to and lives in Appalachia, Lyon knows that her "founding city" is infused with the political, cultural, and aesthetic aspects of the region.

Two of Lyon's prose pieces illuminate her view of poetry and its function in the context of Appalachia: her introduction to *Old Wounds, New Words: Source and Directions* and her essay entitled "Voiceplace." The introduction to *Old Wounds, New Words* is a retrospective in that it surveys Appalachian poetry from the 1920s to the 1980s, beginning with the earliest poets (Byron Herbert Reece, James Still, Elizabeth Madox Roberts), but it ends with her contemporaries (Bob Henry Baber, Fred Chappell, P. J. Laska, Jeff Daniel Marion, Jim Wayne Miller, Robert Morgan). In addition to what the essay tells us about Appalachian poetry, it reveals a number of qualities about Lyon herself as a poet.

First, because she is well read in Appalachian poetry and has worked alongside many of the poets about whom she writes, she understands the power of poetry to mitigate the cultural paradoxes of the region: "The movement of contemporary Appalachian poetry . . . is from a rooted, traditional body of work to a more volatile, politically active, and varied offering."[21] Lyon describes a "burgeoning of poetry" after the seventies, which she credits to a number of factors, but basically to the "cultural crisis" that resulted from the conflict between outsiders' and insiders' awareness of the region and of each other.[22] She asks, "Why poetry?" And the answer is that "poetry is rooted in paradox": "The force of metaphor comes from its wedding of like and unlike to make something new without destroying the separate identities of the old. It is easy to see how this approaches the dilemma of Appalachia itself."[23]

The first quality revealed, then, is that Lyon views poetry as a force in a dialectic. Unlike Robert Frost, who sees poetry as having "not necessarily a great clarification" but a "momentary stay against confusion,"[24] Lyon sees poetry as having more permanent power and influence. The power of words in a dialectic is well illustrated in "Catechisms—Talking with a Four-Year-Old" (33). In this exchange between adult and child, each question-response exchange moves the conversation to a deeper level, starting with "What's the oldest thing that's living?" and ending with "Who will die first?" Appropriately, this question has no response. A question about life evolves into a question about bones and death.

The same process is evident in the picture book *Who Came Down that Road?* The child's first question, "Who came down that road, Mama?" leads backward in time, all the way to "Questions! / Questions crowded like a bed of stars, / thick as that field of goldenrod. . . . the mystery of the making place— / that came before this road."[25] The child's questions (words) in the present move the dialectic backward in time to the ultimate word—a question. The questions are a path backward in time but also very much in the here and now, like the spool of thread and the basket. But the paradox is that the backward movement in time is a forward progression of thought, impelling the exchange toward a conclusion. Words (poetry) are the force in the dialectic; more importantly, Lyon boldly offers up this concept to children in picture-book format.

*Dreamplace* is another picture book that illustrates the power of words to impel a dialectic. *Dreamplace* begins with tourists traveling in Pueblo country in the western United States, territory that is "plain as beans." They visit a cliff-dweller city, once thriving until "water dried up / corn withered / sickness came."[26] The story continues:

> They packed their prayer sticks and grinding stones
> climbed down the cliff face
>
> and set off
> leaving us
> far in the future
> to drive up roads they never knew
> and hike trails to their city
> and stand amazed.

The "words" of this poem perform magic. They achieve an action greater than time shift; they fuse time: The people "set off / leaving us" not far in the past, but "far in the future." The words achieve a dialectic by moving the reader through paradox and antithesis to a new conclusion.

The result of the dialectic force is healing—what Lyon calls the "mission work" of poetry: "Poetry offers, then, some healing, a map of relatedness amid the fragmentation and isolation of modern life and the template sameness that is its deadening connector. Furthermore, its recognition of paradox, its mission work among the irreconcilable forces in our lives, is a form of healing."[27] Elsewhere she explains: "It's important . . . to connect with the deepest sources of who you are. . . . Writing is a way to do that. It's a healing and integrating thing."[28]

The healing power of words is beautifully illustrated in Lyon's poem "Elopement." The persona, Ella May, "cries at the pain" she is causing her family when she slips "out to the bed of a sailor," because her father "killed" the sailor's "question" "with a face of grief." Ella May offers a gesture of healing: "She leaves the zinnias, tongues of the late June morning, / loud in the jar mouth, hoping their words will heal" (16). *Tongue, mouth, words, heal*—these are words on a mission in Lyon's poem.

This healing function of poetry is directly related to the dialectic or the paradox and contradiction. "Crossing" is a dialectic between a father who is dying of cancer and his daughter who is pregnant. The scene is the seaside, the edge of the source of all life, and the paradox is in the cells: "As soon as the sperm / burrows into the egg / a clock starts ticking, / a rhythm to which / billions of cells / are born and learn / their dance" (42). But their conversation turns to pain, and the persona speaks of "cells gone wrong, / hurt out of tempo" (43). The poem ends with healing laughter and a pun on "bellyfull": "each with a bellyfull / laughing / into the waves" (43).

In addition to the healing power of poetry (words), its mission work, the *Wounds* introduction denotes two additional qualities—the power of naming and telling. Lyon says, "And, to the extent that to name and to tell are to know and thus to control, poetry gives us a measure of power over those forces."[29] The power of naming and telling are also part of the dialectic; they impel the dialectic. In "Voiceplace," Lyon notes that she recorded in her journal interesting names that she heard from her grandmother—"Honey-eating Richard, Pie-belly Miracle."[30] The names in *Catalpa* clearly come from Lyon's voiceplace: Oaksie Caudill, Katie Stoddard, Rhody (not Rhoda), Ella May, Dillard, Minnie, Virgil, and plain names like Jim and Jo. But in addition to personal names, Lyon invokes the power of naming. The picture book *A B Cedar* names trees from Aspen, Butternut, Cedar, Dogwood to Willow, Xolisma, Yew, Zebrawood.[31] The act of naming carries power like a talisman, imbuing the trees with spirit and magic. The composite sound of the names is musical and poetic: Kumquat, Laurel, Maple, Nannyberry. There is power in the simplicity of names uttered in succession.

Naming can sometimes be playful, as in *A Day at Damp Camp*, a picture book that "tells" its story through triplicate rhymed pairs: "Damp camp / green screen / hot cot."[32] No connecting verbiage is necessary—the naming is sufficient—from beginning to end: "Far star / steep sleep / long song." But naming can also be painful in that it connects: The poem "My Grandfather Sees the World" relates the tale of the grandfather, at age twelve, moving the neighbors' household goods and livestock on a train from Kentucky to Canada: "He got there. He gave over his warm wordless folk, / he did, smoothing feathers and flanks as if to rub off / names he'd given them . . . " (9). To rub off the name is to disconnect; he leaves his "wordless folk" and returns to Kentucky.

In "For a Time," the connections among work and poem and naming are honed: "There was a poem / like a bowl you break beans into / or a newspaper spread across the lap. . . ." Involved in the action of poem-making and bean-breaking, "We tried to name it all / sitting close, the poem piled high / the damp newspaper blurring / as words came off in our hands" (41). This trying to name it all is, finally, the business, the art of the poet. The transfer of words, like objects, from paper to hands is part of the power of naming. Words take on new roles, cause action, create synesthetic experience.

"For a Time" is, like much of Lyon's poetry, also narrative, and the act of telling is related to the naming. Lyon says she grew up listening to her family talk: "They loved telling stories. I don't mean Jack-tale kinds of stories, but what happened to Great Aunt So-and-So or the time we washed the money in the washing machine—those kinds of things."[33] These stories, the telling, are central to her art. Her poetry is never far from the narrative tradition of Appalachia, and her picture books frequently relate the family story. Examples are *Basket*, *Come a Tide* (both discussed above), *Cecil's Story*, and *A Regular Rolling Noah*. In these picture books, the act of telling is catalyst to the dialectic. *Cecil's Story* grew out of researching her great-great-grandmother who went to Cumberland Gap to tend her husband in the Civil War.[34] The child's telling the story and naming his fears in an internal suppositional monologue has healing power. Though the father returns from war with one arm, it is "strong enough to lift you now."[35] The telling and naming move the child through an emotional dialectic to a place of comfort, and the lines show that Lyon has heard the words in her voiceplace: "You'd think about the plow, though" and "Wounds take awhile to heal."

Frequently, a line in a picture book mirrors a line or a concept from a poem: for example, "I am digging" in "Archaeology" and "digging for home" in *Mama is a Miner*.[36] Though unrelated on the surface, both employ the metaphor of questing and searching. Less frequently, the reader has the opportunity to compare a story in the form of a poem with its picture book version. But "My Grandfather Sees the World" and *A Regular Rolling Noah* both tell the story of a twelve-year-old boy who is charged with tending the neighbor's household goods (nail kegs, seeds, bedding, pot vessels) and livestock (cow, horse, chickens, roosters, guineas) on a train to Canada: "When he saw them safely set down / at the mouth of the north / he was coming right back home" (8). The poem tells and names the journey in "the rolling barn" (9) in more somber and serious language than does the picture book. Compare the opening passages of both. First the poem:

When he was twelve
he walked out his door
climbed in a wagon
full of children
and roosters
nail kegs and seeds
bedding and pot vessels
and neighbors.
Moving to Canada on a train.
Them. Not him. He'd never seen
a train.

(8)

Then the picture book:

Now I'd never seen a train
before today, but I've heard its whistle
down at the mouth of the hollow.
    [page break]
The Creeches are taking it to Canada,
moving their whole farm.
They've hired me to go along and tend the stock. I can do that.
I'm a good hand with animals.[37]

Third-person point of view in the poem is exchanged for first; the picture book story is narrated by the boy, who asserts with conviction, "I can do that." This simple utterance is appropriate for a twelve-year-old; children struggle to develop competence and confidence. The simple sentence of four words defines the character of the child narrator and pulls in the child reader.

Later on in the picture book, people, places, and animals are given names: The boy is identified as "a Gabbard from Pathfork, Kentucky." In the poem's title, he is "My Grandfather," but the poem itself refers to him merely in third person (8). In the poem, the neighbors are unnamed; in the book they become Creeches. And the animals are identified: Rosie the cow, Mossy the calf, Bad Patch the mare. In the poem, as noted above, at the end of the journey the grandfather rubs off "the names he'd given them" (9), but the names are never revealed. These and other examples too numerous to recount here demonstrate Lyon's sensitivity to her audience and her skill as a poet. She can manipulate words—the building blocks of the poem—to suit her audience and her genre, all the while maintaining the integrity of the story and the voiceplace.

Finally, the introduction to *Wounds* and the essay "Voiceplace" demonstrate that Lyon has a firm grounding not only in the poetry of the region but in the region itself. Lyon says that the poem titled "Her Words" was the first "voice poem" she wrote.[38] By that, she means that it is the first poem that drew from the "voice" of the place she was from, Harlan, Kentucky. "Place is not just location, geography; place is history, family, the shape and context of daily life. How can I separate the mountains from my grandparents . . . ? How can I distinguish between where we stayed . . . and the stories of those who left?"[39] How can she separate place from words? In "Voiceplace," Lyon explains that she "sets down" in a journal interesting "things": "One was a sentence I'd seen printed in crayon on a young child's paper at Pine Mountain Settlement School: 'I hope how soon Spring comes.' I loved the way the rising sap of spring, hope itself, lifted the words into a new order. Not standard but rare, expressive. 'How I hope Spring comes soon' is tired by comparison."[40] The interesting feature of this comment is not that the words create a new vision or order through their art; rather "the rising sap of spring . . . lifted the words into a new order." In her journal, Lyon also noted her grandmother's sayings—"I feel like a stewed witch."[41] For all the complexity of Lyon's art, for all the importance of words, her poetry is deceptively simple—akin to Emily Dickinson's. As she learned from Nancy Willard, there is power in the economy of words. The simple declarations in "Her Words" need no illumination: "You gotta strap it on" (3) and "death scalds the dark" (4) and "I scrubbed on a board" (4). These bare-bones statements capture Lyon's voiceplace without succumbing to the complex issues of that place.

The picture book *Come a Tide* is a masterpiece of such simplicity. By paring the poetry down to simple statements, the story of the flood can be told with greater power. The weight of the story rests on the voice of well-chosen words and expressions, such as the grandmother's pronouncement, "It'll come a tide."[42] The horror is blunted by bald humor: "Joe won't go / till he finds his teeth. . . ." and "I've got me a boat / and I'm aiming to find the oars." The sentences are stripped of all unnecessary qualifiers, articles, and verbs: "Rain came down like curtains." "Water up to the piano keys." And finally, the grandmother's wisdom: "'If it was me, . . . / I'd make friends with a shovel.' / And we did."

The introduction to *Old Wounds, New Words* and the essay "Voiceplace" reveal that Lyon relies on the power of words to heal and utilizes their power to name and to tell. In so doing, she takes Appalachian poetry in new directions; she works from a unique aesthetic. Though her art is rooted in Appalachia, with its political and cultural paradoxes, it transcends the conflict and paradox, easily juxtaposing Oaksie Caudill and Virginia Woolf. Her art is dependent upon but not prisoner to the cultural conflicts of the region that she so aptly describes. And the feature of her poetry that characterizes her art is her conceptualization of *words*.

The picture book format has made Lyon's poetry available to a wide audience, ranging from kindergartners to adults; her highly developed style has raised Appalachian children's picture books to a new literary height. And the constrictions of the picture book genre and form (page breaks, 32 maximum pages, illustrations, etc.) have honed her poetry into simple brilliance. Her words shine. Consequently, her poetry collections such as *Catalpa* and picture books such as *A B Cedar*, *Cecil's Story*, and *Come a Tide* place her among the forefront of women who are leading the Appalachian literary renaissance.

## Notes

1. George Ella Lyon, "Voices Rooted in Place: A Conversation," interviewed by Jeff Daniel Marion, *Iron Mountain Review* 10 (Summer 1994): 24.
2. Ibid.
3. Rudine Sims Bishop, "Profile: George Ella Lyon," *Language Arts* 67 (Oct. 1990): 611.
4. George Ella Lyon, "Sidelights," *Something about the Author*, vol. 68 (Detroit: Gale, 1992), 151.
5. "Voices Rooted in Place," 24.
6. George Ella Lyon, *Catalpa* (Lexington, Ky.: Wind Publications, 1993). Unless otherwise noted, all references to Lyon's poetry are from this collection.
7. George Ella Lyon, *A Wordful Child*, photography by Ann Olson (Katonah, N.Y.: Richard C. Owen, 1996), 4.
8. Ibid., 7.
9. Bishop, 613.
10. "Voices Rooted in Place," 25.
11. Quoted in Jim Wayne Miller, "A Heart Leafed with Words Like a Tree: The Poetry of George Ella Lyon," *Iron Mountain Review* 10 (Summer 1994): 7.
12. "Sidelights," 151.
13. Bishop, 612.
14. Ibid.
15. Ibid., 614.
16. *A Wordful Child*, 21.
17. Ibid., 17.
18. John Keats, "Ode on a Grecian Urn," in *Anthology of Romanticism*, ed. Ernest Bernbaum, 3rd ed. (New York: Ronald Press, 1948), 819–20.
19. "Sidelights," 151.
20. George Ella Lyon, *Basket*, illus. Mary Szilagyi (New York: Orchard, 1990), n.p.
21. George Ella Lyon, introd. to *Old Wounds, New Words: Poems from the Appalachian Poetry Project*, ed. Bob Henry Baber, George Ella Lyon, and Gurney Norman (Ashland, Ky.: Jesse Stuart Foundation, 1994), 8.
22. Ibid., 13.
23. Ibid., 14.

24. Robert Frost, "The Figure a Poem Makes," in *Interpreting Literature*, ed. K. L. Knickerbocker et al., 7th ed. (New York: Holt, Rinehart and Winston, 1985), 1148.
25. George Ella Lyon, *Who Came down that Road?*, illus. Peter Catalanotto (New York: Orchard, 1992), n.p.
26. George Ella Lyon, *Dreamplace*, illus. Peter Catalanotto (New York: Orchard, 1993), n.p.
27. Introd., 15.
28. Bishop, 615.
29. Introd., 15.
30. George Ella Lyon, *Bloodroot: Reflections on Place by Appalachian Women Writers*, ed. Joyce Dyer (Lexington, Ky.: Univ. Press of Kentucky, 1998), 169.
31. George Ella Lyon, *A B Cedar: An Alphabet of Trees*, illus. Tom Parker (New York: Orchard, 1989), n.p.
32. George Ella Lyon, *A Day at Damp Camp*, illus. Peter Catalanotto (New York: Orchard, 1996), n.p.
33. Bishop, 612.
34. Ibid., 614.
35. George Ella Lyon, *Cecil's Story*, illus. Peter Catalanotto (New York: Orchard, 1991), n.p.
36. George Ella Lyon, *Mama Is a Miner*, illus. Peter Catalanotto (New York: Orchard, 1994), n.p.
37. George Ella Lyon, *A Regular Rolling Noah*, illus. Stephen Gammell (New York: Bradbury, 1986), n.p.
38. "Voiceplace," 170.
39. Ibid., 171–72.
40. Ibid., 169.
41. Ibid.
42. George Ella Lyon, *Come a Tide*, illus. Stephen Gammell (New York: Orchard, 1990), n.p.

# Linda Parsons Marion

## *House Holder*

To live within these bounds
is enough world for now. To have coffee
in a wicker chair with sun moving toward
my feet, to watch morning unfold on the breast
of a mocker. By noon, its purtygurl, purtygurl
will lodge in the brown grass, full of desire
for rain. For now, the dew beads up like shallows
on the porch. If the air had salt, I would feel
near the sea. I want to sit awhile
on these faded cushions
and wade slowly into day.

My daughter sleeps late and wakes
with damp crosses on her cheek.
I always know when she rummages around
for a lost barrette. A rug will be crooked,
my glass box open or slightly askew.
I know this house better than the children
I've kept from traffic. These rooms are the end
of my grasp, my sleeves falling loosely back,
light tumbling in like the pearl buttons
I searched weeks for.

For now, my daughter can't see
that coming home feels like approaching
the altar, the dry wafer on my tongue,
the little gasp as I take it in. She can't see
that cleaning the kitchen tile feels like
a cool rag on my eyes at the close of day.
I want to be at that table and smooth out the lace.
I want to stand in that kitchen with the blue tile
and feel my mouth water.

## Stitch in Time

Taught to be handy with needle and thread,
once upon a time I spun straw into gold—
chrysanthemums on the pillowcase, bunnies
on my sister's bib, slipstitch and blindstitch,
the pinpricks of my girl's heart embroidered
on the snowy field of cloth. Stretched across
the wooden hoop, I could be a handkerchief
with pink scalloped edges to be taken home
in my teacher's purse. To be taken in hand
and dabbed at nose or eye, to be soaked
in rosewater, to reel in the dance of floss
and fingers, my firstborn skill. I came by it
rightly, my grandmother gunning the treadle
at the garment factory, churning out shirts
like paper from presses to meet her daily quota.
I received the gift of every young bride, a packet
of #2 needles, one bright penny taped inside
to dull the bad luck of sharpness given, blood
drawn on white linen. But for the occasional hem
and iron-on patch, I've put it all aside. Wall hangings
and crewelwork in the attic, wooly alpaca yarn
I always meant for something wonderful—all mislaid
in the fast shuttle of days. My hands now too restless
to point so precisely, too questioning for the enormous
simplicity of buttons. They have other tales to unravel,
their nimble ways cutting down to the moment,
the indelible fabric of remembrance and ever after.
Across the blank page, I sew a tableau more mysterious
than velvet, the weft of this girl's hopes to be kept
in a pocket near the heart, with callouses thick
and proud, my quickness spinning on in low light,
threading over, under, around, and through.

# Listening for the Hello of Home
*A Conversation with Linda Parsons Marion*

Jeff Daniel Marion

L inda Parsons Marion is poetry editor of *Now & Then* magazine, published by the Center for Appalachian Studies and Services at East Tennessee State University. She has received literary fellowships from the Tennessee Arts Commission (1996–97, 1998–99), ArtReach grants from the Knoxville Arts Council (1997–98, 2000–2001), the Tennessee Writers Alliance award in poetry (1996, 2000, 2001), the Tennessee Poetry Prize (1995), and the Associated Writing Programs' Intro Award (1990), among others. Her work has appeared in *The Georgia Review, Iowa Review, Asheville Poetry Review, Prairie Schooner, Apalachee Quarterly, Wind, Appalachian Heritage, Now & Then, Louisiana Literature, Negative Capability, Helicon Nine,* and *Press,* among others. Her column "The Writing Well" appeared regularly in *New Millennium Writings* from 1995 to 2000. She is co-editor of *All Around Us: Poems from the Valley* (Blue Ridge Publishing, 1996). Her first book of poems, *Home Fires,* was published by Sow's Ear Press (1997). Marion is an editor and policy analyst for the University of Tennessee and lives with her husband, poet Jeff Daniel Marion, in Knoxville.

J.D.MARION: In one of your unpublished poems, "Tomato Songs," is the phrase "the hello of home." And in "In My Mother's House" you say, "Home, yet not home, I am a guest / in my mother's house. . . ."[1] I see in much of your writing a search for home, a struggle with the concept of home, an attempt over a series of poems and maybe much of your writing life to define for yourself what home is. Could you talk about that?

L.P.MARION: Yes, that is the central story of my work. Whether in the form of essays or poems, it seems I'm either looking for home or describing the small, comforting objects of home and all of the rituals, the dailiness they represent. I think that is one of my deepest longings—to be at home both in myself and in the physical space I've created.

J.D.MARION: Your first book is titled *Home Fires.*[2]

L.P. MARION: My parents divorced when I was three, in the mid-1950s, when divorce was fairly rare. My mother moved us around a good bit, so I gauged home by my grade in school—I attended nine schools in twelve years. That was how I kept up with where we were and is how I remember the string of places today: in third grade we lived on such-and-such street. As a child, the only long-term place I could call home was my grandmother's. I identified greatly with my maternal grandmother.

J.D. MARION: So she provided a sense of stability, groundedness, an anchor in a specific place?

L.P. MARION: That's the key, a specific place. The home environment at my grandmother's was not what I would call stable because of my grandfather's alcoholism. It was something to be pushed aside and hushed up. Still, there were threatening clouds in the house—it could storm any minute, you didn't know. But as a child, my main concern was the sameness of the place itself and, of course, my grandmother. She was the overriding symbol of home for me, such that my grandfather's failings didn't disturb me much when I stayed with them on the weekends.

J.D. MARION: Your attempts to locate and define home literally seemed to shift about. I'm wondering if the central metaphor in your writing, that writing itself, is an attempt to provide the anchor that daily life did not provide for you. Would you talk about how you came to writing, how that's connected to your search for home? Is writing, in a sense, a home for you?

L.P. MARION: The act of writing is very much an ordering process for me. I gather various possibilities within the flights and confines of imagination, snippets of memory or story, and through the line and particular word choices, I'm able to create a sense of order out of seemingly disparate loose ends. So each time of making the poem or essay is like making home again, making order that has so long escaped me. A place warm and familiar, therefore safe and protected. However, the danger in that is to think the poem doesn't have any rough edges when, of course, it does. There should be a tension, both light and dark sides of the coin. There's the good turn of the line, but also what's between those lines, what's unsaid. That's where some of the darkness and tension can and should come in. Something that should prick your comfort level, somehow move and change you in the moment of reading or hearing.

J.D. MARION: Whereas the poem comes out of a kind of chaos and need for order, that doesn't mean you have a gloss, a complete positive. Instead it becomes, as Donald Hall suggests, a poem with contrary motions, moving forward and backward at the same time.[3] When a poem does not have those motions, it lacks the necessary substance a poem should provide. It seems your poems have both dark and light and the tension of trying to walk the tightrope between those two.

L.P.MARION: Oh! Blessed rage for order!

J.D.MARION: You talk about your grandmother in more than one poem, most recently in a new piece you're working on, "Stitch in Time." Let's discuss your relationship with her, how you viewed her work, calling her the "star buttonholer" in one poem, and how her work becomes a metaphor for your work.

L.P.MARION: I have thought about that connection. She caught a bus before daylight to work in a Nashville garment factory for over thirty years, cutting buttonholes in men's shirts. The foreman always asked her to do the samples, which was a privilege but also increased her regular workload. And of course they had quotas, "making production," she called it. I remember going to a few company picnics—the great sea of "girls" and a handful of men, the foremen and managers. I have been struck with the preciseness of her work, the quickness she had to develop. She worked a machine in which a blade came down to cut the buttonholes. She had to hit her mark, and she had to get her fingers out of the way! I don't recall her ever cutting herself. She was quite efficient and took a lot of pride in her work.

So there is a connection between the two: the precision of writing poetry and capturing just the right image, just enough words, and hitting that mark of craft, language, and emotion. Then making sure the hand of the poet stays out of the way! When the poet's presence is too obvious in a poem, it can feel contrived or forced.

J.D.MARION: Like the old expression "don't show your hand."

L.P.MARION: Right. So there is an interesting resemblance between my grandmother's work at the factory and what I have chosen to do with poetry.

J.D.MARION: She was one of many in a mass production environment, and yet the poet is solitary and separate from the company. In a sense we might call your grandmother one of those vast groups of invisible women—who do amazing work, but they aren't always offered the opportunity to be seen and known for the quality of their work as specific, individual artists.

L.P. MARION: Yes, she "made production" in a collective sense, with a collective pride. If, for example, the button girl was slow, that affected whether my grandmother made production, and so on down the line. They depended on each other to get through the day. And although I'm solitary in my work as a poet, I make production on the shoulders of all who have come before me and who influence my writing today—the rich tradition of Frost, Rilke, Neruda, William Stafford, Mary Oliver, and in the Southern Appalachian region, Jim Wayne Miller, Kay Byer, Robert Morgan, Fred Chappell, and someone named Jeff Daniel Marion. What fine company to be in! Denise Levertov said of William Carlos Williams: "He cleared ground. He gave us tools."[4] All poets are clearing ground, preparing the way for me when I sit down to write. Their words live in my mind's eye, just as my grandmother's needle and thread are working in my blood.

J.D. MARION: In the book of essays *Sleeping with One Eye Open: Women Writers and the Art of Survival*, Colette Inez describes herself as "a woman intent on making herself visible."[5] You speak in admiration of your grandmother, but in the history of your family you are moving toward being the visible woman who is making a contribution opposed to a group of women who were, by virtue of their society, doing invisible work. Can you talk about the difference between the way your life as a woman has moved opposed to your grandmother's as a worker for the company?

L.P. MARION: I've often thought of her as my early savior, a steady presence, someone who did not assert herself. She was the faithful church mother, a quiet woman who lived her faith. She had her share of prejudice, she didn't drive, didn't vote. Yet, because she went to work every day in a time when women weren't expected to work, she made a grand assertion—she was the breadwinner. She was out there like any man, as my father says, "making the beans." My grandfather was a barber and could always get work, but you couldn't depend on him to show up. In that sense, I share her determination, her will to carry on. She carried the burden of my grandfather's illness at a time when alcoholism was considered a weakness, something to be ashamed of. I don't recall any attempts in the family to try and help him, by acknowledging he was ill. She fussed at him and showed her displeasure, sure that church could straighten him out. He responded by hiding his bottles and basically receding into the wallpaper.

J.D. MARION: Do you feel in your writing you are acknowledging this illness? Where she could not, you are trying to fulfill the role of acknowledgment, taking on the burden of history?

L.P. MARION: More and more, I do feel that. For example, in his poetry collection *Eureka Mill*, Ron Rash imagines his parents' and grandparents' lives in the textile mills of South Carolina after they have left their long-held lands in the North Carolina mountains.[6] He acknowledges his debt to their labors and losses, and the poems stand as testaments to their backbreaking work, their dream of a better life. He wrote the book in order to preserve and remember their lives, the history that shaped him before his birth. I identify with that drive to preserve and remember.

When I began writing seriously around 1980 and was in my first marriage, I felt I suddenly had a way to make myself heard and be valued as never before. Through my poems I was able to proclaim that I have words to say, words with substance and meaning. Writing was certainly a giant step in making myself visible.

J.D. MARION: But it's taken several generations of women to find a level of fulfillment in what you are doing, in your acknowledgment of them. You are not only making yourself visible, but also the invisible women of your past—by acknowledging the positive influences as well as the darker aspects of their lives, such as your grandfather's alcoholism and your grandmother's denial of that. It seems the need to become visible goes even deeper. Can you talk about your first marriage and the evolution of your voice? How would you describe the tone of your early poems, as a wife in a marriage where you did not feel valued?

L.P. MARION: I began writing food and kitchen poems, with the wife as mother and caretaker, but quickly moved into the difficult issues of my marriage. Then I started to see some of my anger, which became more and more apparent. Because I didn't bring in a paycheck, technically I didn't own anything (or so I was told).

J.D. MARION: So the poem gave you something specific, an acknowledgment of your own anger.

L.P. MARION: But something I felt I could not express in the relationship. The poems became a mirror for my anger, but a dangerous mirror because I had no outlet for the anger. Young children, no college degree, no economic means to leave and change my life. I had sworn I would never divorce as my parents had. So how could I break up my family and leave my home, a home I had painted and papered and raised my children in? I allowed my poems to be the only outlet for my anger. When I began reading publicly in Knoxville, that provided another outlet, another level of expression.

J.D. MARION: Another step in becoming a visible woman?

L.P. MARION: During the 1970s and '80s, I think many women were struggling to redefine themselves both inside and outside the home.

J.D. MARION: You were starting to realize things about yourself and the women in your history.

L.P. MARION: I was leading a double life—the freedom of the public readings versus the responsibilities and, yes, the suppression of home. These lives were not at all integrated. It's especially wonderful now to be married to a poet where these aspects of myself are much more integrated on a daily basis.

J.D. MARION: I know in your childhood women were often not valued and the relationships were very complicated. Is that where your need to be honored and valued had its roots?

L.P. MARION: My grandfather wanted a son and ended up with four daughters, so my mother grew up not knowing her own worth, not being appreciated.

J.D. MARION: Not being honored goes beyond your individual life, then, back to your mother, your grandmother, your aunts. You're speaking out of a whole tradition. . . .

L.P. MARION: I'm saying, "Yes, we matter, we're important! We have stories to tell!" But because I'm a fairly private person, I do struggle with the idea of publishing and public readings. These activities place two sides of my basic nature in conflict. How much truth do I reveal and still maintain my personal integrity? How do I shape that truth? I don't want to be too raw about it, so that's where craft and restraint are important.

J.D. MARION: Go back to those complicated relationships you experienced as a child. How did those relationships and events shape you apart from your grandparents' drama?

L.P. MARION: In my middle childhood, from age seven to eleven, my world was very black-and-white. My mother was with her third husband, and they were both highly emotional, volatile people. My stepfather was extremely controlling—he got angry if my mother wore slacks, talked to the neighbors, rode the bus, made any move to join the outside world. They were openly sexual around me, but could just as easily explode into violence, especially when they drank. Lots of mixed messages for a child. When you watch your mother get beaten up, you never forget it. I lived in fear wondering if I would be next.

My father remarried when I was seven, so I visited him and his new wife, Judie, on the weekends. She and I were only thirteen years apart, almost like sisters. During the week I lived with a ticking time bomb, and on the weekends I experienced a loving family who did happy things together . . . a normalcy I had never known. The grass was definitely greener on the other side. Judie pulled mother duty when my own mother was not allowed to—or would not—do the essentials like take me to the dentist and attend school programs. Most importantly, Judie read to me, sang, played games. I experienced the world of fairy tales, even felt in some sort of enchanted world. Of course, as a child I wanted to escape into that happy, magic place and live there. As with my grandmother, I was seeking stability, a home on safe ground. Literally, I was seeking *mother*, who embodied home. A mother who was strong enough to protect herself and therefore protect me.

By age eleven, my father and Judie had moved to Knoxville, and it was as if the sun had left the sky. No more weekends with *mother*. No more safe island just a phone call away. I decided I had to live with them. I don't remember what prompted my decision, except I missed Judie terribly. My mother packed my suitcases in a rage, and everyone thought it was a whim, I would get over it and come back. Even at that age, I understood I was leaving one family for another, leaving behind my grandmother, aunts, and cousins—primarily my mother who, despite all the difficulties, was still my mother.

J.D. MARION: This story seems to be one of the incredible price someone pays to be visible. As you make this move from an unstable home with your mother and stepfather to what you perceive as the good home with your father and stepmother . . . to be visible, to be honored and protected, you had to give up what had valued you as well as what had threatened you . . . your connections with your maternal grandmother and your actual mother, but you gained the presence of your father and a loving stepmother. We are hearing the incredible price that must be paid by a woman attempting to become respected for her own sake.

L.P. MARION: Even at age eleven. I suppose I was born old in that I understood some harsh realities and responsibilities before my time, was indeed robbed of certain aspects of childhood by being forced into such decisions at an early age.

J.D. MARION: Even though you have half-brothers and -sisters on both sides, you have always been like an only child.

L.P. MARION: With all the seriousness of the only child! Leaving my first marriage was also an enormous break. But not on the same scale as leaving my mother since that was breaking a blood bond, which has never fully healed.

J.D. MARION: We have an interesting mix of images here. One must leave in order to find. Perhaps it's within the mythology of human stories that we are not given what we need and must journey to find it. But that journey is always made at the greatest price. This seems to be the crux of much of your writing—being forced to leave on one hand, yet knowing on the other hand you must strike out. But you must also leave behind those precious to you in order to move forward.

L.P. MARION: Always moving toward some sort of created home. Whether a physical place or in the poem itself—because the poem is also a physical place. A room you open in your mind when you decide it's time to write.

J.D. MARION: As Yeats says, "I will arise and go now, and go to Innisfree. . . ."[7] The poem is the place we can go to find what we need. Robert Frost described home as the place that, when you go there, they have to take you in.[8] The poem and home can become one and the same.

L.P. MARION: The leaving scenario has played itself out for me in many ways. Two years after I moved in with my father, he was transferred to his home company in Wisconsin, a tiny dairy town near Lake Michigan.

J.D. MARION: How did that affect you?

L.P. MARION: What a culture shock! I essentially learned what it was like to be in a foreign country. Very Germanic people, immaculate farms, snow drifting up to the roof of the house!

J.D. MARION: You became more aware of who you were in a regional sense.

L.P. MARION: Suddenly I was aware of my southernness, every time I opened my mouth! Of course, they were equally foreign to me. That's when my identity as a southerner was really forged. My nickname became "Reb." I fought to remain southern during my years there.

J.D. MARION: This was during your adolescence?

L.P. MARION: Yes, all four years of high school. Leaving my regional home taught me how to love it in a way that, when you are in a place and part of it, you may not truly appreciate it. I felt exiled, a stranger in a strange land, but I learned some valuable lessons about identifying with a particular place. After so many years of jumping around, it's very important for me now to feel rooted—I've been in Knoxville for almost thirty years.

J.D. MARION: You became more conscious of being from the South, being shaped by a place.

L.P. MARION: I saw *Gone with the Wind* for the first time in Wisconsin, and my girlfriends thought Scarlett was a blue-ribbon bitch. They couldn't understand, as she knelt clasping a handful of red Georgia clay, that all of her actions thereafter were from her determination to never allow herself and those she loved to go hungry again. Even more than that, to preserve the ground that was Tara—home. War had never been fought on their soil, and I suddenly understood history in a very personal way. So I defended her.

J.D. MARION: I wonder if this identification with Scarlett goes even deeper . . . such that, as God is my witness, I will do something about this hunger I have for home. I will find myself a home, I will survive against all odds.

L.P. MARION: Like Scarlett, I did hurt people along the way—my mother, my grandmother, my first husband, certainly my daughters. Now divorce is part of their history, and I never wanted it to be. As you say, sacrifice is a terrible part of the journey. There are things offered up to be left behind. And when you offer them up you know it has to be done in order to move forward. I don't look back in anger, but in great sadness. But, as Dorothy Gale found out, home is really within. As I near fifty, more and more I'm learning to mother myself, father myself, to not look outside for a parent figure to fix the brokenness of my past.

J.D. MARION: So this is part of your evolution as a person and a writer to make that discovery: The stability of the physical home is perhaps illusory, whereas the home within the poem has a longer lasting stability?

L.P. MARION: I have come to realize that the real home is the body, the heart, the mind, the spirit. But I do love to surround myself with the comfort and familiarity of things collected and given, things with a history attached to them. Coming from very changeable homes, it is important for me to ground myself with belongings that have meaning. I could write poems for every room in my house, for every object, and they would all speak with their own voices, their own history.

J.D. MARION: Isn't that what you've been doing in your work?

L.P. MARION: I think, within the ordinary, the extraordinary is alive and well. We're surrounded by poems waiting to be born and join their music with the larger song. The most common things shine and speak, if we look and listen hard enough. As you say in "House Holder," "To live within these bounds / is enough world for now" (39).

---

As the stepchild in both my mother's and father's family, the idea of belonging and the poem are very tied together for me. I had an early need to find a home of constancy and to create that space of belonging, yet I always felt there was a pane of glass in front of me.

J.D. MARION: With your nose pressed up against it, wanting in.

L.P. MARION: I think that's why I have chosen poetry. It allows me that door inside rooms where I can walk around, imagine, observe. Often it's a door or room to the past. There I can see and imagine different possibilities, not to remake it into something good and sweet, but to present it in a crafted way of realization and healing for myself.

J.D. MARION: So in the process of presenting so many of these dark memories of the past, you seek a kind of healing.

L.P. MARION: Facing my early anger was a necessary step. In poem after poem I am looking back in difficult truth, writing through to a little more peace and understanding. Flannery O'Connor writes that anyone who survives childhood has enough material to last the rest of her life.[9] I believe that! But in revisiting the past, my objective is also to create art that can exist outside of my particular experience, that moves into the realm of the universal. In the creative process, I'm affirming my own worth as a woman and an artist. All of my leavings have been affirming my worth, but with a price of great loss.

J.D. MARION: With the act of acknowledgment comes an act of witness. Out of that witness comes a new level of self-awareness, and therefore visibility. You create a person who stands before the world and in that sense find the healing you've hoped for. It's never complete, it's always in process.

L.P. MARION: Like turning an object over in your hands, each time you see different light and shadows, new passageways to enter.

J.D. MARION: This is the willingness of the writer to enter pain and hardship to become whole, more self-aware. That is an important gift the writer offers the public—sooner or later you must acknowledge yourself.

L.P. MARION: I've discussed my poems as rooms the reader and I can enter, but they are also an offering cup, a drink offered to the world that's perhaps bittersweet.

J.D. MARION: Your writing is also the cup of remembrance. By remembering the past, we make those things visible and memorable, things at risk of disappearing.

L.P. MARION: Yes, drink this in remembrance of who you were and who you are yet to be. A little magic may be mixed in, but you've got to work for it, open yourself to the possibility of change.

## Notes

1. "In My Mother's House," *Sow's Ear Poetry Review* 10, no. 2 (2000): 27.
2. Linda Parsons, *Home Fires* (Abingdon, Va.: Sow's Ear Press, 1997). Subsequent references to poems are in the text.
3. For more discussion of this concept, see Donald Hall's "Varieties of Pleasure" in *The Pleasures of Poetry* (New York: Harper & Row, 1971), 11–21.
4. Denise Levertov's remarks appear on the dust jacket of William Carlos Williams's *The Collected Poems*, ed. A. Walton Litz and Christopher MacGowan (New York: New Directions, 1986–88).
5. Colette Inez, "Sounds of Hazard and Survival." In *Sleeping with One Eye Open: Women Writers and the Art of Survival*, ed. Marilyn Kallett and Judith Ortiz Cofer (Athens: Univ. of Georgia Press, 1999), 145.
6. Ron Rash, *Eureka Mill* (Corvallis, Ore.: Bench Press, 1998).
7. W. B. Yeats, "The Lake Isle of Innisfree," in *Collected Poems. Definitive Edition* (New York: Macmillan, 1956), 39.
8. Robert Frost, "The Death of the Hired Man," in *The Poetry of Robert Frost*, ed. Edward Connery (New York: Holt, Rinehart and Winston, 1969), 38.
9. Flannery O'Connor, *The Habit of Being: Letters*, ed. Sally Fitzgerald (New York: Farrar, Straus, Giroux, 1979).

# Irene McKinney

## Deep Mining

Think of this: that under the earth
there are black rooms your very body

can move through. Just as you always
dreamed, you enter the open mouth

and slide between the glistening walls,
the arteries of coal in the larger body.

I knock it loose with the heavy hammer.
I load it up and send it out

while you walk up there on the crust,
in the daylight, and listen to the coal-cars

bearing down with their burden.
You're going to burn this fuel

and when you come in from your chores,
rub your hands in the soft red glow

and stand in your steaming clothes
with your back to it, while it soaks

into frozen buttocks and thighs.
You're going to do that for me

while I slog in the icy water
behind the straining cars.

Until the swing-shift comes around.
Now, I am the one in front of the fire.

Someone has stoked the cooking stove
and set brown loaves on the warming pan.

Someone has laid out my softer clothes,
and turned back the quilt.

Listen: there is a vein that runs
through the earth from top to bottom

and both of us are in it.
One of us is always burning.

# Viridian Days

I was an ordinary woman, and so
I appeared eccentric, collecting gee-gaws
of porcelain and cobalt blue, mincing
deer-meat for the cat. I was unhooked

from matrimony, and so I rose up
like a hot-air balloon, and drifted
down eventually into the countryside,
not shevelled New England nor the

grandeur of the West, but disheveled
West Virginia, where the hills are flung
around like old green handkerchiefs
and the Chessie rumbles along, shaking

the smooth clean skin of the river.
If I wanted to glue magazine pictures
to an entire wall, or walk around nude,
I did so, having no standard to maintain

and no small children to be humiliated
by my defection. I spent years puttering
around in a green bathrobe, smelling of
coffee, perfume, sweat, incense, and

female effluvia. Why not. That was
my motto. I collected books like some
women collect green stamps, but I read
them all, down to the finest print,

the solid cubes of footnotes. Since no one
was there, nobody stopped me. Raspberry vines
slashed at the Toyota's sides as I came in.
Flocks of starlings, grosbeaks, mourning doves

lifted the air around the house. Fragments
of turkey bones the dog chewed on, a swarm
of ladybugs made into a red enameled necklace,
hulls of black sunflower seeds piled

on the porchboards. Locust, hickory, sweet gum
trees. Absolute silence stricken by crow calls.
Copper pans, eight strands of seed beads,
dolphin earrings. I climbed over the fence

at the edge of the woods, back and forth
over it several times a day, gathering ferns,
then digging in the parsley—shaggy, pungent, green.

# A Conversation with Irene McKinney

Jeff Mann

West Virginia Poet Laureate Irene McKinney was recently honored by West Virginia University with an Alumni Recognition Award from Eberly College of Arts and Sciences. McKinney earned a master's degree in English from West Virginia University in 1970 before earning a doctorate from the University of Utah in 1994. Her awards include a Bread Loaf Scholarship and a McDowell Fellowship. She is the author of four books of poetry, including *Quick Fire and Slow Fire* (North Atlantic Books, 1988) and *Six O'Clock Mine Report* (Univ. of Pittsburgh Press, 1989). Her poems have appeared in five anthologies and more than sixty journals and magazines. She is a professor and director of the creative writing program at West Virginia Wesleyan College, where she received her bachelor's degree in 1968.

MANN: Your present project at the Virginia Center for the Creative Arts is putting together a volume of new and selected poems. How would you characterize your newest work?

McKINNEY: "Viridian Days" is pretty representative of my more recent work.[1] In tone, it's much more heated up, the imagery is much less systematic. And the subject matter is different, because many of the poems that I'm interested in completing right now have to do with aging, specifically with how I feel each day, each week, each month, as I've just passed my sixtieth birthday. There are a lot of angers that fuel this too. Anger has fueled my work all the way along, it's just that the subject of the anger keeps changing. At various times I was angry at men—which I don't seem to be any longer. I was angry at people who stereotyped people from the [Appalachian] region. And now I'm angry at the way our culture makes women invisible after they pass the age of childbearing. I feel that I still have the same kinds of vitalities and talents and knowledge— perhaps more knowledge. In other words, I have a lot of good, positive things to put into my writing, into my teaching, into my social life, yet when I walk down the street I have the feeling that there's a blank spot there. So even if this is not the direct subject matter of the work I'm writing right now, this is what's powering it.

MANN: One element I've noticed in your poems is a deep awareness of impermanence and thus a desire to be in the moment. This theme appears in "A Freshet in Brattleboro," in "Breathing," and in your comment in the *Kestrel* self-interview: "The house sits here by the woods as a guest, I know this. Never was a house less permanent. It will not stand, I know this. But I wanted only to be truly here for a while."[2]

McKINNEY: Part of being a poet is that realization [of impermanence], but also feeling compelled to remind yourself of that every day, to discipline yourself by saying, "Don't act like you're here forever, or don't act like you're here talking to this particular person forever, because something could happen to either one of you before you meet again." Now this is not, for me, doomsday thinking at all. It's realistic. It sharpens my perception of where I am. I think that most poetry comes out of that kind of awareness, even if it doesn't mention it. It's somebody opening their eyes suddenly, saying "Hey, I'm here, now, and I think this and I feel that." That original sort of perception can be conveyed to other people, so that when I pick up a poem by a poet whose works I find powerful, they're doing that for me. So I want to do the same.

MANN: So poetry is born of a kind of an awakening on the part of the poet, and hopefully it awakens the reader. A mutual waking-up. There's that line in Thoreau: "Only that day dawns to which we are awake."[3]

McKINNEY: I remember the first actual poetry reading I ever went to: Winston Fuller, Maggie Anderson, and I drove to Pittsburgh to hear Denise Levertov read. I remember her reading "I don't want / to forget who I am . . . and hang limp and clean, an empty dress—" and getting the sense that if you get too comfortable, too well laundered, then you've just lost it, you've lost what's valuable, the only thing that's valuable, which is an awareness of where you are.[4] Now, frankly, the more losses that occur in my life, the harder it is for me to remind myself to stay aware, because it's so very painful. When you've lost someone you're close to, staying aware means more pain. So I suppose it's easier to talk about living in the moment when your moments haven't had anything too horrible in them.

MANN: Because then being awake means being in pain. Oh, yes, I understand that. Shifting gears, here's another topic I'd like your perspective on. One definitive element of Appalachian literature is Place. Much Appalachian writing seems tinged with the struggle between Going vs. Staying. I think about Thomas Wolfe describing the sound of the train whistles, the longing for the outside world which that sound evoked. Do you share a desire to escape? Do you suffer from homesickness when away? I recall at the Virginia Tech reading you said that your homesickness in Utah inspired the poem "Twilight in West Virginia" from *Six O'Clock Mine Report* (3).

McKINNEY: Observing my own push-and-pull motion in relation to this region, and other people's, I think that is the primary subject matter. The idea of home; the idea of nostalgia, of being pulled toward something you know you can't live with full-time; the rejection of the outside world sometimes in favor of this world, which truly is a different world—I think all those tensions are right at the heart of the Appalachian experience.

I virtually grew up in the nineteenth century. I lived out on a dirt road, on a self-sufficient farm, and even though it was only about ten miles from the nearest town, that was like a day's trip away. We raised almost all of our own food, most of the people we associated with were relatives or close neighbors. It was a tight-knit community. Everybody knew each other and to a certain extent accepted each other. I'm not saying it was idyllic, but it was a totally different world from the one I find myself living in now, even living back in that region, because that region has changed.

So that push and pull, that idea of there being a home some place for you, this is one of the enduring ideas of literature, not just in Appalachia, the idea of longing for home, the place where you can be yourself and also have a sense of peace and accomplishment and completion. Of course, this is tied up in our case with all of the cultural forces that have been at work for a long period of time. Louise McNeill said some place, "We held to our pioneer ways the longest, the strongest."[5] In other words, West Virginia stayed isolated when everything around us was being exposed to mainstream culture, which has only recently been filtering into the state. So we're in the midst of enormous changes and they're all very, very painful.

MANN: One line in your poem "The Durrett Farm, West Virginia: A Map"[6] from *The Girl with the Stone in her Lap* reminds me of Denise Giardina's work. You say, "my father read to me Emerson, Wordsworth, Poe, and Pinocchio. There is a wall between the words you say and write, the enactments of your body in this place, and the truly literary location, these said to me" (36). Similarly, in *The Unquiet Earth*, the character Jackie says, "I'm not a real writer. Real writers live in New York apartments or sit at sidewalk cafes in Paris." Later she complains, "So there is not a thing to write about, only hillbillies, and nobody cares to hear about hillbillies."[7]

McKINNEY: Yes, that's a very basic lack which we all had: a lack of models. When I teach Appalachian lit, one of the things I try to emphasize about Breece Pancake is that he invented this place. As far as I'm concerned, that's the first real fictional voice that showed us the struggles of poor, rural West Virginians, by someone who'd grown up there. In other words, from the inside out. He is struggling in every sentence, he's a very young man, there are awkwardnesses, and there are Hemingwayesque turns here and there, but what he finally won through to was claiming a literary space that hadn't been claimed before. And I remember feeling that lack [of role models] very much when I was growing up, especially when I first started writing seriously. I remember talking with Maggie Anderson and Jayne Anne Philips about that, about who do we look to, who came before us?

The writers from this region, even when they're very, very different, and even when they're generations apart, were all aiming for something somewhat different, but there are things that we do have in common. And one of the deepest ones which has to do with the actual physical region is a sense of Time. I think of James Still, in *River of Earth*, where he has the preacher Sim Mobberly speaking of riding on the waves of "this mighty river of earth."[8] Things change, the earth itself changes. So geologically there's some kind of awareness in writers of this region, that you don't really see in most other regions. In Breece Pancake's first major short story, "Trilobites," that young man is always out hunting fossils, evidence of when the ocean covered all this land.[9]

MANN: There's that poem by Louise McNeill, "Ballad of New River," which has that whole sweep, from the ancient past right up to the future—dinosaurs at the beginning, dinosaurs she envisions supplanting "the hominids."[10]

McKINNEY: This is something that's pretty rare in literature. I find it very painful and very difficult to understand when people outside the region sneer or look down their noses at what they consider nature writing. So there's that sense of geologic time. Then there's a sense of family time, which I think Jayne Anne Philips' work exemplifies very strongly. To her, as a young writer, the mysteries of the two or three generations before her, what happened in her family, all of these were provocative mysteries to her, made her want to write, made her want to create a past. And finally there's an awareness of personal, autobiographical time. Also there's a kind of necessary humility when you think of nonhuman time. And there's a kind of wonderment that rises up in you when you're out in the countryside and find an old cellar-hole or old chimney or Indian arrowheads or ancient burial grounds or mounds of the Moundbuilders (which also show up in Breece Pancake). You have this realization: "I'm a very tiny thing here on this great big landscape." And to me that's a necessary humility. I think that humility brings us to basic truths. And if you live all the time in an urban setting, it's very, very easy to forget that.

MANN: Yes, my father has always railed against The City. One of his favorite writers is Jacques Ellul, who wrote *The Meaning of the City*.[11] He's always talked to me about how out-of-touch urban dwellers must be, creatures completely deracinated, no sense of roots at all. On the other hand, friends sometimes say to me, "Oh, you're so lucky to have such a sense of roots," but sometimes I feel root-bound!

MCKINNEY: You are lucky, unless you get strangled to death by the roots! It's an enormous love for the people, for the region, for the land, so you suffer for that attempt to pull away. Mary Lee Settle, in her novel *Charley Bland*, says that those of us who grew up here are like trained hound dogs, trained to come back home.[12] We feel a sense of betrayal; if we go anywhere else, we think somehow we've betrayed our roots.

MANN: And as for Place/Home, you're now living on the ancestral farm. How's the Durrett farm at present?

MCKINNEY: The old farmhouse, which was built in 1848, is still standing. It's a very well-built structure; it was built with wood pegs instead of nails and enormous beams. It's a foursquare solid old house. My mother still lives in that house. We had about 350 to 400 acres. That's a tiny farm in other parts of the country, but in this region it's pretty good-sized. With part of a National Endowment grant, I moved back from upstate New York and built my small house, a glorified cabin. I wanted it almost in the woods but not entirely. After my father's death we sold all the cattle, and now the land's going back to wilderness. It's not fully a working farm, the way it was when I grew up on it, but it's still functioning. We sell some of the hay, we occasionally sell a mature oak tree. It made me very sad the first year I moved back there, I would go out and hike around and see things growing up because already my father was aged and ailing and couldn't go out to supervise the clearing of the brush. And I thought, my ancestors worked lifetimes to clear that land. Literally, they gave their lifetimes to clearing that land and making it productive, and here in just a short period of time. . . . None of us will ever farm it. For a couple of reasons: we don't know how, really, not the way my mother's generation did. And we couldn't make a living from it.

MANN: I see that in my father's life. He was born in the twenties, and he's in his late seventies and in absolutely amazing shape. I joke that, like Dorian Gray, he has a portrait in an attic going to hell somewhere. He remembers growing up in Summers County in the twenties and thirties, and it was that nineteenth-century world you talk about. It was almost entirely self-sufficient, except that they'd take the corn down to the mill to be ground, and they'd buy coffee and a few other little things.

McKINNEY: Right. We bought coffee, and sugar sometimes, though during the Second World War there was sugar rationing and so my father decided to plant sugar cane. We made molasses out of it, so then we didn't even have to buy sugar.

MANN: We used to make maple syrup, actually. It's one of my major colorful childhood memories. A lot of work! It's easy to romanticize these memories, but the actual truth of the matter is different.

McKINNEY: Yes, it takes up your whole life, your whole devotion, you have to think about it every day.

MANN: Well, that ties into the next question. Often I see a temptation and tendency to romanticize country life in some Appalachian literature. This contrasts nicely with the pure nasty realism of your prose poem "The Pig's Head" in The Girl with the Stone in Her Lap (4–7).

McKINNEY: From the beginning, with those poems in the first book The Girl with the Stone in Her Lap, I knew I had to be very, very tough with myself. The whole tendency to romanticize country life is one that seems to cut across all times and places. People who lived in London romanticized the countryside three miles away, declared it an entirely different way of life. In this country, as people in urban centers realize that rural life is deteriorating and disappearing, they have even more of a longing for Walton's Mountain, to imagine it as a place full of the salt of the earth, folk who were well intentioned and wonderful. And if they don't do that, they want to Beverly Hillbilly–ize it, and turn them all into ignorant savages. The truth is there's probably more change going on in this region than there is in urban centers right now. Genuine cultural upheavals. I feel it every day. When the highway was built through the edge of the family farm (this is Corridor H, Route 33, which is eventually going to run all the way to Virginia, a big four-lane concrete slab laid down the length of the state) this went through our family farm. When I moved back there and built my place, I saw it as a quiet country retreat, and now this major highway is half a mile away from me.

We're really going through all kinds of cultural upheavals. It is not a settled, certain way of life. So to romanticize it and say that it is, or ever was, would be an enormous lie. I would rather err on the other side, to come down on the tougher, nastier parts, if I have to err at all, rather than to prettify.

MANN: In a poem from the same collection, "The Farm," you state, "A tree's got rights" (24). Later, in "Dear Friend," you say, "People with their indefatigable motors / are rolling away tree branches, / grass, limbs" (50). And you mention strip mines and loggers in "The Durrett Farm, West Virginia: A Map." These references certainly suggest an interest in environmental protection. Has there been much damage about the Durrett farm? And what do you think about that most controversial of West Virginia topics, mountaintop removal?

MCKINNEY: The saddest thing, of course, is that there's nothing new in all of this. I do hate simplification, of course, and yet at the same time it does occur to me now and then that there really are two kinds of people. One kind is on the side of life, and that includes the life of trees, the soil, water and air, animal life. And the other kind of people don't give a hoot and a holler for other forms of life. I've had that awareness very deeply all along, even back there in that first book, that a tree does have rights. And it does me good as a human being to understand that, because it puts me in my proper, humble place. Then I don't have this inflated illusion that I'm the center of the universe. I know I'm not, as an individual human being or as a representative human being.

Living out where I do, I see a lot of wildlife up close and personal, because it's fairly quiet back where I live at the edge of the woods, even with the highway going through that close. There's a great big tract of forest, so the deer come out there every day, raccoons, possums, foxes, crows, every kind of bird that you can think of. And I know, looking at them, I know for a fact that they're just as important in the scheme of things as I am. Whereas the second kind of person I'm talking about here has made a decision, conscious or unconscious, not to really think about or care about other forms of life.

MANN: You often mention Thoreau and say your father read you Emerson. Have these two writers been influential?

McKINNEY: Yes, they really were. I've read them and thought about them over long, long tracts of time, so that each time I came back to them, I'd be a different person. And each time I come back, they keep giving me different things. Their discussions about self-sufficiency and solitude are very, very interesting. When I moved back to West Virginia, I remember talking to a writer friend and she said, "Well, what are you going to do down there in isolation, in the country?" and I said, "I'm going to think about community." The issues of solitude and community, I think, are very real concerns, when you grow up in a place like this. Well, our family was self-sufficient, physically isolated, in many ways emotionally and psychologically isolated, and so I learned how to do that. How you make do. Take pride in it. Have a sense of accomplishment in making do. And in terms of human company, well, human company is limited, and yet you learn to make that stand in for more. And so there's a kind of legitimate pride in that, and a kind of humility in it at the same time.

I think with Thoreau—with Thoreau more than Emerson—and with Emily Dickinson, you see the idea of self-sufficiency taken to the place almost of the ridiculous, so that a bunch of other things start to come into play at that point. And where you're trained to make your very own ego do things it was never intended to do. You're forcing it into artificial functions, to be company for yourself, when really all you may need is a few friends to just sit around and chat with you.

As I get older, these things become more and more important to me. At one time I thought I didn't really want to spend very much time talking to other people because nobody seemed as interesting as me. I honest to God believed that! In my twenties and thirties I thought I could do without people, because I thought, "Well, what are they going to give me?!" Horrible arrogance! This is where you see self-sufficiency going totally insane. Nevertheless, I think that it really is true that one of the great cultural forces in Appalachian life is to teach you to live with your own company. And I meet a lot of people who really cannot stand it. And that seems to me like an awful human disadvantage. If you can't stand to live with yourself fairly alone for a couple of weeks. . . .

MANN: Religion seems to be a real comfort in your poem "Sunday Morning, 1950" from Six O'Clock Mine Report (15). What functions have you seen religion serve in Appalachia?

McKINNEY: My family, for the most part, is not very interested in organized religion. A lot of people in our community went to church every single

Sunday and talked the talk, walked the walk. But my family didn't. They just said, "Ah well, whatever." But at the same time I think I developed a kind of independent sense of the spiritual dimension of human life. A lot of that, of course, has come from my reading, especially my reading of poetry. But also a lot of it came, I think, from observing especially my father's way of conducting himself, what he thought was an honorable way to be. And he never attached it to any orthodox religious position. It wasn't that he was saying, "You ought to do this or that because of what we read in the Bible." He never said that. He never said much of anything at all about how you ought to be; he was just a very honorable man. And so my sense of conducting myself came more from example than anything else. And then with my own leaning toward being responsible for my own life and my own decisions, I have never been drawn at all toward any kind of organized religion. I don't quite understand what it's all about, frankly, because your spiritual awareness is quite obviously a matter of deepest internalization and understandings, and therefore the idea of joining a club that thinks the same way seems to be a terrible diminishment.

MANN: So we're back to that conflict between personal solitude and a sense of community. I feel much the same as you, that spirituality is very much a deeply personal experience.

MCKINNEY: Yes, the real understandings you come to that way are probably not something you're going to be able to talk about with any coherence. I think that the real religious experiences I've had, if I did try to communicate them, would just come out sounding like clichés, and besides, there wouldn't be much point to it. But having said that, I do think that a lot of the social and communal rituals that are associated with organized religion are deeply, humanly comforting.

I was thinking at my father's funeral how grateful I was for the rituals. It was just the right way. I don't know what I would have done without that, and it gave me a place to release my grief, which I had been kind of holding off on, because I was trying to help out and knew I couldn't give way in any other setting. When I was younger I remember thinking that funerals were barbaric. Yet during my father's funeral, I thought, "What a highly civilized way of behavior this is." I was very, very grateful for it. In other words, I didn't have to feel that everybody there had read all the books that I've read, thought all the thoughts that I've thought, had all the confusions that I've had, in order for us to find a meeting place together. The ritual provided the meeting place. And I think that's enormously valuable. Whereas my zeal to get at the real truth, the real basic truth, when I was younger, would have made me say, "Well, they don't know what they're doing, you know, they don't know the history, they haven't read comparative religion." Well, who cares?! When you're in need of comfort and somebody gives you comfort, you'd be an idiot to say, "No, I don't want it!"

MANN: You were appointed poet laureate of West Virginia after Louise McNeill's death. What's the laureate position been like?

MCKINNEY: What I thought about the poet laureateship was this: maybe in the past, or in some states, to get appointed poet laureate was an honorary position and that's the end of it. You don't really do anything with it. And it seemed to me, that since the position was there, that I should take some kind of active role, which I've tried to do as much as possible. I was counting up the other day: I think that I've made 182 appearances as poet laureate. And here I'm including speaking to school groups, college groups, other kinds of organizations. It seemed to me that the position was a wonderful opportunity to talk to people about the value of poetry in their lives. It's not that I'm a zealot and want to go out and convert the world; it's that I feel that people need poetry and can't always find it. Once they find it and realize what a lot of crucial things it answers for them, then they'll keep reading it, they'll seek it out. I was also impressed when, in the first couple of months after I got the appointment, I got a lot of letters from people around the state—letters from nuns, school kids, folks I've known in the past who decided to contact me—and they were all saying what a wonderful thing it was to have a poet laureate. Now, I know a lot of those who wrote to me hadn't read my work and didn't know me from Adam, but yet they wanted to register their approval of the idea of the state appointing a poet laureate. They thought this was a very good thing. I thought a lot about that, about why they would feel that way.

And I finally decided it was something like this: everybody instinctively knows that poetry is the place you go to tell the truth. That it has very little commercial clout of any kind, it has no power in the economic world, it doesn't really figure into our ideas of wealth or personal advancement, or all those other consumer values. The American Dream of success—all those things are irrelevant to the world of poetry—believe me!—I've received none of those! I think that everybody, even if they don't read very much poetry, instinctively knows that here's something outside the usual realm of things, materialism, and they're very glad to know that that exists. Especially the first year or two [of the laureate appointment], it was exhausting because I got a lot of requests to go and speak here and there, and yet I felt that it really was a forum to spread some news about poetry to folk who might not get that otherwise, and also it was a forum to spread some news about our writers from the region. Several of those talks I built around discussing this generation of writers. A lot of people just didn't know about the level of literary activity [in the Appalachian region], and they were very pleased to know.

MANN: Well, one last question. In April 1998, when you came to Blacksburg to read at Virginia Tech, I'd picked up some ramps at a roadside stand in Summers County the weekend before, and for our breakfast I fried them up with potatoes and eggs. As I recall, we both relished them mightily! All those regional peculiarities—local dialects and customs and delicacies like the ramp—which make Appalachia so rich, do you see them diminishing due to the homogenization caused by technology and mass media? Or will they endure?

MCKINNEY: I tend to think that the basic outlines of the region are going to survive quite a long while. One of the reasons I think that is because I'm seeing the younger people coming up who are absolutely determined not to let go of those things. And it surprises me a great deal because I think that probably I grew up in a generation who were the rejectors, the first generation out? And so I'm kind of an anomaly that way. All the pressures told me that if I had any ambition or gumption at all that I'd better get out and not look back. And yet I didn't do that. Most of the ambitious people in my community and also in the little town I lived near really did go away and built their lives elsewhere. They really suffered enormous homesickness but felt it was absolutely necessary in order to be a success in life. Whereas many people of this new generation are saying, "No, I'm going to stay here and build up the life of the region with my abilities and my ambitions." That's a new thing. That's very hopeful.

## Notes

1. Irene McKinney, "Viridian Days," in *Wild Sweet Notes: Fifty Years of West Virginia Poetry, 1950–1999,* ed. Barbara Smith and Kirk Judd (Huntington, W.Va.: Publishers Place, 2000), 237–38. This poem was first published in *American Voice* 49 (1999).
2. Irene McKinney, "A Freshet in Brattleboro," in *Six O'Clock Mine Report* (Pittsburgh: Univ. of Pittsburgh Press, 1989), 10; "Breathing," in *Quick Fire and Slow Fire: Poems* (Berkeley, Calif.: North Atlantic Books, 1988), 40. Page references to other poems are found within the text. Also see "An Interview with Irene McKinney," *Kestrel* 4 (Fall 1994): 9.

3. Henry David Thoreau, "Walden," in *Anthology of American Literature*, vol. 1, ed. George McMichael (New York: Macmillan, 1980), 1661.
4. Denise Levertov, "The Five-Day Rain," in *With Eyes at the Back of Our Heads* (New York: New Directions, 1959), 13.
5. Louise McNeill, *The Milkweed Ladies* (Pittsburgh: Univ. of Pittsburgh Press, 1988), 8.
6. Irene McKinney, "The Durrett Farm, West Virginia: A Map" in *The Girl with the Stone in Her Lap* (Berkeley, Calif.: North Atlantic Books, 1976), 36. Subsequent references to this book are in the text.
7 Denise Giardina, *The Unquiet Earth* (New York: Ivy Books, 1992), 108.
8. James Still, *River of Earth* (Lexington, Ky.: Univ. Press of Kentucky, 1978), 76.
9. Breece D'J Pancake, "Trilobites," in *The Stories of Breece D'J Pancake* (New York: Holt, Rinehart and Winston, 1984), 21–37.
10. Louise McNeill, "Ballad of New River," in *Hill Daughter: New and Selected Poems*, ed. Maggie Anderson (Pittsburgh: Univ. Of Pittsburgh Press, 1991), 42.
11. Jacques Ellul, *The Meaning of the City* (Grand Rapids: William B. Eerdmans, 1970).
12. Mary Lee Settle, *Charley Bland* (New York: Farrar, Straus, Giroux, 1989).

# Lynn Powell

## *Creed*

*for Rebecca Cross*

I'd like to believe God's like you and Heaven's
like Miller's Dry Goods, here by the side of Rt. 557
in Charm, Ohio. Improbable from the outside,
but inside, beyond the vestibule of notions,
steep sunlight falling onto fresh versions
of the world: bolts of forest, river, fire, desert, sky,
and the calicos of human lives.

Women in pious caps come and go to the cutting table,
attending you. You move along the aisles
certain as Solomon, handing out the hues
of your green and purple thought. The shocks
of crimson you pass over now, the reticence
of gray, cool fathoms of blue wait
for their seasons beneath your hand.

A child ventures from the folds of your skirt.
Her patchwork of genes is pieced with keepsakes
from the family story—flaxen hair, cat-delicate bones—
and memories of mothers: one who peered into tea leaves,
one who crocheted blizzards of warmth as she died. . . .
Nothing can harm your angel here but
the open door you keep your glance trained on

where horses clop past with hooves as big as her face
and ramshackle Ford pickups gun by.
She laughs and waves at them all, scooping
buttons from the barrel just inside the door:
coins of color lost from ten thousand spring coats
and Sunday dresses, a fortune of change pouring
through the little hands you made for her.

# Faith

Hard to believe the earth
will come to love again its green life—
the red and yellow, the violet
will tire of all this fragrant asking.

Whatever secret slept
in the white meat of bulb or trunk
erupts now, trespasses
in the hundred shades of desire.

The forsythia blooms helplessly.
The beds openly confess
their lavender, their scarlet.

Even the dogwood's white witness
is more beautiful for its shadow
of flowering Judas.

# "Slowly the Heart Revises"
## Lynn Powell's Old & New Testaments

John Lang

B orn and raised in East Tennessee, Lynn Powell earned her B.A. at Carson-Newman College, where she studied with Jeff Daniel Marion, and her M.F.A. at Cornell University, where Robert Morgan was among her teachers. From both these mentors she learned an attention to image and metaphor and to the music of words that has served her poetry well, as is amply evident in her first book, Old & New Testaments, published when the poet was approaching her fortieth birthday. Winner of the 1995 Brittingham Prize from the University of Wisconsin Press, that volume announced the emergence of a highly accomplished new voice in Appalachian poetry. The artistry, originality, and thematic complexity of Old & New Testaments make it one of the best first books of poems published by an Appalachian poet during the past fifty years.

As its title suggests, Old & New Testaments addresses one of Appalachian literature's most prominent themes: the varied roles played by religion in the mountain South. Like many of the region's best-known writers, Powell resists the dualistic impulse in traditional Christianity that tends to denigrate this world in its eagerness to embrace the next. Earth vs. heaven, body vs. soul, the world vs. God—these are the oppositions that have often defined religious consciousness not only in Appalachia but wherever Christianity has been espoused.[1] Such a theology is insufficiently incarnational. It devalues the body, nature, and much of human experience in the temporal world. In historical Christianity, this metaphysical dualism is paralleled by a moral dualism that divides human beings into two groups: the elect and the reprobate, the saved and the damned, a division that often heightens, ironically, fear and anxiety for believers themselves.

What Robert Morgan has termed "the terrors and exclusions of Calvinism"[2] has led him—and many other American writers—to a rebellion that Morgan labels "coming out from under Calvinism."[3] Emily Dickinson's poems repeatedly enact such rebellion, of course, and it remains a recurring motif in twentieth-century Appalachian literature, from Harriette Arnow's Gertie Nevels in The Dollmaker and Fred Chappell's Joe Robert Kirkman in I Am One of You Forever to the poetry of Morgan, Chappell, Jim Wayne Miller, and Kathryn Stripling Byer. Powell's book not only extends that critique of traditional Christianity but also offers an alternative set of allegiances grounded in human love, in family relationships, and in nature. This "new testament" appears to supplant the "old testament" derived from her Southern Baptist upbringing.

Initial reviews of the book acknowledged the poet's profound ambivalence about her religious heritage. Fred Chappell remarked, for instance, that "[Powell's] deeply felt religion seems to flood into every niche of her life, but more to perplex than to console."[4] Under the title "Theopoetry," Ruby Riemer likewise noted that the book embodies "an argument with God." Yet Riemer saw the poems, despite their skepticism, as working "to bring her [Powell] back to God," though not the God of doctrinal Christianity.[5] Other reviewers tended to emphasize the secular elements in the book, especially its focus on the body and the physical world. Fleda Brown Jackson, for example, declared that "*Old & New Testaments* . . . encounters the Holy directly through the body," celebrating "not God's paradoxes, but our own."[6] Jeff Daniel Marion concluded his review with the statement, "Call this work an extended hymn to the body, to the five senses as gateway to the spirit, to the common processes of living and loving that unite us all."[7] With one exception, *Publishers Weekly*, reviewers praised what Jackson called the book's "winningly energetic poems" and what Chappell termed its "memorable complexities."[8]

The forty-two poems of *Old & New Testaments* are divided into four parts of varying lengths. Part one, with seven poems, is the shortest. Its epigraph from Genesis 18, verses that prophesy Isaac's birth, immediately announces this section's focus on motherhood and on the bearing and raising of children. The opening poem, "Nativity" (3), one of the book's three sestinas, demonstrates Powell's mastery of traditional forms and her careful choice of end words that mirror her major thematic concerns. Of this poem's six repeated end words, the most consistent in orthography are "body," "cross," and "love." The first stanza's "mother" later becomes "Mommy" and "Mom," just as the first stanza's "Jesus" becomes "Christ" and "God." The sixth end word alternates between "birth" and "death"—though by beginning with the former, the poet is able to conclude with "birth" even in a poem that is haunted by the prospect of mortality. As Powell notes, "death / looks back at every birth, even God's."[9] Yet "Nativity" emphasizes how the gift of life is conveyed by and through a woman's body, she herself both manger and throne, her body one of the many instruments not of evil but of grace. Powell's recourse to so complicated a traditional form as the sestina may itself be seen, as Jackson suggests more generally about this poet's use of traditional forms, as a way of "calling attention to the body of the poem"[10] and thus of reinforcing the book's concern for the centrality of the body.

Like most of the poems in Old & New Testaments, "Nativity" is explicitly autobiographical. It intersperses biblical references, the poet's memories, and current experiences. In its focus on the family (Mary's, the poet's), this poem anticipates many others in the book, for family relationships are one of Powell's most pervasive subjects. As Marion notes, "the immediate and extended family" is among Powell's key metaphors for the body.[11] Yet she refuses to sentimentalize the family. Her poetic vision, though celebratory, remains conscious of human vulnerability, of love's liability to betrayal and suffering and death, as her use of the term "cross" underscores. Love is powerful but "not omnipotent" (3), and the heart itself is subject to various disorders—as the second and third poems in part one, "Echocardiogram" and "Poem for the Second Born," both indicate—disorders that are emotional and moral as well as physical.

In addition to "Nativity," two other poems in part one, "After Bonsignori" and "Raising Jesus," invoke the figure of Mary, thus reinforcing the motif of mother and child around which this section revolves. The former is a variant on the sonnet, one of five Powell employs, three of them to conclude part three. "Raising Jesus," in contrast, runs to eight six-line stanzas plus a closing line, a stanza structure that links this poem to the sestinas with which part one begins and ends. While its title might lead readers to expect a poem about Christ's resurrection, Powell focuses instead on Mary's human role as mother and humorously depicts her own children's re-creation of assorted characters from Peter Pan, role-playing that permits the poet to explore the moral implications of human conduct. Of Mary herself the poet asks, "How did she perform that first miracle, teaching him [Jesus] to love?" (10).

Powell fills this poem, as she does many others, with words and phrases borrowed from religious contexts: "converted," "save," "born-again," "mustard seeds," "parable," "miracle." And she closes the poem with a prayer and an allusion to Mark 5:25–34, verses in which a woman is cured of a hemorrhage that has afflicted her for twelve years simply by touching the hem of Jesus' robe. According to Jesus, the woman's faith has made her whole (Mark 5:34). Powell's faith is not that of this woman, however, as the following poem, "Creed" (and the later poem entitled "Faith"), reveals. "Creed" opens with a wish, a statement in the optative mood, not an affirmation of belief: "I'd like to believe God's like you and Heaven's / like Miller's Dry Goods, here by the side of Rt. 557 / in Charm, Ohio" (12). The "you" addressed in this poem, its frequent contractions reflecting the speaking voice, is a serene, loving mother accompanied by her daughter, God as mother displacing God the father and his son. The specificity of the poem's setting directs the reader's gaze toward the here and now, not toward Heaven or toward the transcendent. It is the image of mother as creator that Powell's poem celebrates—the miracles of human love, not divine. Though dangers wait just outside the store, it is the "fortune of change" that temporal life affords which this poem highlights.

The term "change" in the preceding quotation is also meant to remind the reader that not all change signals growth. Decay and death are inescapable elements of human experience. The "memories of mothers" which "Creed" recalls include memories of mothers now dead. Yet love offers a countervailing force amid people's recognition of their mortality, as the final poem in part one, "Myth," attests.

In contrast to the humanizing and particularizing of motherhood that occurs in "Creed" and in contrast to Powell's earlier references to Mary, "Myth" universalizes the Christian nativity story and the Old Testament's account of Isaac's birth by linking the motif of "the longed-for child" (13) to sacred texts in non-Western cultures. Moreover, in this poem Powell focuses more on woman as wife than as mother, thus enlarging the scope of love's activity. The specific myth Powell employs is the widely known Hindu legend involving Savitri and Satyavan, whose relationship affirms love's power over death, however temporary the victory. This couple's tale is told in the Hindu epic, The Mahabharata, and is the basis for Gustav Holst's chamber opera, Savitri.[12] In this marriage it is the wife, Savitri, who is the hero-figure, saving her husband from death, Yama.

Like "Nativity," "Myth" is a sestina. Its end words—"time," "face," "hands," "sun," "child," and the alternating terms "past," "present," and "future"—again evince Powell's commitment to time rather than to eternity, to body rather than soul, to the natural and the human rather than the supernatural or divine. Equally important to the poem's structure is the fact that the narrator is reading the legend of Savitri to her own daughter, who "wants a brighter future / for the bride and groom" than "the future // return of Yama" portends (13). The daughter persuades her mother to read the story backwards, thereby reversing the forward thrust of time and suggesting instead the cyclical nature of human experience, its archetypal patterns of repetition. Just as the alternating terms "birth" and "death" conclude with "birth" in "Nativity," so in "Myth" Powell moves from "past," "present," and "future" to a reversal of those terms before concluding with a vision of Savitri as a sleeping child perched in a goddess's hand, "her corona of futures flaring like the sun's" (14; italics added). It is with a sense of hope, then—the plural noun "futures" indicating immense possibilities—that "Myth" and part one conclude. Yet here, as elsewhere, the poet's affirmations occur in a context shadowed by the prospect of mortality.

Part one is the most tightly structured of the book's four parts. Its images of mother and child, of hearts and hands, of loving family relationships, and of mortality reappear in various guises throughout the remainder of the book. Like part one, each subsequent section bears an epigraph from the Bible—from Song of Solomon, Revelation, and Job, respectively. Many of the poems in these sections have explicitly religious titles: "Vespers," "Balm," "Do This in Remembrance," "Manna," "Faith," "Confession," "Immersion," "Grace," "Promised Land," and "Revelation," among others. Yet while these poems may begin with a religious event or a biblical epigraph, they tend to portray what usually would be called secular rather than sacred subjects. The epigraph to part two, for example, taken from the Song of Solomon, introduces the image of a garden but evokes human love, not divine, for this garden is neither Eden nor Gethsemane but a metaphor for the body, for human sexuality and female fertility. In "Immersion," an account of the poet's baptism, Powell learns as much of the body's insistent needs as she does of the soul's when she finds herself unable to resist the impulse to urinate as she is plunged into the baptistry's waters. The poem's final section, moreover, also includes references to menstruation and to douching, further highlighting the body's role in shaping female identity. In "Balm," the title refers not to a spiritual restorative or to divine consolation but to the scent of a lover's body borne on the poet's flesh throughout the day following their love-making.

The content of these poems often subverts, then, the reader's expectations about the announced subjects. In "Confession," to cite another example, the poet reveals that her once obscured vision has been remedied by new glasses. In "The Calling," the poem's epigraph cites Jesus' words in Matthew 6:20 about laying up treasures in heaven, and Powell initially recounts several childhood experiences at Bible camp, including her decision to become a missionary. But the poem closes with the youthful poet's encounter with a luna moth in the camp's bathhouse, a setting which becomes the locus of what might be seen as an inverted baptism, though the narrator never takes the shower she had intended to have. Awed by the moth's size and its beauty, she views it as one of earth's great treasures, "a flamboyant verse / lodged in a page of drab ink" (19). This experience calls the poet not to a religious vocation but to the things of this world, in a poem whose final line echoes Robert Morgan's "Lightning Bug."

As mother, Powell seeks to insulate her own daughter from the often violent images and events that pervade biblical narratives. The crucifixion is one example already mentioned. Another occurs in the poem "Judgments," in which the poet's grandmother sends Powell's daughter a Picture-the-Bible coloring book. With the book comes a note, censored by the child's mother: "*Jesus / died to save you from your sins*" (45). The poem describes the child's efforts to comprehend the story of Abraham and Isaac, as she colors the lamb that feeds the sacrificial flames in Isaac's stead:

> Abraham, crudely drawn but unmistakable, is serving
> up the scorched ambrosia and beseeching the air,
> while Jehovah, robed in stormcloud, speaks His thunder.
> But the bleated prayer of the panicked animal
> is the loudest thing on the page to a four-year-old girl.
>
> (45)

The same coloring book reappears in another poem when the daughter copies out the caption, "FORASINADAMALLDIE," running the letters together as one word. Death and judgment are the lessons the child learns, just as her mother, in "The Calling," had had quoted to her at Bible camp Jesus' words, "*Every tree that does not bear good fruit is cut / down and thrown into the fire*" (18).

One consequence of the anxiety created by such pronouncements is the mental anguish recorded in the poem "Rapture." Here Powell reveals how, as a child, she worried about Judgment Day, fearing that it would arrive undetected, that others would soar up to heaven, abandoning her. The dread she experiences would have been familiar, of course, to Jonathan Edwards's Calvinist contemporaries, and the poem's mood closely parallels that expressed in Robert Morgan's poems "Signs" and "Face." Such anxiety is yet another of the legacies of the "exclusions of Calvinism" to which Morgan's and Powell's poetry attests.

As a striking contrast to the other-worldliness of her grandmother's outlook, Powell presents her great-aunt Roxy, the dominant figure in part four of *Old & New Testaments*. Roxy first appears in "Witness," the third of the book's sestinas, and she is thus linked to the strong female figures of part one. In fact, as Marion rightly observes, Aunt Roxy is "the grand muse whose feisty love of the world pervades this book."[13] Nearly one hundred years old, Roxy meditates on death and the afterlife, but the repeated terms of the sestina and many of her thoughts align her with the physical world, not with eternity.

Just as Fred Chappell organizes the four volumes of *Midquest* (1981) around the four elements that ancient philosophers saw as the bases for all life, so earth, air, fire, and water (or variations on those terms like "ground" and "flame" and "sweat") provide four of the poem's six repeated end words.

"Touch" and "blind" are the other terms used. In structure, too, "Witness" stresses the earth. The first of its two parts, separated by an asterisk, consists of three stanzas devoted to a plane ride that Roxy takes in 1928 with a blind nephew to afford him the sensation of flight. In the second part, which consists of three sestets and the sestina's closing tercet, Powell portrays Roxy's mother's death and Roxy's response to that event. The setting of the poem thus shifts from the sky, from the heavens, to the earth.

Roxy's vision of the afterlife is one of the central concerns of the four poems in which she appears. In "Witness," for instance, Roxy prepares her mother's body for burial, "trying to believe in hellfire / and prepared mansions, not just the blind / alley into the Jerusalem of dirt" (58). Grief-stricken, she flees into her mother's garden, comforted by the rich array of flowers planted there, "the blaze / her mother had lit on the combustible earth" (59). The fire imagery here contrasts with the threatened hellfires so frequently invoked in fundamentalist mountain religion, but the phrase "combustible earth" also serves to remind readers of the mutability of the physical world, its liability to decay and death.

One of the major themes of part four is human mortality, a theme clearly anticipated in "Nativity" and "Myth" in part one and directly stated in part four's opening poem, "FORASINADAMALLDIE." In part four that theme is also reflected in the attention to time's passage in "Prodigal," with its rhymed tercets, each successive rhyme a diminished form of its predecessor to mirror the reductions that time effects; in the previously mentioned "Rapture"; in "Epochs," which invokes the prehistoric past; and in "Versions of an Elegy." For Aunt Roxy, however, death is not something feared but something longed for, and she envisions an earthy afterlife. The poem "At Ninety-Eight," for example, bears an epigraph from Aunt Roxy herself that reads, "I sure as hell hope the Lord's got beans to break and string in heaven," and the poem's opening lines testify to what "Witness" calls "the body's blind / allegiance to earth" (58):

> Her mind goes blank
> imagining what pearly gates
> and boulevards of gold—what
> contraption of an afterlife—
> could matter more than sweet
> potatoes garden dug, still damp,
> a green bonfire of mustards,
> the pumpkin fattening like a golden calf.
>
> (60)

The alliteration of g in this passage helps to unify the lines but also contrasts the gates and gold of heaven with the green garden of an earthier paradise. In "Promised Land" as well Roxy views the journey over Jordan not as a pilgrimage toward the pearly gates but as an excursion on which she is "bound for a bed of white trillium" (61). That poem begins, moreover, with an argument between the decrepit Roxy and God—an argument that Roxy wins:

> The Lord wrinkles up His nose and admits she's right:
> He *had* forgotten her.
> Well, damn, she says. She knew it.
>
> (61)

The humor that marks these lines and Powell's effective use of dialogue are among the many engaging qualities of this volume's narrative poems.

While Aunt Roxy, with her "Methuselan face," yearns for "the promised new flesh" of a resurrected body (62), Powell is less sanguine about that possibility:

> And I think, how heart-breaking and human, how predictable
> really, this longing to salvage and restore the body—
> as if ruin, written on the flesh at birth,
> could be erased once time has washed over it.
>
> (62)

In "Grace," the sonnet variant with which part three concludes, the title denotes not divine providence but the postponement of inevitable mortality:

> Grief for those already gone in from the weather
> counsels us to prize the quiet damage that the living
> must collect—while the sure unknown tethered
> to our constants is still a blessed x.
>
> (49)

The witty mathematical diction may provide a measure of detachment, but it does not evade the fact that "the sure unknown" is death itself, which "looks back at every birth," as Powell had said in "Nativity." For Aunt Roxy, death is a welcome release from her protracted dissolution.

Powell concludes Old & New Testaments not with poems about death but with three poems—"Epithalamium," "Beulah," and "Concordance"—that celebrate marriage. Despite the religious connotations of the last two titles, she portrays not the mystical marriage of Christ and the church but decidedly human relationships. As in "Myth," so in these poems she offers love as humanity's strongest weapon against death, love and memory and a commitment to incorporating the best of the past into the present. In choosing the title "Epithalamium," for instance, Powell places her work in a long tradition in Western poetry, thus reinforcing her insistence on the present's continuity with the past—what she calls in the closing line of "Epochs," "a comfort built from the bones of what is gone" (63). The second stanza of "Epithalamium" again recalls the figure of Mary invoked as an emblem of motherhood in part one, for Powell writes of the special memories "*stored in a mother's heart*," a heart that "keeps and ponders what each child forgets" (66), the verb "ponder" echoing the account of Mary in Luke 2:19. Addressing the newly married couple in the poem's final stanza, Powell re-emphasizes the present's indebtedness to the past. Although each marriage takes on a shape all its own, Powell reminds the couple, "Yet you have not invented love" (66). The couple's relatives and friends remain a part of the newly-weds' relationship. In simple but sustaining daily actions, Powell notes, "you'll recognize the ones who've loved you well, / and know, that here with you, they live" (66).

In "Beulah," yet another variant on the sonnet, a traditional form accustomed to taking love as its subject, Powell depicts marriage's "midlife," with mothers nursing their children and husbands and wives sleeping quietly side by side. The Hebrew word "beulah" means "married." As a place name, the word also suggests the Promised Land, a realm of wholeness and harmony. Powell had used the term earlier in the poem "5103 Beulah Avenue," her grandparents' address. In the book's penultimate poem, however, "beulah" denotes primarily the contentments of marriage and motherhood, of a life "lush with the ordinary: phlox, / daylilies, jonquils, the evergreen" (67). Here, as so often in Old & New Testaments, the delights of nature and of human relationships overshadow the traditional religious meanings of the terms the poet employs.

The book's final poem, "Concordance," confirms this strategic displacement of the sacred by the secular. The word "concordance" typically refers to an alphabetical listing of the key words in a text or in an author's works. The concord to which Powell testifies, however, is that of married love, for she dedicates these lines to her husband, whom she addresses throughout the poem. Yet as a concordance should, this text provides a key to the book as a whole. Like many of the earlier poems, it draws upon a traditional religious vocabulary, including two passages from the Bible. Yet as it builds to its concluding word "Zeal," it applies that term to human love rather than to religious fervor. The poet has not abandoned a sense of wonder ("A Miracle / it seems to me now"), but that miracle originates not in divine intervention in the human sphere but in humanity's own capacity to love (68).

Alicia Ostriker has written of Powell's book, "*Old & New Testaments* is a reclaiming of spiritual texts and traditions for a woman's life in the body—a life of . . . female sexuality, procreation, and nurturing love."[14] While Ostriker's assessment is generally accurate, her use of the word "reclaiming" does not adequately express the radical revision, if not outright rejection, of traditional Christian theology that is both implicit and explicit in Powell's poetry. Ultimately, Powell's book is closer in outlook to Wallace Stevens's "Sunday Morning" than to Chappell's *Midquest*. Her faith rests in what "Epithalamium" calls "the cathedral of air" (66), not in the church and its doctrines; it resides in the landscape of "the dogwood's white witness" (34) and the heartscape of motherhood and marriage. In these superbly crafted poems Powell offers moving testimony to the force of human love. Not an entirely new testament, certainly, but one she powerfully proclaims.

## Notes

1. Such metaphysical dualism is not, of course, unique to Christianity. It is central as well to Platonic and Neo-Platonic thought and to a non-Western religion like Hinduism.
2. Robert Morgan, "Bryant's Solitary Glimpse of Paradise," in *Under Open Sky: Poets on William Cullen Bryant*, ed. Norbert Krapf (New York: Fordham Univ. Press, 1986), 56.
3. Robert Morgan, "A Conversation with Robert Morgan," interview by Suzanne Booker, *Carolina Quarterly* 37, no. 3 (1985): 22.
4. Fred Chappell, "Five New Southern Women Poets," *Georgia Review* 50 (1996): 181.
5. Ruby Riemer, "Theopoetry," review of *Old & New Testaments*, by Lynn Powell, *American Book Review* 17, no. 6 (Aug.–Sept. 1996): 12.
6. Fleda Brown Jackson, "Temples of the Holy Ghost," *Shenandoah* 46, no. 4 (1996): 123, 119.
7. Jeff Daniel Marion, review of *Old & New Testaments*, by Lynn Powell, *Now & Then* 13, no. 3 (1996): 38.
8. Jackson, 126; Chappell, 182. The reviewer for *Publishers Weekly* was unenthusiastic, referring to Powell's "often prosaic coming-of-age poems" and declaring that "this collection lacks an identifying character"; see *Publishers Weekly*, Oct. 23, 1995, 66.
9. Lynn Powell, *Old & New Testaments* (Madison: Univ. of Wisconsin Press, 1995), 3. All further references to Powell's book will be found in page references within parentheses.
10. Jackson, 124.
11. Marion, 37.
12. "Savitri," *Facts on File Encyclopedia of World Mythology and Legend*, ed. Anthony S. Mercatante (New York: Facts on File, 1988), 576.
13. Marion, 37.
14. Ostriker's remark appears as a jacket blurb on the back cover of *Old & New Testaments*.

# Rita Sims Quillen

## Counting the Sums

I must tell them someday
when they are old enough for memory
about the family of twelve
huddled in a creaking cabin
cracked feet oozing
on splintered floors,
show them the photo album
my father by a '52 Ford
his foot propped on the bumper
with the confidence
only the baby boy
in a clan of doting sisters
could even know,
my mother in a red coat
the hat with fur trim
beaming at the camera
with the smile of a survivor
the strong one
in a house of weakness.

A counting of all their sums
requires the telling
of day after day in two rooms
with four kids and an ironing board
$20 in a drawer
two weeks to payday
the mouth-drying grief
of a busted radiator,
a day of stinging sweat
in a heat-dancing field
coal grit
in the back of the throat.

## Deathbed Dreams

*(for Carrie Freeman 1904-1986)*

In the willows and vines along the river
where white stone and heat glow
the fairest child of morning stands
her heart drumming like nighthawk's wings.

Where white stone and heat glow
bees hover and die by the hundreds
her heart drumming like nighthawk's wings,
the child who answers waits.

Bees hover and die by the hundreds
in the stillness just beyond memory
the child who answers waits
suffering in the heat and day drone.

In the stillness just beyond memory
the daughter of daughters feels the past
suffering in the heat and day drone
like a musty blanket of wish and wait.

The daughter of daughters feels the past
knowing the dawn of her very last morning
like a musty blanket of wish and wait
listening to winds, warnings, and foreign tongues.

Knowing the dawn of her last morning
down the long dark well of stopped time
listening to winds, warnings, and foreign tongues
in the willows and vines along the river.

# Staring at the Wind
## A Conversation with Rita Sims Quillen

Don Johnson

Rita Quillen graduated from the public schools in Scott County, Virginia, where her family has lived for five generations. She received an associate's degree from Mountain Empire Community College in Big Stone Gap, Virginia; a B.S. in English education from East Tennessee State University, and an M.A. in English also from East Tennessee. Currently, she is instructor of English at Mountain Empire Community College. Her most recent book is *Counting the Sums*, (Sow's Ear Press, 1995). Other publications are *October Dusk*, a poetry chapbook from Seven Buffaloes Press (1987); and *Looking for Native Ground: Contemporary Appalachian Poetry*, a critical study (Appalachian Consortium Press, 1989). Quillen was also the associate editor of a popular Appalachian literature textbook, *A Southern Appalachian Reader* (Appalachian Consortium Press, 1989). She has been a staff member of the Appalachian Writers Workshop at the Hindman Settlement School and has given readings and conducted workshops at many colleges and universities in the region. A segment of the Appalshop public radio program *Go Tell It on the Mountain: Appalachian Women Writers* featured a reading and interview. Honors and awards include Northeast State's Outstanding Faculty Award in 1991 and the Outstanding Alumni Award from the Virginia Community College System in 1990.

JOHNSON: When did you first become interested in poetry?

QUILLEN: At East Tennessee State University. I had tried to write fiction and I really struggled with it because everybody who read my fiction said, "Um, this isn't fiction. I mean these aren't typical stories. That's not what you do. I think you're a poet." And I thought that was really strange because to me a poet was sort of the highest calling. I'd never put myself in that category, but people kept saying that to me, both teachers and other students, and then Lee Smith. I had submitted a little piece to a competition that she was judging up at the Virginia Highlands Festival, and she wrote on it the same thing, "This is not a story, but what language," you know. And so I started thinking maybe I can write poetry, and I started playing around with it a little bit. The first ones that I wrote, people really responded to and I got published very quickly so that was kind of the motivational side. So I guess really from college.

JOHNSON: And this is from ETSU?

QUILLEN: Yes.

JOHNSON: So you don't remember as a child being fascinated by any particular poems that you read or any elementary school teachers that got you interested in reading poetry?

QUILLEN: Not so much, no. I love to read but I remember that in elementary school I read primarily biographies, for some reason. That's what I got interested in. Of course, there were always poems that I thought were fun, like Lewis Carroll's poems, but I don't have too much memory of teachers emphasizing poetry. I don't remember being exposed to it all that much. I remember much more reading short stories and plays when I got to high school, but not too much poetry.

JOHNSON: Were there any poems that you read when you were at ETSU that just really got you excited or turned some lights on?

QUILLEN: Well, I think just having teachers who were excited about poetry. I do remember Jack Higgs teaching Whitman and appreciating for the first time the fact that poetry was a lot freer than I thought it was. That was a tremendous eye-opener. Finding out that you weren't as restricted as I thought you were in poetry. That's one really powerful experience from undergraduate study that I recall. The other experiences I had as an undergraduate with poetry came about on my own. One teacher at Mountain Empire Community College (you know I was up at Mountain Empire before ETSU), a teacher there when I started showing him some of my poems, said, "Well, you remind me of Fred Chappell." And I said, "Who's that?" and he said, "You never heard of Fred Chappell?" So he sent me off to the library, and I still remember vividly that day walking in, finding that book of poems, and sitting down in the library reading, and before I ever moved flipping back to the start and reading it again and just being dumbfounded that here was somebody writing, first of all very experimental, to me really experimental, poems; yet they were about things I knew about. Those poems struck so close to the bone with me. From Chappell, then, I discovered Jim Wayne Miller and Danny Marion. After I had found Fred's book of poems in the library, I found theirs next to it and I still remember that vividly as a turning point in my life. I can still see the books on the shelf because it just was a revelation to me that you could write poems about Southwest Virginia or Rogersville or any-where and about people that I knew and even just dialect and all those things. I had just never thought about that before.

JOHNSON: Was this after you had started writing some poems?

QUILLEN: I was actually writing stories. I had written a few poems. I didn't think they were very good, but I was showing them along with some of these fiction pieces to one of my teachers and he was encouraging me more to write fiction. He wanted me to try to write fiction, but he did know poetry well enough to introduce me to Fred Chappell and to encourage me to just explore regional writing, you know, which again was something that no one else had ever mentioned to me before.

JOHNSON: Once you had started reading their poems did you consciously try to imitate what they were doing?

QUILLEN: Somewhat. Just thinking about how I had had similar stories or sim-ilar experiences, I tried to sort of write some of those down. Mostly I think I imitated them in the sense of just being myself. For the first time, like I said, I realized it was just like Lee Smith talks about, she couldn't believe it when she saw the name Grundy, Virginia, in a book and it was sort of the same experience for me. I was finally free of all of my pre-conceived limitations about what I could write about and what was appropriate, whether it's for poetry or fiction, because I'd been trying to write like love stories or these really meaningful pieces about death or something, you know, all young writers do. You always look for these big abstract dreams to go after rather than telling the story of what happened on your grandmother's front porch last Sunday. So it was a freeing expe-rience for me finding out.

JOHNSON: Did you go to school on them in terms of stylistic techniques? Did you consciously say, well he did it this way, can I do it that way also, or was it primarily subject matter?

QUILLEN: I think it was more subject matter, trying to find my own way. I would never be so presumptuous as to think I could imitate Fred Chappell's range or his style anymore than I could imitate, say, Danny Marion, who to me is this amazingly sparse sort of succinct writer. I don't think there's very many people who can approach what Danny does. He can make what I call watercolors, you know, just the most subtle poems. I can't do that. I know I can't. My mind just doesn't work that way. So I guess it was more of just in subject matter and in making me realize that I could experiment. I could do whatever I wanted to in poetry. See, that was why I wanted to write fiction, because poetry was too restricted. I couldn't approach what I wanted to approach. That was a totally wrong idea I found out. So, once I discovered them I knew that poetry was my medium, that it was ideal for my very visual way of thinking and seeing drama in the mundane and all those things, that poetry was perfect for that.

JOHNSON: Were you at all discouraged at not having women poets to serve as role models?

QUILLEN: You know, that never crossed my mind. I don't know why. I guess for some reason it didn't seem to me that poetry had anything to do with gender necessarily at the time. It was just painting a picture of the world and it didn't matter whose eyes were looking at it. As time went on and I look back on it, I was sort of surprised, in a way, that I didn't notice that, you know, when you think about it, but it never occurred to me.

JOHNSON: Who might you have looked toward at that time?

QUILLEN: I don't know, George Ella Lyon was already writing some poetry then, but I didn't know about her at that point. Louise McNeill, up in West Virginia, would have been a female poet I could have looked to.

JOHNSON: But a different generation?

QUILLEN: Exactly, a different generation. To me, even though these guys were about ten years older than me, I felt a real connection with them, because they still remembered that world I remembered too, and yet they had moved out of it also into some more academic world. They were all teachers. They were all thinking about the connection, the growing divide between themselves and that old family, particularly like grandparents and things. All those were things that I was very aware of and so again it just didn't dawn on me to think that, well, these are men, so their experience is different from mine or these are men and their way of looking at nature might be very different from mine. That just never occurred to me at the time.

JOHNSON: Most of the women that I've talked with about your poems identify you as having a point of view uniquely female, which is interesting in the light of what you just said. Can you comment on that?

QUILLEN: Well, again, I think it goes back to that I did not try to imitate them, and I certainly would never try to be a man. I have no motivation to try to think like a man. My interest as an artist is to render my world, so it's got to be female, there is no escaping that. But it wasn't something I did self-consciously. I saw them as people who simply told the truth and they were trying to do something beautiful and original in the medium of words and I just try to do the same thing without making gender an issue at all, but just, "Here's my life." I think it's true, that when you look at my writing, there are obviously big differences between it and, say, Fred Chappell's. I think what my teacher was referring to is that we had some of the same concerns for subject matter. But still our way of looking is very different, and I think that's what I got from them. Not that I tried to imitate them other than just to say, "Here's who I am, this is my world, I'm gonna say what I want to say whether anybody is interested in hearing it or not. I'm gonna talk about my world, and if that turns out to have something to do with gender fine, and if it doesn't fine." It just wasn't an issue.

JOHNSON: Do you think you accurately depict your father in "Letter to my Grandfather" and in the title poem of your second book, *Counting the Sums?*[1]

QUILLEN: One aspect of my father, yes. That poem is one I don't think he would ever comment on. That is such a painful thing, his loss of his father when he was very young. And it's only as I have come to mid-life that I've realized what a tragedy that was for him.

JOHNSON: How old was he?

QUILLEN: He was just, like, five years old and he had three other sisters and no men to look up to except his maternal grandfather. He was only alive for a few more years and then he died. So there were no men in his life. He had to grow up without that model and it's been very hard and I just more fully appreciate that now. As a child that never dawned on me.

JOHNSON: It's interesting how we can understand a lot of things that our parents experienced when we get to the ages at which we can remember them going through those experiences.

QUILLEN: Right.

JOHNSON: At forty you can remember things that happened and that you remember when your parents were forty.

QUILLEN: Right.

JOHNSON: And, you think, maybe they weren't so crazy after all.

QUILLEN: It makes a whole lot more sense.

JOHNSON: There's that great poem by Robert Hayden, "Those Winter Sundays,"[2] where he comes to understand the sacrifices his father made. Does your family generally read all your poems?

QUILLEN: Yes they do, and it's real funny. When *Counting the Sums* came out, to say the least, I was concerned. Because that book explores some family things that are pretty touchy. And one interesting thing is that one of the poems in that book (my mother, she was very old fashioned, which has generated a tremendous amount of interest and comment from people) is actually not autobiographical. It's not about my mother, but it's about her generation and a lot of women I knew growing up, not so much my mother, but other women I grew up with. And it's so funny, my mom said when the book came out a couple of people called her and said, "What did you think about that poem? That doesn't sound like you at all. That's terrible. That's a terrible poem." And my mom just laughed and said, "It's called poetic license." She was great, I was so proud of her, I mean, she knew instinctively that *that* was not her, but it obviously it made my father a little uneasy. That's a touchy poem and I didn't mean it to be some kind of male-bashing poem. That's not what I meant it to be, but I think it's a real portrait of how difficult marriages can be, especially in those times when the attitude was, you put on a good front no matter what. There was no such thing as divorce, you know. You played this role. Yeah, that book was touchy, a little bit touchy, but I was proud of their response.

JOHNSON: But at least they read and understood the poems. That's success.

QUILLEN: Oh ,yeah, definitely, and it's not like, I thought so many times about Jim Wayne telling that funny but awful story about his father after his (I can't remember which book it was that came out. I want to say it was *The Mountains Have Come Closer*),[3] and someone asked his dad, well, have you read Jim Wayne's last book and he said, "Hope so." That was his comment and I thought, oh how awful.

JOHNSON: I have a poem called "Carrying Drunks Up River,"[4] where I describe my father at the slate dump drunk, and it never happened. I've never seen my father drunk in my life, but it was appropriate for that poem.

QUILLEN: Right. And you're exploring something there that's a truth even if it's not literally true about your father. You're exploring some great truth, and that's the way I looked at my mother. She was old fashioned. If I had written that poem in a very detached, objective way, it wouldn't have had the power that it has of a child, saying, this was my parent, this is what I now see. It would have lost that power of that voice, of that first person that counts. So I wrote it that way for artistic reasons.

JOHNSON: Sure. Have you had people in the family come up and ask you, "Is this really what you think of us, is this the way you see this situation?"

QUILLEN: No. Like I said, other than some of those conversations with my mom, nobody has ever challenged me. I think most of them have understood that I take license, you know, I play with the facts and so they're pretty much at ease with it, at least so far.

JOHNSON: That kind of leads to my next question. In many of your poems about rural life, the life of the farm wife, it seems as if you're advocating a kind of knowing stoicism, sort of like saying I know life is filled with hard work and heartache, but we must accept it. Would you comment on that?

QUILLEN: Yeah, I guess that's true and I think that, that's a very common attitude among country people. I mean, you occasionally run into the Whitman-esque person who's sort of naked running into trees and romanticizing life on the farm and all of that. You do run into that, but primarily the country people I know and the country community that I was part of was very much that way. If you live in the country you see . . . well, for instance where we lived, we suffered floods on a regular basis. We had animals killed by disease, which has cost us a fortune. You'd have crops ruined in a flash, money problems. Every farmer wrestles with money, which is why farming is a losing proposition. It was just always something, you know, the wind blowing the roof off your barn, and you just sort of have to learn to roll with it. Otherwise, you're not going to enjoy life in the country because you're going to be so busy worrying about the negative things that you can't appreciate. For instance, the twin does who show up at your creek, and all the sort of miraculous things you witness in the country. So you have to just sort of take it as it comes, both the good and the bad, the blessings and the curses or else you're in the wrong place.

JOHNSON: But Counting the Sums is rather short on the miraculous, isn't it?

QUILLEN: That's a dark book, very dark book. It was a dark time in my life. First of all, I experienced a lot of death in a very short period of time, and I think most poets have that period in their lives where you start losing family members. I lost friends. I lost students, young people who were cut down in the prime of life, so that was going on, plus I had young children and a very demanding job. I felt squeezed because I had so many demands on me and yet I wanted to write. That's always been the tension underneath everything else. That was a time when I was depressed a little bit. I realize now looking back at when I read that book I'm kind of like, oh gosh. I was depressed. I was struggling. I was a little bit angry. That's the sort of shake your fist at God book too, just a little bit. And I think now, I haven't written very many poems recently, but if I did they'll be very different. The next ones will be very different from *Counting the Sums*.

JOHNSON: I had read around in this book and of course heard many of the poems, but going back and reading both books straight through several times I was really struck at how dark *Counting the Sums* was. The cumulative effect.

QUILLEN: Yeah, it's a very somber book.

JOHNSON: In another voice, some of the things that you described might be tinged with irony. For example, "Three Men Bury Their Father" The words you say are something like, they needed to be men.

And then there's the woman in the "Prayer of the Mad Farmer's Wife" crying into her pillow, and I think there is another image in the poems of a woman crying into her pillow. Again, that kind of dutiful stoicism. But from another point of view, one might look at those incidents with some irony: "You need to be a man" really wouldn't mean that, but it would be critical of whoever said it. But, there's none of that there. It's straightforward, from the heart: "Everyone is being a man" (32). Even in your poems about children there seems to be an argument for acceptance, of their learning to accept the bleakness. There's a sense that you protect them as long as you can, as you say in "The Unspeakable,"[8] but ultimately, as in "Nexus," you wait for them to connect with the knowledge that the world hurts. Is that a pretty fair summary?

QUILLEN: Yes. One of those poems . . . I think it is "Unspeakable," maybe, really came out of the conversation I was having with a class at Hindman. I was talking to George Ella Lyon, who was directing the class, and Danny Marion was in there, and we were talking about children's literature, and they were talking about how you shouldn't protect children from everything. You shouldn't assume that children's literature is all sunny and happy. I heard myself say, "That's exactly right, as in the case of my children. I think they've always been curious about despair." And when I said it the room sort of turned and looked at me and I just sort of stopped in my tracks and thought, I had never really considered that before. But they do, and maybe it's because I've encouraged that curiosity. I don't know, but I think to come awake as a human being is to appreciate the possibility of despair and of darkness and bleakness. Again, just as I said about the farm life, if you can't appreciate that, if you don't fully feel the despair and the sadness and the ironies, how can you appreciate the opposite too? The joy, the elation, the surprise that life can offer. To me, just being fully open as a person involves a certain comfort level with despair and cynicism, I guess.

JOHNSON: Your poem "Sunday School Lesson" kind of escapes that, though, doesn't it?

QUILLEN: A little bit. That's a really affirming kind of poem. It's really affirming. But notice that where you find that is in nature. Nature in my world that I create and in the world I live in is a very dangerous place. It's very much a mixed bag, but it's where you find the little daily epiphanies as well as the daily tragedies, too.

JOHNSON: If you were to sum up the themes in Counting the Sums, what would they be? We've already talked about stoicism, the flirtation with despair, is there anything else that we missed?

QUILLEN: One thing that struck me after I finished Counting the Sums is how much less it explores nature as a metaphor. It's a much more internal book. It's an exploration of the world of the heart, in a way and there's something to do with aging in that book. That's an underlying theme. Again, I didn't see that until I could come through it, but I think that I wrote this book as I was approaching forty, and even though I was not overtly conscious of that, evidently underneath a lot was going on about the idea of aging, approaching middle age, how women are, as a woman how I would be regarded differently in middle age as opposed to when I was twenty. All of those issues are circling around in there somewhere and they pop up from time to time.

JOHNSON: Yes, that certainly comes up in your, what's the poem about the vessel, being a vessel?

QUILLEN: Oh, "I Used To Be a Teacup."

JOHNSON: Yeah, that pretty much explicitly states that.

QUILLEN: Even the poem "Women in the City" is about that. The young woman goes to the city and for some reason feels surrounded by all these old women, everywhere she turns there are old women, and it becomes a reflection of her. None of these things were things I was at all cognitive of. When I was writing it, I just was putting down what was on my mind and it was only much later, looking back, particularly with three or four poems as a group in there, and realizing that there's a certain amount of vanity working through there or fear of aging. All that's working through that and I didn't see it at the time. I guess I'm just not self-aware enough of my own writing. Whatever comes I put it down and I don't analyze it too much.

JOHNSON: But speaking about aging, I noticed several times the focus on faces that become the faces of people older than you are, or faces that have passed down through the family.

QUILLEN: Again, that was not conscious. I was astonished by that, when I looked back and really realized what it meant, that there was some meaning perhaps that I didn't see at the time. It was evidently what was going on in my subconscious with regard to my own impending milestone.

JOHNSON: Are you more comfortable with that now?

QUILLEN: Oh yeah. I'm fast approaching that age. George Ella says that I should look forward to it. In five more years I turn fifty and I get to stop being a female impersonator.

JOHNSON: I've called this conversation "Staring at the Wind" after a line from your poem "Poets" (10). I really like that image because it describes an intense fixation on something that can't be captured visually. Why would a poet stare at the wind?

QUILLEN: It's just like I say in that poem. She's trying to do the impossible, trying to capture, you know, what it means to be alive on this planet. You can't capture it. It's about living and loving and dying and grieving, and it's too huge, but you keep trying; you keep, as I said, wasting words on it. You keep casting out and trying to get hold of it and you never really do. But it keeps you off the streets, I guess.

JOHNSON: Tell me about "Deathbed Dreams." Why the formal structure in that piece?

QUILLEN: It was just purely on a dare to myself to see if I could do it. I had read, I guess it was, Robert Morgan's pantoum.[5] He's the first one got this started, by the way. I credit Morgan with starting the revolution. He published that pantoum in *Atlantic Monthly* and pretty soon everybody was talking about it and writing them again. It sort of faded into oblivion. So after I read that, I had some of those lines down in another poem and I had been thinking about my grandmother's death because it was very strange the way it happened. I had read his pantoum, and I had watched *A Trip to Bountiful* on the night that she died. When they called me, I was watching that movie and all of that just sort of started going around in my head and so I thought it makes sense that if she were on her deathbed her thoughts would be circling. We had also been reading "The Jilting of Granny Weatherall,"[6] that was the other thing, in my class. I just sat down and just tried to see if I could make it work and I came close. I don't think it's a perfect pantoum by any means, but it works pretty well. It did what I wanted it to do. It surprised me. There were some lines in there that I feel actually came out of the center of the earth. I don't know, they just arrived and they worked and I was really struck by them. So, pretty much one time through, I had it.

JOHNSON: That's impressive.

QUILLEN: Yeah, it was an amazing poem. It was an amazing experience. It still makes chills run down my neck to think about because I just got the lines whole and it was just like automatic writing. Just came out. I said, "Wow." I tried to do it since then but I've never gotten a pantoum that was anything like the power of the language in that one. I guess it was just a one shot deal.

JOHNSON: How about other formal poems?

QUILLEN: I've tried and I'm not very good at them. Usually I'm not that lucky. A man that used to draw cartoons for the *New Yorker*, he found some of my poems somewhere, I forget the story but, he had read *October Dusk* and he wrote to me and said something to the effect, "Don't try forms. Don't be sucked into this new formalism."[7] Because he said when somebody can write blank verse like you can and just do it naturally, free verse, you should just go for it. Don't try to do what doesn't come naturally to you. So, I've not messed with forms too much. I try not to tinker with what my natural bent is and I've pretty much stuck with free verse.

JOHNSON: Are you reading any poems now?

QUILLEN: I try to read my friends. That's about all I can do at this point. I can't get enough time to read like I'd like to. I always try to read anything that Robert Morgan puts out, Michael McFee. I just finished last year Lynn Powell's book *Old & New Testaments*.[8] That's a wonderful book. I really enjoyed that. I haven't been reading as much poetry lately. The last year or so I've been reading more either novels or religious things. I got interested in Kathleen Norris. Do you know the poet who wrote *The Cloister Walk* and *Amazing Grace: A Vocabulary of Faith*?[9] Those are amazing books. They're wonderful. She's a poet who went to live with a group of Benedictine sisters and recorded her spiritual journey with them. It's amazing stuff and it's really sort of prose poems, some of it. But I've been reading that mostly, so I'm a little bit out of touch. I don't read as much poetry as I used to.

JOHNSON: I know that recently you've turned to writing short fiction, abandoning poems for awhile. Why?

QUILLEN: I don't know. I just try not to question it too much. When I finished *Counting the Sums* I knew I was ready to do something different. I had said all I had to say about that, right now. I had these group of women characters that I'd been messing around with, had all these ideas about for years and I finally got really motivated in trying to complete a cycle of stories about them. These women would be of my mother's generation and I worked on those for a long time, and then while I was thinking about those stories I took time to stop and write down a fictional rendering of a family story from Mack's family. He'd been trying to get me to do it for years. He kept saying, "If you want to write fiction, you want to write a novel, write about my grandfather." I knew the story and I knew it was an incredible story but I hadn't just really sat down and tried to write it. But I did finally do that, at least do a sketch, a skeleton sketch of a story about his grandfather. And it just so happened that about the time I finished that they were playing that radio series *Go Tell It on the Mountain* nationwide, and I read a portion of the other stories, the women stories (I call them the Elizabeth stories) on that radio program, and a filmmaker down in North Carolina heard me read and really liked that character, liked the voice, and called me and said, "I'm looking for new material, I'd like to see everything you've got, any fiction, whatever."[10] And, so I sent him everything, including this outline of this family story. To make a long story short, he went nuts over the family story and so for the last year-and-a-half I've been working with him to create a screenplay based on that, which is now finished mostly.[11] We've still got some tinkering to do, but it is finished and it's the most fun thing I've ever done. I love writing for movies. Poets are great for writing for movies because we see everything or we hear it. So I see it on screen and what I've spent a year doing is trying to get him to see it. You know, trying to find a way to communicate to him what this film could look like, what the characters look like, how they move, how they talk, and he's just sort of been pulling it out of me putting it into a script. I've written a few poems in the last year or two, but like I said, not many. I'm just drawn now to this whole narrative thing and the fun side of creating characters and particularly now seeing that film could offer me the opportunity to in effect write poems and fiction all at the same time. So I've loved it. I've had a great time.

JOHNSON: How old are your children now?

QUILLEN: They're teenagers. My daughter is a senior in high school and my son is a freshman. He'll be fifteen on Christmas.

JOHNSON: Either of them fledgling writers?

QUILLEN: Yes. My daughter is very talented. She's got the jazz, big time. She's already got a huge notebook full of poems, and she writes fiction. She's an excellent essay writer. She edits a literary magazine at her school. She went to Governor's School last year on her writing talent and she's looking to go to Hollins following Lee Smith's footsteps.

JOHNSON: So does momma give advice?

QUILLEN: Not too much. No, I just try to encourage her. She's very interested in politics and debate. She's also good at public speaking. So she's done quite a bit of that competing at the state level. She's an actress. She's been in some things. So she's looking to maybe do a double major in, she says, journalism and political science, and she wants to do newspaper work, a big magazine, New York Times, or something like that or she says, maybe going into some kind of government position with an ultimate goal of running for office. So I said fine, whatever, I'm behind you wherever you want to go. Now my son, he likes to read, but he's just beginning to show an interest in writing.

JOHNSON: Has either of them come to you with one of your poems and asked what did you really mean here?

QUILLEN: Yes, my daughter has several times. She's read the poems very carefully and asked me a lot of questions about them. My son just sort of accepts it, and he comes to a reading and listens. I don't know how much of it he takes in. He's one of these kids who loves video games and computers. He's very different. He likes to read science fiction, things like that, you know. He's very proud of me and he's glad I do what I do.

JOHNSON: You've said you've written a few poems recently. Are those in a different vein from Counting the Sums? Do you see yourself coming back to poetry after this movie business?

QUILLEN: Maybe. I would really like to explore another book of poems about mothering. I think I would like to do that someday. Or again, maybe not so much about mothering, maybe about being a girl, being somebody's daughter. I'm not sure which. Maybe from both directions, but the poems that I've written, as I said, the ones in recent months or years, I don't think they're very good. I'm not sure there's much quality there. They tend to be just memory poems, things I've pulled up from somewhere and played around with them some. Memories from childhood that are just now coming back, as you say I guess because you get to that age sort of where your parents were and you suddenly look back at some things with a new perspective. But, yeah, I think I will eventually. I hope that I will. I hope that I'll write more poems. I'd be sad and disappointed to think that I never would because for me, there's a wonderful exhilaration to writing poems that I don't have with fiction. What I found out about fiction is that it's grunt work. That it's really hard and dirty and exhausting and it takes a long time. I was always really fortunate in that and I don't mean that to sound arrogant or anything, it's just the truth. Writing poetry for me is easy. I can do poems in my head. They appear on their own and by the time they come out onto the page I've already worked them out. I don't have a whole lot of rewriting and stuff. I just put them on the page and they're ready to go. That's great. You go "wow" you've got something solid, to look at and feel good about it and you've not sweated or lost too much blood over it. But fiction isn't like that. So probably at some point my lazy bone's gonna kick back in and I'm going to be looking to do something easier again or at least trying to, so I may write some more poems.

JOHNSON: Good, I think we'd all would be disappointed if you didn't write any more poems.

QUILLEN: That's what Michael McFee's been fussing at me for, saying, "You better not abandon poetry. You'll be sorry if you did." So, I don't know, but for right now I'm going to pursue this fiction angle until I at least get that cycle of stories about those women. I want to finish and I'd like to see that in print someday, if I live long enough. Then, after that I'll probably be ready to go back to poems for a while. I'll get that out of my system, whatever it is. Then I'll be ready to go back.[12]

## Notes

1. Rita Sims Quillen, "Letter to My Grandfather," in *Counting the Sums* (Abingdon, Va.: Sow's Ear Press, 1995), 20; and "Counting the Sums," in *Counting*, 21. Subsequent references to Quillen's poems from this book are found in the text.
2. Robert Hayden, "Those Winter Sundays," in *Collected Poems of Robert Hayden*, ed. Frederick Glaysher (New York and London: Liveright, 1985), 41.
3. Jim Wayne Miller, *The Mountains Have Come Closer* (Boone, N.C.: Appalachian Consortium Press, 1980).
4. Don Johnson, "Carrying Drunks Up River," in *The Importance of Visible Scars* (Green Harbor, Mass.: Wampeter Press, 1984), 19.
5. For examples of Robert Morgan's pantoums, see "Audubon's Flute" and "Mica Country" in *Sigodlin* (Middletown, Conn.: Wesleyan Univ. Press, 1990), 4 and 53. Also see "Oxbow Lakes" in *Wild Peavines* (Frankfort, Ky.: Gnomon Press, 1996), 28.

6. Katherine Ann Porter, "The Jilting of Granny Weatherall," in *The Collected Stories of Katherine Ann Porter* (New York: Harcourt, Brace, and World, 1965), 80–89.

7. Rita Sims Quillen, *October Dusk* (Big Timber, Mont.: Seven Buffaloes Press, 1987).

8. Lynn Powell, *Old & New Testaments* (Madison: Univ. of Wisconsin Press, 1995).

9. Kathleen Norris, *The Cloister Walk* (Hudson, N.Y.: Riverhead Books, 1997); and *Amazing Grace: A Vocabulary of Faith* (Hudson, N.Y.: Riverhead Books, 1999).

10. Quillen, "Hiding Ezra," *Go Tell It on the Mountain*, Appalshop Radio Series, Whitesburg, Ky., 1995.

11. Quillen, *Hiding Ezra*, unpublished screenplay.

12. My thanks to Constance Alexander for the transcription of this interview.

# Rita Sizemore Riddle

## *Hole in the Sky*

I hunger for a hunk of hot cornbread
like Mama used to make, with country butter
dripping on the plate, the inside sticky
and the outside crunchy brown. Daddy used
to stand and hope a bit would stick
to the bottom of the skillet when she turned
the pone out upside down. "Hole in the sky, Rita Ann,"
he'd say, and pick a piece of crust left
in the pan, by luck, for me.

They knew what stuck to your ribs
and kept a soul alive. Porch people,
sky-watchers, they could tell when
the signs were right. And what to do
when they were not.

As the day warms, I open the house
and step outdoors. Rocking on this porch
rooted in the mountains, I stare across the ridge
singing the old hymns I've learned here,
words that say there is nothing to fear.

I can't make cornbread like Mama did,
at least, not like she could in Coeburn
when miners struck and blessed the crust
in 1953. My meal's too white and fine.

Daddy said, "You don't need education
to cook a pot of beans." but Daddy, Daddy,
there's more to me than bread and beans
and different signs from loins and feet.

I know something you don't know, Daddy—
my education is higher than yours.
My AAUP beats the hell out of your UMWA.
The record's cracked you played in G;
that damned circle will be broken
and just one rose won't do.

You called water-bread "poor-do"
and ate it anyway. I won't.
I know something you don't know, Daddy:
nothing less than Lear for mourning you:
poor *perdu*, my lost foolk, I know
(With *hey, ho the wind and the rain*)
my hole in the sky let you drop through.


## Potted Ham and Crackers

"We're going home today," he said
when he came in at six a.m.
"These midnight shifts are killing me."

By nine, they'd quit their jobs in Detroit,
packed their clothes in Kroger bags
and nosed the '54 Plymouth down Telegraph Road.

"We'll go to summer school at ETSU,"
he said, as they reached Pound Gap on 23;
"I'll sign my daddy's name again
for a loan at Coeburn Bank."

Next morning her mother
put a paper poke in her hand.
"Potted ham and crackers," she said;
"It's all I have that'll keep."

That night in Johnson City, the loan papers
on the dresser and the stores all closed,
sitting cross-legged on the floor, they ate
the potted ham and crackers, then slept
on the thin mattress, sheetless.

Thirty years later, she opened up a can of potted meat
which smelled of home, and him, and time.
Her mom was right. That's all there was to keep.

# Rita Sizemore Riddle
## A Coal Miner's Daughter on the National Poetry Scene

## Parks Lanier

Rita Sizemore Riddle, born September 26, 1941, in Fleming, Kentucky, was raised on Sandy Ridge in Dickenson County, Virginia, coal country, in a family of a coal-mining father. Earning a Ph.D. in English from the University of Tennessee, Knoxville, in 1971, she began teaching at Radford University, Radford, Virginia, where she is still teaching creative writing, Shakespeare, American literature, and film. Publications include *Soot and Sunshine*, essays and poems (Radford University Occasional Publications Press, 1993); and *Pieces for Emma* (Radford University Occasional Publications Press, 1994). *Aluminum Balloons* (Pocahontas Press, 1996), a book of poetry, includes three poems that won the Appalachian Writers Association James Still Award for Poetry in 1995: "Reunion at the Winter Solstice," "Bargaining for Breakfast with Emma," and "Too Many Widows on Sandy Ridge." Other poems have appeared in such periodicals as *Asheville Poetry Review* and *Pine Mountain Sand and Gravel*. Termed "an Appalachian feminist with a polemic" by David Huddle, she addresses topics not always stereotypically associated with Appalachia.

LANIER: When you were at places like Bread Loaf, MacDowell, and Spoleto, did you find people who envied your Appalachian roots?

RIDDLE: I don't know that they envied my Appalachian roots, but I think a great many of them envied the Appalachian accent; and, of course, the way Appalachians often speak in metaphors or maxims or clever, witty, sometimes hard, cold phrasing, as illustrated by "Post Annum Matris"[1]:

> Rita Ann Sizemore was barren,
> but only after three sons.
>> Then alternate weekends
>> and half-day Christmases.
> An occasional stepson and slivers of real sons
>> sift through her days like stardust.
>> End. Without world.
>> Amen.
>
> (21)

I think sometimes they were shocked but I think they were intrigued with words or phrases that I would use: "We *leave off* quilting for the day" (5). They would think it was original, but I would say, "No, that's what my mother said. Or what everybody said in Appalachia." More than anything else, it was the language that they found fascinating, language, of course, I can't claim originality for. It's language that we learn when we are little. It's plain. It's sharp. Pointed. And sometimes it's as musical as anything in the King James Bible. My accent and the language always attracted attention. It wasn't a negative kind of attention either. It was a "Say that again!" and of course I was quite pleased.

LANIER: We hear stories about people from the region who have been in conflict about their language, usually when they got to public school, perhaps high school. Did that ever happen to you? Was there ever a time when someone corrected you?

RIDDLE: No. I can remember, though, an incident in elementary school which was the other way around. I can remember that I had teachers who would correct me for pronunciations when mine was correct. And I don't mean just "Appalachianisms." I had people in my family who were very, very particular about pronunciation of words. Not an accent type of thing but correctness, a concern for words. Some of my earliest memories of conflict were about my vocabulary as opposed to the vocabulary of some of the people in the community. But to be corrected because I spoke with an Appalachian accent, dropped the -ings, or said things funny, the only time I can remember being a bit shocked about it was well after I started writing. I had written a piece called "The Reward" in which I used the verb "reach," as in "He reached him a dollar bill." At a party, a friend who had read my work said, "I thought it was wonderful that you used this substandard version of the verb 'reach.'" And I thought, "Let me see! This is as normal to me as love or breath." I had had linguistics courses and never been called on the use of the word before. I used it as part of my vocabulary. That was late in my life to be called upon in a congratulatory way for the use of a word that is not in standard use now, to have it treated as a regionalism, when I wasn't even aware of that. So there may be times when I have used words and been impervious to how people might react. I say whatever comes in my language to express what I mean, whether it be Appalachian or medieval.

LANIER: Do you think perhaps this is rooted in your childhood?

RIDDLE: Yes, I notice in my writing that the language comes back in a way I don't use it today, and I will remember Appalachian colloquialisms and some of them may not be considered straight "Appalachian." They would be terms that my father made up, or carried down from his father. I wrote a poem last week, "No Use in Hunting," and used the phrase "small skimption." Everybody has been asking, "What is a 'skimption'?" It's "a little thing, no big deal." I'd better look it up to see if it is listed somewhere, but it won't bother me if it isn't.

LANIER: Lines?

RIDDLE: I wrote,

> These keys I look for
> are just a small skimption.
> No call to worry,
> I'll get some more made.

The other things the narrator lost include two husbands and a daughter, but she says:

> I never lost anything
> I can't live without.

LANIER: And "dimity," now that's not a word everyone is accustomed to hearing these days.

RIDDLE: Yes, that's in "Piecing":

> I lift out tiny dresses,
> piles of dimity, worn by a brother
> and two sisters I never saw.
> Mama lays the scissors down.

(5)

LANIER: That poem also talks about "britches." Any stories about pronunciation?

RIDDLE: When I did *Soot and Sunshine*, I didn't know how many people in the world pronounce "s-o-o-t" as "sut," but we did and do still. A man who introduced me at a reading said he looked in three dictionaries and found three different pronunciations, but could not find that particular pronunciation. I use what was there in my home and community. And if it's a pocket a little different from other parts of Appalachia, then that's what I use anyway because it's what I know and what is most natural to me.

LANIER: Which is more fun, being a coal miner's daughter or being Shakespeare's sister?

RIDDLE: I teach my children—my blood children as well as my students—that there is no such thing as "or." Everything in the world, so far as I know, is "and, and, and." Being a coal miner's daughter and Shakespeare's sister, who lived, who did not die by the wayside as Virginia Woolf pretends, I don't want to cull anything, cast out anything. I don't want to reduce Appalachia to a narrow little alley that doesn't allow me the depth and breadth of everything else that I am. I want to tell the truth of my own childhood, as in "What Cleaving Means":

> My mom tried to tell me about sex
> the year I turned thirteen.
> "A man will want to bite your breasts,
> she warned, "and push hard things
> up into your body.
> Some times you will bleed."
>
> I learned my lesson
> under his hand.
> I found out
> there was more to marriage
> than making beds and biscuits.
>
> (4)

LANIER: There's a touch of the dramatic in so many of your poems. Even "My Parents Pick Blackberries," the opening poem in *Aluminum Balloons*, sets up a scene and concludes with drama worthy of Milton:

> I'm sure that she did eat,
> not knowing that she was eating death—
> his death, her death, our death—
> as she sucked the berry, bit down hard,
> on pungent flesh and bitter seeds.
>
> (1)

RIDDLE: I have always had an eye for drama. I teach a great deal of modern drama right now, and modern poetry. I am seeing a new way of doing things and seeing things that's maybe not as direct as Appalachian writing. I want to be able to do that. If I learn German, I wouldn't mind using German.

LANIER: In thinking about your work, I had concluded "and" is your favorite conjunction. Some poets like "or." Some poets like "but." It's right there in your title, *Soot and Sunshine*. But you have this oxymoron in your other title, *Aluminum Balloons*. Why did that title appeal to you so strongly?

RIDDLE: I have always had a revulsion about these metallic balloons, these commercialized, cheap, trivialized sayings and greetings to each other on these huge air filled metallic-looking balloons that are so popular now. Unlike the others, they don't seem natural. They don't seem to me to be a part of celebration or joy. I think it's negative to have aluminum balloons. There is nothing of joy in them. Aluminum is the material of the twentieth century. My brother tells me he has read that aluminum is causing Alzheimer's disease, shavings are being found in the brain, so he's buying all stainless steel. It's this mercantile, glossy, metallic concept of greeting and loyalty and love, the worst symbol of what we have to offer one another.

LANIER: How does that relate to the poem?

RIDDLE: I use the images of aluminum balloons and hothouse flowers to accentuate the artificial environment of a hospital room, where someone is recovering from a bullet wound as "phlegm bubbles / in his lungs" (36).

LANIER: This poem, like so many, is about someone you have known. In your writing, have you developed a subject basic to your concerns, something perennially important to you?

RIDDLE: Yes. A good deal of my work is concerned with domestic abuse, domestic violence, the breakup of the home. Several years ago, after a divorce, I was talking with someone who told me, "What you need to do is write what divorce means to an Appalachian."

LANIER: Did you?

RIDDLE: "I Want Him to Feel That Desperate" was a start:

> Desperate enough
> to pick up pop cans for money
>      to buy Christmas toys,
> sell last year's coat to Goodwill
> for this week's gas; stop the newspaper,
> cut the cable bill, turn off the lights
> as soon as the sun comes up.

(25)

Scott Russell Sanders says in *Staying Put: Finding a Home in a Restless Universe* (he has values that are very Appalachian even though he is not Appalachian) that staying in the same home for years is almost necessary for a sense of rootedness in our culture.[2] Almost nobody does it. He thinks there is a great loss because people don't do that. To lose a home because of divorce is unthinkable. Maybe this tearing apart of the family, tearing apart the homeplace, in-laws and out-laws being separated, children being separated, may be horrible across the world, but it is unbelievably horrible to an Appalachian family. In Appalachia, when you marry some-one, his family or her family are like blood kin. You marry the family. You divorce the family, you bleed.

LANIER: Was there something which dramatized that truth for you?

RIDDLE: When I lost my brother-in-law in 1976, I didn't know how to mourn for him. He was killed in a backhoe accident, and I didn't know how to mourn for him. But at the funeral home, my own brother walked in and immediately it dawned on me. It's like losing Charles. This is my brother, too, no matter what label you put on it. It's still family. When it's broken, there is a loss that can never really be healed quite again. There are other things to do, other relationships, other riches in a life, but to break the family into parts, into shreds is something I'm concerned with. It leaves emotional problems for children, for people involved in the divorce, in families related to the divorce. It's a sadness. I keep picking at it, work-ing with it. It's an issue, a strand of grief. It's larger than any other grief. People expect death and they get over it. It's final. It's done. But you don't get over divorces and home wrecking. The healing is not clean. It's always scarred. And so I look at those scars.

LANIER: But there is the paradox of making those beautiful poems out of those horrible moments you are speaking of.

RIDDLE: Listen to the last few lines of "Too Many Widows on Sandy Ridge":

> By the time my parents died,
> I'd been married long enough to fear
> another kind of widow: man-less
> woman singled by divorce, left alone
> to pay the bills, cut out the lights.
>
> (17)

Paradise lost, right? The fortunate fall. You buy that, too? It's the paradox of human life, isn't it? The human condition, as my students would say.

We don't always write about happiness. My students say, "Why do we have such dark things to read? Why is American literature so dark?" I say, "You wouldn't know it is so dark if you hadn't seen the good times. If you didn't know the sunshine and how wonderful it is to be loved and to be happy and to be prosperous, you wouldn't know that the injustices and jags of fortune are what they are."

LANIER: When you have a topic about which you want to write, and you are gifted in many forms of storytelling, story and novel writing, essay, and poetry, what helps you determine whether something should be a story or a poem?

RIDDLE: It is not at all a conscious decision. It just becomes incumbent on me to write this "thing." As I write it, it becomes the form it wants to be. Several years go, I felt that it was really over, and I think writer's block comes to a lot of people. But I just knew at that time that it was over. No more writing. I wouldn't be doing any more writing. But I had a writing group meeting that week. I sat down at my computer to force something. I said, "I will write a poem about my Aunt Ruth, because I can always write about my Aunt Ruth." So I lined it out, lined it out until I had about five lines. And then, all of a sudden, as fast as I could write it, it was there in its entirety. It was not a poem. It was not an essay. It wasn't first person narrative. It wasn't my life. I don't know Aunt Mazelfa Carico. And there is no way I can take her and force her into a poem, or force her into an essay, or force her into part of a novel. I can't redo, I can't make this subject or this particular concept over into something else. I can't say, "Let's write a poem about this and then let's write a short story about it." That's not possible for me to do. I think what I have to say, the tone, the attitude that I'm writing in, the significance of what I'm writing . . . very, very much the tone, determine whether this is going to be a poem. Or is this going to be an essay? Or is this going to spread itself out into a novel? For me, these are never conscious decisions. The subject dictates its own form. And I think that's good. Some writers say a person cannot excel in three forms, or even two forms. And that may be true, but for some of us, there have to be different cups to put it in. We have to have different glasses, different sizes, different shapes, for that wine. I would hate to have to choose one. I'd also like to try drama, or a screenplay. Right now, the other three forms, particularly the essay, are big enough cups for me. "God Comes to Roaring Fork" came to me when I began to write a poem about Aunt Ruth.

LANIER: Going to places like MacDowell and Spoleto allowed you to be the solitary singer and the communal participant. Writing is very often a lonely task, but then you have the joy of sharing. How does that help you as a writer?

RIDDLE: There is nothing that inspires writing more, or makes you want to keep on writing more than having a good reading. A reading is a way to connect. It lets me know that my writing is real, that I am connecting. One of the most blessed things about it is that someone, perhaps someone who has not been a writer, will go home and write and say to me the next day, "Listen. Listen to me!" Of course, that makes me feel very humble about my own writing, and it makes me want to continue because, as one of my friends once said, "The surest test of being a writer is to inspire others to write, to tell their tales." I think that's true. The writing and the sharing in a reading is a communal effort that is so worthwhile. A woman at Bread Loaf was shocked that great writers there were reading their work. She said writing was not meant to be read aloud. But to hear the living voice . . . Appalachia has an oral culture. We learn to speak first, we learn to sing probably before we learn to speak. The ministers, the teachers, the old stories we get from the family . . . we had an oral culture before we ever thought much about reading. I think it is extremely important for Appalachian writers, maybe for all writers, to give readings and have contact with people at the readings afterward, to talk with those people. At MacDowell, a woman on the board of directors was surprised that I agreed to give a reading at the library and was willing to go among the audience to talk, visit, and have coffee later. She thought, "Artists don't do that. They just take their money and get out."

LANIER: And you say?

RIDDLE: No, no, it's a sharing. It's a listening to people in the audience to hear what they have to say, to hear what their father said. For me, much of the gratification of being a writer comes in a public reading.

LANIER: Where has your work appeared in the region?

RIDDLE: In *Stitches* and *ALCA Lines*, newsletters disseminated at Radford University. In the *Radford University Magazine*. Further out, in *Pine Mountain Sand and Gravel*, which is an Appalachian group primarily in Cincinnati, Ohio. At *Asheville Poetry Review*, Keith Flynn has done a lot with publishing my poems. From Kentucky, there was a publication called *A Gathering at the Forks: Writings of the Hindman Settlement School Writers Workshop*, to which I contributed an essay and a poem.[3] I've had work in *Cloverdale*, which is a magazine a little farther north. I like to send my work to magazines in the area, though, to find homes for my material in the area.

LANIER: Would you agree that we need to help to sustain those kinds of publications, not just because they are "ours," but because they do good work for people everywhere?

RIDDLE: I think so. Definitely. People who want to be published should definitely sustain publications that support what they are doing. And if they want to be published in *Ploughshares*, they should keep up with those magazines. Reginald Gibbons speaking at Spoleto wasn't exactly complaining. The editor of *TriQuarterly*, he was concerned about the number of young writers who want to be published but have never bought any kind of journal, have never bought a magazine, don't know what is being published in them, don't know the difference between *Asheville Poetry Review* and another magazine. And he says, and he's right, that supporting a magazine, Appalachian or otherwise, is important for writers who want anybody to be published.[4] Today, when the National Endowment for the Arts is threatened with being cut down almost to nonexistence, who is going to support the arts? Who is going to publish? Publishers can't make it without selling their materials. If we don't support those magazines, we'll find that there will be no way we can be heard. I don't think it's going to go Internet.

LANIER: That was going to be my next question.

RIDDLE: It's just kind of alien for those of us who like to see pretty paper and nice copies and have something we can put in the bookcase or show to relatives. But, it may very well be that publishing on the web will be the thing we will have to do in order to survive as writers. What do you think?

LANIER: I don't know. I like books. I like paper. It becomes a contest sometimes between the writer and the demands of the medium. I think you show a wonderful ability to adapt to your medium. The product and the process. It seems to me the process means as much to you as the product. You love the process and you love getting it to the page, and getting the page to readers.

RIDDLE: I have not sent my essay "God Comes to Roaring Fork" out yet for someone to put in hard copy. And I haven't sent it yet to the Internet. I haven't sent it yet anywhere because right now I am enjoying sending it to friends, reading it at public readings. At a university reading, a nursing teacher was quite taken with this particular essay and asked me if she could have a tape for her class on death and dying. There are so many ways we can use these pieces.

LANIER: What is your attitude toward books on tape?

RIDDLE: I would love for somebody to say, "Hey, Rita, I want you to do a good tape, a choice tape of some poems." For the accent, for the reading, that may be one of the cheapest ways to disseminate work. I haven't pursued that, but I think I would like to. It might be cheaper than print.

LANIER: And for the voice?

RIDDLE: It would be superior. It would enrich, enlighten, and make the page live, and I think that's helpful.

LANIER: It could reveal part of your process that goes cold on the page, that process of loving words, loving sounds that you say is such an important component of your writing.

RIDDLE: An audiotape would pick up exactly the way you say it. And not only that, it would pick up the emotion and the passion behind it. I guess good pieces of writing can do that on the page; I'm sure they can. Shakespeare's soliloquies look wonderful on the page. I used to hate anyone who messed them up in performance, but when you hear Richard Burton, they're alive. Literature takes many forms. I think we should experiment with all of them, audio, video, even the Internet. It's also interesting to hear someone else read your work.

LANIER: Has that happened to you? Have you heard your words in someone else's mouth?

RIDDLE: Yes. When I won an essay award in the Irene Leach Contest for "Getting Ready" and went to the Chrysler Museum in Norfolk, there was a young man from Iran who read it to the audience. Of course, he read it in his accent. He couldn't quite get Sandy Ridge, but it was lovely. He called the parents "Mummy" and "Da-i-ddy." But there wasn't a dry eye in the place when he finished. He didn't sound like Sandy Ridge, but it translated. It worked.

## Notes

1. Rita Sizemore Riddle, *Aluminum Balloons* (Blacksburg, Va.: Pocahontas Press, 1996). Poems cited parenthetically in the interview are from this book.
2. Scott Russell Sanders, *Staying Put: Making a Home in a Restless World* (Boston: Beacon Press, 1994).
3. Riddle, "The Reward" [essay], in *A Gathering at the Forks: Writings of the Hindman Settlement School Writers Workshop*, ed. George Ella Lyon, Jim Wayne Miller, and Gurney Norman (Wise, Va.: Vision Books, 1993), 316; and "Potted Ham and Crackers" [poem], *Gathering*, 318.
4. Reginald Gibbons, lecture (presented at the Spoleto Writers Symposium, Spoleto, Italy, July 1998).

# Bettie Sellers

## *Brasstown Valley*

How fair the mountains
when willows green-out on the valley floor,
feathery light against spruce and pine;
and Jack-in-the-Pulpit thrusts his red-tipped spikes
up through warming leaf mold.

How fair the mountains
when sourwood waves spicy white flags
to tempt the roving bees,
and blue mid-summer's haze hides the distant
ridge indistinct as behind a soft veil.

How fair the mountains
when autumn unfolds a patch-work quilt
of red and gold and brown;
when day is warmed and yellow to touch,
and nights come crisp and cool.

How fair the mountains
when pines, ice-sparkled, bend on Cedar Ridge;
when February snow has hushed all sound
except a passing crow, and Brasstown waits,
asleep in the winter sun.

## Complaint to Betelgeuse

I used to know that stars were stars
and stayed wherever in that distant space
their ordered orbit was. The sky
was snug with Cassiopeia's Chair,
and night had big and little bears to hunt.

Then, winking moving lights began to stitch
an arch from Sunset Ridge to Raven Cliffs—
planes to Birmingham and points beyond
with travelers drowsing past sleeping hills
folded like dark velvet, with ribbons wound
for lake and stream, silver in reflected light.

Now, satellites invade the ridge—
the star I thought was Venus rising
keeps on rising out of sight
to bring the morning's news—and wars
are instantaneously played on beams
that tear Orion's belt, divide Andromeda.

# Stories of the Land, Family, and God
## The Poetry of Bettie Sellers

Robin O. Warren

"**P**oetry is not anything strange," says Bettie Sellers, "it's what I am living, thinking, doing today."[1] Writing the stuff of everyday life has been fruitful for Sellers; she has written seven books of verse: *Westward from Bald Mountain* (n.p., 1974), *Appalachian Carols* (n.p., 1976), *Spring Onions and Cornbread* (Pelican Publishing Company, 1978), *Morning of the Red-Tailed Hawk* (Green River Press, 1981), *Liza's Monday and Other Poems* (Appalachian Consortium Press, 1986), *Satan's Playhouse* (n.p., 1986), and *Wild Ginger* (Morning Glory Ink, 1989).[2] In 1997 her neighbor in Young Harris, Governor Zell Miller, appointed her poet laureate of Georgia. Pervading her poems, says Sellers, are the traditional southern concerns for God, place, family, and stories.[3] Sellers first began to write verse almost four decades ago when she moved to Young Harris, Georgia, where she still lives today. "It was perhaps a magic the valley had," she says, that first inspired her to write.[4] Maybe so, but that magic is invested with her own sensitivity and respect for where she lives.

Like much of Appalachia, North Georgia has not always done well by its writers, especially those who came from elsewhere, as Sellers does; thus, her achievement stands even higher when compared to that of her peers. Lillian Smith lived in Rabun County, next door to Sellers's own Towns County. Though Smith fought bravely and tirelessly against the supremacy of white men, she never deigned to write about her neighbors. According to her biographer, Anne Loveland, Smith felt mostly contempt for the people of Rabun County; yet this disdain even creeps into Loveland's account of Smith's life. For instance, she describes the Rabun County residents whom Smith and her family met when they moved from Jasper, Florida, to North Georgia in 1915: "impoverished and backward, they [Rabun County residents] made a meager living farming submarginal land or selling moonshine whiskey."[5]

When James Dickey set his novel *Deliverance* in Rabun County in 1970, he created characters even more depraved and empty-headed than the people Smith and Loveland described. Dickey's tale of four suburban Atlanta men's disastrous weekend on a North Georgia river soon to be dammed needs no retelling. All the hoary stereotypes of the worst Appalachian writing are there, though: a fecund, lush, nature peopled and spoiled by physically and mentally maimed Anglo-Saxons, one of whom plays a banjo. As Allen Batteau has shown, outsiders like Dickey and (to a lesser extent) Smith have created the idea of Appalachia; consequently, more than reflecting any real part of the southern mountains, the idea serves the needs of those outsiders better than it does the mountaineers themselves. Three symbols, Batteau has said, inform the image of Appalachia in people's minds: beautiful, pristine nature, a prolific folk culture, and ubiquitous poverty.[6]

Other writings about North Georgia lend dignity to the mountains' people in all their virtues and failings; the poetry and novels of Byron Herbert Reece, the Foxfire Project, and the poetry of Bettie Sellers, for example, treat the region and its natives with respect. William R. Ferris, an anthropologist, has written that a place and its people can be studied "from the outside, as anthropologists often do, entering cultures and places foreign to their own, or from the inside, as artists and writers have often done."[7] Though an outsider, Sellers has more than one personal connection to North Georgia. First, her grandmother, the daughter of a Methodist circuit rider, grew up in White County's Nacoochee Valley and graduated from Young Harris College in 1889. When Sellers was a child near Griffin in the Piedmont, her grandmother often told her about her own upbringing in North Georgia. Second, Sellers's husband Ezra also grew up in North Georgia and graduated from Young Harris College, where he was Byron Herbert Reese's student and later his friend. For the first two decades of their marriage, Bettie and Ezra lived in La Grange and Athens, Georgia. While Ezra taught at La Grange College, Bettie attended classes and graduated in 1958 with a B.A. in English. Later, when Ezra moved to the University of Georgia, she earned an M.A. in English, finishing in 1966. Bettie and Ezra then moved to Young Harris, where her husband accepted a position in the art department in his alma mater and Bettie taught English.[8]

Perhaps because of these connections, Sellers says her move to Young Harris "was like coming home to a place I had never seen before."[9] Young Harris may also have seemed like home since it was rural, just as Sellers's childhood home near Griffin was. "I am sure my fellow feeling for these hills comes in part from having grown up on a farm in middle Georgia," she has said.[10] In her second collection, *Spring Onions and Cornbread*, Sellers looks back at her childhood, partly to show her children "what it was like when Mama was little."[11] Sellers's family kept a kitchen garden and raised a few cows and pigs, but the main source of their sustenance was cotton, the cash crop. *Spring Onions and Cornbread* recalls scratching out a living on a small farm, with work and play and eating and sleeping following the seasons. Sellers's childhood had its joy, but it also had its anguish and fear, especially when the cotton failed to make and her father had to find other ways to raise some cash. "Country Store" recalls that kind of year:

> Sometimes during the lean years
> when the mortgage hung like a thunder cloud
> over Septembers, Dad put up a little store
> on the highway. Those of us big enough
> to make change sold crackers and sardines,
> gas and sacks of chicken feed
> afternoons after school and on Saturdays.[12]

Dusty country roads leading to town, farmland watered by swiftly running creeks and dotted with poplars and pines, cavernous barns filled with horses, hay, cows, chickens, or a cat constitute the settings for the poems in *Spring Onions and Cornbread*.

More than a few readers have mistaken Sellers's Piedmont farm in *Spring Onions* for one in the mountains. Sellers herself understands the confusion. "Rural scenes and the kinds of people who live and work in them are much the same no matter where they lie geographically," she says.[13] Perhaps that is an exaggeration; but, even given their occasional nostalgia, Sellers's poems about her childhood show that her raising helped make her a better poet of Appalachia. Through her verse runs a respect for nature, sometimes as provider and other times as destroyer, for land touched and untouched by human hands, and for hard physical labor itself. Sellers's is a far different picture of the mountains than Dickey's *Deliverance*, with its four suburban men confronting their fears and phobias against a green, pristine backdrop. Though Dickey often hunted and fished in North Georgia, he never made a living there; he only knew the outdoors as a tourist. Richard White, the historian, has described how urban environmentalists' perceptions are shaped because their pleasure, not their livelihoods, comes from the out-of-doors. In his aptly titled essay, "Are You an Environmentalist, or Do You Work for a Living?" White notes that not only do environmentalists fail to see the land as the ultimate giver of life, but they also often contemptuously dismiss the people who make their living directly from it.[14] Dickey falls into that trap, while Sellers does not, perhaps partly because of what she learned growing up. Even though agriculture had lost its ascendancy in North Georgia by the time Sellers moved to Young Harris, her own childhood on the farm probably helped her understand her new home better.

Alluding to William Faulkner, Sellers has often said that a writer must tell of the place she knows best: her own little "postage stamp" of soil.[15] When she moved to Young Harris, Sellers paid heed to the natural world more and more, and she began to record her observations in verse, which later appeared in her first book, *Westward from Bald Mountain*.[16] Bald Mountain is the common local name for Brasstown Bald, Georgia's highest peak, which looms over the Young Harris campus. The poems in this first collection observe the passing of the seasons and paint vivid pictures of flora and fauna. In "Brasstown Valley," the culminating poem of the collection, for example, she rejoices at the changing of the mountains through each new season:

> How fair the mountains
> when willows green-out on the valley floor,
> feathery light against spruce and pine;
> and Jack-in-the-Pulpit thrusts his red-tipped spikes
> up through warming leaf mold.
>
> (49)

The poem is unabashedly romantic; but then Sellers, like most of us, sees mountains as Wordsworth ("a Mountaineer by habit," he called himself) and others two centuries ago taught us to see them today.[17] "Brasstown Valley" and the other poems of *Westward from Bald Mountain* are not just warmed-over romanticism, though. At the heart of their power is Sellers's specificity. "I believe in naming," she says. "People have names; plants and animals should too. I tell my students, don't show me a bird in a tree, show me a cardinal in a pine."[18] As William Blake once said, "To Generalize is to be an Idiot. To Particularize is the Alone Distinction of Merit."[19] In her verse, Sellers closely observes the named world she lives in: Double Knob, Brasstown Bald, Raven Cliffs. She describes Indian pipe, plantain, lamb's tongue, wild ginger, joe-pye weed, rufous-sided towhees, killdeers, screech owls, and monarch butterflies.

Without specificity, Sellers cannot consider what to her is a central question: "What is it about the land that impinges upon the person; what has it done to me and to others?"[20] In "A Mortal State," from *Wild Ginger*, the land changes slowly, underneath Sellers's own transient presence:

> I press my littleness
> against Cedar Ridge,
> feel the mountain's
> slow changing,
> my own swift pass.[21]

---

Fleeting as her passage on earth is, though, she is aware that heedlessness can wreak harm. "Complaint to Betelgeuse," in *Morning of the Red-Tailed Hawk*, mourns the loss (to vision) of brightly twinkling constellations that once stood out clearly against dark night skies:

> I used to know that stars were stars
> and stayed wherever in that distant space
> their ordered orbit was. The sky
> was snug Cassiopeia's Chair,
> and night had big and little bears to hunt.
>
> Then, winking moving lights began to stitch
> an arch from Sunset Ridge to Raven Cliffs—
> planes to Birmingham and points beyond
> with travelers drowsing past sleeping hills
> folded like dark velvet, with ribbons wound
> for lake and stream, silver in reflected light.[22]

For all the beauty of its mountains and its skies, North Georgia is not a place apart; and the satellites, for good or ill, tie it in more closely with Atlanta, Birmingham, and Kosovo.

On writing poetry, Sellers remarks, "a poet has to visualize, to imagine, to put herself into a place."[23] Putting herself into North Georgia means watching autumn's falling maple leaves, winter's first snow, and spring's new grass, as well as night skies cluttered by new lights. As the final lines of "Moment at Dusk" declare, however, she still finds strength and solace in her home ground: "My eyes / trace the distance to the farthest star— / but the mountain holds my feet in place" (*Wild Ginger*, 69).

Sellers writes not only of the land but also of the people and families who live on it. Her poetry shows that in addition to physical location, communal and familial relationships provide part of the continuity of Appalachian life. Some of the people who populate her poems are those who make up the Young Harris community. "I came to know the people and hear their stories," she says.[24] Lovick Adams, professor of humanities, is one of those who regaled her over the years with local lore. Indeed, she calls him the "oral historian of the valley" and took delight in watching him work his garden after she began to teach at the college.[25] She wrote "From My Window" in *Westward from Bald Mountain* on the occasion of his ninety-fourth birthday:

Old man, I watch you
across the greening valley;
your spring planting feeds
my soul with scarlet dahlias.
I shall mourn them when you die.

(27)

Her students too sometimes figure in Sellers's work. Always evident in the poems about those she has taught is a concern for their well-being. That heart-felt interest remains even though she has retired now; former students continue to seek her advice, and she encourages their efforts.[26] She recognizes, however, that she cannot always help those under her tutelage; thus, "For a Student Withdrawing" in *Wild Ginger* shows sadness and frustration at being unable to do anything for a disturbed and possibly suicidal young woman:

She has wrung the leaving dry,
collected all the salt drops
in her belljar for future drowning.
She hugs it close under her coat,
warm against the snow
mazed by boot soles.

(28)

Sellers writes too of families, their joys and sorrows. The birth and death of children; relationships between husbands and wives, between parents and children or between brothers and sisters; divorce; incest; and fratricide are all part of her poetry. "Writing is a terrible, awesome responsibility," Sellers says; hence, she does not shy away from the pain that is sometimes part of family life. "Sarah's Quilts" from *Liza's Monday*, for example, relates the story of a mother gathering stones to mark the grave of one son who has been killed by the other.[27] Describing "Sarah's Quilts" as "a sort of Cain and Abel story written in Dante's terza rima," Sellers remarks that before a poet can write abstractly, she must learn to write using the old forms.[28] Since terza rima is one of the most difficult of the traditional forms to master, it is no wonder that Sellers took nine months to write "Sarah's Quilts" and the other poems that make up the inter-connected narrative of *Liza's Monday*.[29]

"Sarah's Quilts" and the other poems in *Liza's Monday* stand out not just for their forms or for what they reveal about families; they also show the importance of religion in the lives of their characters. Explaining the centrality of God in her writing and that of fellow Towns County writers Byron Herbert

---

Reece and Zell Miller, Sellers says, "Our fathers brought their several daily ways, but they also told us how to weave the roots of a family with an even older past that holds the story of faith they carried in their Bibles wherever they might have wandered."[30] At the turn of the century, Appalachia was faced with the supreme irony of being a deeply Christian area proselytized by mainline Protestant missionaries.[31] At that time, the faith of the region was different in many ways from that propounded by the large, metropolitan Protestant churches. Loyal Jones says that Calvinism, "with its dim view of the human condition," persisted in the mountains, while other parts of America had largely abandoned it.[32] In an essay on the religion of the Old South, Richard Weaver, the conservative prodigy of the Nashville Agrarians, perhaps generalizes from his own experience growing up in Weaverville, North Carolina, in the mountains. Weaver says that the heart of southern faith was "the attitude of orthodoxy . . . a simple acceptance of a body of belief." Southern religion, says Weaver, was less speculative and analytical than it was "a matter of profession."[33] Still, as Deborah Vansau McCauley and Jones show, an unwillingness to analyze a faith does not mean that it is lived or acted on without thought or reason.[34]

Running through Sellers's poems is a profound sense of faith and sin. Drawing upon biblical stories and names for inspiration, the narrative poems in Liza's Monday portray a region steeped in faith, though one that by no means makes its believers perfect. Thus, Aaron and Sheba, Mary and Cal all succumb to adultery as do their Old Testament counterparts, David and Bathsheba.[35] Eunice and her sister fight over their mother's heirloom quilts after she has died in much the same way that the biblical characters Jacob and Esau fight over their father's blessing before he dies.[36] Leah patiently lives a lonely life devoid of romantic love since shy, uncertain Nathan cannot bring himself to profess his affection for her; similarly, the Leah of Genesis lives with the knowledge that her husband Jacob loves her own sister, Rachel, more than he loves her.[37] As already mentioned, one of Sarah's boys kills his brother just as the biblical Cain kills his brother Abel, and throughout the whole narrative of Liza's Monday, Preacher Enoch professes an Old Testament religion featuring a vengeful God.[38] "Enoch Preaches at Gumlog" serves as an apt illustration:

> "Jehovah God, convict these miserable sinners,
> bring them to their knees." Mid-morning sun
> strikes new fire from his birthmark swollen as
> blue veins that pulse distended, fierce around

his eyes. "Conceived in mortal sin, we all
are filled with wickedness, dependent on
Your Mercy, damned without Your Grace. Fall
down, you sinners, put your faces on the ground."

(13)

Yet Sellers does not speak solely through Preacher Enoch. Indeed, she notes with some asperity that people in the "Bible Belt" are all too often judgmental.[39] Accordingly, much of her work concerns itself with a "sense of sin and retribution," but a large part also addresses "the possibility of repentance and redemption."[40] Hence poems like "Enoch Preaches at Gumlog" may reveal a harsh and unbending God, but a poem like "Leah's Prayer in August" in *Wild Ginger* portrays faith in a loving God:

In Him no darkness
when the sky is strung with stars
from Raven Cliffs to Sunset Rock,
when fireflies gather distant light
and wing it down to fingers' reach.

(70)

Explaining the biblical allusions that pepper her work, Sellers says, "I have hundreds of Bible passages in my head. You memorize enough, and they have to come out."[41] She cites, for example, the book of Genesis as one inspiration for her long poem, *Satan's Playhouse*. Though published as a separate volume, *Satan's Playhouse* is actually a prologue to the poems of *Liza's Monday*. Her other inspiration came when she awoke to "a dream or a vision" one early morning in January 1981. In a semi-conscious state, she watched as Satan passed through the Young Harris Valley on his way to exile, leaving in his wake a legacy of evil and hard work. The dream led her to think of the pain, grief, and hardship with which women in particular would have had to contend after the devil's visit. The idea for *Satan's Playhouse* engendered others, which in turn became the narrative poems in *Liza's Monday*.[42]

If Sellers relies on the Old Testament for inspiration, she also turns to the New Testament for ideas, as her book *Appalachian Carols* shows. Written to celebrate the birth of Jesus, these poems, like those in *Liza's Monday*, take a biblical subject and transfer it to the mountains of North Georgia. Local flora and fauna imbue these poems with the same sense of place felt in the rest of Sellers's work. The narrator of "Appalachian Carol #1" recalls a little boy who wonders what he would do if Jesus were born in his valley:

If the Christ Child should come to our mountains,
his birth angel-told in these vales,
I would thatch his stable with pine boughs
garnered by steep winding trails.[43]

Sellers attributes her affinity for biblical subjects to the fact that they make for such good storytelling. Likewise, she cites the Greek myths, Dante's poetry, and Shakespeare's plays as fertile sources to which she returns again and again. She recalls her mother reading the classical myths out loud to her as a child and reading voraciously on her own.[44] Attending a performance of *The Merchant of Venice* put on by some traveling players for her elementary school when she was in the third or fourth grade, however, caused her to "fall in love with the sound of words and the way [they] taste and smell" and come together to form stories.[45] "The Day Dick and Jane Bit the Dust" in *Spring Onions and Cornbread* chronicles this first experience with Shakespeare:

I must have been ten the spring
a traveling troupe came to tread
the creaking boards at Orrs Elementary.
"The Merchant of Venice" it was—
and the country girl soared off,
brief in hand, into a grease-paint world.

(26)

Local, personal memory and stories, both ancient and recent, also figure in Sellers's verse. "Our ears have heard the rich stories that tie us to the past," she says. "Oral tradition . . . is the stuff of poetry and fiction, the source for telling and re-telling for all of the generations that we can remember."[46] Thus, her poems relate tales told to her along the way as they simultaneously tell their own stories. "Ghost Flowers," in *Westward from Bald Mountain*, for example, recounts the legend of a dispossessed people, even as it describes finding a hauntingly beautiful early spring wildflower in the woods:

Beneath the pines,
a cluster of tiny Indian Pipes
grows without chlorophyll,
white against the wet black soil—
like small Cherokee children,
torn from freedom and the mountains,
paled in faded lodges
by rocky Oklahoma streams.

(15)

Writer John Elder speaks to the ways that the natural world teaches about history when he says, "nature always has a past, and an awareness of natural history includes and lifts up into coherence the history both of individuals and of humanity as a whole."[47] Since the Cherokee had lived and farmed in the mountain valleys of North Carolina and North Georgia until their removal in 1838, memories of them still abound in local stories; not surprisingly they surface in Sellers's poems. "Indian Corn" in *Spring Onions and Cornbread* also focuses on the Cherokee; it relates their removal while at the same time showing country children at play: "We played at Creeks and Cherokees, / found arrowheads and potsherds in plum thickets / where the Indians used to plant grains . . ." (47). Like others, this poem recalls a history of violence and banishment.

Other poems tell stories that are just funny. "Don't Send Me Off Like Some Three-Legged Dog" in *Liza's Monday*, for example, describes John Lowe's efforts to have a miniature coffin made for a leg he loses in an accident: "The decorated coffin graced the corner // of his room for forty years" before he finally went "to join his other leg" (5). In the same vein, "Miracle at Raven Gap" relates how Mary Dean, "pale and thin," just wishes for "a mess of greens" before she dies. Her kindly neighbor Nell obligingly brings over a plate, but

> Next morning, Nell thought ghosts could walk.
> She started, gave her head a scratch
> when out her window saw at dawn
> Old Mary digging in her turnip patch.
>
> (23)

"I am a damn good storyteller!" Sellers says, and it shows.[48] Most of all, she credits her grandmother for both her way of telling stories and the stuff of many of them. "Of Stories Told in a Garden," from *Morning of the Red-Tailed Hawk*, is a fitting tribute to her revered matriarch: "It was my grandmother's stories, and visions / of running away to Lapland / that made me write at all" (52).

Sellers continues to write poems that tell stories of the land, families, and God in the Young Harris Valley. More than half of the poems she chose to share at a recent reading were written since the publication of her last book, *Wild Ginger*.[49] "Everywhere you turn," she says, "there's a poem to write."[50] Since she has spent a good bit of her time since retirement traveling—either to give readings, to instruct Elderhostel students, or for her own enjoyment—Sellers's poems have sometimes wandered farther afield. She still returns, however, to the same valley that enfolded her in its embrace thirty-four years ago. As she says in *Morning of the Red-Tailed Hawk*, "I have planted my roots deep into mountain granite, / valley soil" (93). That fertile soil has yielded a rich harvest, and that solid rock has held her in place.

## Notes

1. Bettie Sellers, keynote address (presented at the Three Arts Club, Cornelia, Ga., Nov. 5, 1998).
2. References to particular poems are found within the text.
3. Bettie Sellers, lecture (presented at Piedmont College, Demorest, Ga., Apr. 9, 1999).
4. Bettie Sellers, interview by author, Young Harris, Ga., Mar. 10, 1999.
5. Anne C. Loveland, *Lillian Smith: A Southerner Confronting the South* (Baton Rouge: Louisiana State Univ. Press, 1986), 9–10.
6. James Dickey, *Deliverance* (New York: Houghton Mifflin, 1970); Allen Batteau, *The Invention of Appalachia* (Tucson: Univ. of Arizona Press, 1990), 6–8. See also Rodger Cunningham, *Apples on the Flood: Minority Discourse and Appalachia* (Knoxville: Univ. of Tennessee Press, 1987), 122–31; John C. Inscoe, "Appalachian Otherness, Real and Perceived," in *The New Georgia Guide* (Athens: Univ. of Georgia Press, 1996), 166–70; J. W. Williamson, *Hillbillyland: What the Movies Did to the Mountains and What the Mountains Did to the Movies* (Chapel Hill: Univ. of North Carolina Press, 1995), 155–67.
7. William R. Ferris, "Region as Art," in *Regional Studies: The Interplay of Land and People*, ed. Glen E. Lich (College Station: Texas A & M Univ. Press, 1992), 3. Article is 1–6. See also the geographer Yi-Fu Tuan's discussion of the differing perspectives of "visitor and native" in Yi-Fu Tuan, *Topophilia: A Study of Environmental Perception, Attitudes, and Values* (Englewood Cliffs, N.J.: Prentice-Hall, 1974; reprint, New York: Columbia Univ. Press, 1990), 63–66.
8. Bettie Sellers, "Westward from Bald Mountain," in *Bloodroot*, ed. Joyce Dyer (Lexington: Univ. Press of Kentucky, 1988), 234.
9. Sellers, interview by author.
10. Sellers, "Westward from Bald Mountain," 238.
11. Sellers, interview by author.
12. Bettie Sellers, *Spring Onions and Cornbread* (Gretna, La.: Pelican Publishing Co., 1978), 50. Subsequent references to this volume will be noted parenthetically in the text.
13. Sellers, "Westward from Bald Mountain," 238.
14. Richard White, "'Are You an Environmentalist, or Do You Work for a Living?'" in *Uncommon Ground: Rethinking the Human Place in Nature*, ed. William Cronon (New York: W. W. Norton, 1995), 171–85.
15. Sellers, interview by author.
16. Sellers, "Westward from Bald Mountain," 236.
17. See Marjorie Hope Nicolson, *Mountain Gloom and Mountain Glory: The Development of the Aesthetics of the Infinite* (Ithaca: Cornell Univ. Press, 1959; reprint, Seattle: Univ. of Washington, 1997). Wordsworth's self-appellation appears on 12.
18. Sellers, interview by author.
19. David Perkins, introd. to *English Romantic Writers* (New York: Harcourt Brace Jovanovich, 1967), 9.
20. Sellers, interview by the author.
21. Bettie Sellers, *Wild Ginger* (Atlanta Morning-Glory Ink, 1989), 74. Subsequent references to this volume will be noted parenthetically in the text.

22. Bettie Sellers, *Morning of the Red-Tailed Hawk* (Univ. Center, Mich.: Green River Press, 1981), 17.
23. Sellers, keynote address.
24. Sellers, "Westward from Bald Mountain," 237.
25. Bettie Sellers, interview by Stephen R. Whited and Frank Gannon, *Habersham Review* 8, no. 1 (1999): 15–22. As Sellers was leaving from her interview with Whited and Gannon, she noted that she was going to meet with a former student now doing graduate work at the University of Georgia who wanted Sellers's "stamp of approval" on her thesis; see 19.
26. Sellers, keynote address.
27. Bettie Sellers, *Liza's Monday* (Boone, N.C.: Appalachian Consortium Press, 1986), 3.
28. Sellers, interview by Whited and Gannon, 15.
29. J. A. Cuddon defines terza rima as "a series of interlocking tercets in which the second line of each one rhymes with the first and third lines of the one succeeding, thus: aba, bcb, cdc." Although Dante, Chaucer, and Boccaccio favored the form, few other poets have chosen to use the difficult rhyme scheme. See J. A. Cuddon, *A Dictionary of Literary Terms* (Oxford: Basil Blackwell, 1991), 961–62. Sellers wrote "Sarah's Quilts" with a slight modification on the Italian poet's preferred form; she added an unrhymed fourth line in each stanza.
30. Bettie Sellers, "Westward from Bald Mountain: Valleys for Writers" (lecture presented at the annual meeting of the Georgia Humanities Council, Atlanta, Georgia, 1998), 1–2.
31. Henry D. Shapiro, *Appalachia on Our Mind* (Chapel Hill: Univ. of North Carolina Press, 1978), 46–57.
32. Loyal Jones, *Faith and Meaning in the Southern Uplands* (Urbana: Univ. of Illinois Press, 1999), 4.
33. Richard M. Weaver, "The Older Religiousness in the South" (1943), in *The Southern Essays of Richard M. Weaver*, ed. George M. Curtis III and James J. Thompson Jr. (Indianapolis: Liberty Press, 1987), 134–35.
34. Deborah Vansau McCauley, *Appalachian Mountain Religion: A History* (Urbana: Univ. of Illinois Press, 1996).
35. See 2 Samuel 11:2–5.
36. See Genesis 27:1–41; note also that the two boys had "struggled together" within Rebekah's womb before their birth (Genesis 25:22) and that they had fought over their birthright as young adults (Genesis 25:29–34).
37. See Genesis 30:16–30.
38. See Genesis 4:2b-8.
39. Sellers, keynote address.
40. Sellers, "Westward from Bald Mountain," in *Bloodroot*, ed. Dyer, 240.
41. Sellers, interview by author.
42. Sellers, "Westward from Bald Mountain," in *Bloodroot*, ed. Dyer, 239.
43. Bettie Sellers, *Appalachian Carols* (n.p., 1976), 10.
44. Sellers, interview by author.
45. Sellers, interview by Whited and Gannon, 19.
46. Sellers, "Westward from Bald Mountain: Valleys for Writers."
47. John Elder, *Reading the Mountains of Home* (Cambridge: Harvard Univ. Press, 1998), 101.
48. Sellers, interview by Whited and Gannon, 21.
49. Sellers, "Westward from Bald Mountain: Valleys for Writers."
50. Sellers, interview by author.

# Betsy Sholl

## *Lament*

Spring
and a delicate depression
swells within you—
all this tenderness
falling like rain, seeds
onto asphalt

You drive
and see tree limbs
that have hung stiff all winter
begin to blur

At first you think it's your eyes

You close them at night
then in darkness you can see
magnolias with tiny buds
like stars on their branches
incredibly distant and sparse

You walk
and the slight tinge of green
growing on willows across the field
seems more like rain
like dusk or fog dripping its veil

All this tenderness
and no place to go

You enter your house alone
hair wet, arms laden
with unbloomed forsythia sprigs
darkened by rain—trying to pretend
it is not always yourself
who is last, hardest to open

# Appalachian Winter

1

I sit in darkness
beside the stove, rocking

like Gretel come back alone
to the old, tight place—
away from her father and brother now,
lonely as the witch herself.

I stoke the fire.

When I close my eyes
the forest returns. Flickers of trail
disappear like snakes under rocks,
ledges drop sudden as guillotines.

I see that others who came here before me
have left no more of themselves than
pieces of chimney crumbling like bread.

2

The change I want I cannot name—
perhaps the ability to live anywhere
not fearing the little shacks
scattered throughout the hollows
where women stare, grim with silence,
growing thinner each year.

I have crawled through briars
until I cannot recognize
the woman on my face.

I have cut stems, set stalks on fire.
Nights I dream of luring children
to join me.

These mountains were opened by men
unashamed of slaughter, mapped
by the crisscrossing of bootleggers.
Now night after night, they are held in place
by women left alone, aging too quickly in shacks,
their shotguns pointed at shadows

Something rustles at my window.

*Hansel? Hansel?*
I rummage the sheets all night.

In the morning I pull out the vines
that brush and scrape against the glass.
I sift dirt through my fingers.
Learn not to hate myself.

*Hansel? Hansel?* I continue
to speak out loud for months.

When our new mother moved in
she stood in the doorway
staring at the forest that held her
like a madwoman screaming in the attic.
Her face was so hard, Hansel and I
broke just looking at her.

We took off through the flickering of leaves.

At each cabin we came to
she appeared before us, grim, hungry.

Father was a woodsman. He taught us
to cut down everything in our paths
till we were left standing in a clearing.

Later, we played house. Hansel deepened
his voice and disappeared through the trees.
He left me raising mine
to screech at our imaginary children
till my face was stiff.

Once I thought I could live forever
tip-toeing on the edge of his shadow.
I tried to burn down the woods for him.

Now I tie bright cloth to branches,
hike in further and further.

Hansel! Do you hear me? I walk alone.
The bushes do not jump out and grab.
I shed layers of anger and fear
as easily as leaves falling
first from the maples on the ridge,
then in flame-colored waves moving down.

### 6

The sun rises. The ridge
separates itself from the sky,
comes forward with what scant color
the cold has left it.

I see that land has tides.
Our mother sank. The dirt closed over her.
But the waves of disturbance
did not spread out and fade as on water.

Father was the last part of her
I clung to—last root of the pain
that swelled within her, crying
for a life of its own.
I cannot go home.

### 7

I cut, trowel,
burn my roots like fuses.
I belong in this strip-mined land.

Perhaps it's her death I fear—
that body shriveling before me.

I turned and ran. The flames grew
smaller through the leaves.

Her voice cracked like dry wood.
It hissed, licked through my thoughts.

Now it is gone, that hunger
scorching the tree limbs black.

I heat my oven with sticks.
It is not so hard after all
to keep from burning myself,
to forgive the lonely women
whose love curdled inside me.

As the day warms, I open the house
and step outdoors. Rocking on this porch
rooted in the mountains, I stare across the ridge
singing the old hymns I've learned here,
words that say there is nothing to fear.

# The Place of the Poet, the Poet's Place
*An Interview with Betsy Sholl*

## Richard Jackson

B etsy Sholl grew up in New Jersey, lived in Boston and Big Stone Gap, Virginia, and now lives in Portland, Maine. Her experience in Big Stone Gap has led her to maintain literary ties with the Appalachian region, in her poetry as well as her commitment to the region. Educated at Bucknell University, the University of Rochester, and Vermont College, she now teaches at the University of Southern Maine and the Vermont College M.F.A. program. A commitment to social service first illustrated in her work with Christ Hill, a residential community in Big Stone Gap, continues in her work on the board of directors for the Wayside Evening Soup Kitchen. Sholl has received a number of awards including a Woodrow Wilson Fellowship and an NEA Fellowship. She teaches at the University of Southern Maine and in the writing program at Vermont College. She has published five books of poems including *Appalachian Winter* (alicejamesbooks, 1978), *The Red Line* (Univ. of Pittsburgh Press, 1992) which won the 1991 Associated Writing Programs Award, and *Don't Explain* (Univ. of Wisconsin Press, 1997), winner of the Felix Pollak Prize in Poetry.

JACKSON: What were some of your early influences?

SHOLL: Talking about early influences often seems pompous to me; and I'm wary of being seduced by my own self-absorbed semi-fictions, but I'll try.

I came to blues and jazz well into adulthood, and am amazed by how little I know. But I love both, and listen to them sometimes like instructions to keep from drowning. The music I grew up with was my sister's. She was a bit of a prodigy, who practiced several hours every day. So I'd hear Chopin and Tchaikovsky, Mozart—and one of those yellow books said Scriabin—but always in process, with key banging, sighs and sobs, tossed books, restarts, passages slowed down or slammed onto the keys, and then a flourish of wholeness, a run of fulfillment. There was something very precious about it all—shhh, your sister's practicing. But also something excitingly makeshift, impromptu, improvisational—my sister wrestling with these huge Russians and manic Austrians. . . . It seemed arduous, anguished, and between her being good and me being lousy at piano, I kept my distance. So, later, the music I could make on my own needed to be pretty different from that classical mode that always in some ways seemed to shut me out. But the blues had room for a clutzy listener. And jazz with its multiple doors let me in.

JACKSON: Music and the life you had created a stimulating room for you.

SHOLL: Yes, and speaking of making room. . . . Sometimes I think about class connections to poetry. I grew up in an all-female household, a family fallen on hard times after the death of my father. My mother moved us from an upscale Cleveland suburb to a pretty working class part of the Jersey shore where her parents had retired. We were displaced in a sense, we were strangers in a town where it took generations to belong, culturally rich (more or less) and economically poor, with class pretensions in a blue collar town. I think those tensions are with me still. Though I understood the loss and nostalgia behind it, I hated my mother's attempts to make us elite culturally. In some ways this background caused me to view the literary establishment as a shop closed to me. The great liberation movements I got to participate in—Civil Rights, the women's movement, the burgeoning free verse and small press scene of the '70s—all gave people in my general situation openings we might not have had otherwise. Misguided as it probably was, I associated formal verse with a kind of classical patriarchal world, and free verse with something proletarian, energetic, open to the likes of me.

This probably relates to the blues too, which sings of the underside, mourns and celebrates and makes fun of hard times and hard bosses. It gives a voice to sharecroppers, workers, women making do. Jazz with its great improvisation, its constant transformations also gives a sense of openness, of every note or riff opening a new world.

JACKSON: When did you first begin to write?

SHOLL: About beginning to write? I don't remember not writing. I was a stutterer—another huge influence, I'm sure. At times it nearly silenced me. So as early as I could hold a pen and make letters, I wrote. I filled tiny little spiral notebooks with poems. All terrible, of course. I had a speech teacher in second grade who would ask me what I wanted her to write about, then before my eyes she'd compose quatrains about rabbits or cats or dolls, all full of thr's or some other consonant cluster I couldn't pronounce..Writing was fluency, and fluency was the longed for, the gold, the grail of my childhood.

JACKSON: Who did you read, and who are you reading now?

SHOLL: In the beginning, after college and an unhappy stint in a Ph.D. program, I read mostly women—Levertov, Plath, Rich, Atwood. I picked up *Ariel* by chance and started reading it in the bathtub, and remember thinking if I didn't get out of that water I'd be electrocuted by her metaphors. I loved Rich's syntax, those intelligent poems struggling to define their terms: "Necessities of Life."[1] Those ghazals. All that serious intellectual inquiry matched by an equal use of poetic resources. I loved Atwood's chutzpah, those acidic one-liners, that cool and humorous tough-woman tone. Around then I also read Simic and Tate, which fed a part of me that the more earnest women didn't always speak to.

Later, I found myself reading passionately James Wright, Denis Johnson, Czeslaw Milosz. Elizabeth Bishop. Cesar Vallejo. Others of course, but right now, today, these stand out. The draw was different with each of them. But I think—either by style or by translation—each combines something very formal with something contingent, something spontaneous, makeshift, something struggling to find itself. Butterfly nudging cocoon. I didn't feel that my childhood taught me generosity, and I wanted to learn that in all its forms. I didn't want monuments. But maybe ruins would be okay, half-forms with cracks and water stains. Of course, describing Bishop that way seems sacrilegious. But it was her colloquial self-corrections, her little jokes, the vast shadowy weight of emotion behind the poems that seemed so moving. Denis Johnson's diction shifting, his coming at things from such wild slants. Wright's colloquial, dark angers, and what can one say about Vallejo? That Peruvian soulfulness, that kind of fused poetic, looking at the external world and then recording it through the inner lens. You can't imitate it, you just have to love it.

Too many books right now are on my floor, a couple week's worth of whatever my students are reading. I've been taking longer looks at Bill Matthews, Heather McHugh and Belle Waring. Plus a lot of Muldoon. Dickinson. Whitman.

JACKSON: What influences did living in the South, Appalachia, really, have on your work? Has place been an influence? Do you see poems as transcending place? Place seems to play an important part as memory in poems.

SHOLL: I remember the shock of moving from Boston to Big Stone Gap, Virginia. My husband promised me fresh air—as if I cared, being a smoker at the time—but when we got there the air was acrid with coal smoke. I was an obnoxious twit for months and months. A sad, grieving, obnoxious twit. But in a great gesture of generosity, Appalachian writers reached out to me, included me in festivals and conferences, various gatherings. Well, not right away, but soon enough. Once I reminded someone that I wasn't really Appalachian, and she answered that she lived in Lexington now, but I was still out there in the hills. "You need us," she said. And I did.

Place as memory is interesting. Place is often a way into a poem. Setting the scene before the action starts, or even finding the action growing out of the scene. I think one's childhood landscape is most influential. And then other landscapes reinforce or resist that. The ocean, the shore, those wide open edges are my childhood landscape. The mountains were foreign. I learned to love them, especially our house on the edge of a huge cornfield. In the fall when the farmer cut it down, it went on for miles and had that same wide-open feel as the shore. It always annoyed me that you couldn't ever see the sun rise or set in Big Stone Gap because of the mountains. But there were wonderful spider webs, birds, pools of wildflowers, long tongues of fog, spring rising up the mountain, fall coming back down. And poverty. And a culture that grew itself out of an indigenous grit and richness of spirit. A music at times hauntingly dissonant. But I don't know really what the influence of place has been on my writing.

JACKSON: How did living there affect your writer's life? I mean, all those details; it's as if you were living inside a poem itself.

SHOLL: Personally, the influence was huge. It was another experience of being an outsider, which I seem to half-love for the way it cleanses the eyes and makes everything intense. It was immersion in another culture, which enabled me to start seeing what parts of myself were culturally derived. It was the most beautiful landscape I'd ever seen. We lived six years on a dairy farm with indigo buntings, blue birds, orioles. Those things make it into my poems sometimes through a back door. I've never figured out how to write about the natural world head-on. It seems most people do it via meditations that combine the natural world with some philosophical brooding. Living in the south, in Appalachia—two miles from the town of Appalachia, Virginia—also strained my emotional resources, plopping me down in an isolated situation I'd always managed to avoid. I had to confront a lot of my own shadows. That's probably given me whatever depth I have. Being the Bible Belt it also gave me a chance to come to terms and find a place for myself in the religious tradition I'd grown up with and gleefully abandoned. We shared land with a community of people who were left wing, Christian, artsy, and social activists.

You can't hardly find that combination any more. But it existed down there; we ran a sort of safe house for troubled people. Women at first, but then it shifted toward whoever was the poorest of the poor at the moment. I don't want to inflate my role in this. For me there was always a conflict between that work and trying to write. Writing required solitude and peace, and that work involved constant disruption. I lived a mile or two down the road and pretty much made sure I controlled when I joined in the work.

During those years it seemed impossible to keep up with contemporary fiction, something I deluded myself into thinking I was doing in Boston. So, instead I read classics—Augustine, Tolstoy, Dostoevsky, Abigail Adams, Flannery O'Connor—all sorts of wonderful things.

For sure, there are poems I'd never have written without that landscape and those years. And I assume there will be more poems that draw on it, just because living there was so germinal for me, and the landscape was so stunning. There are people I knew there—still know—that I'd love to make room for in a poem.

JACKSON: There's that room metaphor again. In fact, your poems are very populated, and the people themselves are tied to places.

SHOLL: I had dear, dear friends. There was something wonderful about the people, wise, cagey even, unpretentious, genuine. In contrast to my years in the city, it seemed like people down there did things in a less self-conscious way. My neighbor on his front porch whistling back and forth to an owl wasn't going to tell anybody about that or write a poem or song about it. It was just between him and the owl—and me eavesdropping, I suppose. My friend Emmy, while her children napped, would go out into our cornfield and fly a kite—no intention of being watched, no internal camera filming her.

JACKSON: The poems in *Don't Explain* seem to me to be structured in a more complex way than earlier poems.[2] For example, "redbud" counterpoints a story about Keats, a car wreck, and the notion of beauty, and love—among other things. And the title poem counterpoints the Raritan River scene, allusions to jazz, Woodstock, current music, your father, the tape, questions of responsibility into a poem about including what has been excluded. I guess I'm seeing the poems as more inclusive in general, scooping more and more of a varied world into them.

SHOLL: At some point I became aware that most of my older poems were focused on one moment in time, a moment of realization or intense feeling.

Becoming aware of that pattern was almost synonymous with realizing it was a pattern, and not a necessity. In fact my earlier sense that a poem had to be about an intense in-your-face moment of change suddenly seemed very limited. I remember reading your interview with Donald Hall, where he talked about starting to break away from ending all his poems on an epiphany.[3] That was extremely helpful. Surely most of our days are not about hitting bottom or being struck by metaphysical lightning. So, I think I started reading poets who had a different sense of time, maybe a little more detachment in their poems, and therefore an ability to step back from the pure present and move around in time. From there it seemed pretty natural to follow threads of association wherever they led, mixing present-tense observation with memory with second and third thoughts.

I'm sure most people experience multiple things going on in their minds at once, becoming aware of a sweet happiness looking at the sunset, and instantly thinking of earthquake victims hovering in the cold. I guess I wanted to get those mixed thoughts into poems, those mixed realities, both as a way of tracking how the mind works, and also of trying to honor something of the complexity in the world.

JACKSON: Take a poem like "Test Patterns," which operates like a conceit poem, radiating out from its basic image, "big blobs / the shape or your head, or your shadow on the wall" (45–46). Can you describe how this—or any other poem—comes to be written, some of the ways you work?

SHOLL: "Test Patterns" was a little different for me because it began with just random typing, emptying my head into the computer. I was probably frustrated about something, and just clacking away to discharge energy. I don't remember exactly what was in that first little mess—the opening images for sure, the Martian business, maybe the moon. I suspect there was something that pleased me so I kept trying to build on it. Every time some incident or thought came up that brought the poem to mind I'd just make a note or add it to the draft until a pattern emerged. A friend of mine was complaining that one of my poems was too lugubrious and asked, "Why don't you write in the voice of *The Red Line*," a sort of fast-paced slangy voice of emotional extremity. I remember thinking that voice wasn't available to me any more, so one of the problems I was trying to work out in "Test Patterns" was how to have energy and interesting diction without trying to imitate a voice that had escaped me.

In general, at least for me, that kind of braided or highly associative poem usually starts when several incidents come together at once. Often there's an external trigger, an incident with images that are already connected to language and seem rich with associations. Often I can tell when those kinds of things are coming together, I can feel the resonance tugging at me. Then I have to write and write until the more subtle linkages become clear. Later in the process, of course, there's the need to cut and shape, make sure the lines of connection are clear. Of course, having said all that, I have to add that the process is at least half mystery or chance.

JACKSON: You structure your books very carefully. I was tracing several links from image to image in *Don't Explain*, especially towards the end. There is a kind of interweaving—like what Pavese calls the "image story," which is a set of building associations. Can you talk about this?

SHOLL: It's nice to hear the books look carefully structured. When you're putting them together the possibilities seem so endless—it's never clear if you actually landed on something satisfying that makes a whole. I lay the poems all out on the bed and start shuffling, seeing what various combinations might to do. It's hard to talk abstractly about these structures, but I did hope that there would be echoes, reverberations from one poem to the next. The trick is to let them be as subtle as possible without dissolving. In *Don't Explain* I had a kind of loose "image story" in mind. It's pretty hard to miss those birds. But I also found myself thinking in terms of themes. One had to do with a process of relinquishment, letting go of some insistence on control in order to be open to experience. Another had to do with imagination. I wasn't especially conscious of this until putting the poems together, but at some point I noticed how many poems seemed to revolve around the imagination, characters finding sustenance in books or art, or having fantasies, using imaginative means (sometimes in good, sometimes in questionable ways) to deal with the pressures in their lives. I don't know if anybody else sees that, but it struck me, and I remember thinking about how to arrange poems to try to make that a kind of understory.

Putting a book together seems to involve a process of discovery, realizing certain things have been on your mind that you might not have consciously articulated. I was surprised by how many children appeared in the poems. There's also a need to balance tones, not bunch up all the dark stuff.

JACKSON: What are you working on now? What new directions is your work taking?

SHOLL: After the talk about those longer associative poems, it seems ironic to say I've been trying to write shorter poems lately. But I guess whenever you find yourself getting used to working in a certain way—as soon as it starts to feel like habit—it's time to break it. So, for one thing, I've been trying to write poems that can do their work in thirty lines or so. I'm not getting fanatical about that, but just trying to vary what I do, and learn to work with slightly more concise structures. It's meant a different kind of poem, less rambling, a bit more philosophical than narrative. I've also been trying to let more music into my poems, more sound, assonance, alliteration, what I call random rhyme. For years I seemed to be afraid of that, and it feels good to just let sound lead a little more.

The autobiographical poem is seeming pretty tired to me right now, at least my autobiographical poems. I've been thinking that while poetry probably needs to be personal or individual, that doesn't necessarily mean it needs to be about the poet directly. I've been looking at a few stories that move me, thinking about ways to tell them, or see them, that don't have to involve me as a character. Along with that, I've been thinking lately that we talk so much about process we almost ignore or even dismiss the notion of subject matter. I wonder if there's a way to incorporate the notion or content or subject into this process of discovery. I've been brooding some on how to make poems more responsive to the world, or to history or social concerns. So many of the poets we think of in this light—Neruda, Vallejo, Herbert, Szymborska, Milosz—are Latin American or Eastern European. So, that's on my mind, how to open poems up to subjects that often get left out. I think of the poor, and what's happening to them as the world gets more and more obsessed with economics. I think about how much popular American history is mythologized, glossing over anything that makes us look bad as a people. William Carlos Williams comes to mind, as an American poet whose work was open to these issues. There's also the way a consumer society is so at odds with anything we might call spiritual, or so ready to sell it. These things really interest me. I'm just stumbling around with them, but hope they're bubbling and stewing inside, staining my brain, so whatever I write, these concerns will have to be part of it.

## Notes

1. Adrienne Rich, "Necessities of Life," in *Poems: Selected and New, 1950–1974* (New York: W. W. Norton, 1974), 69.
2. Betsy Sholl, *Don't Explain* (Madison: Univ. of Wisconsin Press, 1997). Subsequent further references to this book are found in the text.
3. Richard Jackson, "Donald Hall, On the Periphery of Time," in *Acts of Mind: Conversations with Contemporary Poets* (Tuscaloosa: Univ. of Alabama Press, 1983), 191–95.

# Bennie Lee Sinclair

## The Vegetable Queen

Her breasts swinging
like great golden squash
she moves through the rows of time
hoeing; hoeing.

And I have sometimes moved
on her bare feet myself,
going step by step
more naked from the house—
leaving teeshirt, panties, jeans
like scales of some other skin
discarded on the path.

Wherever she gardens,
phalluses shimmer and swim
into seed: the slaughtered
richen her furrows.

Now, secret
beneath their leaves,
my firm cucumbers wait.
Cantaloupe split and spill
into halved and pulpy moons—
tomatoes fall, erupt, and drip
convincingly as blood.

Always, for her, hard work.
Even her image, unearthed,
has a sheen
like perspiration.

Whenever I stoop or bend,
sweat blinds me. Phalluses
shimmer and swim, seed spill.
My hair wrung tight like a crown
I harvest my way down the rows—
the chill
merely her fear I dream

growing old, growing cold;
withering.

## My Father. His Rabbits

In my dreams they return as they should,
my father's rabbits I loosed one day
when I was four, the year
that he, too, left—
not suspecting how wildly they strained

toward field and wood,
or that even our deep yard, rimmed with roses,
seemed merely extension of cage.
They appeared reliable and tame
as I whispered through the wire, worked the latches,

remained with me for awhile
browsing clover—their fur, their markings
intact, in health and lovely.
Perhaps it would not have occurred
to desert roof, kin, feed—pit hunger against hunger

in a dark rife with owls and traps—
if I have not thought to free them.
Most, we never saw again.
But one or two came
back to the edge of our lawn

thinner, harried—like him
to visit, but never quite within.
It is only in my dreams
I welcome them truly home.
Salving their wounded eyes, patching

ears torn by gun and thunder
I lift them into their pens, shut the doors,
making all as it was before.

My father. His rabbits.

# Stewardship and Sacrifice
## The Land and the People of
## Bennie Lee Sinclair's South Carolina

## William B. Thesing and Gilbert Allen

I n 1986, Governor Richard Riley appointed Bennie Lee Sinclair as South Carolina's poet laureate. Born on April 15, 1939, she was a native of Greenville, South Carolina, and a lifelong resident of the mountains in the northwestern part of the state until her death on May 22, 2000. She worked as a teacher in the Poets in the Schools program and as the director of the creative writing division of the South Carolina Governor's School for the Arts. A gifted author of poems, fiction, and essays, she held a bachelor's degree in philosophy and English. While a student at Furman University, she married Don Lewis in 1958 and became one of the first married women ever to graduate from that institution in 1961. In subsequent years, her *alma mater* honored her with an alumna membership in Phi Beta Kappa and a doctor of literature degree.

The Appalachian Center for Poets and Writers Press published her collection of short fiction, *Appalachian Trilogy*, in 1991. Her novel, *The Lynching* (Walker and Company, 1992), is based on the story of Willy Earle, a black man who was lynched in Greenville County, South Carolina, in 1947. But Bennie Lee Sinclair's primary literary achievements have been as a poet. She has published four collections of verse: *Little Chicago Suite* (Drummer Press, 1971; Wildernesse Books, 1978), *The Arrowhead Scholar* (Wildernesse Books, 1978), *Lord of Springs* (Rowan Mountain Press, 1990), and *The Endangered: New and Selected Poems* (Ninety-Six Press, 1992). She received the Stephen Vincent Benét Award from *Poet Lore* in 1970 for "The Arrowhead Scholar," an elegy both for her brother Walt [Waldo Graham Jr. or "Buster"] and for the land he once roamed in Oconee County. In 1978 she received the Winthrop College Excellence in Writing Award (for *The Arrowhead Scholar*) and in 1990, the Appalachian Writers Association Book of the Year Award (for *Lord of Springs*). In her poems, she often celebrates the ordinary wonders of her native state: a young mother named Kathy, living in a trailer, not quite understanding her own grief; a small white hen "tactfully aglow" in the "everyday sun"; the Appalachian wildflowers that, "indomitable as kin," bloom "like psalms" around her. Her longtime residence at Wildernesse, a 130-acre sanctuary for native animals and plants in northern Greenville County, reflected her abiding concern for her fellow creatures.

Although her intellectual and cultural life in South Carolina was distinguished and fulfilling, Bennie Lee Sinclair struggled with many physical disabilities. A "brittle" diabetic, she briefly chronicled the recurring problems with her vision in the poem "Going Blind" (*The Endangered*, 54). She endured dialysis for fifteen months before receiving a kidney transplant in 1993. Her three-part broadside poem, "The Dying. The Donor. The Phoenix." is a heartfelt account of her gratitude to a young person from Georgia whose posthumous gift provided her with a new life:

> Conjoined, we have become
> miraculous as the phoenix, borne
> on our new wings, raised from ashes
> by forces old as love and sacrifice,
> recent as state-of-the art technology.

Because of the medicines that she had to take, however, she was vulnerable to infections and broken bones. Near the end of her life, she walked with two canes or used a wheelchair. She retained some, but not all, of her eyesight: when she wrote or read her poems, she had to work with pages that held only three or four lines of large type.[1]

Poetry was an important means for her to deal with these physical difficulties and with earlier sorrows: principally, the death of her father in 1960 and of her brother in 1967. Compassion, suffering, and death are the attendant muses for many of her poems. As she once reflected: "It is the bad memories, the painful experiences, the losses that nevertheless shape us. . . . In a strange way, the sad life experiences, the tragic ones, are loaves and fishes also, for they truly do build character, as well as wisdom for writing."[2] Her other most prominent inspiration was an abiding love for the wilderness areas of her native state.

Bennie Lee Sinclair wryly remarked that early in her writing career, "I . . . had editors tell me they accepted my first poem because they thought mine was a man's name."[3] In a 1996 essay, Fred Chappell laments the relative obscurity of southern women poets:

> My best guess is that if you ask someone knowledgeable
> to list a few prominent living Southern poets, you will hear
> of James Dickey, A. R. Ammons, Robert Morgan, Dave Smith,

Charles Wright, A. B. Spellman, Andrew Hudgins. . . . You might hear of Ellen Bryant Voigt and perhaps of Kelly Cherry, but I have my doubts. . . . Female Southern poets get short shrift.

I can't say why this is so. The feminists will offer their predictable elucidation, the conservative canonists will offer theirs, yet neither explanation will seem conclusive. . . . It may be that the tradition of the deep drinking, recklessly womanizing, varmint-slaughtering, good-ole-boy Southern Poet makes such testosterone racket that the softer voices are drowned out. . . .

If I may be allowed a large, perhaps inaccurate, but (I hope) dimly suggestive analogy: the differences in presentation between the two genders of Southern poets are a little like the differences between D. H. Lawrence and Virginia Woolf. It is easy to say which of those figures made the greater stir in their contemporary world, but not easy to claim he was the better writer.[4]

All recent South Carolina poets, both male and female, have labored in the shadow of the late James Dickey's literary reputation and public notoriety. More than any other poet in South Carolina, however, Bennie Lee Sinclair has had an impact upon the general culture of the state: in her earlier years, through her teaching and public readings, and, after 1986, through her visibility as poet laureate. One of her last public appearances was at the inauguration of Governor Jim Hodges, where she read her new poem "South Carolina 1999." Like Carl Sandburg—who shared her affection for the Carolina mountains and her respect for working-class people—she was an unusual poet for attracting more attention from the general public than from the literary community.

And, like the socialist Sandburg and the conservative Southern Agrarians of the 1930s, she regarded the blessings of modern technology as decidedly mixed ones. She would have wholeheartedly agreed with the conclusion of Lyle H. Lanier's essay "A Critique of the Philosophy of Progress":

> Industrialism bears its own antidote, but it is a bitter one: the consequences of its course of action are scarcely justified, even by that foremost American contribution to world-culture, the billionaire. If there exists any effective social and political intelligence in the country it might profitably be mobilized for the conduction of a specific program of the rehabilitation of the

agrarian economy and the "old individualism" associated with it. This program is not conceived in a spirit of pathological regression to the past, stimulated by repugnance toward contemporary conditions; it is the definition of a concrete social aim. The instrumentalities of intelligent political leadership, informed social science, and a definitive social philosophy could have no more important problem than that of trying to effect a synthesis, in some sense, of the unified manner of living inherent in the agrarian family and community with the energy and inventiveness which have been diverted into industrialism.[5]

It would be difficult for anyone who owed her life to surgeons and anti-rejection drugs to be wholly critical of technology—just as it would be difficult for such a person to be indifferent to the anonymous decency of organ donors and their families, whose actions cannot be explained in economic terms. In her early work—most notably in the title poem of *The Arrowhead Scholar*—Bennie Lee Sinclair often emphasized the destructive, ahistorical violence of technology. In more recent works—perhaps "My Appalachian Wildflowers," from her 1990 volume *Lord of Springs*, is the best example—the land she loved seems more resilient, capable of surviving even within a world increasingly dominated by machines.

Throughout her career as a poet, Bennie Lee Sinclair emphasized the need for responsible stewardship. Human beings must recognize that their actions have consequences in two spheres: the social and the natural. They must strive to fulfill both sets of responsibilities. The childlike protagonist of the poem "Sidney" in *Little Chicago Suite* intuitively understands this. "Speeded by taunts," defying public decorum by urinating along the roadside as he tows his red wagon, he still acts in accordance with his generous spirit:

> Intoning heaven, as he has seen the reverend do,
> he digs a hole, deposits, covers;
> adds another stone to the small scattering
> that mounds this secret graveyard:
> dogs, cats, rabbits, possums, and a fox
> unable to manage the walking of these roads.
>
> (11)

The irony, of course, is that Sidney himself has difficulty walking the same roads: in part because of his disabilities (his "vague face" and "spastic gait") and in part because of the willful cruelty of many of his fellow human travelers.

In "Landmark," the first poem in *The Arrowhead Scholar*, the reader is again placed on the roadsides of upstate South Carolina. Here, however, the only visible object is a stove by a former home site. The poet must provide the erased history: the last residents literally had to burn their own house, piece by piece, to survive a harsh winter. Sinclair eloquently described the poem's origins in *Conversations with South Carolina Poets*:

> [I]t suggests something . . . about . . . my sense of responsibil-
> ity as a poet. . . . I put a lot into "Landmark": my regularly pass-
> ing an old house whose occupants were slowly tearing it down
> and using it for firewood; my watching some poor people burn
> their furniture during a very cold spell; my teaching a class of
> rich kids at a posh private school who had no idea of what
> being truly cold or controlled by the weather meant.[6]

Both "Sidney" and "Landmark" silently lament the absence of a nurturing social order visible in "Decoration Day." In that poem from *Little Chicago Suite*, the individuals gathered for the annual clearing of graves are not equally diligent, but each has his or her place in the drama of human mortality:

> Each pilgrim as of age assumes his role:
> the old knead deeply in ancestral
> dust, upending spiny threats upon
> their own sure home, while those of lesser
> urgency resolve themselves unmossing faded
>
> elegiacs. It is the young who take
> no part. Escaping one by one to ride
> the afternoon, they do not hear the gentle chime
> of hand-tool hitting rock; this knelling
> for green bones as well as brittle.

(13)

In their own good time, those "green bones" of the young will hear the sound of their own mortality and assume a new role that befits them.

The most withering criticism in Sinclair's early poems is reserved for human beings in positions of power who have renounced their responsibilities to the natural world. In "Ivorybill," from *The Arrowhead Scholar*, the poet describes the "solitary drumming" of the last ivorybill woodpecker in a cypress swamp menaced by loggers. Then she outlines the biblical ideal of stewardship:

Out of the grounded ark
God led each lesser pair
(each bird, and fragile creeping thing,
and beast) and delivered them
into our care.

(26)

As the poem ends, however, it is abundantly clear that "our care" has been woefully inadequate.

Nowhere is this inadequacy more powerfully evoked than in her tribute to her brother Walt, "The Arrowhead Scholar." To appreciate the poem fully, a reader should have some historical background concerning the Keowee-Toxaway Project and the Sinclair family. In the 1960s, Duke Power announced that a dam and nuclear power facility would be built in Oconee County on the site of two of the oldest Native American villages in the Southeast. The towns Keowee and Toxaway, along with all of their cultural artifacts, were to be buried under tons of water. It was an event of the sort that Raymond Williams would describe in *Culture and Society* as the destruction of "a whole way of life, material, intellectual, and spiritual."[7] The news astonished Bennie Lee and her elder brother—both of whom had roamed the area as children in the 1940s. Walt was especially distressed, because over many years he had sought and studied the artifacts—mainly arrowheads and pottery—in the villages. He also had a profound reverence for the native plants of the area, particularly the mountain laurel (which would become one of the recurring motifs within his sister's poem).

"The Arrowhead Scholar" is an elegy for the area's beauty and history— the beauty irrevocably changed, the history lost—and for her brother him- self, who died in 1967 of kidney failure resulting from a brain aneurysm. All of these events come together in an expression of grief and outrage that is at once public and personal. Sinclair spoke angrily of the public events behind the poem: "Building the facility was one of the greatest crimes against his- tory that has ever been committed. It was a sin. Technology has done in everything in the area: everything that used to be there is gone. The prettiest area of South Carolina, and the one with the richest heritage, is now under water. . . . Technology does not look back. It's blind to everything, even the future. The Keowee-Toxaway plant is built on an earthquake fault! To me, the whole thing is human folly at an idiotic level."[8]

These prose sentiments are echoed in the poem from *The Arrowhead Scholar*. Although the poet ruefully acknowledges the apparent gentleness of the completed dam's form and the "shimmering Visitors' Center" nearby, the overwhelming emphasis is upon loss. In the poem's first section, "1967," the new construction is a growing, malevolent shadow upon the land: "Now, a dam / begins to shroud it, locking in the secrets / of the Cherokee, and those tribes older / who survived prehistory // to civilize this valley—only / tenacious drifts of laurel / high, at the new crater's rim, hide / some final relic // for those who care to race / the drowning hour" (41). The poem bemoans a past that has been "brutally uprooted" (43) and the indifference of government and industry towards a culture that the poet and her brother had touched with their own hands. In the poem's second section, an exhibit presents "the Story // of Nuclear Energy woven of films, recordings, / animation— but little is said / of what once was here; / of our lost Indian villages, only // the names" (44). Within such a landscape, the deaths of her father and brother cannot inspire the poet to embark upon a redemptive "pilgrimage" (45). The poem concludes with personal despair and a public warning:

> . . . Technology
> has done this place in, in trust
> of the future, but I know
> (of the Arrowhead Scholar)
> that the past must be suffered again
>
> as it is today,
> in my brother's form,
> moving with his magnificent grace
> among the laurel there, which is no more.
>
> (45–46)

Her conviction is strong and prophetic: our society is in mortal danger of mistaking technological convenience for enduring value. She does hold on to the memory of her brother's example, but the places that helped define his being are "no more."

Bennie Lee Sinclair acknowledged that "The Arrowhead Scholar" was an important catharsis for her: "I felt an obligation to make my brother exist in some way for the future—and to get across the idea that technology does not believe the past matters at all. . . . And when I had finished the poem, I was ready to enter a second stage of writing poetry, although at the time I didn't think of it that way."[9] Many of these newer poems are more celebratory: the gracious acceptance of aging in "August Light"; the meditation upon her husband's sensuous kinship with the waters of Wildernesse in "Lord of Springs";

the simple, glorious image of a white hen in sunlight in "Aureole"; her praise for a dedicated conservationist and his autistic son in "The Endangered." The poem that best embodies this resilient spirit, and that has the most sustained connections with "The Arrowhead Scholar," is "My Appalachian Wildflowers."

Both poems have their roots in Emersonian tradition. The very title of "The Arrowhead Scholar" recalls Emerson's 1837 address, "The American Scholar." And both Walt Sinclair and Emerson's idealized Man Thinking are "the world's eye," "the world's heart," and a force against "the vulgar prosperity" that regards money and power as absolute goods.[10] The epigraph to "My Appalachian Wildflowers" in *Lord of Springs*, attributed to Emerson, reads as follows: ". . . whereby contrary and remote things cohere, and flower out from one stem . . ." (29). As the poem proceeds, those "contrary and remote things" become the wildflowers themselves, in their amazing persistence and diversity, and their parallel in human culture: the phenomenon of kinship.

In the prologue to this four-part poem, the wildflowers are "fragile" and "delicate as tears," yet they have endured "ten million years." Like human beings, "they do not last, but resurrect," transforming themselves into faces as we behold them, "connecting us" (29). In the poem's first section, the poet assumes the role of "this student of flowers," analogous to the role of Walt in "The Arrowhead Scholar." The poet still perceives the destruction wrought upon the land by human technology. Yet "though the mountains be slaughtered around us / these preglacial, anteholocaust flowers / will remain" (30). The second section continues the celebration of "flowers strange as their names // like generations past" (31). Terms such as *generations, root, gene,* and *family* have dual significance as the floral and the human world graciously mirror and echo one another. Section three celebrates the astonishing variety of violets: violets which feed "a pencil-legged doe and her fawn" (paralleling the poet and her poem-in-progress) and which hold "remedies, dyes, superstitions" that "the true student" cannot even begin to enumerate (31–32). The poem's fourth section provides a final elaboration upon the trope involving mountain flowers and mountain people—an elaboration at once sad and consolatory:

> Whether camp or mine or town
> has been, or been
>
> moved on, the cabin gone,
> indomitable as kin
> these flowers peculiar to place
> whenever we climb toward home

welcome us. Out of the evening mist
like ghosts they bloom:
faces we have known,
connecting us.

Like psalms they bloom:
music that we live,
connecting us.

(32–33)

Sinclair reprises the abandoned home site of "Landmark" and the vanished towns of "The Arrowhead Scholar," providing an image of endurance that, like the human family, is mortal but persistent, imperfect but comforting.

For more than thirty years, Bennie Lee Sinclair was an important part of the cultural landscape of her native state. As she once stated in an interview, she tended to write poems "about things that bother [her]."[11] Many of these "things" are centered in upstate South Carolina, yet she resisted being marginalized as merely a poet of place:

> The label "regional" offends me when it is used in a derogatory way, like the word "local." . . . But most good writers are the ones who learn to write about what they know best. I am Southern. This part of South Carolina is where I am. It's where I want to be. And I consider this region both as my home and as the subject I want to write about. . . . [W]hen you become . . . well known . . . the most wonderful thing people can say about you is that you are from some little corner of somewhere—like Eudora Welty from Jackson, Mississippi. I would like to be called "regional" in that sense![12]

She asserted that she "found audiences of farm and mill families to be just as sensitive to poetry as academia-oriented people."[13] Indeed, she found the snobbishness of many contemporary poets and literary critics "a terrible misstep."[14] Throughout her career, she strived to make her poems accessible to everyday South Carolinians who behold the rapid changes around them with both fear and hope.

## Notes

1. Claudia Smith Brinson, "Bennie Lee Sinclair Writes Poetry for South Carolinians," *The Columbia, S.C., State*, Mar. 25, 1999, A14.
2. Bennie Lee Sinclair, "Appalachian Loaves and Fishes," in *Bloodroot*, ed. Dyer, 270, 271.

3. Gayle R. Swanson and William B. Thesing, *Conversations with South Carolina Poets* (Winston-Salem, N.C.: John F. Blair, 1986), 32.

4. Fred Chappell, "Five New Southern Women Poets," *Georgia Review* 50 (1996): 174–75.

5. Lyle H. Lanier, "A Critique of the Philosophy of Progress," in *I'll Take My Stand: The South and the Agrarian Tradition*, introd. by Louis D. Rubin Jr. (Baton Rouge: Louisiana State Univ. Press, 1977), 153–54.

6. Swanson and Thesing, 37–38.

7. Raymond Williams, *Culture and Society, 1780–1950* (New York: Penguin, 1963), 16.

8. Swanson and Thesing, 40.

9. Ibid.

10. Ralph Waldo Emerson, *The Collected Works of Ralph Waldo Emerson*, vol. 1, ed. Robert E. Spiller and Alfred R. Ferguson (Cambridge, Mass.: Belknap Press, 1971), 62.

11. Swanson and Thesing, 42.

12. Ibid., 34.

13. "Bennie Lee Sinclair," *Contemporary Authors*, New Revision Series (Detroit: Gale Research Group, 1985), vol. 1: 601–2.

14. Brinson, A14.

# Barbara Smith

## Death Watch

Bonedust grates inside my eyes.
I watch you dying,
Warm the hand that once held mine,
Bring you the bedpan
And take away your pride.
Old man, that body's not worth dwelling on,
Though I shall miss it sorely,
The thin white hair once thick and handsome
Trimmed now the very best I can,
The pencil legs that wrote a thousand times
Their way around the golf course
And down the river bank to pull in
Fat, black catfish.
Nothing but bones now,
Dust motes held in shape
For one more day or two
By slick, dry skin and watchful eyes
Refusing to give in,
Those blue, blue eyes that see me still
A little girl
And call me still to love.

## From Where I Am Now

I would rather be with you again,
Listening to the swimming hole,
Big Blue, so cold as to turn us purple.
I would rather be with courage
Imagining, at least, the leap from Top Dog Rock
Into the depths to which you drew me.
I would rather be balancing
Barefoot down the railroad tracks
Where you, so many-few years ago
Balanced in the footsteps of a little-known father.

Instead, I remember, so many-few hours from you,
The jewelweeds by the side of the road,
The black-eyed susans and the black-eyed woods,
The talk of fern-blossomed mimosa trees.
I remember a tipsy merry-go-round
And the windows of a broken school,
The baseball field in the sun abandoned,
The slagheap burned to half its childhood size.
From where I am I imagine you fourteen
Stealing apples from a long-gone tree,
Hopping the freight train back to town,
Climbing the creek to where it begins.

Oh, I can see you from where I now am,
And I would be there, waiting.

# From Image to Epiphany
## Barbara Smith's Poetic Moments

## Felicia Mitchell

**B**arbara Smith is a free-lance writer, editor, workshop leader, teacher, bio-ethicist, and social and religious activist. She is former chair of the Division of Humanities at Alderson-Broaddus College in West Virginia, where she was also professor of literature and writing with specializations in technical communication, Appalachian literature, and issues (e.g., world hunger, war and peace, ecology) courses. In her career, she has published almost three hundred poems, short stories, journal articles, plays, and feature articles, along with seven books of nonfiction and one novel. She is a regular workshop leader at the Appalachian Writers Workshop of the Hindman Settlement School in Kentucky.

MITCHELL: Tell me something about where you come from, how you came to be here, how you came to associate yourself with writing in Appalachia.

SMITH: I was born in Milwaukee and raised in one of its suburbs, but I have very weak connections there. We spent our vacations and holidays and long weekends on my grandparents' farm in southern Illinois, outside of Jerseyville, where both of my parents grew up and where almost all of my relatives are buried. Our family was small but very close. I have lived in Madison and Minneapolis and, for eight years, in Manhattan—New York—and I enjoyed all of those settings and learned from them, but I have always felt more at home in rural settings. I have felt most at home in West Virginia, rural and with hills and rivers and trees and mountain people.

MITCHELL: Could you mark a specific time when your move to this region began to make an indelible mark on your poems?

SMITH: No, I can't name a specific time unless it was the first time I woke up here in the fall of 1960. I knew then that this was truly home, the place I belonged.

MITCHELL: You felt connected. . . .

SMITH: Lawrence Raab talks about how readers of poetry have "imagination, combined with the ability to make sympathetic connections—with words first, and through them all they represent in the world."[1] I think of the process as reversed for the writer: sympathetic connections and then words.

MITCHELL: So when you woke up here the first time, you felt that connection.

SMITH: The poet must, I believe, listen for and then record or interpret the voices of the world, the universe. One's perspective on this world is rooted somewhere: for me, West Virginia.

MITCHELL: Some people might easily see an influence in a poem such as your unpublished "Naming the Bones," which responds to the mystery of four skeletons found in an abandoned mine in 1896:

> Oh, yes, I know that boy's bones, and I know his name.
> I know his bones, and were they to ask,
> I could tell them to look for the break above his left wrist,
> His right toe which was hammered by too-small boots,
> The tear in his left ear from a bear slap in '59.

SMITH: Yes, this is a "voice poem," the voice of a mother whose son, I speculate, has deserted the army. I took the story from an 1896 piece in the *Randolph Enterprise*, about several bodies found in a deserted coal mine near Colliers: "As no relatives of the dead men could be found their remains were given in charge of an undertaker for burial."[2]

MITCHELL: You might say that what makes the poem yours, really yours, is not just the context of a war that—especially in these parts—created conflicts within families but the way you have allowed the image of the bones to help create a larger message, an epiphany of sorts. I understand that you do, in fact, view your poems as growing from an image into something of an epiphany.

SMITH: Yes, I believe that before or during or after the fact, every good poem is an epiphany, a revelation or, in somewhat less dramatic terms, an experience of insight. Alberto Rios says, "I used to look for language only in words, rather than in the things those words were . . . [now] I look for things that have a voice of their own and I try to listen before I speak."[3] I agree. All creative endeavors are, in a sense, mystical.

MITCHELL: So poetry is more than fact, more than the obvious.

SMITH: I think it was Susan Goldsmith Wooldridge who said in *Poemcrazy*, "What's real may lie below the surface of fact, and we have to stretch the apparent truth to reach it. So, in poems, with the help of lies, we can tell what's real like nowhere else, and sometimes arrive at the emotional truth."[4]

MITCHELL: As in inventing a mother for a lost man. Give us another example of a poem in which you lie.

SMITH: "Folksong in the Cemetery." It's an example of what I consider double vision, ordinary to extraordinary, going below—or above—the surface situation.

MITCHELL: In this poem that you shared with me recently, you enhance a visit to the cemetery with memories of relatives buried there.

SMITH: Yes, the middle of the poem goes like this:

> But there are voices,
> Grandpa's forbidding me to watch him
>
> milk the nervous cow,
>
> Grandma's applauding my clean weeding
> of what seemed a hundred rows of beans,
> My sister telling secrets
> in the darkness of the trundle bed,
> My own voice whispering back.

MITCHELL: Your reference to the redbud captures an emotional embrace of spring and a stark contrast between life and death, certainly a subject for a writer interested in spiritual concerns, or for an "Appalachian" writer.

SMITH: And yet there is my own voice, lying, "Look, everyone, look—the redbud is in bloom!" Does it matter that the cemetery is really in Illinois where redbud, my favorite flowering tree, does not grow? I hope not. I hope my desire to offer the best to the loved and missed is as meaningful to someone in North Dakota or New Mexico as it might be in redbud country.

MITCHELL: Before you told me the inspiration was Illinois, I was seeing Appalachia in the redbud and the barn of that same poem:

> The house is dark, its siding gray
> As is the empty barn,
> The fields stubbled like an old man's face.

Your decades in this region have certainly influenced your imagery, but am I assuming too much of the stereotypes to sense an "Appalachian" feel in this poem?

SMITH: No, you're right. Appalachia has become an important part of my identity, my "place." Not long ago, I unexpectedly drove past the Talbott Community Church outside of Belington, West Virginia. I stepped on the brakes and pulled over. Here was the church of Irene McKinney's poem "Sunday Morning 1950." Here was the cemetery of her "Visiting My Gravesite, Talbott Churchyard, West Virginia," which concludes,

Once I came in fast and low
in a little plane and when I looked down at the church,

the trees I've felt with my hands, the neighbors' houses
and the family farm, and I saw how tiny what I loved or knew was,

it was like my children going on with their plans and griefs
at a distance and nothing I could do about it. But I wanted

to reach down and pat it, while letting it know
I wouldn't interfere for the world, the world being

everything this isn't, the unknown buried in the known.[5]

MITCHELL: A striking experience to be reminded of. . . .

SMITH: As I wandered among the gravestones, my eyes burned and my pulse increased. Being physically present reinforced the poetic experience and gave it new meaning, more meaning. Such an out-of-the-way, specific setting. Such universal truth! For me, much of that truth can be found here in West Virginia, in Appalachia.

MITCHELL: "Universal" seems key here, a way of bridging where we are with the rest of poetry.

SMITH: Truths are everywhere, really: old cemeteries, red wheelbarrows, misplaced car keys, freshly washed windows—a current television commercial reminds us that God is in the details.

MITCHELL: So writing can be a religious experience?

SMITH: Every writer will agree that the most exciting writing experience—what for me is a religious experience—occurs when the writing takes over, when the woman who keeps her son in a cage on her front porch begins telling her own story, when the old doctor being interviewed provides exactly the anecdote that will bring the feature article to life, when the meaning of a poem reveals itself with no help whatsoever.

MITCHELL: For example?

SMITH: I remember this happening to me in a class I was teaching. I had asked the students to write something based on their viewing of a film on mountain climbing. One of the students dared me to write too. I had done my share of hiking and had climbed many West Virginia hills, but I had never done any serious rock-climbing. My pen, rather than my conscious mind, recorded what for me was an epiphany.

MITCHELL: In this poem, "Lines," you insert your son. Let me read a few lines from your manuscript:

> Anchoring, I watched him climb,
> His legs still smooth, his ringless hands
> Grasping, inching at the cliff,
> His eyes turned upward toward my own,
> My own downsmiling at my son.

SMITH: That's another example of stretching the truth. I've had many, many meaningful moments with my three kids, but my son and I have never mountain-climbed together.

MITCHELL: What remains true in poems that lie, it seems, is their honest appraisal of what it feels to be alive and a part of one's surroundings.

SMITH: Yes. The poetic lie is only a tool, like a simile or a symbol. It provides the vehicle for the reader to move into the experience. Raab also wrote that "a poem can't work unless a reader's imagination is lured into responding to it."[6]

MITCHELL: And for the writer?

SMITH: We might think of the process as reversed for the writer: sympathetic connections and then words.

MITCHELL: Thus a sympathetic connection offers the beginning of an epiphany, the ability to make those connections that help to create poets.

SMITH: Clay-footed beings that we writers are, what makes us poets? What makes us susceptible to epiphanies? I believe that it is what Robert Frost referred to as seeing double.[7] And I believe that we can train ourselves to be double-visioned, to practice insightfulness. That doesn't have to result in poetry, of course. It may be expressed through painting or dance—or it may simply result in increased appreciation for life.

MITCHELL: I know that poets spend a good bit of time reading other poets, learning the tradition as they hone their craft, just as painters and dancers hone theirs. But how do poets train themselves to be insightful?

SMITH: When we allow ourselves to live on at least two levels—double or triple vision—these wonders will occur. It rained yesterday, the first time after weeks of 90-plus degree weather and drought, drought, drought. I went out to the backyard and just stood in the downpour for about ten minutes. When I came back in, I had to remove my muddy shoes. I suddenly realized how many meanings can be communicated by muddy shoes: longed-for rain, mountaintop removal, burials, imminent punishment, an aborted round of golf, and on and on and on.

MITCHELL: I guess I should tell young writers to stand in the rain more.

SMITH: But they should also read. I urge every writer to read Emerson, particularly "The Poet": "The poet knows that he speaks adequately . . . only when he speaks somewhat wildly, or 'with the flower of the mind'; not with the intellect, used as an organ, but with the intellect released from all service, and suffered to take its direction from its celestial life; or, as the ancients were wont to express themselves, not with the intellect alone, but with the intellect inebriated by nectar."[8]

MITCHELL: Which Appalachian poets do you tend to turn to in the classroom?

SMITH: Irene McKinney, Maggie Anderson, James Still, Louise McNeill, Richard Currey (whose prose is really poetry), Robert Morgan, Jeff Daniel Marion, Michael McFee—the list goes on and on.

MITCHELL: What might you say they have in common with Emerson?

SMITH: A connection with the earth, with the common, with the immediate, all touched with something metaphysical.

MITCHELL: To whom do poets offer their insights?

SMITH: I think William Stafford said it best: ". . . some language may start experiences that resonate with the self, with the being we have become amidst our apparently random encounters with this alien world."[9]

MITCHELL: Could you offer an example of how this has happened to you as a reader?

SMITH: Ellen Kort has a poem called "Letter from McCarty's Farm" in which she expresses insight and emotion that extend from her Wisconsin to my West Virginia—and beyond. This piece represents not only double vision but also the power of "thinking globally but acting locally," of making extraordinary a specific and ordinary setting.

MITCHELL: Could you quote a few lines from Kort's poem?

SMITH: After two stanzas of vivid natural description, the poem concludes,

> If it's true
> that landscape
> is to be read as text
> I will take it as wafer
> the whole complete
> roundness of it
> and place it on my tongue[10]

MITCHELL: This deep connection with landscape and religion in her poem is what some see as typical in Appalachian poetry, as I mentioned earlier when we were discussing "Folksong in the Cemetery," but Appalachian poets obviously don't have the monopoly on such a subject.

SMITH: Well, Appalachia has always been a survivalist culture, from the earliest days of Native American hunting villages through European settlement through early industry—particularly coal and timber—to our current attempts to stabilize the economy and the population. Anyone who has lived outside of Appalachia or has even spent vacations in other cultures—New Orleans or Minneapolis or Coos Bay, Oregon, or Bloomington, Illinois—can sense the differences. All cultures are to some extent survivalist, but the focus in other places lies somewhere other than on the land and family and religion—the three major foci here in Appalachia. Perhaps the other extreme is exemplified by Silicon Valley or Fifth Avenue, New York. Not much land-family-religion centering in those settings! And of course, what a person focuses on determines to a large extent that person's identity.

MITCHELL: What more, then, do you think a particular relationship with the Appalachian region has done to inform your "double vision"?

SMITH: Let me clarify that a little. I believe that the ability or predilection to "see double" is what affects a writer's identity. It's not the mountains or the rivers themselves. A good and sensitive writer will respond to the seashore or the desert or to the London subway, to a sunbonneted woman churning butter or to a Wall Street broker or a Hopi tribal chief. The writer's own identity will affect the perspective, however. No matter how hard I may try to abide by the "when in Rome" dictum, I will always be a West Virginian writing about or in Rome. I can be happy and productive anywhere, but my gyroscope is centered in Appalachia.

MITCHELL: Some lines to illustrate?

SMITH: "From Where I Now Am" begins,

> I would rather be with you again,
> Listening to the swimming hole,
> Big Blue, so cold as to turn us purple.
> I would rather be with courage
> Imagining, at least, the leap from Top Dog Rock
> Into the depths to which you drew me.

MITCHELL: Again you take us from an image grounded in experience into a spiritual connection. Is this what is meant by a writer's mystical vision?

SMITH: First of all, though I do believe the act of writing is mystical, I would never use the word "mystical" or the word "vision" as related to my own writing. Those words both sound lofty, even presumptuous. Let's just leave it at "double vision" in that sense of the word. Or let's use the term that so many writing coaches use—the "what if—."

MITCHELL: And how do you keep that "what if" going? What do you encourage other writers to do to keep it going?

SMITH: First of all, you have to work at it, force yourself to see a mop as something other than a mop, a carburetor as first cousin to the Grand Coulee turbines, a maple leaf as an inside-out lung. Second, we should be fraternizing with other double-thinkers—reading, corresponding, going to workshops and conferences—anything that will keep the juices flowing. And then, very important, spending time just seeing and hearing and tasting and touching—and thinking.

MITCHELL: You mentioned workshops. Which conferences or workshops have influenced you most or suited you best? I know you're a regular at the Appalachian Writers Workshop in Hindman, Kentucky. Any others?

SMITH: Yes, I go to Hindman every year and to the Writers Conference at Green Lake, Wisconsin. They're very different settings, but I learn a lot—and write a lot—at both.

MITCHELL: But aren't you one of the workshop leaders at both? What do you teach?

SMITH: I'm a workshop leader at both, but not a teacher—a coach. That's been my intention throughout my teaching—and workshopping—career. At Hindman I've coached everything from poetry to nonfiction to fiction and drama. I think the only sessions I've not done there are the children's lit. At Green Lake, it's always fiction.

MITCHELL: How do you find time to write?

SMITH: There are snatches of moments here and there, but most of the writing related to the conference or workshop comes before and after, especially after. One conference will keep me going until the next. There's so much energy! So much good writing! It's contagious, and I always hope and pray that I'll stay infected until the next conference.

MITCHELL: And do you?

SMITH: Oh, there are down times. We'd all burn out—or up—otherwise. But I also belong to a local writers' group, the Barbour County Writers' Workshop—which meets every two weeks. It's funny. Almost every time I'm reluctant to go—too busy, too tired, no new work to share—but I go anyway, and I'm always glad I did. I come away revitalized, ready to take another crack at it.

MITCHELL: If these workshops revitalize you, are your friends, what is the poet's enemy? What would you tell a writer early in her career?

SMITH: Unfortunately, as Russell Edson suggests, "Words are the enemy of poetry."[11] He reminds us of the fact that because the tool we use for poetry is the same as that used for instructions on the Bisquick package, many of the epiphanies of poets are recorded as zeros on readers' or listeners' scoreboards. Few readers today have the patience or the mindset to deal with Andrew Marvell or T. S. Eliot. But there are many, more accessible, exceptions like "The Red Wheelbarrow" and other poems by William Carlos Williams.[12]

MITCHELL: I'm thinking of your "On the Crossing of Bridges." Could you recite from that manuscript?

SMITH:

> If you cross a footbridge early enough,
> Before the sun does,
> You will be touched by dew,
> Thick on the cables and floorboards,
> Suspended like a virgin's tears
> On the breath-holding cobwebs,
> The cobwebs thus outlining, highlighting,
> And framing in crystal the whole waking world. . . .

MITCHELL: And a bridge is more than a bridge, a cobweb an infrastructure larger and less literal than a cobweb. I understand.

SMITH: Granted, we may still have readers ask, "What is that supposed to mean?" when we write one poem or the other, and in classes I have gone with students through the process of trying to help them understand the inexplicable. The interesting aftermath is that years later, some of the questioning students, even if they do not say "I understand," do say "I remember." That memory is of the connection with that double vision to which I, and other poets, aspire. It transcends the instructions on the Bisquick package and is visceral. The memory is what the epiphany engenders, provided that the imagery gets it there.

## Notes

1. Lawrence Raab, "Poetry's Weakness," *Writer's Chronicle* 31, no. 6 (Summer 1999): 11.
2. David Armstrong, "A Mystery Solved: Story of Four Skeletons Found in an Abandoned Mine," *Randolph, W.Va., Enterprise,* Mar. 4, 1896, n.p.
3. Alfredo Rios, foreword to *Approaching Poetry,* ed. Peter J. Schakel and Jack Ridl (New York: St. Martin's, 1997), xxv.
4. Susan Goldsmith Wooldridge, *Poemcrazy* (New York: Three Rivers Press, 1996), 71.
5. Irene McKinney, "Visiting My Gravesite: Talbott Churchyard, West Virginia," in *Six O'Clock Mine Report* (Pittsburgh: Univ. of Pittsburgh Press, 1989), 31.
6. Raab, 6.
7. Robert Frost discusses this concept in his favorite preface, "The Figure a Poem Makes," which is collected in *Robert Frost on Writing,* ed. Elaine Barry (New Brunswick, N.J.: Rutgers Univ. Press, 1973), 125–28.
8. Ralph Waldo Emerson, "The Poet," in *Essays and English Traits,* ed. Charles Eliot (New York: P. F. Collier and Sons, 1909), 180.
9. William Stafford, introd. to *Since Feeling is First,* ed. James Mecklenburger and Gary Simmons (Glenview, Ill.: Scott, Foresman and Company, 1971), 7.
10. Ellen Kort, "Letter from McCarty's Farm," in *Letter from McCarty's Farm* (Appleton, Wis.: Fox Print, 1994), 20.
11. Russell Edson, interview by Peter Johnson, *Writer's Chronicle* 31, no. 6 (Summer 1999): 32.
12. William Carlos Williams, "The Red Wheelbarrow," in *The Collected Poems of William Carlos Williams,* vol. 1, ed. A. Walton Litz and Christopher MacGowan (New York: New Directions, 1986), 224.

# Bibliography

Anderson, Maggie. *Cold Comfort.* Pittsburgh: Univ. of Pittsburgh Press, 1986.

———. Correspondence with Ellesa Clay High, 2000.

———. *The Great Horned Owl.* Baltimore, Md.: Icarus Press, 1979.

———. "The Mountains Dark and Close around Me." In *Bloodroot: Reflections on Place by Appalachian Writers*, edited by Joyce Dyer. Lexington, Ky.: Univ. Press of Kentucky, 1998.

———. "Saving the Dishes." *Poetry East* 20 and 21 (1986): 88–95.

———. *Space Filled with Moving.* Pittsburgh: Univ. of Pittsburgh Press, 1992.

———. "Two Rivers." In *Liberating Memory: Our Work and Our Working-Class Consciousness*, edited by Janet Zandy. New Brunswick, N.J.: Rutgers Univ. Press, 1994.

———. *Windfall: New and Selected Poems.* Pittsburgh: Univ. of Pittsburgh Press, 2000.

———. *Years That Answer.* New York: Harper & Row, 1980.

Anderson, Maggie, Alex Gildzen, and Raymond A. Craig. *A Gathering of Poets.* Kent, Ohio: Kent State Univ. Press, 1992.

Angelou, Maya. *I Know Why the Caged Bird Sings.* New York: Random House, 1969.

Armstrong, David. "A Mystery Solved: Story of Four Skeletons Found in an Abandoned Mine." *Randolph, W.Va., Enterprise*, Mar. 4, 1896, n.p.

Awiakta, Marilou [Thompson, Marilou Bonner]. *Abiding Appalachia: Where Mountain and Atom Meet.* Memphis: St. Luke's Press, 1978. Reprint, Bell Buckle, Tenn.: Iris Press, 1995.

———. Interview by Grace Toney Edwards. Memphis, Sept. 16, 1999.

———. *Rising Fawn and the Fire Mystery.* Memphis: St. Luke's Press, 1983.

———. *Selu: Seeking the Corn-Mother's Wisdom.* Golden, Colo.: Fulcrum Publishing, 1993.

———. "Sound." In *Bloodroot: Reflections on Place by Appalachian Women Writers*, edited by Joyce Dyer. Lexington, Ky.: Univ. Press of Kentucky, 1998.

Baker, Houston A., Jr., and Charlotte Pierce-Baker. "Patches: Quilts and Community in Alice Walker's 'Everyday Use.'" In *"Everyday Use" / Alice Walker*, edited by Barbara T. Christian. New Brunswick, N.J.: Rutgers Univ. Press, 1994.

Bakhtin, Mikhail. "From the Prehistory of Novelistic Discourse." In *The Dialogic Imagination*, edited by Michael Holquist. Austin: Univ. of Texas Press, 1981.

———. *Problems of Dostoevsky's Poetics.* Edited by Caryl Emerson. Minneapolis: Univ. of Minnesota Press, 1984.

Batteau, Allen W. *The Invention of Appalachia.* Tucson: Univ. of Arizona Press, 1990.

Battlo, Jean. "Frog Songs." *Small-Cast One-Act Guide Online.* Edited by Lewis W. Heniford. <www.heniford.net/1234/1m1f_fs.htm>

Beaver, Patricia D. "Women in Appalachia and the South: Gender, Race, Region, and Agency." *NWSA Journal* 11, no. 3 (1999). Online. Infotrac.

Bishop, Rudine Sims. "Profile: George Ella Lyon." *Language Arts* 67 (Oct. 1990): 611–16.

Booker, Suzanne. "A Conversation with Robert Morgan." *Carolina Quarterly* 37, no. 3 (1985): 13–22.

Brinson, Claudia Smith. "Bennie Lee Sinclair Writes Poetry for South Carolinians." *The State* (Columbia, S.C.), Mar. 25, 1999, A14.

Byer, James. "The Woman's Place Is in the House." In *The Poetics of Appalachian Space*, edited by Parks Lanier Jr. Knoxville: Univ. of Tennessee Press, 1991.

Byer, Kathryn Stripling. *Black Shawl*. Baton Rouge: Louisiana State Univ. Press, 1998.

———. "Deep Water." In *Bloodroot. Reflections on Place by Appalachian Women Writers*, edited by Joyce Dyer. Lexington, Ky.: Univ. Press of Kentucky, 1998.

———. *The Girl in the Midst of the Harvest*. Lubbock, Tex.: Texas Tech Press, 1986.

———. Interview [Jeff Daniel Marion]. *Mossy Creek Reader* 11 (Spring 1987): 28–31.

———. *Wildwood Flower*. Baton Rouge: Louisiana State Univ. Press, 1992.

Carson, Jo. "The Brown Dress." In "Out Loud: Telling Real Stories in Front of People Breaks the Tradition of Silence." *Southern Exposure* 24 (Winter 1996): 44–45.

———. "His Father's Work," "The Last of the 'Waltz across Texas," and "Stories from the Night the Family Received Friends at a Kentucky Farmer's Funeral." In *The Last of the 'Waltz across Texas' and Other Stories*. Frankfort, Ky.: Gnomon, 1993.

———. Interview by Jo Harris. *Appalachian Journal* 20 (Fall 1992): 56–67.

———. "Jump." *Iron Mountain Review* 14 (Summer 1998): 7.

———. "Jump." In *Preposterous: Poems of Youth*. Edited by Paul B. Janeczko. New York: Orchard Books, 1991.

———. "Out Loud: Telling Real Stories in Front of People Breaks the Tradition of Silence." *Southern Exposure* 24 (Winter 1996): 42–47.

———. "Some Thoughts on Direct Address and Oral Histories in Performance." *Drama Review* 40 (Summer 1996): 115–17.

———. *Stories I Ain't Told Nobody Yet: Selections from the People Pieces*. New York: Theatre Communications Group, 1991.

———. "Thou Shalt Not Covet." In "Out Loud: Telling Real Stories in Front of People Breaks the Tradition of Silence." *Southern Exposure* 24 (Winter 1996): 42–47.

———. "The Wealth of Story: A Conversation." Interviewed by Pat Arnow. *Iron Mountain Review* 14 (Summer 1998): 31–37.

Chappell, Fred. "Five New Southern Women Poets." *Georgia Review* 50 (1996): 174–84.

———. "Two Modes: A Plea for Tolerance." *Appalachian Journal* 4 (1978): 335–39.

Coffman, Lisa. *Likely*. Kent, Ohio: Kent State Univ. Press, 1996.

———. "Judges Notes: Poetry." From the *Philadelphia Citipaper.net* web page. Online. Available: <http://www.citypaper.net/articles/122895/article009.shtml>.

Crabtree, Lou V. *The River Hills and Beyond*. Introduced by Lee Smith. Abingdon, Va.: Sow's Ear Press, 1998.

———. *Sweet Hollow*. Baton Rouge: Louisiana State Univ. Press, 1984.

Cuddon, J. A. *A Dictionary of Literary Terms and Literary Theory*. Oxford: Basil Blackwell, 1991.

Cunningham, Rodger. *Apples on the Flood: Minority Discourse and Appalachia*. Knoxville: Univ. of Tennessee Press, 1987.

———. "Writing on the Cusp. Double Alterity and Minority Discourse in Appalachia." In *The Future of Southern Letters*, edited by Jefferson Humphreys and John Lowe. New York and Oxford: Oxford Univ. Press, 1996.

Cutler, Rupert. Review of *Selu: Seeking the Corn-Mother's Wisdom*, by Marilou Awiakta. *Now & Then* 12, no. 1 (Spring 1995): 37.

davenport, doris. "All This, and Honeysuckles Too." In *Bloodroot: Reflections on Place by Appalachian Women Writers*, edited by Joyce Dyer. Lexington, Ky.: Univ. Press of Kentucky, 1998.

———. Correspondence with James A. Miller. Aug. 13, 2000.

———. *eat thunder & drink rain*. Los Angeles: privately printed, 1982.

———. *it's like this*. N.p., 1980.

———. "The Pathology of Racism: A Conversation with Third World Wimmin." In *This Bridge Called My Back: Writings by Radical Women of Color*, edited by Cherrie Moraga and Gloria Anzaldua. Watertown, Mass.: Persephone Press, 1981.

———. Selected Poems. In *DAY TONIGHT/NIGHT TODAY* 21 (1984).

———. *Soque Street Poems*. Sautee-Nacoochie, Ga.: Sautee-Nacoochie Community Association, 1995.

Dickey, James. *Deliverance*. Boston: Houghton Mifflin, 1970.

Dickinson, Emily. *Emily Dickinson, Selected Letters*. Edited by Thomas H. Johnson. Cambridge, Mass.: Belknap Press, 1986.

———. *Letters of Emily Dickinson*. Edited by Thomas H. Johnson. Cambridge, Mass.: Harvard Univ. Press, Belknap Press, 1958.

Dillard, Annie. *Pilgrim at Tinker Creek*. New York: Harper & Row, 1974.

Diyanni, Robert. *Modern American Poets, Their Voices and Visions*. New York: Random House, 1987.

Dodson, Angela. "Patches: Quilts as Black Literary Icons." *Black Issues Book Review* 1, no. 3 (May–June 1999): 41–42.

Dyer, Joyce, ed. *Bloodroot: Reflections on Place by Appalachian Women Writers*. Lexington, Ky.: Univ. Press of Kentucky, 1998.

Edson, Russell. Interview by Peter Johnson. *Writer's Chronicle* 31, no. 6 (Summer 1999): 32.

Edwards, Grace Toney. "The Hum of Black Oak Ridge in the Poetry of Marilou Awiakta." Paper and slide presentation given at the Appalachian Studies Association's Annual Conference, Univ. of Tennessee, Knoxville, Tenn., 2000.

Elder, John. *Reading the Mountains of Home*. Cambridge, Mass.: Harvard Univ. Press, 1998.

Ellul, Jacques. *The Meaning of the City*. Grand Rapids: William B. Eerdmans, 1970.

Emerson, Ralph Waldo. *The Collected Works of Ralph Waldo Emerson*. Vol. 1. Edited by Robert E. Spiller and Alfred R. Ferguson. Cambridge, Mass.: Belknap Press, 1971.

———. "The Poet." In *Essays and English Traits*, edited by Charles Eliot. New York: P. F. Collier and Sons, 1909.

*Facts on File Encyclopedia of World Mythology and Legend*. S.v. "Savitri."

Ferris, William R. "Region As Art." In *Regional Studies: The Interplay of Land and People*, edited by Glen E. Lich. College Station, Tex.: Texas A & M Univ. Press, 1992.

Ford, Karen Jackson. *Gender and the Poetics of Excess*. Jackson: Univ. Press of Mississippi, 1997.

Fowler, Virginia C. *Nikki Giovanni*. New York: Twayne, 1992.

Freeman, Roland. *A Communion of the Spirits: African-American Quilters, Preservers, and Their Stories*. Nashville: Rutledge Hill Press, 1996.

Frost, Robert. "The Death of the Hired Man." In *The Poetry of Robert Frost*, edited by
   Edward Connery. New York: Holt, Rinehart and Winston, 1969.
———. "The Figure a Poem Makes." In *Robert Frost on Writing*, edited by Elaine Barry.
   New Brunswick, N.J.: Rutgers Univ. Press, 1973.
———. "The Figure a Poem Makes." In *Interpreting Literature*, 7th ed., edited by K. L.
   Knickerbocker et al. New York: Holt, Rinehart and Winston, 1985.
Gallup, Dick. *Shiny Pencils at the Edge of Things*. Minneapolis: Coffee House Press, 2001.
Geer, Richard Owen, and Debra Jones. "Gathering Mayhaws: Jo Carson and Writing
   for Community Performance." *Iron Mountain Review* 14 (Summer 1998): 24–30.
Giardina, Denise. *The Unquiet Earth*. New York: Ivy Books, 1992.
Gibbons, Reginald. Lecture presented at the annual Spoleto Writers Symposium,
   Spoleto, Italy, July 1998.
Gilbert, Sandra M., and Susan Gubar. *No Man's Land: The Place of the Woman Writer in the
   Twentieth Century*. New Haven and London: Yale Univ. Press, 1988.
Giovanni, Nikki. *Blues for All the Changes*. New York: William Morrow, 1999.
———. *Gemini: An Extended Autobiographical Statement on My First Twenty-Five Years of Being a
   Black Poet* (1971). New York: Penguin, 1985.
——— Lecture at Longwood College. Farmville, Va., Apr. 20, 2000.
———. *Like a Ripple on a Pond: A Golden Classics Edition*. Narberth, Pa.: Collectables
   Records, 1993. Audio CD.
———. *Love Poems*. New York: William Morrow, 1997.
———. *Racism 101*. New York: William Morrow, 1994.
———. "Racism, Consciousness, and Afrocentricity." In *Lure and Loathing: Essays on
   Race, Identity, and the Ambivalence of Assimilation*, edited by Gerald Early. New York:
   Allen Lane, Penguin Press, 1993.
———. *Sacred Cows . . . and Other Edibles*. New York: William Morrow, 1988.
———. *Selected Poems of Nikki Giovanni*. New York: William Morrow, 1996.
———. *Truth Is on Its Way*. Narberth, Pa.: Collectibles Records, 1993. Audio CD.
Gray, Amy Tipton. *The Hillbilly Vampire* (1989). Blacksburg, Va.: Rowan Mountain Press,
   1992.
Griffin, Farah Jasmine. *"Who set you flowin'?": The African-American Migration Narrative*. New
   York: Oxford Univ. Press, 1995.
"The Guid Scots Tongue." Videocassette. Part 3 of *The Story of English*. BBC TV co-
   production with MacNeil-Lehrer Productions in association with WNET.
   Chicago: Public Media Video, 1986.
Haddix, Cecille, ed. *Who Speaks for Appalachia?* New York: Washington Square Press
   Pocket Books, 1975.
Hall, Donald. "Varieties of Pleasure." In *The Pleasures of Poetry*. New York: Harper & Row, 1971.
Hayden, Robert. "Those Winter Sundays." In *Collected Poems of Robert Hayden*, edited by
   Frederick Glaysher. New York and London: Liveright, 1985.
Hernadi, Paul. "So What? How So? And the Form That Matters." *Critical Inquiry* 3, no. 2
   (Winter 1976): 369–86.
Higgs, Robert J. "Hicks, Hillbillies, Hell-Raisers, and Heroes: Traditional Mythic
   Types of Southern Appalachian." In *Appalachian Literature: Critical Essays*, edited by
   Ruel E. Foster. Charleston, W.Va.: Morris Harvey College, 1976.

hooks, bell. *Talking Back: Thinking Feminist, Thinking Black*. Boston: South End, 1989.

Howard, Julie Kate. "'Having Become Their Own Voices': The Third Stream in Kathryn Stripling Byer's *Black Shawl*." *Asheville Poetry Review* 6, no. 1 (Spring and Summer 1999): 37–44.

Hughes, Langston. *The Collected Poems of Langston Hughes*. Edited by Arnold Rampersad. New York: Random House, Vintage Books, 1994.

Inez, Collette. "Sounds of Hazard and Survival." In *Sleeping with One Eye Open: Women Writers and the Art of Survival*, edited by Marilyn Kallett and Judith Ortiz Cofer. Athens: Univ. of Georgia Press, 1999.

Inscoe, John. "Appalachian Otherness, Real and Perceived." In *The New Georgia Guide*, edited by Thomas G. Dyer. Athens: Univ. of Georgia Press, 1996.

Jackson, Fleda Brown. "Temples of the Holy Ghost." *Shenandoah* 46, no. 4 (1996): 118–29.

Jackson, Richard. "Donald Hall, On the Periphery of Time." In *Acts of Mind: Conversations with Contemporary Poets*. Tuscaloosa: Univ. of Alabama Press, 1983.

Johnson, Don. "The Appalachian Homeplace as Oneiric House." In *The Poetics of Appalachian Space*, edited by Parks Lanier. Knoxville: Univ. of Tennessee Press, 1991.

———. "Carrying Drunks Up River." In *The Importance of Visible Scars*. Green Harbor, Mass.: Wampeter Press, 1984.

Johnson, James Weldon. *God's Trombones: Seven Negro Sermons in Verse*. Rei Edition. New York: Penguin Books, 1990.

Johnson, Jennifer. Review of *The Girl in the Midst of the Harvest*, by Kathryn Stripling Byer. *Mossy Creek Reader* 11 (Spring 1987): 22–25.

Johnson, Patricia A. *Spirit Rising*. Elks Creek, Va.: S.P.A.R.K.S., 1999.

———. *Stain My Days Blue*. Philadelphia: Ausdoh Press, 1999.

Jones, Loyal. *Faith and Meaning in the Southern Uplands*. Urbana: Univ. of Illinois Press, 1999.

Keats, John. "Ode on a Grecian Urn." In *Anthology of Romanticism*, 3rd ed., edited by Ernest Bernbaum. New York: Ronald Press, 1948.

Kendrick, Leatha. *Heart Cake*. Abingdon, Va.: Sow's Ear Press, 2000.

———. "No Place Like Home." *American Voice* 49 (1999): 96–106.

———. *Sharing a Love of Sunlight*. Self-published chapbook, 1992.

Killens, John Oliver. Introduction to *Black Southern Voices: An Anthology of Fiction, Poetry, Drama, Nonfiction, and Critical Essays*, edited by Killens and Jerry W. Ward Jr. New York: Meridian, Penguin, 1992.

Kort, Ellen. "Letter from McCarty's Farm." In *Letter from McCarty's Farm*. Appleton, Wis.: Fox Print, 1994.

Lang, John. "The Editor's Page." *Iron Mountain Review* 10 (1994): 2.

———. "Means of Grace." Paper presented at the annual meeting of the South Atlantic Modern Language Association, Savannah, Ga., 1996.

Lanier, Lyle H. "A Critique of the Philosophy of Progress." In *I'll Take My Stand: The South and the Agrarian Tradition*. Introd. by Louis D. Rubin Jr. Baton Rouge: Louisiana State Univ. Press, 1977.

Lanier, Parks, Jr. ed. *The Poetics of Appalachian Space*. Knoxville: Univ. of Tennessee Press, 1991.

Larkin, Philip. *High Windows*. London: Faber and Faber, 1974.

Lee, Ernest. "Sources of Light in Awiakta's *Selu*." Paper presented at the Appalachian Studies Association's Annual Conference at the University of Tennessee, Knoxville, Tenn., 2000.

Leidig, Dan. Foreword to *The River Hills and Beyond*, by Lou V. Crabtree. Abingdon, Va.: Sow's Ear Press, 1998.

Levertov, Denise. "The Five-Day Rain." In *With Eyes at the Back of Our Heads*. New York: New Directions, 1959.

Lindbergh, Anne Morrow. *A Gift from the Sea*. New York: Random House, 1991.

"Lisa Coffman." Pew Fellowship for the Arts web page. Available: <http://www.pewarts.org/93/Coffman/main.html>.

Lorde, Audre. *The Uses of the Erotic: The Erotic as Power*. Milford, Conn.: Out and Out Books, 1978.

Loveland, Anne C. *Lillian Smith: A Southerner Confronting the South*. Baton Rouge: Louisiana State Univ. Press, 1986.

Lyon, George Ella. *A B Cedar: An Alphabet of Trees*. Illustrated by Tom Parker. New York: Orchard, 1989.

———. "Appalachian Women Poets: Breaking the Double Silence." *American Voice* 8 (Fall 1987): 62–72.

———. *Basket*. Illustrated by Mary Szilagyi. New York: Orchard, 1990.

———. *Catalpa*. Lexington, Ky.: Wind Publications, 1993.

———. *Cecil's Story*. Illustrated by Peter Catalanotto. New York: Orchard, 1991.

———. *Come a Tide*. Illustrated by Stephen Gammell. New York: Orchard, 1990.

———. *A Day at Damp Camp*. Illustrated by Peter Catalanotto. New York: Orchard, 1996.

———. *Dreamplace*. Illustrated by Peter Catalanotto. New York: Orchard, 1993.

———. *Mama Is a Miner*. Illustrated by Peter Catalanotto. New York: Orchard, 1994.

———. *Mountain*. Hartford: Andrew Mountain Press, 1983.

———. "Old Wounds, New Words: Sources and Directions." In *Old Wounds, New Words: Poems from the Appalachian Poetry Project*, edited by Bob Henry Baber, George Ella Lyon, and Gurney Norman. Ashland, Ky.: Jesse Stuart Foundation, 1994.

———. *A Regular Rolling Noah*. Illustrated by Stephen Gammell. New York: Bradbury, 1986.

———. "Sidelights." *Something about the Author*. Vol. 68. Detroit: Gale, 1992.

———. "Voiceplace." In *Bloodroot: Reflections on Place by Appalachian Women Writers*, edited by Joyce Dyer. Lexington, Ky: Univ. Press of Kentucky, 1998.

———. "Voices Rooted in Place: A Conversation." Interviewed by Jeff Daniel Marion. *Iron Mountain Review* 10 (Summer 1994): 22–28.

———. *Who Came down That Road?* Illustrated by Peter Catalanotto. New York: Orchard, 1992.

———. *A Wordful Child*. Photographed by Ann W. Olson. Katonah, N.Y.: Richard C. Owen, 1996.

Lyon, George Ella, Jim Wayne Miller, and Gurney Norman. *A Gathering at the Forks*. Wise, Va.: Vision Books, 1993.

Marion, Jeff Daniel. Review of *Old & New Testaments*. *Now & Then* 13, no. 3 (1996): 37–38.

Marion, Linda Parsons. "In My Mother's House." *Sow's Ear Poetry Review* 10, no. 2 (2000): 27.

McCauley, Deborah Vansau. *Appalachian Mountain Religion: A History.* Urbana: Univ. of Illinois Press, 1996.

McKinney, Irene. *The Girl with the Stone in Her Lap.* Berkeley, Calif.: North Atlantic Books, 1988.

———. Interview. *Kestrel* 4 (Fall 1994): 9.

———. *Quick Fire and Slow Fire: Poems.* Berkeley, Calif.: North Atlantic Books, 1988.

———. *Six O'Clock Mine Report.* Pittsburgh: Univ. of Pittsburgh Press, 1989.

———. "Viridian Days." In *Wild Sweet Notes: Fifty Years of West Virginia Poetry, 1950–1999,* edited by Barbara Smith and Kirk Judd. Huntington, W.Va.: Publishers Place, 2000.

McNeill, Louise. "Hill Daughter." In *Hill Daughter: New and Selected Poems,* edited by Maggie Anderson. Pittsburgh: Univ. of Pittsburgh Press, 1991.

———. *Hill Daughter: New and Selected Poems.* Ed. Maggie Anderson. Pittsburgh: Univ. of Pittsburgh Press, 1991.

———. *The Milkweed Ladies.* Pittsburgh: Univ. of Pittsburgh Press, 1988.

*Merriam-Webster's Collegiate Dictionary.* S.v. "Appalachian."

Miller, Jim Wayne. "A Heart Leafed with Words Like a Tree: The Poetry of George Ella Lyon." *Iron Mountain Review* 10 (Summer 1994): 6–8.

———. *The Mountains Have Come Closer.* Boone, N.C.: Appalachian Consortium Press, 1980.

Mitchell, Sean. "Eavesdropper Jo Carson Spins a Personal Story." *American Theatre* 7, no. 1 (Jan. 1990): 56–57.

Morgan, Robert. "Audubon's Flute" and "Mica Country." In *Sigodlin.* Middletown, Conn.: Wesleyan Univ. Press, 1990.

———. "Bryant's Solitary Glimpse of Paradise." In *Under Open Sky: Poets on William Cullen Bryant,* edited by Norbert Krapf. New York: Fordham Univ. Press, 1986.

———. "Oxbow Lakes." In *Wild Peavines.* Frankfort, Ky.: Gnomon Press, 1996.

Morrison, Toni. "Rootedness: The Ancestor in Afro-American Fiction." In *Black Women Writers at Work: A Critical Evaluation,* edited by Mari Evans. Garden City, N.Y.: Anchor Press, 1984.

Nicolson, Marjorie Hope. *Mountain Gloom and Mountain Glory: The Development of the Aesthetics of the Infinite.* Ithaca, N.Y.: Cornell Univ. Press, 1959. Reprint, Seattle: Univ. of Washington, 1997.

Norris, Kathleen. *Amazing Grace: A Vocabulary of Faith.* Hudson, N.Y.: Riverhead Books, 1999.

———. *The Cloister Walk.* Hudson, N.Y.: Riverhead Books, 1997.

O'Connor, Flannery. *The Habit of Being: Letters.* Edited by Sally Fitzgerald. New York: Farrar, Straus, Giroux, 1979.

Ong, Walter J. *Orality and Literacy: The Technologizing of the Word.* New York: Methuen, 1982.

Ostriker, Alicia Suskin. *Stealing the Language.* Boston: Beacon Press, 1986.

Orwell, George. *1984.* London: Martin Secker & Warburg, Ltd., 1949.

Pancake, Breece D'J. "Trilobites." In *The Stories of Breece D'J Pancake.* New York: Holt, Rinehart and Winston, 1984.

Parsons, Linda. *Home Fires.* Abingdon, Va.: Sow's Ear Press, 1997.

Pennsylvania State University–Altoona English Department faculty web page. <www.personal.psu.edu/faculty/k/a/kaw16/Facultybiographies.htm>.

Perkins, David. Introduction to *English Romantic Writers*. New York: Harcourt Brace Jovanovich, 1967.

Pew Fellowship for the Arts web page. Online. Available: <http://www.pewarts.org/abpfmaintcxt.html>.

Phillips, Jayne Anne. *Sweethearts*. Berkeley, Calif.: Truck Press, 1976.

Porter, Katherine Ann. "The Jilting of Granny Weatherall." In *The Collected Stories of Katherine Ann Porter*. New York: Harcourt, Brace, and World, 1965.

Powell, Lynn. *Old & New Testaments*. Madison: Univ. of Wisconsin Press, 1995.

Quillen, Rita Sims. *Counting the Sums*. Abingdon, Va.: Sow's Ear Press, 1995.

———. "Hiding Ezra." *Go Tell It on the Mountain*. Appalshop Radio Series. Whitesburg, Ky., 1995.

———. *Looking for Native Ground: Contemporary Appalachian Poetry*. Boone, N.C.: Appalachian Consortium Press, 1989.

———. *October Dusk*. Big Timber, Mont.: Seven Buffaloes Press, 1987.

Raab, Lawrence. "Poetry's Weakness." *Writer's Chronicle* 31, no. 6 (Summer 1999): 11–15.

Rash, Ron. *Eureka Mill*. Corvallis, Ore.: Bench Press, 1998.

Review of *Likely*, by Lisa Coffman. *Publisher's Weekly*, Nov. 25, 1996, 72.

Review of *Old & New Testaments*, by Lynn Powell. *Publishers Weekly*, Oct. 23, 1995, 66.

Rich, Adrienne. "Necessities of Life." In *Poems: Selected and New, 1950–1974*. New York: W. W. Norton, 1974.

Riddle, Rita Sizemore. *Aluminum Balloons*. Blacksburg, Va.: Pocahontas Press, 1996.

———. *Pieces for Emma*. Radford, Va.: Radford Univ. Occasional Publications Press, 1994.

———. "The Reward" and "Potted Ham and Crackers." In *A Gathering at the Forks: Writings of the Hindman Settlement School Writers Workshop*, edited by George Ella Lyon, Jim Wayne Miller, and Gurney Norman. Wise, Va.: Vision Books, 1993.

———. *Soot and Sunshine*. Radford, Va.: Radford Univ. Occasional Publications Press, 1993.

Riemer, Ruby. "Theopoetry." Review of *Old & New Testaments*, by Lynn Powell. *American Book Review* 31, no. 6 (Aug.–Sept. 1996): 12.

Rilke, Rainer Maria. "Sonnet to Orpheus 3." In *Sonnets to Orpheus*, translated by C. F. MacIntyre. Berkeley, Calif.: Univ. of California Press, 1960.

Rios, Alfredo. Foreword to *Approaching Poetry*, edited by Peter J. Schakel and Jack Ridl. New York: St. Martin's, 1997.

Sanders, Scott Russell. *Staying Put: Making a Home in a Restless World*. Boston: Beacon Press, 1994.

Santayana, George. "The Philosophy of Travel." In *"The Birth of Reason" and Other Essays*, edited by Daniel Cory. New York: Columbia Univ. Press, 1968.

Schott, Penelope Scambly. Review of *Black Shawl*, by Kathryn Stripling Byer. *Sow's Ear Poetry Review* 8, no. 3 (Sept. 1998): 23–24.

Sellers, Bettie. Interview by author. Young Harris, Ga. Mar. 10, 1999.

———. Interview by Stephen R. Whited and Frank Gannon. *Habersham Review* 8, no. 1 (1999): 15–22.

————. Keynote address at the Three Arts Club, Cornelia, Ga., Nov. 5, 1998.

————. Lecture at Piedmont College, Demorest, Ga., Apr. 9, 1999.

————. *Liza's Monday and Other Poems*. Boone, N.C.: Appalachian Consortium Press, 1986.

————. *Morning of the Red-Tailed Hawk*. University Center, Mich.: Green River Press, 1981.

————. *Spring Onions and Cornbread*. Gretna, La.: Pelican Publishing Co., 1978.

————. *Westward from Bald Mountain*. N.p., 1974.

————. "Westward from Bald Mountain." In *Bloodroot: Reflections on Place by Appalachian Women Writers*, edited by Joyce Dyer. Lexington, Ky.: Univ. Press of Kentucky, 1998.

————. "Westward from Bald Mountain: Valleys for Writers." Lecture presented at the annual meeting of the Georgia Humanities Council, Atlanta, Ga., 1998.

————. *Wild Ginger*. Atlanta: Morning Glory Ink, 1989.

Settle, Mary Lee. *Charley Bland*. New York: Farrar, Straus, Giroux, 1989.

Sewell, Marilyn, ed. *Cries of the Spirit: A Celebration of Women's Spirituality*. Boston: Beacon Press, 1991.

Shapiro, Henry D. *Appalachia on Our Mind*. Chapel Hill: Univ. of North Carolina Press, 1978.

Sholl, Betsy. *Appalachian Winter*. Cambridge, Mass.: alicejamesbooks, 1978.

————. "Big Stone Gap." In *Bloodroot: Reflections on Place by Appalachian Women Writers*, edited by Joyce Dyer. Lexington, Ky.: Univ. Press of Kentucky, 1998.

————. *Don't Explain*. Madison: Univ. of Wisconsin Press, 1997.

————. *The Red Line*. Pittsburgh: Univ. of Pittsburgh Press, 1992.

Showalter, Elaine. *Sister's Choice: Tradition and Change in American Women's Writing*. New York: Oxford Univ. Press, Clarendon Press, 1991.

Sinclair, Bennie Lee. "Appalachian Loaves and Fishes." In *Bloodroot: Reflections on Place by Appalachian Women Writers*, edited by Joyce Dyer. Lexington, Ky.: Univ. Press of Kentucky, 1998.

————. *The Arrowhead Scholar*. Cleveland, S.C.: Wildernesse Books, 1978.

————. *The Endangered: New and Selected Poems*. Greenville, S.C.: Ninety-Six Press, 1992.

————. *Little Chicago Suite*. 2nd ed. Cleveland, S.C.: Wildernesse Books, 1978.

————. *Lord of Springs*. Blacksburg, Va.: Rowan Mountain Press, 1990.

"Sinclair, Bennie Lee." *Contemporary Authors*. New Revision Series. Vol. 1 (1985): 601–2.

Smith, Barbara Ellen. "The Social Relations of Southern Women." In *Neither Separate nor Equal: Women, Race, and Class in the South*, edited by Smith. Philadelphia: Temple Univ. Press, 1999.

Smith, Dave. "Assays." In *First Person Singular: Writers on Their Craft*, compiled by Joyce Carol Oates. Princeton, N.J.: Ontario Review Press, 1983.

Smith, Lee. "Every Kind of Ritual: A Conversation." Interview by Dorothy Hill. *Iron Mountain Review* 3, no. 1 (Winter 1986): 25–27.

Snyder, Robert. "Image and Identity in Appalachia." *Appalachian Journal* 9 (1982): 124–33.

Spacks, Patricia Meyer. *Gossip*. New York: Knopf, 1985.

St. Catherine of Siena. *Dialogue of St. Catherine of Siena*. Designed by Algar Thorold. Rockford, Ill.: Tan Books and Publishers, 1991.

Stafford, William. Introduction to *Since Feeling is First*, edited by James Mecklenburger and Gary Simmons. Glenview, Ill.: Scott, Foresman and Company 1971.

———. "The Tradition of Total Experience." In *First Person Singular:Writers on Their Craft*, compiled by Joyce Carol Oates. Princeton, N. J.: Ontario Review Press, 1983.

Stahl, Sandra K. D. "Style in Oral and Written Narratives." *Southern Folklore Quarterly* 43 (1970): 107–20.

Still, James. *River of Earth*. Lexington, Ky.: Univ. Press of Kentucky, 1978.

Struzzi, Diane. "A Trial in Grayson County. *Roanoke,Va.,Times*. Feb. 15, 1998.

Swanson, Gayle R., and William B. Thesing. *Conversations with South Carolina Poets*. Winston-Salem, N.C.: John F. Blair, 1986.

Thomas, Dylan. "A Refusal to Mourn the Death by Fire of a Child in London." In *Collected Poems*. New York: New Directions Books, 1957.

Thoreau, Henry David. "Walden." In *Anthology of American Literature*, vol. 1, edited by George McMichael. New York: Macmillan, 1980.

Torsney, Cheryl B., and Judy Elsley, eds. *Quilt Culture:Tracing the Pattern*. Columbia: Univ. of Missouri Press, 1994.

Tuan, Yi-Fu. *Topophilia:A Study of Environmental Perception,Attitudes, andValues*. Englewood Cliffs, N.J.: Prentice-Hall, 1974. Reprint, New York: Columbia Univ. Press, 1990.

Vaschenko, Alexandr. Review of *Selu: Seeking the Corn-Mother's Wisdom*, by Marilou Awiakta. *North Dakota Quarterly* 62 (Summer 1995): 229–32.

Walker, Alice. "Everyday Use." In *Love and Trouble: Stories of Black Women*. New York: Harcourt Brace Jovanovich, 1973.

Walker, Frank X. *Affrilachia*. Lexington, Ky.: Old Cove Press, 2000.

Wallace, Robert, and Michelle Boisseau. *Writing Poems*. 4th ed. New York: HarperCollins, 1996.

Weaver, Richard M. "The Older Religiousness in the South." (1943). In *The Southern Essays of Richard M.Weaver*, edited by George M. Curtis III and James J. Thompson Jr. Indianapolis: Liberty Press, 1987.

White, Richard. "'Are You an Environmentalist, or Do You Work for a Living?'" In *Uncommon Ground: Rethinking the Human Place in Nature*, edited by William Cronon. New York: W. W. Norton, 1995.

Whitfield, Stephen J. *A Death in the Delta:The Story of Emmett Till*. New York: Free Press, 1988.

Wilbur, Richard. "Love Calls Us to the Things of the World." In *New and Collected Poems*. San Diego: Harvest/HBJ, 1988.

Williams, Raymond. *Culture and Society, 1780–1950*. New York: Penguin, 1963.

Williams, William Carlos. "The Red Wheelbarrow." In *The Collected Poems ofWilliam CarlosWilliams*, vol. 1, edited by A. Walton Litz and Christopher MacGowan. New York: New Directions, 1986.

Williamson, J. W. *Hillbillyland:What the Movies Did to the Mountains andWhat the Mountains Did to the Movies*. Chapel Hill: Univ. of North Carolina Press, 1995.

Wooldridge, Susan Goldsmith. *Poemcrazy*. New York: Three Rivers Press, 1996.

Woolf, Virginia. *A Room of One's Own*. New York: Harcourt, Brace, and Company, 1989.

Wordsworth, William. "Preface to *Lyrical Ballads, with Pastoral and Other Poems*" (1802). In *WilliamWordsworth:The Oxford Authors*, edited by Stephen Gill, 595–615. New York: Oxford Univ. Press, 1984.

Yeats, W. B. "The Lake Isle of Innisfree." In *Collected Poems. Definitive Edition*. New York: Macmillan, 1956.

# Contributors

Gilbert Allen, a poet and scholar, teaches at Furman University. His books of poetry include In Everything (Lotus Press, 1982), Second Chances (Orchises Press, 1991), and Commandments at Eleven (Orchises Press, 1994). His scholarly essays have appeared in many publications, including The American Book Review, College English, Southern Humanities Review, and Contemporary Poets, Dramatists, Essayists, and Novelists of the South. With William Rogers, he co-edited 45/96: The Ninety-Six Sampler of South Carolina Poetry (Ninety-Six Press, 1994).

Grace Toney Edwards directs the Appalachian Regional Studies Center and chairs the interdisciplinary Appalachian Studies Program at Radford University in Radford, Virginia, where she serves as Distinguished Professor of Appalachian Studies. She currently directs the Appalachian Arts and Studies and English in the Schools Project. Among Dr. Edwards's publications are the foreword to A Circuit Rider's Wife (University of Georgia Press, 1998); "Emma Bell Miles: Feminist Crusader in Appalachia" (Appalachia Inside Out, University of Tennessee Press, 1995); "Place and Space in Breece Pancake's 'A Room Forever'" (The Poetics of Appalachian Space, University of Tennessee Press, 1991); "Appalachia: The Effects of Cultural Values in the Production and Consumption of Alcohol" (The American Experience with Alcohol, Plenum, 1985).

Virginia Fowler is Professor of English at Virginia Tech, where she teaches courses on African American writers and Black Studies. She has published four books: Henry James's American Girl: The Embroidery on the Canvas (University of Wisconsin Press, 1984); Nikki Giovanni (Twayne/Macmillan, 1992); Conversations with Nikki Giovanni (University Press of Mississippi, 1992); and Gloria Naylor: In Search of Sanctuary (Twayne/Macmillan, 1996).

Patricia M. Gantt received her Ph.D. at University of North Carolina–Chapel Hill and now teaches English education and American literature at Utah State University, where she is an associate professor. Her published work includes essays on Wilma Dykeman, August Wilson, Rebecca Wells, and William Faulkner, as well as folklore studies on traditional basket weaving in the hot-air balloon industry and the power politics of cake in the South. She is presently completing books on Dykeman's fiction and nonfiction and on interviews with southern women from the Federal Writers' Project.

ROBERTA T. HERRIN, Professor of English, has taught college-level English for twenty-six years and has for the last seven years served as Associate Dean of the Graduate School at East Tennessee State University. She took the Ph.D. degree at the University of Tennessee, writing a doctoral dissertation on H. L. Mencken as a philologist. Her primary area of research is Appalachian literature with emphasis on Appalachian children's literature, the area in which she has published most frequently. Gloria Houston, Cynthia Rylant, Jo Carson, and George Ella Lyon are among the Appalachian children's writers about whom she has written. From 1988 to 1992, she created and directed the NEH-sponsored Institute in Fantasy Literature at ETSU; in 1992–93, she was awarded the Howard Fellowship from Brown University, a funded sabbatical during which she began the development of a bibliography of Appalachian children's literature, under contract with McFarland Press. She is active in a number of professional organizations, such as SAMLA and the Appalachian Studies Association, and serves as trustee of a number of professional and community organizations such as the Tennesseana Publications of the University of Tennessee Press and the Jonesborough/Washington County Heritage Alliance.

Although raised in suburban Louisville, Kentucky, ELLESA CLAY HIGH has lived her adult life in Appalachia and currently resides in rural Preston County. Since receiving her Ph.D. from Ohio University in 1981, she has taught Appalachian literature and American Indian literature in the English Department of West Virginia University. Her fiction, nonfiction, poetry, and scholarly work have appeared widely. She has received an Andrew W. Mellon Foundation Award and a James Still Fellowship in Appalachian Studies, and her *Past Titan Rock: Journey into an Appalachian Valley* (University Press of Kentucky, 1984) received the Appalachian Award in 1983.

RICHARD JACKSON is the author of several books of poems including *Heartwall* (winner of the 1999 Juniper Prize from the University of Massachusetts). He is also the author of two award-winning critical books, *The Dismantling of Time in Contemporary Poetry* (University of Alabama Press, 1988) and *Acts of Mind: Conversations with Contemporary Poets* (University of Alabama Press, 1983); two anthologies of Slovene Poetry; and a selection of poems, *Half Lives*, based on Petrarch (Invisible Cities Press, 2002). He is U.C. Foundation Professor (Ph.D., Yale University) at University of Tennessee–Chattanooga where he teaches creative writing and classical and twentieth-century poetry, as well as humanities, in the university's interdisciplinary program. He is also on the staff of Vermont College.

DON JOHNSON is Dean of the College of Arts and Sciences at East Tennessee State University. He has published two books of poems, *The Importance of Visible Scars* (Wampeter Press, 1984) and *Watauga Drawdown* (Overmountain Press, 1990), and edited *Hummers, Knucklers, and Slow Curves: Contemporary American Baseball Poems* (University of Illinois Press, 1991). He is also editor of *Aethlon: The Journal of Sport Literature.*

JOHN LANG has taught American literature at Emory & Henry College since 1983. There he also directs the college's annual literary festival celebrating writers with roots in Appalachia and edits *The Iron Mountain Review*, which publishes the proceedings of these festivals. A graduate of St. Olaf College, he received his Ph.D. from Stanford University. He has published essays on a number of Appalachian and other southern writers, including Wendell Berry, Doris Betts, Fred Chappell, John Ehle, Ernest Gaines, Cormac McCarthy, Robert Morgan, and William Styron. His book *Understanding Fred Chappell* was published by the University of South Carolina Press in 2000.

PARKS LANIER is a Professor of English at Radford University who has produced archival television interviews with Appalachian writers and musicians for the university's annual Highland Summer Conference. He has edited journals and books, including *The Poetics of Appalachian Space*, a collection of scholarly essays (University of Tennessee Press, 1991). He also writes poetry.

A native of West Virginia, JEFF MANN is Instructor of English at Virginia Polytechnic Institute, where he teaches courses in poetry and Appalachian literature, among others. His poems have been widely published in journals such as the *Evergreen Chronicles*, *Spoon River Poetry Review*, *Wormwood Review*, and *Prairie Schooner*. His poetry collections include *Bliss* (Brick House Books, 1998), *Mountain Fireflies* (Poetic Matrix Press, 2000), and *Flint Shards from Sussex* (Gival Press, 2000). He lectures on Appalachian literature and reads his poems regularly.

JEFF DANIEL MARION is Poet-in-Residence and Director of the Appalachian Center at Carson-Newman College. He has published six collections of poetry, most recently *Letters Home* (Sow's Ear Press, 2001). His children's book *Hello, Crow* was published by Orchard Books in 1992. His poems have appeared in numerous journals and anthologies. In 1978, Marion received the first Literary Fellowship in Poetry awarded by the Tennessee Arts Commission. He served for several years as Poet-in-Residence for the Tennessee Governor's School for the Humanities. In 1993, he participated in a Distinguished Authors Series sponsored by the National Endowment for the Arts and the University of Tennessee, Knoxville. His many achievements were honored at Emory & Henry College's 1994 Literary Festival in Emory, Virginia. Marion lectures widely and conducts workshops on teaching and writing poetry throughout the Appalachian region.

MICHAEL MCFEE was born in Asheville, North Carolina, and educated in the Buncombe County Schools. He took his B.A. and M.A. from University of North Carolina–Chapel Hill, where he now teaches poetry-writing and literature. He has published six books of poetry, including *Sad Girl Sitting on a Running Board* (Gnomon Press, 1991) and *Vanishing Acts* (Gnomon Press, 1989). He has also edited two anthologies published by the University of North Carolina Press: *The Language They Speak is Things to Eat: Poems by Fifteen Contemporary North Carolina Poets* (1994) and *This is Where We Live: Short Stories by 25 Contemporary North Carolina Writers* (2000).

Previously Professor of English and Director of the African American Studies Program at the University of South Carolina, JAMES A. MILLER is Professor of American Civilization and English at the George Washington University. He received his A.B. degree from Brown University and his Ph.D. from the State University of New York at Buffalo, where he directed the Black Studies Program from 1969 to 1971. His book contributions include *Harlem: The Vision of Morgan and Marvin Smith* (University Press of Kentucky) and, as editor, *Approaches to Teaching Wright's* Native Son (Modern Language Association, 1997). He is the editor of the *Dictionary of Literary Biography: 21st Century African American Literature* and co-editor, with Jerry Watts, of *The Crisis of the Negro Intellectual Revisited*. Essays and reviews have appeared widely, in publications including *Critical Studies in Mass Communications, The Year Left, Callaloo, American Literature,* and *The Nation*.

For more than ten years, JUDY MILLER has worked with student writers at Virginia Highlands Community College in Abingdon, Virginia, teaching both composition and creative writing. Just as important has been her community service in promoting poetry and fiction through a series of readings and workshops. In the early nineties, she served as Chairperson of the Appalachian Center for Poets and Writers, a grassroots organization whose goal was to organize literary events in southwest Virginia. Additionally, she continues to serve on the board of the Appalachian Writers Association. She has published poems in *Appalachian Journal, Greensboro Review,* and *Arts Journal,* among others.

FELICIA MITCHELL, a native of South Carolina, received a Ph.D. from the University of Texas at Austin in 1987 and has since resided in southwest Virginia, where she is Professor of English at Emory & Henry College. Her poems have been widely published and appear in several anthologies and a chapbook from Talent House Press, *Earthenware Fertility Figure* (1999). Her critical essays on contemporary poetry have appeared in *Mid-American Review, Dictionary of Literary Biography, Poets and Writers,* and elsewhere. *Words and Quilts: A Selection of Quilt Poems,* an edited book of poems and quilt art reproductions, was published by Quilt Digest Press in 1996.

A native Virginian with a Ph.D. in nineteenth-century British literature from the University of Kentucky, JENNIFER MOONEY came to the study of Appalachian literature a bit accidentally. In 1996, she joined the faculty at Virginia Tech, and a year later she prepared a web site for and helped team-teach an online course in Appalachian literature. The experience sparked her interest in what for her was a largely unexplored area. Since then, in addition to working in her area of specialization, she has published and presented on Harriette Arnow, Denise Giardina, and Jo Carson. She is particularly interested in the ways in which writers deal with speech acts and vocalization. Currently she is revising her dissertation on nineteenth-century writer Elizabeth Gaskell for possible publication.

ANN RICHMAN, M.A. at Duke University, was an English professor for almost twenty years. She is editor of *The Plow Reader,* a collection of essays from an alternative newspaper of the 1970s; she recently won second place in the tenth annual Rainmaker Awards of *Zone 3,* a literary journal. She is associate editor and co-publisher of the Sow's Ear Press. She has followed the work of Kay Byer since the early 1980s when she heard her read the then unpublished "Alma" poems.

CHRISTINA SPRINGER is an interdisciplinary advocate of theatre, dance, music, film, and other visual expressions. She was one of eighty-four Pennsylvania artists to receive a 2000 Individual Arts Fellowship from the Pennsylvania Council on the Arts in Poetry. In 1998, she received a scholarship and fellowship in Cave Canem, and in 1998 was a runner-up in the 1998 Paul Laurence Dunbar Poetry Contest. She serves as Administrative Director of Sun Crumbs, where she produces and hosts the monthly Sun Crumbs Poetry Series and the Pittsburgh Poetry Slam. Her poems have appeared widely in journals, including *Fireweed* and *Sinister Wisdom*, and in anthologies including *In Our Own Words: A Generation Defining Itself*, vol. 2, edited by Marlow Peerse Weaver (MW Enterprises, 2000).

WILLIAM THESING is a Professor of English at the University of South Carolina. A specialist in Victorian poetry, he has also worked with Bennie Lee Sinclair. His recent publications include, as editor, *Robinson Jeffers and a Galaxy of Writers: Essays in Honor of William H. Nolte* (University of South Carolina Press, 1995).

ROBIN WARREN is a Ph.D. student in English at the University of Georgia. She earned an Ed.S. (1992) and an M.Ed. (1988) in English education at the University of Georgia, and a B.A. in English at Agnes Scott College (1984). She was recently awarded the University of Georgia Award for Excellence in Research by a Graduate Student. She lives in Clarkesville, Georgia.

# Permissions

"Marginal" from *A Space Filled with Moving*, by Maggie Anderson, © 1992. Reprinted by permission of the University of Pittsburgh Press.

"Self-Portrait" from *Windfall: New and Selected Poems*, by Maggie Anderson, © 2000. Reprinted by permission of the University of Pittsburgh Press.

Excerpt from "The Artist" from *Cold Comfort*, by Maggie Anderson, © 1986. Reprinted by permission of the University of Pittsburgh Press.

Excerpt from "Marginal" from *A Space Filled with Moving*, by Maggie Anderson, © 1992. Reprinted by permission of the University of Pittsburgh Press.

Excerpt from "Long Story" from *A Space Filled with Moving*, by Maggie Anderson, © 1992. Reprinted by permission of the University of Pittsburgh Press.

Excerpt from "Abandoned Farm, Central Pennsylvania" from *A Space Filled with Moving*, by Maggie Anderson, © 1992. Reprinted by permission of the University of Pittsburgh Press.

Excerpt from "Self-Portrait" from *Windfall: New and Selected Poems*, by Maggie Anderson, © 2000. Reprinted by permission of the University of Pittsburgh Press.

Marilou Awiakta, "Where Mountain and Atom Meet" and "Star Vision," *Abiding Appalachia: Where Mountain and Atom Meet* (Bell Buckle, Tenn.: Iris Press, 1995).

"Black Shawl" from *Wildwood Flower* by Kathryn Stripling Byer, © 1992, Louisiana State University Press. Reprinted by permission of the author.

"Wildwood Flower" from *Wildwood Flower* by Kathryn Stripling Byer, © 1992, Louisiana State University Press. Reprinted by permission of the author.

"#11, "Went over at George's get some eggs" from *Stories I Ain't Told Nobody Yet* by Jo Carson. Published by Orchard Books, an imprint of Scholastic, Inc. Copyright © 1989 by Jo Carson. Reprinted by permission.

"Faith in Words" by Jo Carson, from *Iron Mountain Review*, volume XIV, Summer 1998, published by Emory & Henry College. Copyright © 1998 by Jo Carson. Reprinted by permission of the author.

"A Mill Worker in Rockwood" from *Likely*, by Lisa Coffman, © 1995, Kent State University Press. Reprinted by permission of the author.

"Rapture" from *Likely*, by Lisa Coffman, © 1995, Kent State University Press. Reprinted by permission of the author.

"He Cut My Garden Down" from *The River Hills and Beyond*, by Lou V. Crabtree, © 1998. Reprinted by permission of the author.

"Husband" from *The River Hills and Beyond*, by Lou V. Crabtree, © 1998. Reprinted by permission of the author.

"And that's another thing" from *Soque Street Poems*, by doris davenport, © 1995, Sautee-Nacoochie Community Association. Reprinted by permission of the author.

"Ceremony" from *Soque Street Poems*, by doris davenport, © 1995, Sautee-Nacoochie Community Association. Reprinted by permission of the author.

"Knoxville, Tennessee" from *Selected Poems of Nikki Giovanni*, by Nikki Giovanni, © 1996, William Morrow. Reprinted by permission of the author.

"Train Rides" from *Blues for All the Changes*, by Nikki Giovanni, © 1999, William Morrow. Reprinted by permission of the author.

"Notes on Commercial Theatre" from *The Collected Poems of Langston Hughes*, by Langston Hughes, copyright © 1994 by The Estate of Langston Hughes. Use by permission of Alfred A. Knopf, a division of Random House, Inc.

"First, Grief" from *Heart Cake*, by Leatha Kendrick, © 2000, Sow's Ear Press. Reprinted by permission of the author.

"Zen Laundry" from *Heart Cake*, by Leatha Kendrick, © 2000, Sow's Ear Press. Reprinted by permission of the author.

"The Kink Fell Out of My Hair" from *Stain My Days Blue*, by Patricia A. Johnson, © 1999, Ausdoh Press. Reprinted by permission of Ausdoh Press.

"My People" from *Stain My Days Blue*, by Patricia A. Johnson, © 1999, Ausdoh Press. Reprinted by permission of Ausdoh Press.

Excerpt from "The Five-Day Rain" by Denise Levertov, from *Collected Earlier Poems 1940-1960*; copyright © 1960 by Denise Levertov. Reprinted by permission of New Directions Publishing Corp.

"Archaeology" and "Papaw" from *Catalpa* by George Ella Lyon, © 1993, Wind Publications.

Excerpt from "My Grandfather Sees the World" from *Catalpa* by George Ella Lyon, © 1993. Reprinted by permission of *Appalachian Journal*.

"House Holder" from *Home Fires*, by Linda Parsons Marion, © 1997, Sow's Ear Press. Reprinted by permission of the author.

"Stitch in Time," by Linda Parsons Marion, © 1999. Reprinted by permission of the author.

"Deep Mining" from *Six O'Clock Mine Report*, by Irene McKinney, © 1989, University of Pittsburgh Press. Reprinted by permission of the author.

"Viridian Days," by Irene McKinney, © 2000. In *Wild Sweet Notes: Fifty Years of West Virginia Poetry 1950-1999*, edited by Barbara Smith and Kirk Judd, Publishers Place. Reprinted by permission of the author and *The American Voice*.

"Creed" from *Old & New Testaments*, by Lynn Powell. Winner of the 1995 Brittingham Prize in Poetry. © 1995. Reprinted by permission of The University of Wisconsin Press.

"Faith" from *Old & New Testaments*, by Lynn Powell. Winner of the 1995 Brittingham Prize in Poetry. © 1995. Reprinted by permission of The University of Wisconsin Press.

"Counting the Sums" from *Counting the Sums*, by Rita Sims Quillen © 1995, Sow's Ear Press. Reprinted by permission of the author.

"Deathbed Dreams" from *Counting the Sums*, by Rita Sims Quillen © 1995, Sow's Ear Press. Reprinted by permission of the author.

# Index

Bold type signifies full chapters and full poems.

Jack Tales, 51, 173
Jackson, Dick, 166
Jackson, Fleda Brown, 209
Jackson, Richard, xvii
Janeczko, Paul, *Strings: A Gathering of Family Poems*, 166
Jesus Christ, 209, 210, 212, 215. *See also* Christianity.
Jim Crow, 128, 146
Johnson, Denis, 268
Johnson, Don, xv; "Carrying Drunks Up River," 225
Johnson, G. P., xxii, 141–42
Johnson, James Weldon, *God's Trombones*, 144–45
Johnson, Jennifer, 39
Johnson, Patricia A., xxi, **138–49**; "Chairman of the Bar," 146; "Corn Meal Mush," 147; "In a Place Where," xxii, 140–42; "The Kink Fell Out of My Hair," **136**, 142; "My People," **137**, 143; Pearl Johnson, 141; "Snow Cream," 139; "Somebody's Child," 144; *Spirit Rising*, 138; *Stain My Days Blue*, 138; "Stain My Days Blue," 142
Jones, Debra, 56
Jones, Loyal, 255

Keats, John, 145, 270; "Ode on a Grecian Urn," 168
Kelly, Patrice, 112
Kendrick, Leatha, xx, **152–64**; "Beauty's Bitter Smell," 154, 162; "Black Stallion Sleeping Beauty,"157; "First, Grief," **151**, 159; *Heart Cake*, 152; "Knotty Pine," 158; "A Life Spent in Contemplation of a Single Thought," 156; "My Great Awakening," 154–55; "No Place Like Home," 163; "Photograph on the Steps Before the Dance, 1948" 157; "Postcard," 160; *Sharing the Sunlight*, 160; "A Simple Thing," 161; "Touching the Cat," 156; "Translating Daddy," 153; "The Visible Transformations of a Summer Night," 155, 156; "Waking Up," 161; "Zen Laundry," **150**, 157, 162
Kent State University, 4
Kentucky, 9, 166, 172; Eastern, 152, 160; Fleming, 237; Franklin, 152; Harlan,

175; Hindman, 295; Pathfork, 174; Prestonburg, 152; Summers County, 199
Kentucky Arts Council Fellowship, 152
Kentucky Foundation for Women, 152–53
Keowee-Toxaway Dam Project, 281
Killens, John Oliver, 122
King, Reverend Martin Luther, 130
kitchen existentialism, 40
Komunyakaa, Yusef, 141
Kort, Ellen, "Letter from McCarty's Farm," 293
Kosovo, 253
Kunitz, Stanley, 145

La Grange College, 250
Lang, John, xviii, 42
language, 10, 14, 15, 58, 71, 72–74, 106, 153, 166, 182, 220, 238
Lanier, Parks, xvii, xix; *The Poetics of Appalachian Space*, xvii
Larkin, Philip, 71
Laska, P. J., 170
Laveau, Marie, 98
Leidig, Dan, xx
L'Engle, Madeleine, 163
lesbian, xxi, 96, 98, 101
letter-writing, 44
Levertov, Denise, 183, 195, 268
Lewis, Don, 276
Lincoln, Abraham, 155
Lindbergh, Anne Morrow, *A Gift from the Sea*, 157
line, 5, 29, 39, 40, 46, 74, 79, 161
litany, 58
literary journals and magazines: *ALCA Lines*, 244; *Apalachee Quarterly*, 180; *American Voice*, 152, 163; *Appalachian Heritage*, 180; *Asheville Poetry Review*, 180, 237, 244, 245; *Atlantic Monthly*, 229; *Aurora*, 152; *Beloit Poetry Journal*, 70; *Cincinnati Poetry Review*, 152; *Cloverdale*, 244; *Connecticut Review*, 152; *DAY TONIGHT/NIGHT TODAY*, 101; *Georgia Review*, 180; *Helicon Nine*, 180; *Iowa Review*, 180; *Jet Magazine*, 129; *Kestrel*, 195; *Licking River Review*, 152; *Louisiana Literature*, 180; *Mossy Creek Journal*, 47; *Negative Capability*, 180; *New Millennium Writings*, 180; *New Yorker*, 230; *Nimrod*, 152; *Now & Then*, 152, 180; *Painted Bride*

literary journals (contd.)
Quarterly, 70; Passages North, 52; Pine Mountain Sand and Gravel, 237, 244; Ploughshares, 245; Poetry Alive!, 138; Poetry East, 5, 11; Prairie Schooner, 180; Press, 180; Publisher's Weekly, 75, 77, 209; Southern Review, 70; Spud Songs, 152; Stitches, 244; Tennessee Poetry Journal, 38; Trellis, 69; Village Voice, 40; Wind, 166, 180
literary theory, 59–60
Little Deer, 23, 27
local color, 38–39, 69
Lorde, Audre, 156
love, 88, 122, 216, 217, 263
Loveland, Anne, 249
lynching, 129
Lyon, George Ella, xiv, xix, xxi, xxii, 153, 161, **166–77**, 223, 227, 229; "1941," 167; A B Cedar, 172, 176; "Archaeology," **165**, 169–70, 173; "At the Lodge," 167; Basket, 169, 173; "Border," 167–68; Catalpa, 166, 172, 176; "Catechisms—Talking with a Four-Year-Old," 170; Cecil's Story, 173; Come a Tide, 173, 175, 176; "Crossing," 172; A Day at Summer Camp, 172; Dreamplace, 171; "Elopement," 171; "Evidence," 167; "For a Time," 173; "Her Words," 175; "How the Letters Bloom Like a Catalpa Tree," 168–69; "In the Garden," 167; Mama is a Miner, 173; Mountain, xiv; "My Grandfather Sees the World," 173; Old Wounds, New Words: Source and Directions, 170; "Papaw," **165**; A Regular Rolling Noah, 173; Something About the Author, 68; "Thirteen Ways of Looking at a Mean Poem," 168; "Visions," 167; "Visiting Monk's House," 167; "Voiceplace," 170, 172, 175; Who Came Down that Road?, 170; A Wordful Child, 166, 167
lyric poetry, 39, 47, 58, 71, 73, 76

magical realism, 103
Mahabharata, The, 211
Maine: Portland, 266
Mamaw. See grandmother
Mann, Jeff, xviii
marginalization, 56
Marion, Jeff Daniel, xv, xxii, 161, 168, 170, 183, 208, 221, 222, 293

Marion, Linda Parsons, xv; **180–90**; All Around Us: Poems from the Valley (editor), 180; Home Fires, 180; "House Holder," **178**, 188; "Stitch in Time," **179**, 182; "Tomato Songs," 180; "The Writing Well," 180
Marvell, Andrew, 296
Mary Anderson Center for the Arts, 152
Massachusetts: Boston, 268
masturbation, 87
material culture, 168
Matthews, William, 268
maxims, 237
McClintock, Dr. Barbara, 32
McDowell Writers Colony, 237, 244
McFee, Michael, xx, 230, 233, 293
McHugh, Heather, 268
McKinney, Irene, xviii, 5, **194–205**, 293; "Breathing," 195; "Dear Friend," 200; "Deep Mining," **191**; "The Durret Farm, West Virginia: A Map," 196, 200; "The Farm," 200; "A Freshet in Brattleboro," 195; The Girl with the Stone in her Lap, 196–99; "The Jewelry Box," xviii; "The Pig's Head," 199; Quick Fire and Slow Fire, 194; Six O'Clock Mine Report, 194, 201; "Sunday Morning, 1950," 201; "Twilight in West Virginia," 196; "Viridian Days," **192–93**, 194; "Visiting My Gravesite, Talbott Churchyard, West Virginia," 291
McNeill, Louise, 196, 203, 223, 293; "Ballad of New River," 197; "Deserted Lumber Yard," 14; A Gathering of Poets, 4; "Hill Daughter," 13
meditation, 157
memo poem, 32
memoir, 106
metaphor, 10, 20, 41, 43, 44, 45, 77, 112, 113, 114, 121, 128, 138, 161, 169, 170, 173, 181, 208, 212, 228, 237, 268, 270
metaphysical dualism, 208
meter, 40, 54. See also rhythm
Meyer, Patricia, 60
migration, xviii, xxii, 78, 115, 119, 120, 196
Milam, J. M., 129
Miles, Emma Bell, 38, 44
Miller, James A., xxi

Miller, Jim Wayne, xv, xxii, 161, 170, 183, 209, 221; *The Mountains Have Come Closer*, 225

Miller, Judy K., xx

Miller, Zel, 249, 255

Million Man March, 118

mills, 8, 10, 14, 70–71, 77, 78, 182, 184, 199, 284

Milosz, Czeslaw, 268, 273

Mingus, Charles, 128

mining, 289. *See also* coal-mining

Minnesota, 288

Mississippi, 129

mock-epic, 72

Monk, Thelonious, 128

monologue, 59–60

Montgomery Improvement Association, 130

Mooney, Jennifer, xiv

Mooney, William, 38

Moore, Lenard D., 142

Moore, Marianne, 74

Moraga, Cherrie, *This Bridge Called My Back*, 99

Morehead University, 152

Morgan, Robert, xxii, 161, 170, 183, 208, 229, 230, 277, 293; "Face," 213," "Lightning Bug," 212, "Signs," 213

Morrison, Toni, 103, 119, 147; *The Bluest Eye*, 117; *Selu*, 131

mother, 15, 19, 22, 26, 28, 33, 34, 41, 43, 46, 77, 89, 113, 114, 129, 139, 159, 160, 173, 185, 186, 188, 209, 211, 213, 225, 226, 231, 238, 257, 267, 290

Mother Earth, 20, 28, 31, 32. *See also* Corn Mother

motherhood, 42. *See also* mother

motif, 103, 130, 208, 210, 211

Mountain Empire Community College, 220

mountain people, 4, 22, 25, 38, 46, 61, 250, 283, 288

mountains. *See* Appalachian mountains

Mozart, Wolfgang Amadeus, 266

Muldoon, Paul, 268

music, xvi, 20, 41, 54, 80, 116, 128, 157, 166, 168, 172, 188, 208, 238, 266. *See also* songs and singing

myth and legend, 19, 24, 27, 28, 33, 45, 51, 98, 153, 157, 167, 187, 211, 257, 273

naming, 172–73, 252

narrative poetry, 53, 56, 71, 77, 154, 173, 212, 254, 255, 273

narrator, 33, 56, 62, 71, 73, 75, 76, 78, 80, 119, 121, 169, 171, 174, 239, 256

native, xviii

Native American, 19, 20, 24, 26, 28, 32, 92, 103, 126, 143, 198, 281, 294. *See also* Cherokee

Neruda, Pablo, 183, 273

New Jersey, 266

New York, 3, 10, 12, 64, 146, 288, 294

*New York Times*, 232

New York University, 69

Norris, Kathleen, *Amazing Grace: A Vocabulary of Faith*, 230; *The Cloister Walk*, 230

North Carolina, 46, 184, 258; Asheville, 138; Chapel Hill, 152; Charlotte, 97; Cullowhee, 38; 46; Cullowhee Valley, 39; Weaverville, 255

nostalgia, 26, 251

nuclear power, 281, 282

Oak Ridge National Laboratory, xxi, 24

O'Connor, Flannery, 189, 270

O'Hara, Scarlett, 188

Ohio, 4; Bowling Green, 97; Cincinnati, xxii, 115, 130; Cleveland, 6, 267

Oliver, Mary, 145, 183

Olson, Ann, 161

Ong, Walter J., 52

open forms, 39

oral history, xvi, 46, 51, 52, 53, 55, 56, 64, 77, 129, 244, 257

orishas, 98

Orwell, George, *1984*, 15

Ostriker, Alicia, 70, 217; *Stealing the Language*, xxii

outer space, 89, 271

oxymoron, 241

Paine College, 96

Pancake, Breece, "Trilobites," 197–98

pantoum, 229, 230

Paradise, 90

paradox, xxi, xxii, 170–71, 172, 175, 182, 201, 209, 242

*HER WORDS* was designed and typeset on a Macintosh computer system using QuarkXPress software. The body text is set in 10.5/14 Joanna and display type is set in Letter Gothic. This book was designed and typeset by CHERYL CARRINGTON and manufactured by Thomson-Shore, Inc.